KT-446-899

Spatial Vision

OXFORD PSYCHOLOGY SERIES

EDITORS
Donald E. Broadbent
James L. McGaugh
Nicholas J. Mackintosh
Michael I. Posner
Endel Tulving
Lawrence Weiskrantz

SPATIAL VISION

RUSSELL L. De VALOIS

Departments of Psychology and Physiological Optics
University of California, Berkeley

KAREN K. De VALOIS

Departments of Psychology and Physiological Optics
University of California, Berkeley

OXFORD PSYCHOLOGY SERIES NO. 14

New York   Oxford
OXFORD UNIVERSITY PRESS
CLARENDON PRESS

Oxford University Press

Oxford   New York   Toronto
Delhi   Bombay   Calcutta   Madras   Karachi
Petaling Jaya   Singapore   Hong Kong   Tokyo
Nairobi   Dar es Salaam   Cape Town
Melbourne   Auckland

and associated companies in
Berlin   Ibadan

Copyright © 1990 by Oxford University Press

First published in 1988 by Oxford University Press, Inc.,
200 Madison Avenue, New York, New York 10016

First issued as an Oxford University Press paperback, 1990

Oxford is a registered trademark of Oxford University Press

Library of Congress Cataloging-in-Publication Data

De Valois, Russell L.
  Spatial vision.

  (Oxford psychology series; no. 14)
  Bibliography: p.
  Includes index.
  1. Space perception—Physiological aspects.   2. Visual
perception—Physiological aspects.   I. De Valois, Karen K.
II. Title.   III. Series.
QP491.D46   1988   152.1'42   88-7660
ISBN 0-19-505019-3
ISBN 0-19-506657-X (pbk)

2 4 6 8 10 9 7 5 3 1
Printed in the United States of America

To Chad and Kamala

Preface

Although we have given this volume the extremely generalized title *Spatial Vision*, we must issue an immediate disclaimer. We have made no attempt to cover all of spatial vision in this one volume. Since the nineteenth century when Helmholtz succeeded in doing so in the second volume of his *Handbuch der Physiologischen Optik*, the literature in the field has increased by many orders of magnitude. Even a bibliographic listing of all the relevant literature would now require more than a single volume. This is a consequence both of the ever-increasing fragmentation and specialization in this field (as in all of science) and of the much larger number of scientists who work in the area.

What justification is there then for such a book as this and for our choosing such an ambitious title as *Spatial Vision*? We realize that specialization is inevitable, given the extent of knowledge and the diversity of research techniques employed in studying vision. On occasion, though, we believe it is useful to sit back and take a broader view, to try to see the shape of the forest instead of the nature of the individual trees, to attempt to get a feeling for how the parts all fit together. This represents our attempt to do that.

We believe there is now another reason for attempting an overall synthesis of the field. For the first time a single unifying framework and a common language are available with which to consider both visual perception and the underlying physiological processes. Since vision has become so fragmented into many subareas, each with its own problems and microtheories, the field as a whole has had little to unify it or give it structure. In our opinion, this has recently changed as a result of two developments. One is the introduction of the techniques of linear systems analysis to the study of both psychophysical and physiological problems in vision. The other is the evidence, both psychophysical and physiological, for multiple spatial channels in the visual system. These developments have given us the hope of being able to interrelate physiology and psychophysics, as far as early visual processing of spatial information is concerned, and to give a coherent picture of the transformations that occur in the initial visual stages.

Given the vast vision literature, it is obviously impossible to encompass in any one book the whole of the anatomy, physiology, and psychophysics of early spatial vision without giving only very perfunctory treatment to many complex topics. We cannot begin to compete in thoroughness of coverage with handbook chapters, reviews, or books that go into great depth on one or another of the topics we have addressed. Such has not been our intention. Since we necessarily must be selective, we have unabashedly concentrated on those problems which we consider most tractable at this time, those which most interest us, and those which we ourselves have studied. Due to space limitations, we have also either ignored or given no more than a passing reference to certain whole areas, such as movement perception and temporal properties of vision in general. Although we have attempted to strike a balance between broad coverage of the whole area of spatial vision and an account only of our own work and interests, we have perhaps inevitably concentrated on the work from our laboratories. The many to whose work we have not given adequate attention will no doubt question the extent to which we have maintained any balance at all. To them we sincerely apologize.

Berkeley, California   R.L.De V.
July 1987   K.K.De V.

Acknowledgments

Our task in writing this book has been made immeasurably easier by the generous cooperation of our colleagues and students. In many cases we have reprinted figures that were originally published elsewhere, or we have published here for the first time either photographs or figures that are based on the work of various colleagues. We gratefully acknowledge the kindness of the authors and the publishers for allowing us to reprint material from their journals or books. We have attempted to acknowledge each of these in the appropriate figure caption.

We wish here also to acknowledge and express our gratitude for other kinds of assistance that we have received. At several stages in the preparation of this manuscript we have benefited from discussions with colleagues and students about either the substance or the presentation of this material. In particular, the following individuals have read all or parts of the book and have given us the benefit of their advice and criticism: Arthur Bradley, Vasudevan Lakshminarayanan, Bernd Lingelbach, Eugene Switkes, Lisa Thorell, Roger Tootell, and William Yund. We have also received very helpful comments from the students in our laboratories and from those in our classes. Since we (doubtless foolishly) did not accept all of their suggestions, the errors of fact and interpretation that remain are, of course, our responsibility.

We are also grateful for the assistance of Pat Charley, Bob Tarr, and Paul Haller in the preparation of figures and photographs. Our editor at Oxford University Press, Shelley Reinhardt, has been both patient and helpful.

The research in our laboratories, upon which much of this book is based, has been supported for many years by the National Eye Institute of the National Institutes of Health, and by the National Science Foundation. We are grateful for their continued support.

Contents

Spatial Vision

1

Linear Systems Analysis

Linear systems analysis has found wide application in physics and engineering for a century and a half. It has also served as a principal basis for understanding hearing ever since its application to audition by Ohm (1843) and Helmholtz (1877). The successful application of these procedures to the study of visual processes has come only in the last two decades, but it has had a considerable impact on the field. It provides in fact much of the *raison d'être* of this book.

It is not our intent in this chapter to discuss the mathematical basis of linear systems analysis, but rather to give the uninitiated reader enough of a background and intuitive feel for the procedures to be able to follow those applications to visual problems which we will be discussing in this book. The reader who wishes to pursue these issues further is strongly urged to read any of a number of more comprehensive treatises on linear analysis (e.g., Bracewell, 1965; Goodman, 1968). An excellent short mathematical treatment of two-dimensional linear analysis and its application to visual problems is given in D.H. Kelly (1979a).

FOURIER THEOREM

Linear systems analysis originated in a striking mathematical discovery by a French physicist, Baron Jean Fourier, in 1822. He demonstrated that a periodic waveform of any complexity could be broken down (analyzed) into the linear sum of harmonically related sine and cosine waves of specified frequencies, amplitudes, and phases. (Harmonics are waves whose frequencies are integer multiples of some lowest, or fundamental, frequency). See Figure 1.1 for examples of sine waves. This is now known as Fourier analysis. Conversely, by the inverse Fourier transform, any desired periodic waveform could be built up (synthesized) by adding together harmonically related sine waves of appropriate frequency, amplitude, and phase. Later, it was shown that any nonperiodic waveform could also be described as the sum of sine waves if all frequencies (not just harmonically related ones) were included.

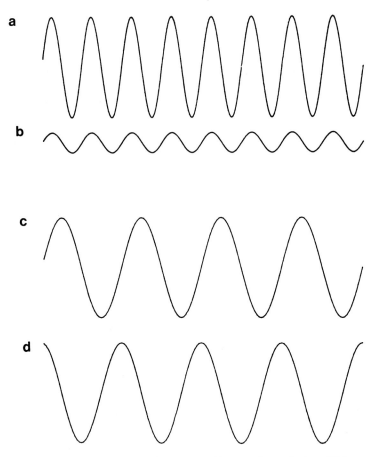

FIG. 1.1 Examples of sine (and cosine) waves. The waveforms in A and B have a spatial frequency which is twice that of the waveforms in C and D. The sine wave in A is equal in frequency and phase to that in B, but its amplitude is 5 times as great. The waveforms in C and D are equal in frequency and amplitude but differ by 90° in phase.

Formally, the Fourier transform of a spatial (or temporal) waveform is

$$F(\alpha) = \int_{-\infty}^{\infty} f(x)e^{-j2\pi\alpha x}dx$$

where x is the location in space (or time, if it is a temporal waveform), α is spatial (or temporal) frequency, and $j = \sqrt{-1}$. The inverse Fourier transform from spatial or temporal frequency to space or time is

$$F(x) = \int_{-\infty}^{\infty} f(\alpha)e^{j2\pi\alpha x}d\alpha$$

The usefulness of Fourier analysis is largely that it provides a way in which complex waveforms or shapes can be described and dealt with quantitatively. One can, of course, specify a complex waveform such as that shown in the top of Figure 1.2 by its amplitude at each point in space: it is "so high" at this point, and "so high" at that point, etc. But there is little that one can say in summary about it except that it is wavy and has several bumps. It would be difficult to make any but the vaguest comparisons of this to some other similar waveform. Breaking it down into elemental units with Fourier analysis, however, allows

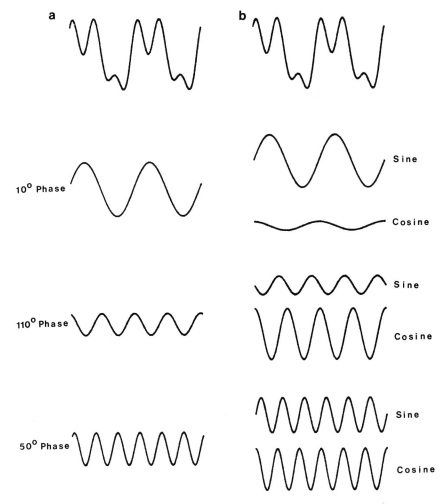

FIG. 1.2   The arbitrary waveform shown at the top can be analyzed into (or synthesized from) either the sine waves of specified frequency, amplitude, and phase shown in A or, alternatively, the three pairs of sine and cosine waves of specified frequency and amplitude shown in B.

one to specify it quantitatively and compare it to other waveforms in an economical way.

A second aspect of Fourier analysis that makes it very useful in many applications is that any waveform can be specified by combinations of a limited number of elemental components, the number depending on the degree of precision required. Sine waves thus provide a universal representation for complex waveforms.

Sine Waves

Examples of sine waves, the basic elements in Fourier analysis, are shown in Figure 1.1. We are most accustomed to dealing with such sinusoidal oscillations in the time domain, e.g., a rapid oscillation of air pressure, a sound wave, produced by a tuning fork or a bell. In our consideration of spatial vision, however, we shall be more concerned with oscillations across space, e.g., ripples on a lake.

The frequency of a sine wave is the number of oscillations per unit distance or time. The patterns in Figures 1.1A and B are of twice the frequency as those in Figures 1.1C and D. So a certain *temporal frequency* might be 3 cycles (or complete oscillations) per second, commonly abbreviated Hz (after the physicist Hertz, and so pronounced). A particular *spatial frequency* (an oscillation of luminance or color in space) might be 3 cycles per centimeter. Since the dimensions of visual stimuli are much more usefully specified in terms of the angle subtended at the eye (visual angle), the usual specification of spatial frequency in vision is in cycles per degree visual angle (c/deg), as described in Chapter 2.

The amplitude of a sine wave is the distance from peak to trough of the wave divided by 2. The sine wave in Figure 1.1B is the same frequency and phase as that in Figure 1.1A, but is of ⅙ the amplitude. For a more complex waveform the amplitude of the overall pattern is not necessarily the same as the amplitude of the fundamental or any other harmonic component. For instance, the amplitude of the sine wave fundamental in a square wave pattern (see Figure 1.3) is greater than that of the pattern as a whole.

The contrast of a visual pattern is related to the amplitude in the sense that both are measures of the height of the waveform, but it is important to distinguish between them. The *contrast* of a visual pattern is conventionally given by the Michelson contrast:

$$\frac{L_{max} - L_{min}}{L_{max} + L_{min}}$$

where L_{max} and L_{min} are the luminances of the peak and trough of the waveform, respectively. As can be seen, then, contrast is a relative measure. Waves are sometimes described not by their amplitude but by their power, which is amplitude squared. The power spectrum is the power at each of the various frequencies, irrespective of phase.

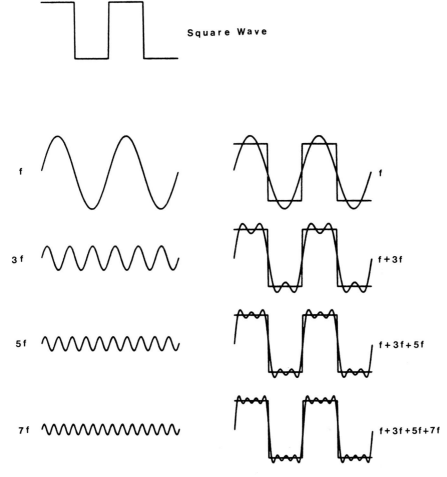

FIG. 1.3 Analysis of a square wave into its components. On the left are shown a section of a square wave and its first four components in appropriate relative phases and amplitudes. On the right is shown the superposition of these components on the original square wave.

The third critical variable is the phase, which refers to the position of the sinusoidal wave with respect to some reference point. In Figure 1.1D, the sine wave is of the same amplitude and frequency as that in Figure 1.1C, but it is shifted 90° in phase. One can distinguish between two different usages of the term "phase" in describing sinusoids. We will refer to these as absolute and relative phase, although strictly speaking all phase must be relative. By "absolute phase" we will mean the position of a sinusoidal wave with respect to some particular fixed spatial location. By "relative phase" we will refer to the relative phase angles (differences in absolute phase) among the multiple frequencies in a pattern. A sine wave and a cosine wave are identical except that one is shifted 90° in phase with respect to the other. The sine wave has a zero at the spatial location used as a phase origin, while the cosine wave has a maximum at that point. Since a sinusoidal wave of a given phase can be expressed as an appropriate combination of sine and cosine components of fixed (0) phase, an analysis of a complex waveform in terms of sines and cosines is equivalent to one utilizing sine waves of varying phase. In many ways it appears that using sine and cosine components is more similar to the way in which the visual system itself might deal with phase, a possibility we shall discuss later.

Examples of Fourier Analysis

An illustration of Fourier synthesis and analysis is shown in Figure 1.2A. The arbitrary waveform shown at top can be "synthesized" or built up from the particular three sine waves, specified in frequency, amplitude, and phase, shown below at the left. That is, if at each point the values of the three sinusoids are added together linearly, their sum will produce the top waveform. In the reverse process, one can decompose (analyze) the top waveform into the sum of the three sine waves below. In Figure 1.2B is shown the analysis of the same waveform into sine and cosine components (of fixed phase), with the amplitudes being specified for each of the three frequencies. Again, the sum of these (six) sinusoids adds up the complex waveform at top.

In Figure 1.3 we show another example of a complex waveform analyzed into its component sine waves. This waveform is called a square wave, and it is of particular importance to vision for several reasons. It is a not uncommon distribution of light, being, for instance, what one would obtain from running a photocell across a picket fence. A square wave also has sharp edges, which have often been thought to be of particular importance for vision. Further, square wave gratings have been widely studied in psychophysical and physiological experiments.

By the use of Fourier analysis, a square wave, which is a periodic function, can be broken down into harmonically related sine waves. The fundamental sine wave component, f, is of the same frequency and phase as the square wave itself, but it has an amplitude which is $4/\pi$ times that of the square wave. If it is added to a sine wave of the same phase but of 3 times the frequency ($3f$) and ⅓ the amplitude as the fundamental, the resulting waveform can be seen to be closer to the square wave. The addition of $3f$ tends to sharpen up the edges a bit, and to cut back the too large peaks and troughs of the original sine wave. As one continues to add odd harmonics in decreasing amplitude at appropriate phases, the resultant waveform more and more closely approximates that of a square wave. So a square wave of frequency f and amplitude 1 can be analyzed into the sum of sine waves which are the odd harmonics of f (i.e., odd integral multiples). Specifically, it is equal to

$$4/\pi \; [\sin(f) + \sin(3f)/3 + \sin(5f)/5 + \sin(7f)/7 + \ldots + \sin(nf)/n].$$

One way to grasp the nature of Fourier analysis is to consider it as a correlational process. In the Fourier analysis of a waveform, one is specifying the extent to which this waveform is correlated with (or overlaps) sine waves of different frequencies and phases. A sine wave is obviously perfectly correlated with a sine wave of the same frequency, amplitude, and phase and can thus be specified by a single point in the frequency domain. A square wave is highly correlated with a sine wave of the same frequency, f, completely uncorrelated with a sine wave of frequency $2f$, partially correlated with a sine wave of $3f$ (but less so than with f), etc. Its Fourier spectrum, the extent to which it is correlated with sine waves of various frequencies, thus consists of f and its odd harmonics in decreasing amplitude.

Filters can be considered as devices that carry out such a correlation. A filter passes information insofar as the input matches, or correlates with, the filter function. Imagine a bank of filters tuned, respectively, to f, $2f$, $3f$, etc. A sine wave of frequency f would activate just the f filter; a square wave would activate the f filter and also the $3f$ and $5f$ and . . . filters, to decreasing extents.

The Fourier amplitude spectrum of a waveform can be graphically represented in various ways. Two useful ones are shown in Figure 1.4. In Figure 1.3, an example of a spatial square wave was shown. The representation of this in the frequency domain is shown in Figure 1.4A, with frequency along the x-axis and amplitude along the y-axis. Another form of frequency representation (which in general is more useful since it can also be used to show the spectrum of two-dimensional patterns) is a polar plot, as shown in Figure 1.4B. Here, spatial frequency is indicated by the distance out from the center and orientation by the polar direction. Amplitude, in such a plot, is often arbitrarily shown by the size or intensity of the spot at a particular frequency and orientation. (Neither plot shows the phase of the components.) Such a two-dimensional plot is similar to the actual two dimensional power spectrum of a pattern obtained by a simple optical diffraction technique (Goodman, 1968).

It can be seen that in terms of its Fourier spectrum, a square wave is a rather complex waveform. Paradoxically, a single narrow bar is an even more complex waveform: since it is a nonperiodic pattern, its synthesis requires not just harmonically related sine waves, but contributions from a continuous spectrum of frequencies across a wide range. In fact, it is by no means intuitively obvious that one could find any combination of sine waves that would add up to a single bar on a uniform background, but it can be done by adding together many sine waves that are in phase at this one location yet cancel everywhere else.

Frequency Domain Versus Space Domain

We pointed out above that a bar, strictly localized in the space domain, has a broad, continuous spectrum in the frequency domain. This raises the general question of the relationship between the frequency and space domains in Fourier analysis. Recall that one can go back and forth between the space domain

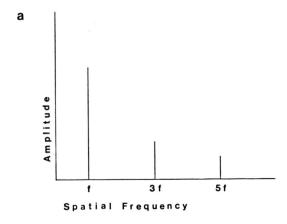

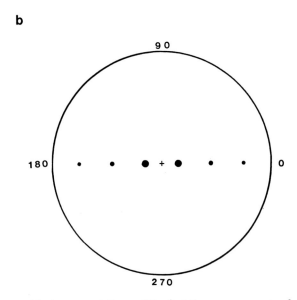

FIG. 1.4 Two graphical representations of the first three components of a square wave. In A, frequency is plotted along the *x*-axis, and amplitude along the *y*-axis. Phase is not represented. In B, the spatial frequency corresponds to the distance from the center, and orientation to the polar direction. Amplitude is here represented by the diameter of the spot. This would be the spectrum of a *vertical* square wave.

and the frequency domain representations by the Fourier transform and the inverse Fourier transform, respectively. There are some interesting, contrasting relationships between these two domains. The simplest, most discrete pattern in the frequency domain, a single spatial frequency, corresponds to a sine wave grating in the space domain that covers all of space, extending infinitely in all directions. On the other hand, the Fourier transform of a single, infinitely small, discrete spot in space covers the whole two-dimensional spatial frequency spectrum, since it contains power at all orientations as well as at all spatial frequencies. So a spot of light, chosen by many visual scientists in an attempt to use the simplest stimulus, is from the point of view of Fourier analysis one of the most complex patterns of all! The spatial frequency spectrum of a spot is very similar to the temporal frequency spectrum of a click. A spot of light and an auditory click appear in the space and time domains, respectively, to be elementary stimuli, but in the spatial and temporal frequency domains they are very extensive, complex patterns. A single spot has very little power at any spatial frequency and orientation. (It is interesting that a large array of randomly positioned dots, e.g., the night sky full of stars, has essentially the same power spectrum as a single dot, but with much more power at each spatial frequency, and a different phase spectrum.)

Sampling Theorem

It is a theorem of euclidean geometry that two points determine a line. This is readily grasped intuitively. A somewhat less obvious geometric finding is that three points determine a circle. The question we wish to raise here is how many points determine a complex waveform. How often must one sample the waveform in order to specify its frequency components? The answer is that with a certain number of appropriately spaced point samples, N, all frequencies below $N/2$ can be specified. So, for instance, 30 regularly spaced samples across 1° visual angle will specify the frequency, amplitude, and phase of all frequencies below 15 c/deg. Thus only slightly more than two samples per cycle of the highest frequency present are required to specify the contributions of all sine waves in a complex pattern. Further data points add no additional information. This is known as the sampling theorem.

The sampling theorem has relevance to the study of the visual system in considering the number and spacing of the visual receptors and other elements in relation to the resolving power of the system, as discussed further in Chapter 2. If the optics of the eye are such as to pass patterns of only, say, less than 60 c/deg, there would be no point in having more than 120 receptors per degree visual angle. The argument can also be put the other way: if receptors can only be packed in at 120 per degree visual angle, there is nothing to be gained from developing a better optical system than one which cuts off at 60 c/deg. This discussion only considers one-dimensional patterns, and the retina is of course a two-dimensional structure. The optimum sampling of such two-dimensional structures is a somewhat more complex question (Crick, Marr, & Poggio, 1981), but the results do not significantly change the conclusions stated above.

Nonsinusoidal Basis Functions

The Fourier theorem states that any waveform can be analyzed into its component sine waves. Sine waves, then, are the elementary units, or basis functions, in this analysis. It is also possible to carry out analogous analyses utilizing other basis functions. For instance, in the Hadamard transform, waveforms are analyzed into square waves rather than into sine waves. So Fourier analysis into sine waves is by no means the only possible linear decomposition procedure. However, sine waves have certain properties that which make them attractive as a basis function, particularly for analyzing optical and visual systems. Sinusoidal waves are of interest and importance because spatially invariant linear systems do not alter their shape. Lenses, and perhaps also certain arrays of visual cells, are to a first approximation such linear systems. For example, a sinusoidal pattern of light passed through a lens with aberrations is not changed in waveform or shape but merely in amplitude and possibly in phase. It is still a sine wave. Thus, even with imperfect optics, no additional frequencies are introduced for sine wave basis functions. That is not the case, however, for square wave basis functions. For these reasons, we will discuss here only Fourier analysis, and only sine waves as a basis function. (Systems with certain symmetries, e.g., two-dimensional circular symmetry, may also pass combinations of sine waves, for instance Bessel functions, without change of shape.)

APPLICATIONS TO VISION

The Fourier theorem can be applied to any sort of oscillation and to variations in either time or space. It has found wide application to many sorts of problems. For instance, in audition one deals with oscillations of sound pressure in time. A physicist might be concerned with variations in heat across space or in time (Fourier in fact developed the mathematics named after him as a tool to study heat waves). A meteorologist might apply Fourier analysis to the study of oscillations in rainfall or temperature across the year. In vision, we are concerned with variations in both time and space, and with variations in either the intensity or the wavelength of light.

Consider, for instance, an ordinary visual scene. If you were to run a photocell across the scene at some constant level, say in a horizontal line from left to right, the output of the photocell would go up and down as it encountered light and dark areas. The result would be a complex waveform related to the spatial pattern of light across the scene. Correspondingly, if such a pattern were imaged on the retina, the output of an array of receptors would constitute samples of this complex waveform. In its application to vision, then, the Fourier theorem and its extension states that these, like any other waveforms of variations in light across space or time, could be analyzed into the sum of sine wave components, or synthesized by adding together sine waves of appropriate frequency, amplitude, and phase.

In applying Fourier analysis to vision, we can first consider a one-dimensional pattern, such as the grating shown at top in Figure 1.5. If this pattern were of

FIG. 1.5   Square (top) and sine wave (bottom) gratings of the same spatial frequency.

infinite height, there would be a variation in light only from left to right across the pattern, not from up to down. We can thus consider it a one-dimensional pattern, although of course any real object terminates in the other dimension as well and is thus really two-dimensional. The shape of the waveform that would result from running a photocell with a narrow acceptance angle across such a pattern and plotting the light intensity would be a square wave such as was shown in Figure 1.3. This pattern is thus called a square wave grating. As we discussed earlier, a square wave is really a fairly complex pattern, from the point of view of Fourier analysis, being made up of an infinite series of odd harmonics of a sine wave of the same frequency as the pattern. The simplest one-dimensional spatial stimulus, then, would be a grating pattern like that shown at the top of Figure 1.5, but with a sinusoidal variation in light across it from left to right. The luminance, L, at each point in x across this pattern would then be

$$L(x) = L_m [1 + c \sin(2\pi fx + \phi)]$$

where L_m is the mean luminance, c is the contrast, f is the spatial frequency, and ϕ is the spatial phase. Such a *sine wave grating* is shown at bottom in Figure 1.5. By the fundamental theorem of Fourier analysis, then, any one-dimensional visual pattern could be synthesized from the sum of such sine wave gratings of the appropriate frequencies, amplitudes, and phases.

In the various waveforms we have been discussing and whose Fourier spectra we have diagrammed, we have implicitly assumed that the values vary from positive to negative across the waveform, with a mean of zero. Such would have to be the case, for instance, for a pattern (a true sine wave) to have all its power at just one frequency. Since negative light does not exist, however, any visual pattern must consist of variations in light about some mean level. This introduces a zero spatial frequency, or DC component, into any actual visual pattern, the DC level being the mean luminance level of the pattern.

Two-Dimensional Fourier Analysis

The actual retinal image of most scenes varies not just from left to right, as in the grating patterns we have been showing, but in the vertical dimension too. Ignoring depth, the visual world is two-dimensional, as is the retinal image. Two-dimensional patterns can be dealt with by the same procedures of Fourier analysis, except that the orientation of the sine wave components must also be specified. Any two-dimensionally varying pattern can be analyzed into sinusoidal components of appropriate spatial frequency, amplitude, phase, and *orientation.*

Formally, the two-dimensional Fourier transform is

$$F(\alpha,\beta) = \int_{-\infty}^{\infty} \int_{-\infty}^{\infty} f(x,y) e^{-j2\pi(\alpha x + \beta y)} dx dy$$

and the inverse transform is

$$f(x,y) = \int_{-\infty}^{\infty} \int_{-\infty}^{\infty} F(\alpha,\beta) e^{j2\pi(\alpha x + \beta y)} d\alpha \, d\beta$$

where x and y are spatial coordinates, and α and β are horizontal and vertical frequencies.

On a polar plot a vertical grating, such as that shown at top left in Figure 1.6, has all its power along a horizontal axis, since the pattern varies only horizontally, see top right in Figure 1.6. Correspondingly, a horizontal grating has its power along the vertical axis. The simple, two-dimensional plaid pattern shown at bottom left in Figure 1.6 was made by the addition of the vertical grating shown at top plus a horizontal square wave grating of the same frequency. It thus has energy at each of these orientations (see bottom right). Also shown, at middle left in Figure 1.6, is a checkerboard pattern. This also is made from a vertical and a horizontal square wave grating, but in this case it is the mathematical *product* of the two rather than their sum. The *Fourier fundamentals* are thus on the diagonals, at 45° with respect to the original gratings, and the spatial frequencies of the fundamentals are $\sqrt{2}$ times that of the grating fundamentals. The numerous higher harmonics, cross products of the various fundamentals and higher harmonics, are at a variety of other orientations and frequencies (middle right). It is thus apparent that there are vast differences between the usual description of a checkerboard in the space domain (vertical and horizontal edges; one particular bar or check width) and in the frequency domain (no power at vertical or horizontal; various spatial frequency components at a variety of orientations).

Two-dimensional spatial frequency analysis and synthesis is of course not limited to simple repetitive patterns such as checkerboards. In Figure 1.7 are photographs of the progressive synthesis of a very complex non-repetitive pattern. At top left is shown a grating of the frequency and orientation whose amplitude in the figure is the largest (a very low frequency vertical grating), with its power spectrum alongside. At top right is the sum of the two largest components in the pattern (the next largest component being a horizontal low frequency), with again their power spectra alongside, etc. By the time 64 components have been summed together, the shape of the pattern becomes recognizable, and 164 frequencies are enough to easily make out the specific picture portrayed. It is unlikely that the pattern could be so economically encoded in the pure space domain, with just 164 points (the original picture had some 65,500 points). Note also that the largest frequency components are all at low spatial frequencies. Just a small number of these low frequency components contain enough information to identify the picture.

Local and Global Analysis

Fourier analysis is in principle a completely global process. That is, the Fourier amplitude at a given spatial frequency and orientation is determined by the waveform at that orientation extending infinitely in space. In the case of a temporal Fourier analysis, one is dealing with infinitely extended time. However, in applying Fourier analysis to any real-life situation it is clear that such completely global analyses cannot operate, since measurements in neither time nor space can extend to infinity. So any practical application of Fourier analysis must

FIG. 1.6 Square wave grating, checkerboard, and plaid patterns. On the left are three related patterns: (top) a square wave grating, (middle) a checkerboard produced by the *cross multiplication* of vertical and horizontal square waves of this frequency, and (bottom) a plaid that results from the *addition* of vertical and horizontal square waves. On the right are polar plot representations of the spatial frequency spectra of these patterns.

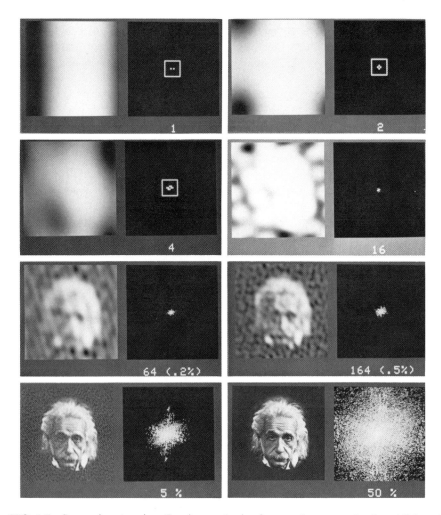

FIG. 1.7 Successive steps in a Fourier synthesis of a complex pattern by the addition of progressively greater numbers of those components which have the highest amplitudes. Alongside each pattern is its power spectrum, the central part of which has been enlarged for each of the first three combinations, for ease of seeing which frequencies are involved. See text for further explanation. We are grateful to Eugene Switkes for preparing this figure. (Derived from a photograph kindly provided by the American Federation of Teachers, with permission for its use).

involve an approximation, dealing with waveforms that must be at least somewhat localized in time and space.

In the applications of Fourier analysis to vision, the question of global versus local analysis refers to still further limitations on the process. Visual space is not infinite, but the visual field does extend some 200° or more; the duration of a single visual event, or visual time, is not infinite, but it could potentially extend for minutes or hours. It appears, however, that in analyzing spatial and temporal variations the visual system fragments patterns much more than is demanded by the spatial extent of the retina or the length of the day. Temporal events are analyzed into small time segments, and space into fairly small parts. Thus, in applying Fourier analysis to the operation of the visual system, or in considering the question of whether the visual system may itself utilize something like Fourier analysis in solving its problems, only a fairly localized analysis should be considered. What we shall be concerned with, then, is something intermediate between a totally global Fourier analysis and a totally localized point-by-point analysis. We can think of this intermediate condition as being a spatially and temporally patchwise approximation to a Fourier analysis.

A sine wave of an infinite number of cycles has a single frequency. However, if the number of cycles is curtailed somewhat (as it is in any practical application), it no longer has a spectrum consisting of one point, but rather of a group of nearby frequencies: its spectrum is somewhat broadened. The smaller the number of cycles, the broader will be the band of frequencies in its spatial spectrum. The breadth can be described by its bandwidth: the distance between the points at which the amplitude falls to half its maximum. This is usually specified in octaves (an octave being a 2/1 ratio).

A filter that correlated the input pattern with a sine wave of infinite extent would have absolutely precise spatial frequency information, since the only thing it would pass would be a sine wave of that precise frequency. If the filter contained only a limited number of cycles, it would pass a band of frequencies, and thus there would be some uncertainty in interpreting its output. A given output could have been produced by any of several nearby frequencies within its passband.

Although an extended sine wave filter would have very precise spatial frequency information, it would have considerable uncertainty with respect to the spatial location of a spatially delimited pattern. That is, a spatially restricted pattern that contained spatial frequencies within the filter's passband could be located at any of several positions within the field and produce the same output from the filter. If the filter were of limited extent (had a limited number of cycles), it would have a broader spatial frequency passband, but it would have reduced uncertainty about spatial location. There is thus a trade-off between uncertainty with respect to spatial frequency and uncertainty with respect to spatial location. A similar situation holds in the auditory system between specification of temporal frequency and the time at which an event takes place. An extended temporal frequency sample gives good temporal frequency resolution at the expense of information about time of occurrence, and vice versa. This problem was examined by Gabor (1946), who showed that a temporal filter with a gaussian fall-off (in both time and frequency, since a gaussian shape is a Fourier transform of itself) would minimize the product of the time and frequency uncertainties. A large number of cycles within the envelope would produce little frequency (but much time) uncertainty; a limited number of cycles would produce little time (but much frequency) uncertainty. But the total uncertainty would remain constant, given an overall gaussian envelope.

A further aspect of the Gabor functions (localized frequency filters with gaussian envelopes) is that, like pure sine and cosine waves, they can provide a complete description of any complex waveform (Helstrom, 1966). These functions can therefore give the concept of a spatially localized spatial frequency analysis, such as we were discussing earlier, mathematical precision. Although Gabor was considering one-dimensional temporal frequency analysis, his equations can equally well be applied in the spatial frequency domain (Marcelja, 1980), and expanded to two-dimensional patterns, with a gaussian taper in the second (orientation) dimension as well (Daugman, 1980). If localized spatial frequency filters have an overall two-dimensional gaussian profile, they would optimally specify the combination of spatial frequency and spatial location information, and could be utilized to characterize any complex stimulus. Thus a visual scene could be broken down into a mosaic of, say, 1,000 patches and the total information in the scene could be represented by the outputs of an array of Gabor filters with different frequency, orientation, and phase tuning within each patch. A cross section of such a localized spatial filter is shown in Figure 1.8.

Arrays of Gabor functions (gaussian-tapered sinusoids) are not the only possibility for a patchwise specification of a two-dimensional scene. Young (1986) points out that arrays of gaussian derivatives of different widths in each patch could serve the same purpose. These also have the property of being a complete set, that is of being able to encode any waveform.

Underlying Assumptions

All of our statements thus far about the analysis of complex waveforms into sine wave components are mathematical truisms, but the assumptions underlying them may or may not make them applicable to any given real-life situation. The most critical determinant of whether they can in fact be validly applied to any

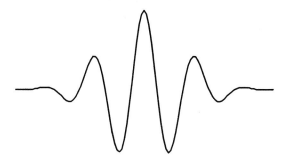

FIG. 1.8   Cross section of a localized spatial frequency filter. This Gabor filter is the product of a sinusoid and a gaussian distribution.

practical situation is the underlying assumption of linearity of summation, or superposition. For instance, suppose that when tested with individual sinusoids a cell gives 10 spikes to a pattern of frequency f and 5 spikes to a pattern of $2f$. Will it give 15 spikes to the combination of $f + 2f$ when they are simultaneously presented? Slight deviations from linearity of summation will only slightly change the result, but clearly any large nonlinearities would render the process of Fourier analysis or Fourier synthesis invalid.

An assumption of linearity is justified in the case of the physics of light, but it is much less obviously so in the case of the physiology of the retina or brain, or in the operation of the visual system as a whole. In fact, it is well known that some visual processes are very nonlinear indeed. For instance, the first quantitative visual relationship historically established—Weber's law—implies a logarithmic rather than a linear relation between light intensity and brightness. A number of nonlinearities have also been shown between certain physical variables and the output of cells in the visual system. It can thus not be assumed automatically that linear analysis can be meaningfully applied to any physiological or psychophysical process. However, most large deviations from linearity occur only under restricted and often rather unusual circumstances. For instance, the large deviations from linearity seen in Weber's Law demonstrations become apparent when brightness is measured over, say, a millionfold range of light intensities. But under ordinary visual circumstances, the range of light intensities within a given scene is usually no more than about 20 to 1. Within such a restricted range, the difference between a linear and a logarithmic function would be slight indeed. In practice, then, the visual system may approximate a linear system to a greater extent than one would assume from classical studies.

A further assumption underlying Fourier analysis is that of homogeneity or spatial invariance, namely, that the underlying structure is everywhere uniform in its properties. This is generally true for any but rather poorly constructed lenses, but it is certainly not so for the retina. As is well known, the central, foveal region is quite different in its properties from the periphery. Foveal cones are smaller and much more densely packed than those in peripheral regions, for instance. So the visual properties of the system are very nonhomogeneous across the whole retina. However, as discussed in the section on global versus local Fourier analysis, we will be concerned exclusively here with quite local properties of the system, rather than of the system as a whole. It is clear that the system itself deals (in the early processing at least) with purely local characteristics of the environment. Over such small distances, the retina is in fact quite homogeneous.

Different Applications of Fourier Analysis

We will be making use of the techniques of Fourier analysis in much of this book. It is important in this regard to differentiate between its application to the study of visual problems and the possibility that the visual system itself may be utilizing such techniques in dealing with visual stimuli. We will be concerned with both of these applications, but it is crucial to distinguish between them.

Linear systems analysis can be (and of course has been) applied to the study of complex waveforms in many physical systems, e.g., voltage waveforms in electronics, light going through optical systems, and seismic waves in the earth. The essence of such an analysis is that of breaking complex waveforms down into separate frequency components, thereby providing a means by which one can quantitatively characterize the shape of the waveform. Insofar as the visual system is approximately linear, a similar application can reasonably be made to quantify neural or psychophysical responses to complex waveforms (patterns) of light. For instance, if it is known (as it is) that the visual system cuts off at a particular high spatial frequency and attenuates low spatial frequencies as well, one can make certain predictions about how a visual scene will be perceived. Some details or overall characteristics of the scene will be invisible, others less prominent, etc.

Quite different from applying Fourier analysis to a quantitative study of some complex waveform such as seismic waves is the construction of a machine (or a computer program, or some other device) to *carry out* a Fourier analysis. For instance, one could build a bank of electronic filters tuned to different temporal frequencies into which a complex voltage waveform could be fed. The various outputs of the individual filters would then indicate the extent to which the input pattern had power in each frequency band, and this system of filters would thus act as a Fourier analyzer. Physiological mechanisms, as well as electronic or mechanical or computational ones, could conceivably be built to carry out such a frequency analysis. In fact, it has long been considered that the cochlea of the ear performs such an analysis of auditory waveforms, the different regions of the basilar membrane being tuned to different temporal frequency bands, so that each cochlear region responds insofar as the input sound wave has power at the frequencies to which that region is tuned. It is conceivable that the visual system is so built as to do a similar frequency analysis of the distribution of light across localized regions of space. An essential requirement for that to occur (and for which we will examine the psychophysical, physiological, and anatomical evidence) is that among the cells processing information from each given region in space there be ones tuned to each of a variety of different spatial frequencies. In the last chapter of the book we have a discussion of possible advantages and disadvantages of the visual system's having apparently evolved a physiological organization at early synaptic levels that approximates a patchwise Fourier analysis of visual space.

SUMMARY

Fourier analysis is a powerful tool for the study of complex waveforms, allowing one to specify quantitatively the characteristics of any complex waveform or shape. An additional major advantage in its application to vision is that it gives a common basis by which one can examine optical, physiological, and psycho-physical data. The principal limitation in its application to visual problems is the underlying assumption of linearity, a condition that is only met by the visual system under limited conditions. Finally, it is also possible that the visual system is so constructed as to itself carry out something approximating a local Fourier analysis in its attempt to deal with complex visual patterns.

2

Optics

Our ability to perceive the spatial relations in our visual world depends on a host of factors: on the nature of light, on the image-forming characteristics of the eye, on the photochemical changes within the receptors, on the transformation of the photochemical reactions into neural activity in the receptors, and on the analysis of the receptor output by neural networks in the retina and cortex. Volumes could be (and have been) written about each of these topics. To cover them all within one volume requires at best a superficial discussion of each topic. On the other hand, we do not wish to skip over these areas, because one of our main intents in writing this book is to present an integrated view of spatial vision, covering the anatomical, physiological, psychophysical, and perceptual aspects of the problems.

NATURE OF LIGHT AND VISUAL OBJECTS

Electromagnetic radiation can be alternatively thought of as consisting of waves of varying amplitude and wavelength, or as consisting of a stream of photons, with variations in number per unit time and in energy per photon. In discussing vision, we will use whichever terminology is most convenient for the topic under consideration.

The raw materials from which the visual system builds our percept of the world are the variations in electromagnetic radiation reaching the eye from different locations in space. The light from any given location in visual space (i.e., the light coming to the eye from any given direction) can vary in intensity (amplitude of the light wave, or number of photons/unit time), in wavelength (or energy per photon), and plane of polarization. Some birds and insects utilize polarization information (Waterman, 1981), but higher vertebrates use only intensity and wavelength. Since the light coming to the eye from neighboring objects may differ in wavelength but not in intensity, or in intensity but not in wavelength, an organism that can detect both wavelength and intensity variations and differentiate between them potentially has available two different, supplementary maps of spatial relations in the environment.

Quantum Fluctuations

A fundamental tenet of quantum physics is that there is a basic statistical character to the emission of photons from a radiating source: the number of photons
emitted per unit time fluctuates randomly about some mean value even for a
"steady" light source. There is therefore a basic indeterminacy about the intensity of a light: one can only give a statistical description of its value. The variable
number of photons emitted per unit time from a "steady" source is described
by a Poisson distribution (see Figure 2.1A). Thus if a group of receptors were
receiving photons emitted by a region of a luminous source at a mean rate of 5
photons per ⅒-s, the actual number recorded in successive time intervals might
be 4, 5, 2, 9, 7, 3, etc., rather than 5 in each interval, as would be true in the
absence of quantum fluctuations. Now suppose that the light is slightly increased
in intensity, to a mean photon emission of 6 per ⅒-s interval. It is obvious that
any one sample would be indistinguishable from those earlier; the increment
could only be detected by an analysis over repeated measures. The situation
would of course be even more difficult if one looked at the output of only one
receptor, rather than a group of them (see Figure 2.1B).

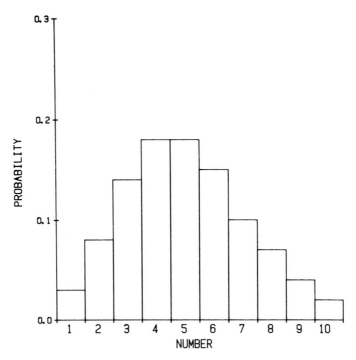

FIG. 2.1A   Poisson distribution. This histogram shows the probability of a given number
of photons being emitted in a given period from a source with a mean emission rate of 5
photons per unit time.

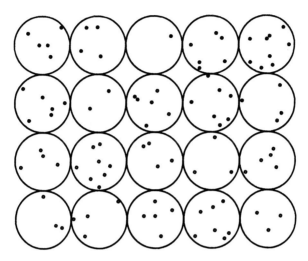

FIG. 2.1B Receptor stimulation by such a light source imaged on a particular retinal area. The large circle at top circumscribes a retinal area containing 19 receptors. The 20 circles below represent the same retinal area at 20 successive instants. Each dot represents a single photon. The individual receptors have been omitted from the lower drawings for the sake of clarity. This figure shows a possible distribution of photons emitted by a "steady" source with a mean rate of 5 photons per unit time, at each of 20 successive time intervals.

One can think of this random variation in number of photons emitted, the quantum fluctuation, as being "noise." Any variation in intensity and/or wavelength to be detected by the visual system can be thought of as a signal embedded in this noise: the basic limiting factor is the signal/noise ratio. There are also many potential sources of visual noise in more central visual processes, e.g., random fluctuations in neuronal membrane potentials, or in the amount of transmitter released at a synapse in response to a given amount of depolarization, etc. It appears, however, that the quantum fluctuations in the actual physical stimulus can account for most of the variability both in the neural responses and in the detection of flashes of light by observers under controlled laboratory conditions (Barlow, 1981).

It is clear that the reliability of an estimate of the intensity and/or wavelength can be increased by increasing the size of the sample. The signal/noise ratio of the quantum fluctuations in fact is proportional to the square root of the sample size (De Vries, 1943; Rose, 1948). Thus increasing the sample size by a factor of 100 would increase the signal/noise ratio 10-fold. So one can gain a more accurate measure by averaging over larger and larger areas, or over longer and longer times. Such averaging, however, occurs at the expense of spatial and temporal resolution, respectively. As one averages over larger and larger areas the ability to resolve fine spatial detail is increasingly lost; averaging light over time produces a similar loss of temporal detail. Thus the visual system is continually faced with a trade-off between accuracy of luminance (and wavelength) specification and spatiotemporal resolution.

The relative importance of the quantum fluctuations—the extent of the statistical indeterminacy—would clearly also be a function of the light level. The signal/noise ratio can be increased not only by averaging over larger areas and times, but also by an increase in the mean light level. The visual system can thus potentially judge intensity and/or wavelength more accurately at high light levels than at low. Alternatively, the visual system might increase its spatiotemporal resolution as light levels increase, while keeping the same accuracy of judgment. As we shall see, both of these processes in fact occur.

Self-Luminous Versus Reflecting Objects

For the purposes of vision it is important to distinguish between two different types of light sources, self-luminous objects and reflecting objects. The major self-luminous object in the natural world is of course the sun, but there are also such sources as other stars, fireflies, and fire. Even with the invention of many additional artificial light sources, however, most objects of visual interest are not these self-luminous sources but rather objects such as trees, people, and other things that do not themselves emit light but rather reflect some portion of whatever light falls on them.

The reason for making this distinction is not, of course, that emitted and reflected light are different physically, but that their sources behave quite differently as visual objects. Self-luminous objects emit an amount of light that is independent of the general illumination. To detect and characterize such objects, an ideal visual system would have the ability to code absolute light level. A reflecting object, on the other hand, will transmit very different amounts of light to the eye, depending on the illumination. It will reflect very high intensities if it is in direct sunlight at high noon and very low intensities at dusk or in deep shadow. Knowing the absolute level of light coming from a reflecting object in isolation, then, tells the organism much about the illuminant, e.g., time of day, but little or nothing about the nature of the object. That which characterizes a reflecting object, for example that which distinguishes a white object from a black object, is not the *amount* of light it reflects to the eye. That will be high for both objects in direct sunlight and low for both in the dark. But a white object reflects a higher *proportion*, say 80%, of whatever light is incident on it, whereas a black object reflects only a small proportion, perhaps 5%, of incident light. The critical information for vision, then, is not the absolute amount of light coming from different locations, but the amount of light coming from a location relative to that coming from other locations. That which remains invariant about an object, and thus allows us to identify its lightness, is the amount of light coming from the object relative to that coming from other objects in the field.

IMAGE FORMATION BY THE EYE

Most sources that emit or reflect light do so diffusely in many directions. Light from all visual locations thus arrives at each point in space. If this were not the case, visual objects would appear and disappear as we moved about putting our eyes in different locations. The light from objects in different locations or from different parts of a given object differs, however, in the *direction* from which it arrives at the eye.

Our spatial vision, our ability to determine the shape and location of objects, depends on our ability to determine the direction from which the light rays emanate. A first step toward accomplishing this would be to have light from different directions go to different receptors. In some invertebrate compound eyes, the receptors themselves have a significant degree of directional selectivity and are aimed in different directions. In vertebrate eyes (and in many invertebrate simple eyes) the receptors themselves have relatively little directional selectivity, but the optical system of the eye is so arranged that light from each particular location goes to a different retinal region and thus to a different group of receptors.

To a first approximation, light can be considered to travel in a straight line, as a ray, and to be unaffected by nearby edges. The principles by which light rays are reflected and refracted at interfaces between different materials constitute the field of geometrical optics. Many of the optical properties of the eye can be understood from geometrical optics, and these will be discussed first. Under some circumstances, the approximations of geometrical optics are no longer sufficient and one must turn to the principles of physical optics.

Refraction

The velocity of light in a vacuum, c, is about 3×10^8 m/s, and is one of the fundamental physical constants. It is equal to the product of the wavelength, λ, and the frequency, ν, of light:

$$c = \lambda\nu.$$

When light passes through any medium other than a vacuum, its velocity is decreased. Since the frequency of the light remains constant, the wavelength is

decreased by some amount, depending on the medium through which it is passing. The velocity of light in a given substance also depends somewhat on the
frequency of the light, this being the cause of chromatic aberrations of the eye,
as discussed below.

When a ray of light passes from one medium to another at an angle (see Figure
2.2), it will be bent or refracted by an amount proportional to the angle of incidence and to the ratio of the velocity of light in the two substances. The ratio of
the velocity of light in air to its velocity in some other substance is called the
index of refraction of that substance. For water this is 1.33, and for glass it is 1.5
or more. Since the velocity differences vary with wavelength, the index of refraction of these substances is slightly different for each wavelength.

Optics of the Eye

The property of refraction is utilized in the construction of lenses. The surface
of a lens may be shaped to focus the beam of light entering the lens onto a point

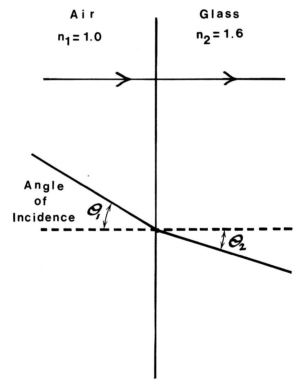

FIG. 2.2   Refraction of light. The refraction of light is described by Snell's law: $n_1 \sin \phi_1$
$= n_2 \sin \phi_2$, where n_1 is the index of refraction in the first medium, n_2 is the index of
refraction in the second medium, ϕ_1 is the angle of incidence, and ϕ_2 is the angle of
refraction.

some distance from the lens. The refractive power of a lens is specified in diopters, a diopter being the reciprocal of the focal length of the lens in meters. Thus a 1-diopter lens will bring a parallel beam to a focus at 1 m; a 10-diopter lens will focus a parallel beam at $\frac{1}{10}$ m or 100 mm.

The average human eye is of such a length that for a parallel beam of light coming from a distant object (say beyond 10 m) to be brought to a focus on the retina at the back of the eye, the eye must have a total optical power of about 60 diopters (Gullstrand, 1924; Le Grand, 1957). For the diverging rays coming from an object closer to the eye than 10 m, a still more powerful optical element is required.

Light is refracted in the eye by two principal structures, at the cornea and at the lens. Of these, the greater refraction occurs at the front surface of the cornea, both because of the considerable curvature of the corneal surface and because of the large difference in the indices of refraction of air (1.0) and the corneal tissue (1.3). The cornea normally has a total optical power of about 40 diopters, so it alone would bring a parallel beam to a focus $\frac{1}{40}$ m or 25 mm back. The additional optical power required to bring it to a focus on the retina is furnished by the lens. The lens has the additional advantage of having variable optical power because it is elastic. When the capsule enclosing the lens is tensed (by the relaxation of the surrounding ciliary muscle) the lens is stretched into a flatter shape with less optical power. The changing of the shape of the lens to provide focus at different distances is called accommodation. In a young child the lens supplies a variable optical power of about 10 to 30 diopters. With increasing age, the elasticity of the lens decreases, and it eventually assumes a fairly rigid elongated shape. Past the age of about 45 years, therefore, few people can focus on nearby objects without the additional aid of reading glasses.

The path of the light rays through the eye's optical system is represented diagrammatically in Figure 2.3A. The visual object AB can be considered either self-luminous (radiating light in all directions) or reflective (reflecting light in all directions). Only a small part of the light coming from this object will reach the eye, and we will just consider those rays coming into the eye from the end-points of the object, A and B. The central ray from point A, hitting the cornea normal to the surface, will not be bent at all and will strike the retina at point A'. The slightly diverging rays from point A will be bent increasingly more as the angle with which they strike the cornea becomes increasingly steep. As a result, they will also strike the retina at point A'. The corresponding process will operate from point B to retinal locus B', and for all points between A and B. The result will be an inverted image on the retina from A' to B' of a line from A to B.

A simplified version of Figure 2.3A is shown in Figure 2.3B, where only the central rays from A to A' and from B to B' are shown, and these central rays are assumed to go through the eye's optics unrefracted. The point within the eye where these beams cross is called the *nodal point* of the eye. The diagram in Figure 2.3B would hold precisely only if the refraction in the eye occurred at only one surface, e.g., at the air-corneal interface. More complicated optical systems can be modeled accurately with two nodal points, the rays from A to nodal point 1 and from nodal point 2 to A' being parallel. The eye, then, has two nodal

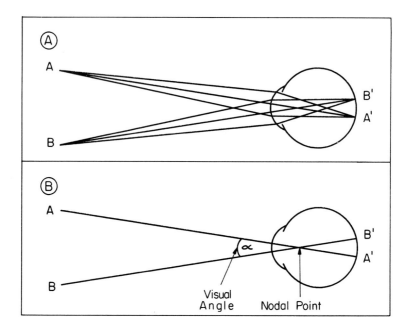

FIG. 2.3   A simplified drawing (A) of the path of light rays through the eye's optical system, ignoring refraction by the lens. In drawing B, only the chief rays from A and B are shown.

points, but they are so close together that Figure 2.3B is in fact a satisfactory first approximation.

Specifying only the physical dimensions of an object is an insufficient way of describing its retinal image size, since the size of the retinal image is obviously a function of the object's distance as well as of its physical dimensions. Rather than stating that an object is x meters long at a distance of y meters, its retinal size can more usefully be represented by specifying the visual angle it subtends with respect to the nodal point of the eye (see Figure 2.3B). This visual angle is the dimension which we will henceforth use, not only to specify the size of outside objects but also intraocular dimensions. For a normal eye having a length of about 24 mm, and a nodal point 7 mm behind the cornea, 1° of visual angle corresponds to about 300 μm on the retina. Thus the foveal pit in the retina subtends about 2° visual angle, and the optic disk is about 6° in diameter (see Chapter 3).

In the idealized pictures shown in Figure 2.3A, all the light coming into the eye from point A is shown coming to a precise focus at retinal point A′, and correspondingly for B and B′. If points A and B, then, are infinitesimally small points, A′ and B′ will also be infinitely fine points. And if line AB is infinitely narrow, so will be its image A′B′ on the retina. The real world is, of course, never quite so simple. In fact, not all of the light from point A will fall at point A′. It will instead be smeared around to some extent onto neighboring retinal areas.

Correspondingly, not all the light falling on retinal point A′ in fact comes from point A in space; some will have come from neighboring regions. This optical smearing or blurring, whatever its origin, can be considered an imperfection since it leads to a loss of information in going from spatial points AB to retinal points A′B′. There are a number of sources of such blurring, among them spherical aberrations in the optics of the eye, chromatic aberration, light scatter off objects or surfaces inside or outside the eye, diffraction, and imperfect focus of the eye. These will be discussed in turn.

IMPERFECTIONS OF THE EYE

Spherical Aberrations

In Figure 2.3A all the diverging rays from point A would fall at A′ if and only if the optical surfaces of the eye—the front and back surfaces of the cornea and of the lens—had precisely the correct curvature and the correct variations in refractive indices. The optical surfaces of the eye all approximate segments of spheres of various diameters. With such spherical lenses, the rays going through the edge of the lens are brought to a focus closer than are the central rays. This imperfection is called spherical aberration. Spherical aberrations cannot be completely corrected in two dimensions by changes in the shape of the lens, although aspheric surfaces can help. The optimal solution is a constant decrease in refractive index of the lens with distance out from the center. The primate eye generally has a slightly aspheric shape that minimizes spherical aberrations, but the cornea does not have the regional variation in refractive index that would eliminate the problem. Given the fact that the eye is built out of limited materials shaped under the control of what must surely be extremely sketchy genetic instructions, the wonder is not that the eye does not have precisely the right shape but rather that it comes so close.

Chromatic Aberration

In the diagrams of Figures 2.2 and 3, the light was implicitly assumed to be all of one wavelength. The situation is more complex when more than one wavelength of light is involved, e.g., with the broad spectrum of white light. At any interface, such as that shown in Figure 2.2, the amount of refraction depends on the wavelength of the light as well as on the angle of incidence and the indices of refraction, as discussed earlier. The shorter the wavelength, the greater the amount of refraction. Thus if the middle wavelength (green) light from a point is focused on the retina, the short wavelength (blue) light will come to a focus in front of the retina and will therefore be blurred on the retina itself. The long wavelength (red) light will be focused behind the retina and will also be blurred.

Even the cheapest camera has color-compensating lenses that minimize if not eliminate chromatic aberration through the use of two or more different varieties of glass of different refractive characteristics. The eye, however, has no such color-compensating elements. Having produced an optical system with much chromatic aberration, however, the eye has a variety of strategies for minimizing the damage. Many of these will be discussed later; we merely note here that chromatic aberration is a nontrivial problem for the visual system.

Light Scatter

If there were absolutely clear air, we could not see the beam from a car's headlights when standing slightly to one side. Almost always, though, the air contains particles of dust or fog or other substances that produce some scatter of the light beam in many other directions. So the light arriving at retinal point A' will not all have come from point A in space; some light from point B and many other close or even distant points might also arrive there.

Light scatter is by no means restricted to the air outside the eye; there is also considerable scatter within the eye itself. This scatter is from two main sources: particles within the eye, and reflection off various intraocular surfaces. In the normal eye there are relatively few internal particles, but it is not unusual for there to be scraps of tissue, often remnants of an incompletely resorbed hyaloid artery, that float in the vitreous humor behind the lens. Light bouncing off such "floaters" will be scattered considerably. A much more severe but still common abnormality is the formation of a cataractous lens. This consists of the development of various forms of opacities within the lens. The dispersion of light caused by a cataract can in the extreme case almost totally prevent the formation of an optical image: light from some point in space is almost equally likely to end up in any one point as in any other on the retina.

Light scatter by floating intraocular particles can be considered an abnormality, but the scatter due to reflections from normal retinal structures is of course not. There are reflections off all the optical surfaces, the front and back surfaces of the cornea and of the lens. The portion of the reflection that comes directly out of the eye can be seen as spot-like images on the cornea if a light is shined into someone's eye (these are called the Purkinje images, after the man who first discussed them). The small amount of light that is scattered from these surfaces into the eye produces some degradation of the optical image. Far more scatter, however, is caused by reflection off retinal structures, in particular the blood vessels that nourish the inner retinal layers, and the highly reflective optic disk, where the nerve fibers gain their opaque, reflective myelin sheath on exiting from the eye. Both of these structures play a considerable role in degrading the optical image.

To initiate vision, light must reach rod and cone receptor cells that lie at the back of the retina, behind all the other visual neurons. In general, the neural elements of the retina are quite transparent, and little light scatter occurs as the light traverses them to reach the receptors at the back of the eye. These neurons lying in the light path are therefore not a major source of blur. A significant amount of reflection occurs from the pigment epithelium cells at the very back of the eye, however. In some nocturnal animals such as cats and deer this reflection from behind the retina is enhanced by the presence of a highly reflective surface behind the receptors, called the tapetum. As a result, their eyes glow in the light from a car's headlights. The function of such a tapetum would appear to be to increase the chance of capture of a photon by reflecting back any photons that were not captured on their first pass through the receptors. Some of the reflection will go laterally to neighboring receptors, though, and thus degrade the optical image. We and other diurnal animals do not have a reflecting tapetum, but rather a highly absorptive pigment epithelium behind the receptors. Nonetheless, enough light is reflected back out of our eyes that it can be used to study photopigment function by a technique known as reflection densitometry (Rushton, 1957; Weale, 1959).

Diffraction

According to the principles of geometrical optics, light rays travel in straight lines unaffected by the presence of nearby edges. This is a reasonable approximation except when the beam passes through a narrow aperture (opening). When that occurs, diffraction and the principles of physical optics must be taken into consideration.

Light can be considered as a wave that covers a certain area. When there is an edge in this area the light interacts with it. The part of the beam passing near the edge will be bent and dispersed laterally much as if it had passed through a prism. So if a pinhole aperture of a diameter equal to the wavelength of the light were put in a parallel beam (see Figure 2.4), one would expect from geometrical optics that all of the beam would be blocked by the aperture except for the one ray that would go through unaffected to form a sharp image of the pinhole on the far wall. This is not at all what in fact does occur. Rather, the portion of the beam going through the aperture is subject to diffraction and a whole fan of rays comes out of the pinhole to illuminate a large area of the wall instead of just a spot. If the size of the aperture is increased more and more, the region subject to diffraction, at the perimeter of the circle, increases in proportion to the radius of the aperture. The total beam, however, increases with the area of the circle and thus the square of the radius. Therefore, the proportion of the beam subject to diffraction becomes smaller and smaller with increasing aperture size.

Were it not for diffraction, one could eliminate problems of spherical and chromatic aberration of lenses (and problems of focus of the image as well) by substituting a pinhole aperture in the eye for the cornea and lens; this would form a perfect (if very dim) image of the world on the retina. However, with physical optics to be considered, there is a trade-off between aberrations and

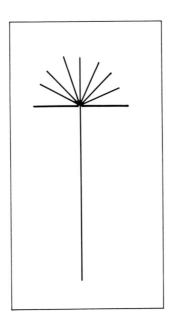

FIG. 2.4   Diffraction of light. This figure illustrates the diffraction produced by passing a parallel beam through a pinhole aperture.

diffraction as aperture size varies. As the pupil of the eye constricts, the effects of aberrations decrease but diffraction increases. The optimum pupil size is thus some intermediate value, as discussed further below.

Imperfect Focus

A final factor we should consider among those which produce imperfections in the optical image is imperfect focus of the image. Referring back to Figure 2.3A, it can be seen that under ideal circumstances the whole beam of light emanating from a given spatial locus would be brought to a focus at a given retinal point. If, for whatever reason, the optical power of cornea and lens is either too strong or too weak, however, the beam will be brought to a focus either in front of or behind the retina and will thus be blurred at the retina itself. We can categorize the potential causes of imperfect focus as structural abnormalities, a slow focusing process, and the fact that in a three-dimensional world objects are at different distances and thus cannot all be in focus at once.

Structural Abnormalities

Many potential defects in the shape of the eye can compromise its ability to focus light on the retina (in addition, of course, to the limitations which the optics of even the best eyes show, as discussed earlier). The cornea and lens may have the "correct" curvature for the particular species in question, but the eyeball itself may be too long or too short. If the eyeball is of the correct shape (see Figure 2.5A), objects at optical infinity will come to a focus at the retina with a relaxed lens. Nearby objects can then also be brought to a focus with an accommodative increase in refractive power of the lens. When the eye is too long, a condition referred to as myopia or near-sightedness (see Figure 2.5B), distant objects will come to a focus in front of the retina with a relaxed lens. Since any increase in accommodation will only worsen the problem, distant objects are always out of focus. Nearby objects will be in focus even without accommodation in such an eye, hence the term near-sightedness.

With too short an eyeball (see Figure 2.5C), distant objects will come to a focus behind the retina when accommodation is relaxed, but can be brought to a focus on the retina with accommodative effort. Nearby objects, however, will come to a focus so far behind the retina that they cannot be focused even with accommodative effort. This condition is often thus referred to as far-sightedness, or hyperopia.

Although eyeballs that are either too long or too short are the most common structural bases of such abnormalities, an incorrect curvature of the cornea with

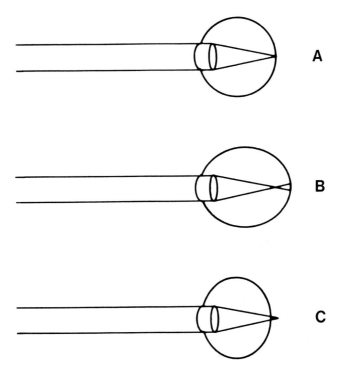

FIG. 2.5   Illustrations of (A) emmetropic, (B) myopic, and (C) hyperopic eyes. Given identical corneas and (relaxed) lenses, the images will be brought to a focus either on the retina (A), in front of the retina (B), or behind the retina (C), due to differences in the length of the eyeball.

correct eye size would have the same effect. A common defect of this sort is a cornea that does not have the same curvature in all directions. The resulting astigmatism produces images that are in focus at some orientations and out of focus at others. Besides these abnormalities of eye size or shape, a natural consequence of aging is the loss of accommodative power in the lens. An increasing portion of the visual world is thus out of focus in older individuals.

One can legitimately point out that almost all of these structural abnormalities can be eliminated with the use of proper spectacles or contact lenses. However, very few cats or monkeys or other animals go around wearing glasses (outside of vision laboratories, where we sometimes do indeed fit them with glasses). It was only recently in human history that spectacles were invented for our use, and even today very many humans do not have access to them. The point we are making here is that the visual system must be able to function reasonably well despite all these imperfections: it did not evolve in anticipation of the invention of spectacles in the fourteenth century.

Slow Focus

We have extremely mobile eyes and are constantly shifting our gaze from one place to another, seldom fixating one spot for more than ¼ to ½ s. Lateral fixational movements of the eyes (versional movements) are very rapid, the eyes being thrown in parallel with sudden muscular bursts from one position to another at rates up to 800°/s (Hyde, 1959). However, when points that are fixated successively are at different depths, the eyes must either converge or diverge; such vergence movements are very much slower than versional movements. The visual system must also take in and process the input from the new locus, decide that it is out of focus (and if so, whether too close or too far), and finally make the appropriate muscular response with the ciliary muscles to change the shape of the lens. During all this time, a significant fraction of a second or more, the optical image will be out of focus and blurred. Since changing fixation from an object at one depth to one at another is by no means a rare visual occurrence, the optical image on the retina must be out of focus for this reason alone a significant proportion of the time.

Multiple Depths

Since our visual world is three-dimensional, objects at different depths are almost always present. So except for that limited segment of our lives that we spend looking at scenes painted on the wall of a cyclorama, not all the objects in a visual scene will be simultaneously in focus on the retina. When we focus on an object at some depth, the images of objects nearer and farther (indeed even perhaps other parts of the same object) will be blurred. Nonetheless, vision goes on.

Finally, it should be pointed out that our focusing mechanism operates mainly on information from the central (foveal) portion of the retina. It is the image in this part of the world that we try to maintain in focus by changing the shape of the lens. Whether the peripheral image is in focus or not depends purely on the chance that it is at the same depth as the field in the center of gaze. It is thus doubtless far more common for the central than the peripheral portion of the optical image to be in focus.

We must now qualify somewhat this picture we have been painting of a very fuzzy visual world. First of all, objects beyond a certain depth, approximately 3 to 4 m, are all equivalently at optical infinity. If one is in focus so will they all be.

Second, the eye has a certain depth of focus, so that even in the case of nearby objects, those at somewhat different depths can at times be simultaneously sharply focused. The range of the depth of focus depends on pupil size, just as it does with the f-stop in a camera. The reason for this can be readily grasped by considering that the central rays in a bundle (see Figure 2.3A again) go through the eye's optics essentially unrefracted and are therefore "in focus" regardless of depth. If diffraction were not a factor, a pinhole aperture would thus transmit an image in which objects at all depths would be equally in focus. As the pinhole is enlarged, however, noncentral rays will be let through; these must be refracted by the optical elements to bring them to a common focus with the central rays. But the noncentral rays will be hitting the cornea at different angles depending on the depth at which they originate, and increasingly so as more and more lateral corneal regions are involved. Thus the depth of focus decreases with increasing pupil size. Under bright daylight conditions the pupil is small and we have a large depth of focus; in dim light, with a large pupil, only objects very close to the fixation plane will be in sharp focus. Depth of focus is more of a problem with nearby than with distant objects, since everything beyond a few meters is essentially at optical infinity and thus effectively at the same depth. The visual system corrects for this with a reflex constriction of the pupil when an object is brought close to the viewer, even though there is no change in overall light level.

As should be abundantly clear by now, the simplistic picture of the optics of the eye forming a precise, sharp image of the world on the retina is quite misleading. Under the best of circumstances, the retinal image is considerably blurred and degraded by spherical and chromatic aberrations and diffraction. There are numerous factors that further degrade the optics in normal life, such as, for instance, the fact that in a three-dimensional world much of the visual image is necessarily out of focus and thus blurred.

Instability of the Eye

In our discussion so far we have been implicitly assuming that the whole process of image formation and the resulting transfer of information to the nervous system occurs instantaneously. This is not the case. Rather, the image must be kept steady on the retina for a period of time; the eye, like a camera, requires a finite exposure duration. A camera with an excellent lens possessing little spherical or chromatic aberration can have an image well focused on the film, but if one uses a one-s exposure and jiggles the camera during the shot, the picture will be blurred. The actual "exposure duration" of the eye is a variable quantity which the visual system changes as a function of light level and other factors, but it is always long enough to make the instability of the eye a serious optical problem.

There are at least two reasons why the visual system has a significant (roughly 10-100 ms or more) "exposure duration" or integration time. One is that it requires some time, particularly in dim light, for the system to gain enough light to specify a scene (just as is the case for photographic film). The other is that the physiological signaling of information, from the ganglion cells in the retina on through later parts of the brain, is by bursts of nerve impulses at varying rates. Each burst requires a finite period of time, so the system cannot give an instantaneous message, but can only signal what has occurred during this time period.

Vibration of the Eye

In a typical visual sequence, the eyes make rapid movements to fixate a given point, then pause (typically for 200-400 ms), then make another movement to a new fixation point. During the eye movements themselves, the optical image of any two-dimensional object will be grossly blurred on the retina, but we seem somehow to discard most of the visual input from these intervals (Latour, 1962; Volkmann, 1962). What concerns us here is the extent to which the eye is stable during the fixational pauses, when visual information *is* being taken in and integrated.

The eye lies cushioned in fat in the bony orbit, held in place mainly by the six relatively massive muscles that move it. It is thus admirably adapted for rapid movement, but not very well designed for holding still (these being somewhat contradictory requirements). Studies of the eye during fixation periods indicate that, in fact, it is not very stable (Ditchburn & Ginsborg, 1952; Riggs, Ratliff, J.C. Cornsweet & T.N. Cornsweet, 1953; Steinman, 1965). There are numerous very small oscillations with an average rate of about 80 Hz, and an average extent of about 20 to 30″ arc (Yarbus, 1967). These presumably reflect the random variations in discharge rate of the eye muscles, each of which must be under some degree of constant tension to hold the eye in a given location. In addition, there are microsaccades of 5′ arc or more, as well as occasional gradual drifts of the eye in one direction or another which will eventually be detected and compensated for by a rapid flick back to roughly the original point of fixation (Steinman, 1965). The net effect of these tremors and drifts is to produce a certain amount of optical blur even under optimal conditions of fixation.

Head Movements

Most visual experiments are conducted with the subject's head more or less rigidly stabilized with a head rest or bite bar. Under ordinary viewing conditions, of course, we rarely attain such stability of head position. Indeed, when we are walking or driving, our head and eyes are moving continuously, not only with the direct forward movement but with numerous accompanying jiggles and bounces. The blur produced by these movements must also be considered in evaluating the nature of the optical image. The bounces made at each step as we walk or those which occur while driving produce blurring of the whole optical image. If you fixate a point toward which you are moving, that part of the image will not change much as you approach, except to enlarge. Other more peripheral parts of the retinal image, however, will be undergoing more movement and thus blur. The same holds for objects to one side that one fixates while moving past them. During rotational (rather than translational) movements of the head, the entire retinal image will be displaced. Although we have well-developed compensatory eye movements that rotate the eyes opposite to the head movement to keep the image roughly constant on the retina, such compensation is far from complete.

The principal effect of these various types of movement of the retinal image is a loss of high spatial frequency information. For instance, a random tremor of 2' arc would essentially obliterate information for spatial frequencies with that period or less, that is, those of more than 30 c/deg. Lower spatial frequencies would be affected less and less the lower the frequency. For a given velocity of eye movement, the temporal frequency (the rate of on-and-off stimulation of a particular retinal location) increases with higher spatial frequencies. Very rapid movements or bounces would likely move high spatial frequency components faster than the maximum discriminable rate. Again, medium and low spatial frequencies would be less affected.

CORRECTIVE MECHANISMS FOR IMPERFECTIONS OF THE EYE

Considering all the imperfections of the human optical system we have been listing, one may quite reasonably wonder whether we are leading up to the final conclusion that vision is impossible, perhaps like the proverbial scientist who, after considering the aerodynamic properties of the bumblebee, supposedly concluded that it could not possibly fly. Our conclusions are not so drastic. First, as we shall discuss here, there are a number of mechanisms that correct or at least ameliorate the effects of certain of the optical imperfections. Secondly, however, we are led to the conclusion that vision would indeed be impossible under many circumstances if it depended on the resolution of fine detail or high spatial frequencies.

Pupil Size

The central rays from A and B in Figure 2.3 are bent little if at all, so spherical aberration would be slight if only central rays entered the eye. As larger and larger bundles of rays from these points pass through increasingly larger segments of the imperfect curvatures of the cornea and lens, the aberrations become significantly worse. A decrease in pupil diameter, restricting the light from various objects to the central rays, lessens not only spherical aberration, but chromatic aberration as well: the minimally refracted rays of all wavelengths will come to a focus at virtually the same point.

The size of the optical bundles getting through to the retina is regulated in the eye by the *iris*, an annular pigmented structure just in front of the lens. When a circular muscle in the iris contracts, the size of the opening, the *pupil*, decreases; as this muscle relaxes, the pupil enlarges. (In cats and certain other animals the iris movement is more like that of two curtains sliding toward each other to form a variable-width slit, which allows a greater range of pupil sizes.)

In determining the optimal pupillary diameter, as with many visual functions we will be discussing, there are opposing processes operating. A decrease in pupil size as a corrective mechanism is accomplished at two major costs. One is that as the pupil size decreases optical quality improves but the amount of light decreases. As the pupil expands, one gains more light but at the expense of increased spherical and chromatic aberration and blur due to accommodative errors. One might therefore expect that the optimum pupillary diameter varies with illumination level, small pupils being better in bright light, large pupils in dim light. Such a variation of pupillary diameter with light level is, of course, found.

The second factor is light scatter due to diffraction. As pupil size decreases, diffraction increases and at some point will more than overcome the improvement in the retinal image due to the minimization of spherical and chromatic aberration and other blur. The pupil size at which the increased diffraction will just balance the decreased aberration is to some extent a function of the spatial frequencies being considered. Aberrations affect high spatial frequencies much more than low. Decreasing pupil size, then, does little to improve the resolution of low spatial frequencies. Scatter due to diffraction also mainly reduces high spatial frequencies, but it affects low spatial frequencies to some extent as well. The pupil size that optimally balances diffraction against aberration is thus very small (ca. 2 mm) for the very highest spatial frequencies, but somewhat larger if only low spatial frequencies are considered.

At high light levels there is potentially enough information available for the visual system to resolve the highest spatial frequencies that the optics can transmit. It is thus advantageous for the visual system to have a small pupil size in bright light in order to optimize the high spatial frequency content in the visual image. Under dim light conditions, however, there is not enough information, given quantum fluctuations in the light, to resolve the highest spatial frequencies even if they were passed by the optics. Under these conditions, a larger pupil size is advantageous both in letting more light into the eye to provide more visual information, and in attaining the best balance between diffraction and aberration for the lower spatial frequency range which is now the highest resolvable by the system.

Directionality of Receptors

An important visual mechanism that has the effect of minimizing the deleterious effects of both aberration and light scatter was discovered by Stiles and Crawford (1933), and is commonly known as the Stiles-Crawford effect. They found that human observers are considerably more sensitive to light coming through the center of the pupil than they are to the off-center rays (see Figure 2.6). (The central rays also have a somewhat different color appearance, an effect known as the Stiles-Crawford effect of the second kind.)

The Stiles-Crawford effect can best be explained if one assumes that cones are pointed toward the entrance pupil of the eye, and if light coming directly into

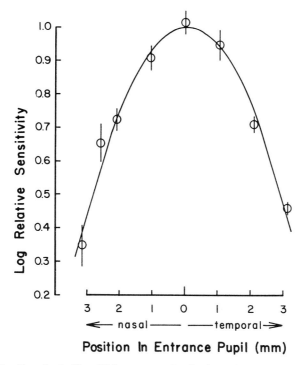

FIG. 2.6   Stiles-Crawford effect. Light rays coming in through the center of the entrance pupil and thus hitting the cones straight on are more effective than those which come in through the periphery of the entrance pupil and thus strike the cones obliquely (data kindly provided by V. Lakshminarayanan).

the cone is more effective than that coming in from an angle. Light coming through the center of the pupil would thus hit the cones straight on and be more effective than the off-center rays, which would strike the receptors at an angle.

There is now good evidence for both of these assumptions. The cones not only are aimed toward the center of the pupil, but they have also been shown to make phototropic movements over a period of days to so orient themselves if the center of the pupil changes. So an individual with an eccentric pupil, resulting from trauma, has a correspondingly eccentric Stiles-Crawford effect (Bonds & MacLeod, 1978), and the center of the Stiles-Crawford effect can be shifted over days by wearing an artificial pupil centered at some other point (Applegate & Bonds, 1981; Enoch & Birch, 1981).

The basis for the directionality of the cones is presumably their tapered shape and the indices of refraction of cones compared with the surrounding fluid (Sidman, 1957; Walraven & Bouman, 1960). The result is that rays coming directly into a cone would be reflected down the tapering inner segment to reach the outer segment, which contains the photopigment. Rays deviating too much from this angle, however, would hit the inner segment walls at too abrupt an angle and would pass out of the receptor rather than being reflected down to the pigment (Walraven & Bouman, 1960). The fact that observers show little Stiles-Crawford effect with rod vision is well established (Crawford, 1937), but the explanation for the difference is not. It may be due to a lack of precise orientation of the rods toward the entrance pupil, or to a basic lack of directionality to the individual receptors, because of their lack of taper. Support for the second possibility comes from the observation that the Stiles-Crawford effect is reduced in the fovea, where the cones are less tapered than they are in the periphery.

The overall consequence of the Stiles-Crawford effect is to counteract the deleterious effects (but to some extent the benefits as well) of increased pupil size for cone but not rod vision. In particular, the effect of the blurring produced by light scattered inside the eye would be considerably reduced by this directionality of the cones.

Limiting Spectral Range

With a non-color-correcting optical system, the human eye has a serious problem with chromatic aberration, the light from different spectral regions coming to a focus at different depths. The more extreme the spectral range, particularly toward shorter wavelengths, the greater the problem. The various corrective measures taken by the visual system are all based on that fact and its natural solution: narrowing the spectral range, particularly in the blue. This spectral narrowing is accomplished in a variety of ways: (1) The rods and the two cone types (L and M cones) that constitute ca. 90–95% of the cone population have their peak sensitivities in the middle of the visible spectrum. The contribution of rays from the spectral extremes, which are most out of focus, is thus minimized. Furthermore, the eye probably usually focuses at a midspectral region. (2) The one cone type (S cones) that does peak near a spectral extreme apparently has no input to the part of the visual system that detects intensity variations. (3) The lens is rather yellow, absorbing short wavelengths and thus curtailing the spectrum at that end. Light below 400 nm is virtually eliminated, and significant absorption occurs up to 450 or even 500 nm, particularly in older observers (Said & Weale, 1959). (4) A further elimination of short-wavelength light takes place in the central retina where the macular pigment filters the light reaching the central receptors. This pigment has considerable absorption in the short wavelengths up to about 500 nm (Wald, 1949). (5) In the central foveal area, the already scarce S cones are further reduced in number and are perhaps missing altogether (Wald, 1967; Marc & Sperling, 1977; De Monasterio, Schein, & McCrane, 1981).

One may legitimately wonder whether it would not have been more reasonable for the visual system to have evolved a color-corrected optical system. To have done so, however, we would not only have to have evolved a second lens material of different refractive characteristics from the current cornea and lens (and of course of the right shape), but to have developed some more complex way of changing accommodation than by changing the shape of a single lens.

Inverted Retina, and Fovea

An intriguing mystery which has prompted wide-ranging speculation (e.g., Walls, 1937) is the fact that the vertebrate retina is inverted, with the receptors facing the back of the eye rather than toward the light. Light must thus traverse the layers of neural elements as well as the main body of the receptors before it reaches the photopigment in the receptor outer segments. It is hard to escape the conclusion that the inverted vertebrate retina is an unfortunate evolutionary accident, but one that was not so disastrous as to be eliminated. There are numerous compensating mechanisms that limit the deleterious effects, but it is clearly not the optimal design. In particular, the inverted retina results in a large gap in the receptor mosaic at the optic disk, to allow the optic nerve fibers to leave the eye. Such a relatively enormous hole in the retina would not be needed if the vertebrate retina, like that of the invertebrate simple eye, had developed facing the other way around.

The neurons that lie in the optical path are as transparent as the vitreous humour and thus do not provide any optical problem. The numerous arteries, veins, and capillaries, which form a rich plexus among these neural elements, are, however, far from transparent. They are a significant source of light scatter in the eye. These retinal blood vessels nourish the postreceptor neural elements; the receptors themselves get their nutrients from the choroid outside the retina. Since the metabolic requirements of the receptors exceed those of all the later elements together, it can be argued that the inverted retina has the advantage of getting the main blood supply out of the optical path and thus minimizing light scatter. However, this might be better accomplished with a verted retina in which the blood vessels for the receptors surrounded them just behind the outer segments, thus totally out of the optical path.

A second way in which the inverted retina minimizes light scatter is by providing a dense, absorbing pigment layer, the pigment epithelium, immediately behind the receptors and extending to some extent between the receptors as well. It seems logical, however, that a verted system with the pigment epithelium in close proximity behind the receptors could work as well.

Finally, in the foveal pit the retina appears to have a localized optimum arrangement. The obstructive blood vessels are displaced to the side, along with the later neural elements, while the receptor tips are still embedded in the pigment epithelium behind. This optimization is, of course, accomplished at the expense of the surrounding, parafoveal region, which is, as a result, encumbered with a considerably increased number of blood vessels in the optical path. The shape of the foveal pit may also serve as a slight lens to magnify the central part of the image (Walls, 1937).

Using Low-Frequency Information

Almost all of the degradations of the optical image we have been discussing—in particular spherical and chromatic aberration and blur due to various types of movement—have very different effects on different spatial frequencies. The amplitude of high spatial frequency components in the optical image will be considerably attenuated by these various optical imperfections, but low spatial frequency components will be changed little or not at all. If there are mechanisms by which the organism can separate out the low from the high spatial frequency components (and we shall see that there are), an optical image which is little degraded by blur can be obtained. Such a middle- or low-frequency image will of course not contain all the information in the scene: it will be missing information on fine detail, for instance, but the information that is there will remain stable in the presence of these multiple imperfections, which can degrade the high spatial frequency information.

MEASURES OF OPTICAL QUALITY

In the above discussion, we have given only a qualitative account of image formation and aberrations within the eye. We would now like to discuss some of these issues in a somewhat more quantitative fashion.

Point Spread Function

Figure 2.3A diagrams an optimal optical system in which the whole beam of rays from a point A arrives, through appropriate refraction by the cornea and lens, at point A′ on the retina. In fact, as we have been discussing, various optical aberrations will result in the light from point A actually spreading over some considerable retinal region surrounding A′. The actual distribution on the retina of light coming from a point is the *point spread function* of the eye under the particular conditions being considered. The distribution on the retina of light from a point source, then, will not be a point but will be distributed over a bell-shaped region, as shown in cross section in Figure 2.7. The light from two nearby points in space will not be two punctate spots of light on the retina, but two normal distributions which overlap to varying extents, forming a single-peaked

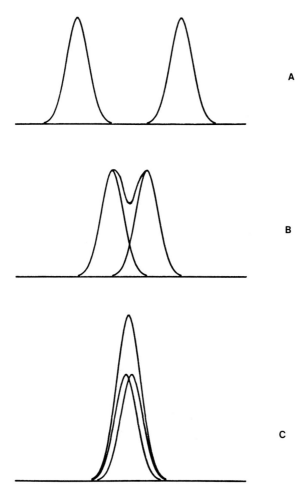

FIG. 2.7 The point spread function of the eye. The images of two single point sources which are separated by some considerable retinal distance will be two bell-shaped curves relating image intensity to retinal distance (A). As the visual angle between the two sources decreases, their retinal images will overlap (B), producing a single image with two distinct peaks. If the images overlap sufficiently (i.e., if the visual angle between the sources becomes small enough), the resulting image will have but a single higher peak (C).

distribution in image space when the points in object space get close together. The amount of, say, spherical aberration or defocus will be reflected in the standard deviation of the retinal light distribution. With small optical aberrations, the retinal light distribution will be narrow around point A′; with large optical aberrations the distribution will be flatter and will cover a considerably larger retinal area. This analysis can be expanded by considering the related *line spread function*, which is the actual distribution of light on the retina from a line in space.

Knowing the point spread function of the eye under some particular condition, one can then in principle calculate what happens to a whole complex visual scene as it is imaged on the retina. The light distribution in space would have to be convolved with the point spread function of the eye to obtain the retinal light distribution. This would be a very tedious but feasible procedure.

Spatial Frequency Analysis

A mathematically equivalent and in many ways more attractive approach to quantifying the effects of various degradations in the optics of the eye is to specify them in the spatial frequency domain. The particular approach that we will emphasize and consider in some detail here is chosen not just for its usefulness in specifying the transformations in the optical image going from space to the retina, but because it can also be usefully applied to later neural transformations and to psychophysical data. Spatial frequency analysis of spatial information, in fact, has the great virtue of providing a common language by which problems of spatial vision can be discussed in optics, physiology, psychophysics, and perception.

A modulation transfer function (MTF) is a measure of the extent to which each spatial frequency gets through (is transferred by) a given optical system. An MTF can be directly obtained for an ordinary optical system by imaging gratings of various spatial frequencies and known contrast, then measuring with a scanning photometer the modulation (i.e., the contrast) of each grating in the resulting image. If the optical system perfectly transmits a particular spatial frequency, the image of a grating of 100% modulation will also have 100% modulation. Such a straightforward procedure can obviously not be carried out for the optics of the eye, for the retinal image cannot be directly measured, although one can measure the distribution of light reflected back out of the eye, after having traversed the optics of the eye twice, as has been done by Campbell and Gubisch (1966). This study shows that the eye's optics pass virtually nothing beyond about 60 c/deg.

Another approach to the problem has led to much the same conclusion: comparing the psychophysical detection of the grating imaged by the eye's optics with those produced directly on the retina by laser interference patterns (Campbell & Green, 1965). The difference between these provides a measure of the optical characteristics of the refractive components of the eye. With laser interferometry, the retina is diffusely illuminated with a laser beam presented in maxwellian view so that aberrations in the optics of the eye play no role. If, from the same laser, a second beam is added which has been shifted in phase by a certain amount by slightly increasing its path length, an interference grating will be produced at the level of the receptors. The spatial frequency of the resulting grating on the retina will be a function of the phase shift. A contrast sensitivity function (CSF: the contrast required by an observer for the detection of each of a variety of different spatial frequencies) for such gratings of different spatial frequencies gives the sensitivity of the whole visual system minus its optics. The CSF measured with patterns that have been imaged by the eye's optics gives a sensitivity function for the whole system including the optics. This study (Campbell & Green, 1965) shows a close agreement between the CSF with and without degradation by the eye's optics, although one has somewhat slightly greater high spatial frequency sensitivity with the laser patterns (see Figure 2.8). Several conclusions can be drawn from these results. One is that since the CSF through the eye's optics is slightly worse than without the optics, the optics must be degrading the image to some extent. Another is that the neural components (the receptors and later neural elements) have their own spatial limitations which are well adapted to the range of inputs presented to them by the optics.

These measurements, as we indicated, were made under optimal conditions. But under many viewing conditions the various factors we have been discussing will degrade the optical image even more. Many of these—spherical aberration, chromatic aberration, wrong focus—will effectively defocus the image, or certain wavelengths within the spectrum of the image, by various amounts. It is thus of interest to examine the effects of defocus. In Figure 2.9 is shown a plot of the way in which different amounts of defocus would affect different spatial frequencies. The main effect of defocus is to attenuate high spatial frequencies, with less and less effect the lower the spatial frequency. Spatial frequencies below about 1 to 2 c/deg are nearly unaffected even by amounts of defocus up to 1 diopter or more. This is because blur tends to distribute light which should go to one place to nearby retinal areas. This will attenuate high spatial frequencies, whose peaks and troughs are near each other, but low spatial frequencies, whose peaks and troughs are much more distant on the retina, will be affected much less.

Light scatter, on the other hand, has a quite different effect across spatial frequencies. Light reflected off the optic disk, for instance, might hit some part of the retina some degrees distant. The overall effect of scatter is thus flatter across spatial frequencies than the effect of defocus.

Receptor Spacing

As discussed in Chapter 1, only slightly more than two points per cycle are necessary and sufficient to determine a sine wave. No further information is to be gained by sampling a waveform more frequently. The other side of this same

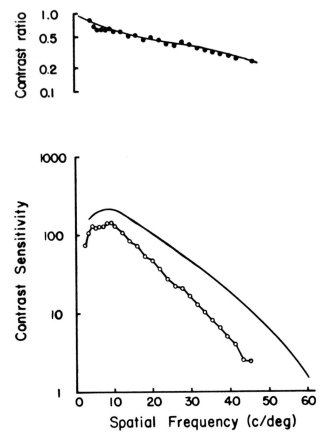

FIG. 2.8   Modulation transfer function of the human eye's optical system. In the bottom figure are measures of contrast sensitivity. The lower curve represents performance when the stimulus is imaged by the eye's optical system. The upper curve is the performance when the eye's optics are bypassed by producing the grating directly on the retina by a laser interference procedure. At top is the difference between these two curves (after Campbell & Green, 1965. Reprinted by permission).

argument is that the number of points per degree visual angle at which a waveform is sampled determines the highest spatial frequency that can be resolved.

In our discussion of the optics of the eye we stated that under optimal conditions the highest spatial frequency passed by the optics of the eye is about 60 c/deg. From the Fourier sampling theorem, then, we can conclude that there would be no advantage to the visual system's having more than about 120 spatial samples (that is, individual receptors) per linear degree visual angle. This statement is based only on optical considerations and does not involve any of the somewhat questionable assumptions about the linearity of physiological processes. One degree visual angle in distance on the human retina is approximately 300 μm. The sampling theorem would thus state that there would be no advantage in having receptors closer than 300/120 or about 2.5 μm center to center. This in fact agrees reasonably well with estimates of the spacing of cones in the central rod-free foveola (see Figure 2.10). One arrives at much the same estimate from considering the total number of cones in this central rod-free area. Polyak (1957) estimates that there are about 25,000 cones in the central 400 μm diameter rod-free foveola. This would work out to an average linear spacing between receptors of about 2.2 μm. (The receptors, of course, lie in a two-dimensional array, and thus the two-dimensional rather than the one-dimensional approximation we have discussed above is really the relevant parameter, but it does not significantly change these arguments.)

We can thus see that the eye has a retinal spacing good enough but no better than that required to extract the most detailed spatial information passed by the optics of the eye. Alternatively, we can state that the optics of the eye, poor as they are, are about good enough to transmit the highest spatial frequencies which the receptor mosaic is capable of sampling. The same conclusion was reached by an examination of the resolving power of the visual system with and without optical limitations (Campbell & Green, 1965), as discussed earlier.

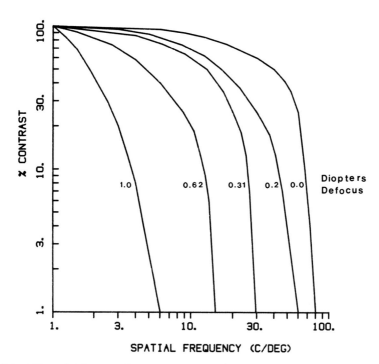

FIG. 2.9 Effect of defocus on image contrast as a function of spatial frequency. Increasing amounts of defocus produce increasing degradations of the optical image. Note that the effect of defocus is much more severe for higher spatial frequencies (after Westheimer, 1964, *Vision Res., 4*, 39–45. Copyright 1964, Pergamon Journals, Inc. Reprinted by permission).

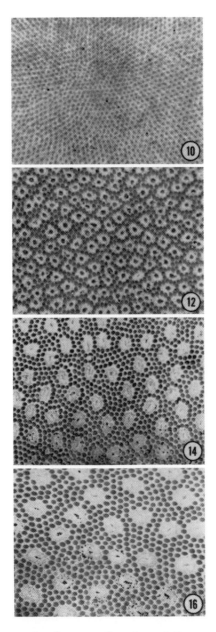

FIG. 2.10 Photomicrographs of cross sections through the receptor mosaic in monkey eye. At top, labeled 10, is a section through the fovea. Those below are increasingly peripheral. In the foveal section the receptors are all cones, which here are very small and tightly packed. In the section labeled 12, from the edge of the fovea, the cones are larger in diameter and there are interspersed rods. The white regions are the gaps caused by the large diameter of the cone inner segments. Note in 14 and 16 that with increasing eccentricity the cone diameters increase still further and more rods are interspersed (from R. W. Young, 1971. Reprinted by permission).

Implicit in this discussion of cone spacing in the foveola and the resolving power of the system is the assumption that all the cones are equivalent, with respect to the luminance-varying stimuli used in the measures of the CSF. However, there is not just one, but rather three different cone types, with different spectral sensitivities. As discussed further below, the L and the M cones have very similar spectral sensitivity functions, peaking at about 560 and 530 nm, respectively. The physiological evidence (see Chapter 3) suggests that these two cone types *are* treated as interchangeable in the visual system's analyses of luminance-varying patterns. The S cones, on the other hand, have a very different spectral peak—but they are almost, if not totally, absent from the central fovea.

The correspondence we have seen between the highest spatial frequencies which are resolvable and the cone spacing (and thus the maximum possible spatial sampling) extends at least qualitatively to more peripheral retinal areas as well. By the edge of the fovea, the cone diameters have increased at least twofold (Polyak, 1957), and rods now become interspersed among the cones as well (see Figure 2.10). Psychophysical measurements of acuity under photopic conditions (with cones alone presumably functional) (Westheimer, 1981) or high spatial frequency cut (Robson & Graham, 1981) show a corresponding drop to one half or one third the central resolution capability with just off-foveal patterns. Intercone spacing increases further (with larger cone diameters and increased rod density), and acuity correspondingly decreases as one goes still further toward the periphery. However, the close correspondence seen in the fovea between the optical limits and the receptor sampling limits no longer holds in the periphery.

Although, as we have been discussing, cone diameters and spacing in the central retina correspond closely to those predicted by visual acuity, a paradox arises with respect to rod diameters and acuity. The highest spatial frequencies resolvable with rod vision are on the order of 5 c/deg (Daitch & Green, 1969), which would suggest an interreceptor spacing of about 30 μm and thus perhaps 25-μm diameter rods. However, rods throughout the retina have diameters of about 1 to 1.5 μm, roughly comparable to foveal cones, and average interrod distances are similar to those of foveal cones (in some cases larger because some cones are interlaced among the rods throughout the peripheral retina). It could be (see below) that rod size is determined by chance factors, or set by some other, nonoptical, considerations. However, one should note that rod and cone diameters are interrelated, since these receptors are intermingled everywhere that rods are present. Rods of, say, 25 μm in diameter everywhere in the retina would produce drastically larger *cone* separations in the near parafoveal retina. So perhaps small rod diameters are demanded not by the sampling requirements of rod vision, but to permit cones to be fairly closely spaced in regions near the fovea where rods and cones are interspersed. However, this does not explain why rods are not increasingly larger in size with increasing eccentricity, as is true for cones.

As we discuss in Chapter 3, the initiation of neural activity in rods probably involves the diffusion of chemicals, released by the photon capture in disks within the receptor outer segments, to the outside membrane of the receptor.

Such diffusion takes a considerable time, and a time which is variable, depending on whether the capture was near or far from the outside membrane. Perhaps if rod outer segments became as large as 25 μm in diameter, the resulting latency and spread in time would be intolerably long.

Finally, we can consider the spacing among cones of different types in relation to information about spatial variations in color. As we discuss at length in Chapter 7, color information lies not in the output of a single receptor, rod or cone, but in a comparison of the outputs of two or more receptors containing different photopigments. Thus, in the case of the red-green color system, the smallest basic element of the system is a pair consisting of one L and one M cone. Even if the retina consisted of only L and M cones (with no S cones or rods), and these cones were completely regularly spaced, the effective "interreceptor distance" or spatial sampling period for color vision would be double that for luminance vision. On this ground alone, we would predict that the color CSF would cut out at considerably lower spatial frequencies than the luminance CSF. Because of chromatic aberration, this lower spatial sampling frequency might not in fact result in loss of information. Between 510 nm in the green and 650 nm in the red there is about 0.7 diopter difference in focus (Wald & Griffin, 1947). If the eye were in optimum focus for 570 nm, as it tends to be under most circumstances, the red and green parts of a red-green pattern would each be about 0.35 diopters out of focus. This amount of defocus (see Figure 2.9) would shift the optical high-frequency cut-off from about 60 c/deg to below 30 c/deg (Westheimer, 1964). Again, then, the retinal receptor spacing seems in remarkably good agreement with the optimum sampling for the spatial information involved.

In the case of yellow-blue color vision the problem of chromatic aberration is considerably greater, for two reasons. One is that the total difference in focus between blue and yellow is somewhat greater than that between a typical green and red. For instance, there is about 1.0 diopter difference in focus from a 460 nm (blue) light to a 570 nm (yellow) light, whereas from 510 to 650 is only 0.7 diopter, as mentioned earlier. A second, even more critical factor is that the eye is usually focused, as we have stated above, at the midspectral region, e.g., 550–570 nm. A 560-nm focus is about optimum for red-green color vision and for luminance vision based on the L and M cones, both of which have peak sensitivity in the middle of the spectrum. However, the effect of such a long-wave focus on yellow-blue vision is to put the blue part of a pattern 1 diopter or more out of focus. (In the highly atypical circumstance in which only yellow-blue variations were present in a stimulus, the optical blur could of course be diminished by the eye's focusing at a shorter wavelength than 560 nm.)

Yellow-blue color vision is based on a comparison of the S cones against the L and M cones (R.L. De Valois, Abramov, & Jacobs, 1966; R.L. De Valois & K.K. De Valois, 1975). From the considerations of chromatic aberration discussed above, we would expect that only fairly wide spacing would be required for the S cones, or for the L and M cones being compared with them in the yellow-blue system. The distribution of L and M cones is of course to a large extent determined by the requirements for the luminance and the red-green systems, to which they also form the inputs. The S cones, however, need not be as numerous as the other cone types.

We need to go one step further and consider the optimum receptor distribution and focus for all three systems considered together, for all are interrelated. For instance, as the number of S cones increases, the average spacing between L and M cones, on which the luminance and red-green systems are based, must get coarser. And the optimum focus for yellow-blue patterns would not be the best for red-green ones. Clearly the best overall strategy (which our visual system in fact adopts) is to optimize both focus and receptor spacing for the luminance and red-green systems. That is accomplished by focusing at midspectral wavelengths and having the maximum number of L and M cones. The net result is to introduce so much blur in the blue that few S cones are required to adequately sample the highest spatial frequencies left. The best psychophysical (Williams, MacLeod, & Hayhoe, 1981) and anatomical (Marc & Sperling, 1977; De Monasterio et al., 1981) studies agree fairly well in estimating that the S cones constitute only about 5–10% of the total cone population.

Aliasing

There is one aspect of sampling theory which we have ignored so far, but which must be taken into consideration in considering receptor distribution and the optics of the eye, namely, aliasing. An unstated assumption in the sampling theorem as we discussed it above and in Chapter 1 is that spatial frequencies above half the maximum sampling rate are absent from the stimulus. That is, 120 samples per degree visual angle would completely specify the waveform of spatial frequencies below 60 c/deg, but if the input contained frequencies *above* 60 c/deg, the sampling would artifactually produce energy at lower frequencies (see Figure 2.11). A spatial frequency f would be aliased to $120-f$, so 80 c/deg,

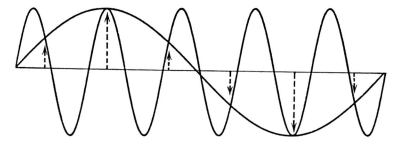

FIG. 2.11 Aliasing produced by undersampling. The arrows indicate the six evenly spaced sampling points across the distance represented. These are insufficient in number to specify the $5f$ grating shown. Note that at the sampled points the $5f$ grating and the $1f$ grating shown have exactly the same values, and the system therefore cannot discriminate between them. The energy of the $5f$ pattern would thus be aliased to $1f$.

for instance, would be aliased to 40 c/deg. We stated above that since the receptor spacing in the foveola is about 120 per degree visual angle, there would be no advantage for the optics of the eye to be better than they are, with a high cut of 60 c/deg. We can now go further and state that it would be an actual *disadvantage* for us to have a much better optical system, given the receptor spacing, since the highest spatial frequencies would then be aliased to produce artifacts. (There would, however, be some compensating increase in contrast at high spatial frequencies if the optical attenuation were somewhat higher than the receptor sampling limit.)

From a consideration of aliasing it is clear that the eye's optics are roughly optimal for resolution in the foveola. What about outside the central fovea? Since the optic axis falls to one side of the fovea (see Figure 3.1), the optics actually improve away from the fovea on that side. The optics of the eye are somewhat degraded further off the optic axis, but less than would be required to prevent the coarse peripheral cone spacing from producing aliasing problems. There appear to be at least two compensating processes. First, the peripheral receptor spacing is not totally regular. In the fovea, the receptors at the level of the inner segments are arranged in a very regular hexagonal array. [Yellott's (1982) measurements showing irregular spacing in the fovea were based on sections through the outer segments, but light collection is determined by the spacing of the inner segments, which serve to funnel the light to the outer segments.] However, this regularity of spacing is increasingly lost with eccentricity, and this would have the effect of cutting down to some extent the sampling of the highest frequencies, but doubtless much more than compensates for that loss by minimizing the aliased representation of frequencies above the sampling rate (Yellott, 1982). A second mechanism is that a peripheral cone has a diameter that is quite large with respect to the interreceptor distances. It therefore does not act as a point sample, but rather averages together the input over the area of the receptor cross section. Very high spatial frequencies would thus tend to cancel. These mechanisms would thus act to compensate for the fact that while the optics of the eye are appropriate to the high resolution of the fovea, they are too good for the periphery.

3

Retinogeniculate Anatomy and Physiology

The eye contains not only the optical elements that perform the critical task of forming an image of the visual world at the level of the receptors, but also the receptors to transduce the light energy into neural activity and the neural structures that carry out the initial analysis of the visual information. Crucial visual processing takes place within the receptors themselves and at the two synaptic levels within the eye before the information is sent on to more central neural levels.

The retina, an outgrowth of the brain which is located in the eye (and thus much more accessible than other brain nuclei), is by far the best understood neural structure. It is the only part of the brain that can be directly observed in the intact individual, and its electrical activity was studied long before that of most neural structures. Many features of brain function were therefore first discovered in the retina. For instance, from early studies of the spinal cord and motor neurons, all-or-none spike discharges were thought of as the characteristic neural process. However, recordings made from early stages in the retina found only graded potentials; we now see these as the crucial type of neural activity for information processing everywhere in the brain, with spike discharges being a specialization needed for long-distance communication of neural messages. Distances within the retina are sufficiently short not to require such all-or-none transmission. It was also within the retina that adjacent regions of membrane were first found that can act both as dendrites receiving information and as axon endings transmitting the information to the next stage. In this as in other cases, processes first seen within the retina were later found to operate generally elsewhere within the nervous system.

Our emphasis in this treatment of the retina, however, will be less on this structure as a model for the nervous system in general than on the ways in which it contributes to the analysis of visual information. The visual system faces many daunting problems in trying to extract useful information about the world from the welter of photons flying through space after being reflected from various objects. Many of these problems are sufficiently urgent to require handling at the very first neural stages in the eye.

In this chapter we will attempt to present a general account of the structure and function of the retina and lateral geniculate, concentrating in particular on issues bearing directly on spatial vision. For those who want to investigate the subject in more depth, an excellent, fairly up-to-date book on the retina is available (Rodieck, 1973), as are two relevant volumes in the *Handbook of Sensory Physiology* (Vol. 7/1 and 7/2).

We would also like to concentrate on understanding human vision. Although virtually all the physiological studies and many of the more detailed anatomical studies (particularly those which combine anatomical and physiological procedures) have necessarily been carried out only on lower animals, there are anatomical, photochemical, and psychophysical grounds for considering the macaque monkey an excellent model for the human visual system, at least up to the level of the striate cortex. The anatomy of macaque and human appears very similar (Polyak, 1957), and the basic processes of spatial sensitivity, brightness and color discrimination (R.L. De Valois, Polson, Mead, & Hull, 1974; R.L. De Valois, Morgan, & Snodderly, 1974), and binocular vision (Bough, 1970) appear to be virtually identical. The cat appears to afford a fair model for non-color, peripheral human vision, although large anatomical differences between cat and primates appear at cortical levels, as well as in the central retina. We will therefore concentrate on the physiology of the monkey, and to a lesser extent the cat, in this account. This leaves one severe gap: there have been (for technical reasons) few systematic physiological studies of units before the ganglion cell level in monkey. Thus for studies of interreceptor interactions and the receptor-bipolar-horizontal cell processing we must still depend to a large extent on studies of such animals as the mudpuppy *Necturus* and the turtle, which have large and accessible retinal neurons. In these areas in particular, then, generalizations from retinal physiology to physiological studies of higher visual structures or to visual behavior must necessarily be more tentative.

ANATOMY

A striking feature of the gross anatomy of the visual system at every level is its prominent stratification. This is seen in the three distinct layers of cell bodies in the retina, and is even more pronounced at the next level, the lateral geniculate nucleus (LGN), which is the most distinctively laminated structure in the thalamus. The unusual stratification of the visual cortex is reflected in its common designation as the striate cortex. This pattern of striation at retina, lateral geniculate, and primary visual cortex reflects the extremely ordered and systematic arrangement of anatomical connections in the early levels of the visual system. The information from each level goes to cells at the next level in a fairly strict serial or hierarchical manner, differing sharply from the arrangement seen in other sensory systems, e.g., the auditory system, where fibers from one level take multiple paths to various other levels or nuclei. However, in many ways the striate cortex appears to be functionally similar to the auditory cochlea (as our later discussions in this book will make apparent). Given this resemblance, the difference between the complexity of the visual and auditory paths is not so pronounced, for the visual path beyond the striate cortex is as complex and convoluted as is the auditory projection from the cochlea.

Gross Anatomy of the Eye

The diagrammatic cross section of the eye shown in Figure 3.1 shows the retina covering more than 200° along the back of the eye. Lying just behind the retina is the pigment epithelium, containing a very black pigment which absorbs most of the light that is not captured by the receptors. This layer also plays a role in providing nutrients for the receptors and contributes to the regeneration of the receptor photopigments.

In the center of the retina is a slight depression, the foveal pit, which is devoid of intraretinal blood vessels (see Figure 3.2). Although the fovea subtends only about 1 to 2° visual angle, it plays a disproportionately large role in vision. The retina is approximately radially symmetric about the fovea, and many anatomical and physiological features of the eye, as well as various visual capabilities, change systematically with distance from the fovea. For instance, the density of cones and of the later neural elements drops progressively with increasing eccentricity. The radial symmetry of the retina is broken at one point, about 15° to

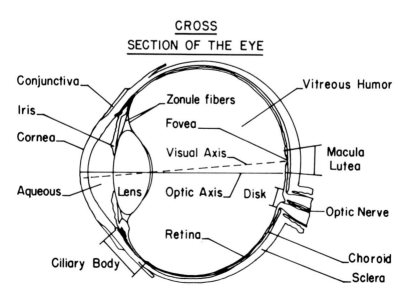

FIG. 3.1 Diagrammatic horizontal section of the human eye. Major structures and axes are labeled.

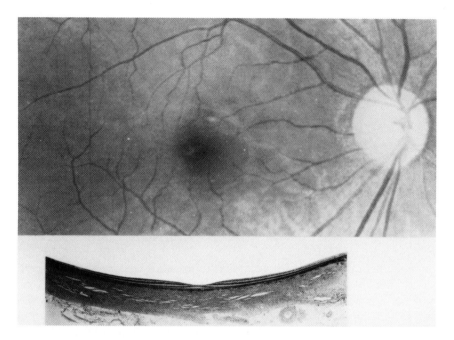

FIG. 3.2 Fundus of the human eye and a corresponding retinal cross section. The top photograph shows the fundus of a normal human eye. The white circular area to the far right is the optic disk. The dark region near the middle is the macula lutea, at the center of which is the fovea. Note that the blood vessels, which enter and exit through the optic disk, fan out across the entire retina except for the foveal area. The bottom photomicrograph shows a cross section through the human retina, magnified to the same scale and aligned with the fundus photograph. In the center can be seen the foveal pit. To the far right, the photomicrograph ends at the edge of the optic disk (fundus photograph courtesy of M. Fendick; photomicrograph from Hogan et al., 1971. Reprinted by permission).

the nasal side of the fovea, by the optic disk, a ca. 6° diameter, roughly circular region where the optic nerve fibers exit the eye and the retinal blood vessels enter and leave (see Figure 3.2).

As can be seen in the crosssection shown in Figure 3.3, the retina contains three distinct layers of cell bodies. At the very back of the retina are the receptors with their outer segments, which contain the photopigments, penetrating the pigment epithelium (see Figure 3.8). Extensions of the receptors lead from the receptor cell bodies, in the outer nuclear layer, to the outer plexiform layer, in which synaptic connections are made among receptors, bipolars, and horizontal cells. Next, the inner nuclear layer contains the cell bodies of the horizontal, bipolar, and amacrine cells. The next plexiform layer (which is itself broken into sublayers) is the region in which synapses are made among bipolar, amacrine, and ganglion cells. Finally, there is the layer of ganglion cell bodies, several cells thick in the central retina but thinning greatly further toward the periphery. The

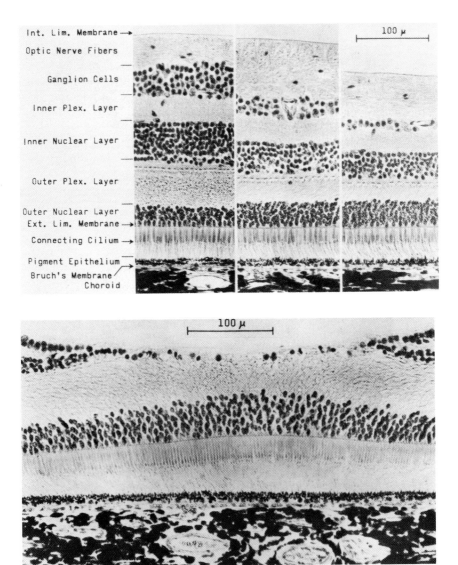

FIG. 3.3 Highly magnified cross sections through the macaque monkey retina. In the top photomicrograph are three separate sections: from the edge of the fovea, from a parafoveal region, and from near the optic disk, respectively from left to right. Note that with increasing eccentricity the inner nuclear layer and the ganglion cell layer become increasingly thinner as the cone density decreases. At the same time, however, the outer nuclear layer increases in thickness, reflecting the greater absolute number of receptors due to the increasing number of rods. With still greater eccentricity, however, all the cell body layers shrink as the total number of receptors drops (see Figure 3.4). In the bottom photomicrograph is shown (at a slightly greater magnification) the central fovea in this same monkey eye. The receptors in this region are all cones. Note that in this central foveal area the inner nuclear layer cells and ganglion cells are almost all displaced to one side, hence the foveal pit. Note also the increased density and greater length of the cones in the very central foveal region (from Brown et al., 1965. Reprinted by permission).

innermost layer of the retina consists of the unmyelinated axons of the ganglion cells, which converge from all over the retina onto the optic disk, where they exit the eye. To reach the receptors, the light must traverse all these layers of cells [except in the central fovea, where the bipolar, amacrine, and ganglion cells are displaced to the side (see Figure 3.3 bottom)].

A region subtending about 1/3° visual angle in the very center of the fovea, the foveola, contains only cones. There are about 2,500 cones in this tiny region (Missotten, 1974), and they are here very thin, long, and tightly packed (see Figure 3.3 bottom). Rods start to intermingle among the cones further out in the fovea and actually outnumber cones by the edge of the fovea (B. Borwein, 1981); see Figure 2.10. Still further parafoveally, the thin cylindrical rods form clusters in rings about each cone. The cones decrease in number with increasing eccentricity, while their inner segments become thicker and thicker. As shown in Figure 3.4, rods reach their highest density about 20° from the fovea, and gradually fall off in number with further eccentricity. Overall there are some 120 million rods and 6 million cones in the human (and macaque monkey) retina. These figures by themselves give the impression that our vision is dominated by rods, but that is not so, for the later neural elements, including the ganglion cells which project to the thalamus and cortex, are concentrated in the central retina where there are many cones. Cones rather than rods thus make the largest contribution to the information going to later brain centers.

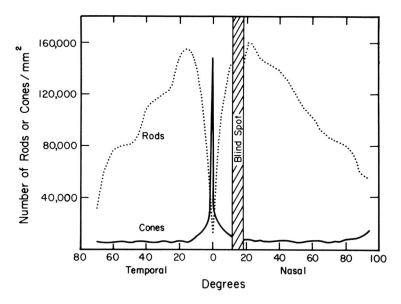

FIG. 3.4   Diagram showing the density of receptors as a function of eccentricity in the human retina (from Østerberg, 1935. Reprinted with permission).

Receptor Anatomy

In Figure 3.5 is shown an enlarged view of the receptor array, as seen in scanning electron microscopy. Figure 3.6 shows a cross section of a rod inner and outer segment, as seen with transmission electron microscopy. The most distinctive feature of the outer segments of both rods and cones is the presence of some 500-1,000 disks stacked up like pancakes. These disks are formed by the infoldings of the outer membranes, but then largely or totally pinch off and separate from the outside membrane. The disks contain, indeed are largely made up of, the photopigment molecules which initiate the visual process by capturing the photons of light. These multiple layers of photopigment membrane in the light path greatly increase the probability of capture of a photon.

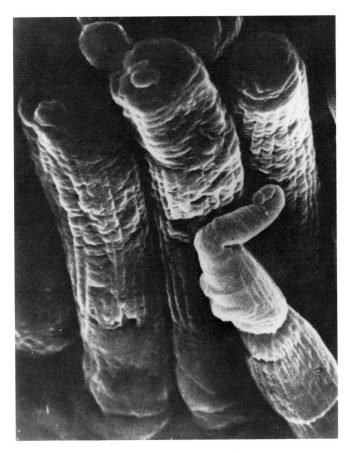

FIG. 3.5   Scanning electron photomicrograph of retinal receptors. This is an external view, looking down on the outer segments of three rods and one cone of the mudpuppy eye, enormously magnified. The tapering cone outer segment was bent during preparation (courtesy of F. Werblin).

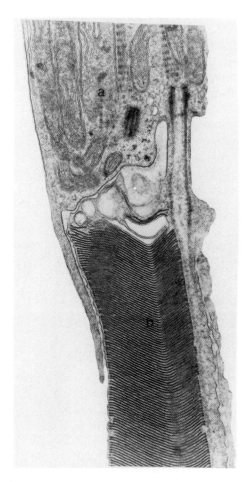

FIG. 3.6   Cross-sectional view of part of the inner and outer segments of a rod, from a transmission photomicrograph. The inner segment (A) can be seen above, and the outer segment (B), with its stack of flattened disks, can be seen below (from Hogan et al., 1971. Reprinted with permission).

The distinct taper of the cone inner and outer segments (see Figure 3.7) funnels the light to and thus concentrates it on the photopigments in the outer segments (Enoch, 1961). The cones in the foveola presumably compensate for their relative lack of taper by a doubling in the total length of the outer segment, with resulting increase in probability of photon capture (B. Borwein, D. Borwein, Medeiros, & McGowan, 1980). The manner in which the pigment epithelium cells surround the tips of the receptors can be seen in Figure 3.8.

The inner segment and the cell body of the receptor contain most of the metabolic and genetic machinery. From the cell body a filament leads to the enlarged synaptic region, the rod spherule or cone pedicle. There the receptor makes physiological contact with other neural elements. These contacts are of two types: electrotonic coupling with other receptors, and chemical synapses with horizontal and bipolar cells. The interreceptor contacts are made at the ends of long filaments that extend laterally from the terminal to contact similar filaments from nearby receptors (Raviola & Gilula, 1973). The synaptic contacts of receptors onto bipolar and horizontal cells take place either within distinctive synaptic invaginations (pouches) in the receptors or on the nearby receptor surfaces (Dowling & Boycott, 1966). Each rod typically has just a single invagination and thus contacts only one invaginating bipolar cell (which also will be picking up from several neighboring rods). Cones, on the other hand, typically have one to two dozen invaginations (B. Borwein, 1981) within which contact is made with more than one bipolar cell. In the foveola, where many bipolars contact one cone each, there are therefore two to three times as many bipolars as there are cones (Missotten, 1974).

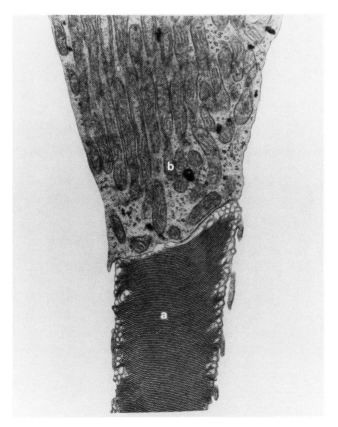

FIG. 3.7   Electron photomicrograph of portions of the inner and outer segments of a cone. Note the taper of both the outer (A) and inner (B) segments (from Hogan et al., 1971. Reprinted with permission).

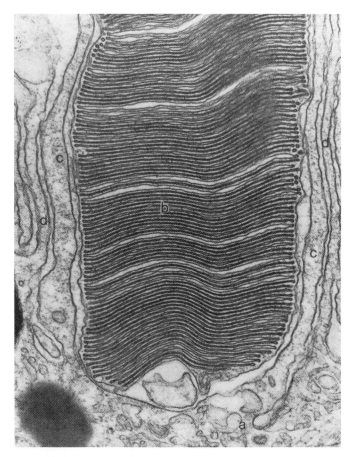

FIG. 3.8   Cross-sectional electron photomicrograph of the tip of a rod outer segment (B) embedded in the pigment epithelium. Note that the pigment epithelial cell (A) at bottom sends out processes (C and D) which actually surround the tip of the outer segment (from Hogan et al., 1971. Reprinted with permission).

Horizontal and Bipolar Cells

There are two different types of neural elements at each successive level through the retina: those that conduct information toward higher levels and those that conduct information laterally between neurons at the same level. At the first synaptic level one finds bipolars, which conduct from receptors to ganglion cells, and horizontal cells, which make lateral connections across the retina at the level of the receptor-bipolar synapse. Further along the visual path, and perhaps in the retina as well (Dowling & Ehringer, 1975), there are also feedback connections from "later" to "earlier" levels.

Bipolar cells are so named because one process extends up to contact receptors, and a second process (or "pole") extends down to contact ganglion cells. The number of receptors contacted by a bipolar cell increases going from fovea to periphery. Many foveal bipolars only make direct contact with one cone (but, we hasten to emphasize, even these bipolars receive inputs from a considerable number of cones either through receptor-receptor coupling or by way of horizontal cells); further peripherally a similar bipolar may make direct contact with several cones. Rod and cone pathways are largely separate through the retina, there being in addition to these cone bipolars others which contact only rods. The rod bipolars receive a direct input from a considerably larger number of receptors than do the cone bipolars (Boycott & Dowling, 1969).

Although bipolar cells have a variety of shapes and sizes (and perhaps functions), we can consider the majority of them to be of one of two functional types. Some bipolars depolarize to increments of light falling in the center of the area from which they pick up; others depolarize to decrements (see below). We will therefore refer to these as incremental and decremental bipolars, respectively. These two bipolar types appear to make different types of receptor contacts, one invaginating the receptor pouch, the other making contact on the receptor surface; see Figure 3.9 (Famighetti & Kolb, 1976; Nelson, Famighetti, & Kolb, 1978). These two bipolar cell types end at different levels in the inner plexiform layer as well (Famighetti, Kaneko, & Tachibana, 1977; Nelson et al., 1978).

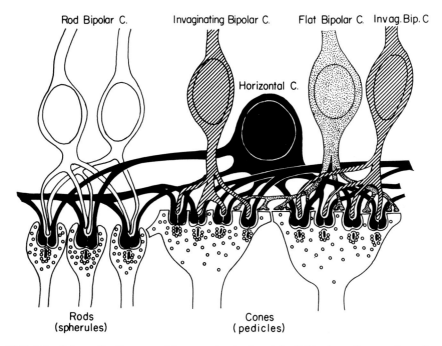

FIG. 3.9 Schematic diagram of the receptor-horizontal cell-bipolar cell synaptic region (after Dowling & Boycott, 1966. Reprinted with permission).

Synaptic contacts are also made in the outer plexiform layer by horizontal cells, which send up numerous processes to contact a number of nearby receptors and bipolars. The size of the lateral spread of horizontal cell contacts varies from a half dozen or so cones foveally to 30-40 cones in the periphery (Boycott & Kolb, 1973); since peripheral cones are much more widely spaced, the areal extent of peripheral horizontal cells is many hundreds of times that of those near the fovea. Some horizontal cells contact only cones (and presumably cones of only one photopigment type, Fuortes, Schwartz, & Simon, 1973); others contact only rods; still others have two groups of connections, one with cones and one with rods (Fisher & Boycott, 1974).

It is useful to consider that each bipolar is connected to receptors by two separate paths: a direct path in which the receptors synapse onto the bipolar, and an indirect path in which receptors contact horizontal cells which in turn synapse onto the bipolar. Since the lateral spread of the interconnections made by the horizontal cells is larger than the spread of the direct contacts made by the bipolars, the indirect path via horizontal cells is considerably more extensive laterally than the direct path from receptors to bipolars. By the direct path, then, a bipolar gets an input from (some of) the receptors in a disk-shaped area of retina; from the indirect connections via horizontal cells the bipolar receives a second input from a larger, overlapping, concentric disk-shaped area.

Many of the synaptic contacts made by horizontal cells are within pouches in the receptors. Here the most common arrangement is for there to be three processes going up into the pouch, the central one being from a bipolar cell and the two lateral ones from horizontal cells (Dowling & Boycott, 1966; Stell, 1967; Dowling, 1968; Boycott & Kolb, 1973); see Figure 3.9. The receptor therefore directly contacts both bipolar and horizontal cells, and the horizontal cell in turn feeds into the bipolar and/or back onto the receptor. Horizontal cells are sometimes seen to contact bipolars outside the pouches as well (Brown, Major, & Dowling, 1966; Werblin & Dowling, 1969).

Amacrine and Ganglion Cells

In the inner plexiform layer are found the connections among bipolar, amacrine, and ganglion cells. The amacrine cells here resemble the horizontal cells of the outer plexiform layer in that they form a largely lateral pathway, interconnecting various bipolar-ganglion cell synaptic regions. The typical type of connection made by cone bipolars is also similar, consisting of a dyad in which the bipolar contacts both an amacrine and a ganglion cell. The amacrine cell in turn synapses with the ganglion cell and/or back onto the bipolar. Some, perhaps all, rod bipolars end just on amacrine cells, which in turn contact ganglion cells. Such a pathway thus consists of four rather than three sequential retinal levels.

Ganglion cells, like bipolars, have quite different extents to their dendritic fields at different retinal eccentricities. In the central retina, many ganglion cells may get a direct input from only one bipolar; further peripherally the typical ganglion cell receives direct input from several bipolars. The indirect input via amacrines also expands in area toward the periphery.

Ganglion cells are the first cells in the visual path to have processes that are clearly differentiable on both anatomical and physiological grounds as dendrites versus axons. Their dendrites extend up into the outer plexiform layer where they tend to branch out at one or more distinct levels (Boycott & Wässle, 1974). The ganglion cell axons traverse the inner retinal surface to exit the eye at the optic disk. Fibers whose direct path to the optic disk would cross the fovea curve to bypass it. The axons are unmyelinated within the retina (the opaque myelin sheath would otherwise block the light from reaching the receptors) and become myelinated at the optic disk as they leave the eye.

We have mentioned that there are two bipolar cell types, those that depolarize to increments of light and those that depolarize to decrements, and that these end in different strata of the inner plexiform layer. Correspondingly, there are two ganglion cell types, whose dendritic branches are in different layers (Famighetti et al., 1977; Nelson et al., 1978). Ganglion cells that depolarize and increase their sustained spike discharge rate to light increments contact incremental bipolars, while decremental ganglion cells contact decremental bipolars. These two ganglion cell types taken together will be referred to as X cells in our physiological discussion below. There are in addition ganglion cells, called Y cells, which give a transient depolarization to both increments and decrements of light (Enroth-Cugell & Robson, 1966).

Anatomical studies of the overall size and shape of ganglion cells have identified several different types. Some have small cell bodies and tiny dendritic fields (termed β cells); others (α cells) have much larger cell bodies and dendrites (Boycott & Wässle, 1974). There is evidence that these two cell types have a different central projection, α cells to the magnocellular layers of the LGN and β cells to the parvocellular layers (Leventhal, Rodieck, & Dreher, 1981). As discussed below, the further relationship between these morphological types and the X and Y functional classes is, however, not so clear-cut.

Central Projection

The axons of ganglion cells leave the eye in what is referred to as the optic nerve. The optic nerve is in fact a central neural tract rather than a true peripheral nerve, since the retina is an outgrowth of the thalamus. There is a partial decussation at the optic chiasm, the nasal fibers from each eye crossing to the other side, and the resulting optic tract leads into the thalamus (see Figure 3.10). The partial crossing of the optic fibers at the chiasm effects a functional crossing of the whole path from the visual world to the cortex. Light coming from regions to the left of the fixation point will strike the nasal retina of the left eye and the temporal retina of the right; ganglion cell axons from both these regions project to the *right* lateral geniculate. The geniculate fibers in turn project only to the cortex on the same side, so information from the left visual field will arrive at

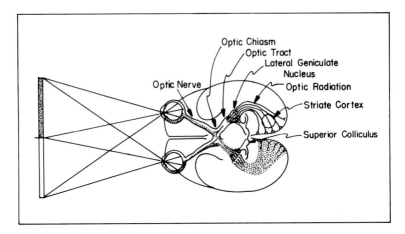

FIG. 3.10   Primary visual projection pathway. Note that due to the partial decussation of the optic nerve, with temporal fibers projecting to the ipsilateral and nasal fibers to the contralateral visual cortex, the left visual field is represented in the right visual cortex, and vice versa.

the right cortex. Light from the right visual field will correspondingly activate the left cortex.

The two main destinations of ganglion cell axons are the LGN and the superior colliculus. A very small number of fibers, part of the circuit controlling pupillary movements and accommodation, go to the pregeniculate and from there to the pretectal area. An even smaller projection goes to the accessory optic nuclei and to the hypothalamus, a pathway crucial for light entrainment of the diurnal rhythm (Stephan & Zucker, 1972). These pathways and functions, however, fall outside the range of topics we will discuss.

About 20% of the optic tract fibers go to the superior colliculus, which in primitive vertebrates is the main central visual center. With the evolution of the geniculate and cortex, the superior colliculus no longer has a dominant role in vision, but it is very important in control of eye movements (Wurtz & Goldberg, 1971). In particular, the superior colliculus may very well control the fixational process by which we build up a detailed picture of the world through successive fixations. Furthermore, there are anatomical interconnections between the colliculus and visual cortex. Ultimately, any explanation of spatial vision will surely find other critical roles for the superior colliculus; at the moment, however, such roles are not clear enough to justify an extended discussion of collicular anatomy and physiology.

Lateral Geniculate Nucleus

The ganglion cell axons subserving the contralateral visual field project to the LGN. The fibers from each half retina break up into three distinct layers, interwoven with those from half of the other eye to form a distinctive 6-layered structure in primates (see Figure 3.11). Labeled from ventral to dorsal, layers 1, 4, and 6 receive their input from the contralateral (nasal) retina and layers 2, 3, and 5 from the ipsilateral (temporal) retina. The lamination is not based on retinal region since each LGN layer contains a mapping of an entire visual hemifield. Rather, it must reflect some functional division of the optic path. There is a conspicuous histological and, as we shall see, functional difference between layers 1 and 2, which contain large cells (magnocellular layers), and the four small-cell (parvocellular) layers.

The incoming ganglion cell axons synapse on the dendrites of the LGN principal cells, which in turn send their axons to the striate cortex. In addition, the LGN contains interneurons which also receive optic tract (and other) input and which also contact the principal cells (Szentagothai, 1973). The LGN interneurons thus functionally resemble retinal horizontal and amacrine cells. There are also a large number of fibers from layer VI of striate (and prestriate) cortex which feed back onto retinotopically corresponding regions of the LGN (J.S. Lund, R.D. Lund, Hendrickson, Bunt, & Fuchs, 1975). Finally, the LGN receives large inputs from the reticular formation and other regions of the brain.

The various cell layers of the LGN are separated by incoming optic tract fibers. There appears to be little if any crossing of the boundaries between layers:

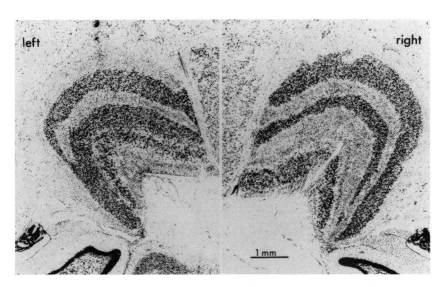

FIG. 3.11 Cross section through the lateral geniculate nucleus (LGN) of the macaque monkey. These sections were taken from the LGN of a monkey from which the right eye had been removed. It can be seen in the right LGN section that layers 1, 4, and 6 (numbered from ventral to dorsal), which receive input from the (intact) contralateral eye are normal, whereas layers 2, 3, and 5, which receive from the (missing) ipsilateral eye are degenerated and pale. The left LGN section shows the intact layers 2, 3, and 5 and degenerated layers 1, 4, and 6 (from Hubel & Wiesel, 1977. Reprinted with permission).

the incoming fibers end exclusively within one layer, and only occasionally do interneurons spread from one layer to another. Thus the anatomical arrangement indicates little binocular interaction at this synaptic level, despite the arrangement of corresponding parts of the projection from the two eyes above each other in adjacent laminae. Physiological studies (R.L. De Valois, 1965; Wiesel & Hubel, 1966) confirm the lack of major binocular interaction at the LGN.

PHOTOCHEMISTRY AND TRANSDUCTION

The initial physiological events in a visual system are the absorption of light by a photopigment and the transduction of this into neural activity. Both of these processes have been extensively studied and are described in detail elsewhere (Wald, 1964; Hubbell & Bownds, 1979). We will here merely give a selective overview of the process.

Photopigments

A problem which has been studied with many different techniques for over a hundred years is that of the spectral absorption curves of the visual receptors. This clearly is a question of critical importance for color vision, but it is vital for several aspects of spatial vision as well. The rod pigment, rhodopsin, can be readily extracted from the rod outer segment, and its spectral absorption curve has been measured with great precision. This curve, which peaks at ca. 500 nm, has been found to coincide with the behaviorally measured sensitivity of human vision measured in the near periphery at low ambient light levels, if appropriate corrections are made for preretinal absorption (Wald, 1964).

Cone pigments have yet to be extracted from primate receptors, but a variety of psychophysical, physiological, and microspectrophotometric experiments have converged to describe functions that are doubtless very close to the correct spectral absorption curves. These studies have shown the presence of three cone types in the macaque monkey and human retina; these we will call the S, M, and L cones. They contain photopigments that peak around 420, 530, and 560 nm, respectively (Bowmaker, Dartnall, & Mollon, 1980); see Figure 3.12. These cone and rod photopigments all have broad spectral absorption curves (although much of that of the S cones is outside the range of wavelengths that are allowed to reach the retina). A characteristic of each is that the drop in sensitivity at long wavelengths is sharper than at short; as a result, all the receptors absorb significantly at short visible wavelengths.

Although the precise photochemistry is known only for the rod pigment, rhodopsin, there are good grounds for assuming that the process is essentially the

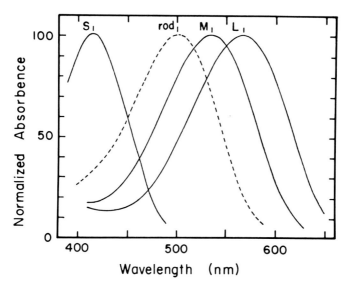

FIG. 3.12 Normalized photopigment absorption curves. Note the considerable overlap between the functions, particularly those of the M and L pigment curves (after Bowmaker et al., 1980. Reprinted with permission).

same in cones as well. The photopigments are large protein molecules, one part of which, termed the chromophore, is photosensitive. Rhodopsin molecules float in the lipid membranes of the disks in the receptor outer segments. The chromophore, retinal (which is vitamin A aldehyde; Wald, 1964), can occur in a variety of different structural configurations, or isomers. When attached to the rest (termed the opsin portion) of the protein molecule, retinal is in the less stable 11-cis isomeric form. The absorption of a photon of light isomerizes the 11-cis retinal to the more stable all-trans isomer. This change in shape breaks its bonds with the opsin, and the all-trans retinal eventually drifts away from the membrane, later to be reisomerized and reattached to the opsin in a very slow regeneration process. At some early point in this breakdown of rhodopsin, physiological processes are triggered that eventually produce a change in polarization of the receptor outer membrane.

Rhodopsin is found in rods. It seems very likely that cones possess the same 11-cis retinal as rods, but attached to three different opsins in the different cone types. The spectral absorption curve is determined both by the structure of the retinal and by that of the opsin to which it is attached. Thus the rod pigment and the three cone pigments have somewhat similar shapes of spectral absorption curves, but they peak at different spectral regions.

An important feature of this process is that it has reached the ultimate in sensitivity: absorption of only a single photon, the minimum quantity of electromagnetic energy, is required to isomerize 11-cis retinal, and the isomerization of only a single photopigment molecule can produce a change in receptor membrane potential. Since the average photon catch in dim light may be less than one photon per receptor per unit integration time, it is essential that the system have this ultimate sensitivity at the receptor level.

A critical point with respect to this photochemical process is what has been termed the principle of univariance (Rushton, 1972): all that the breakdown of a photopigment molecule can signal is that a photon was absorbed. No information about the nature of the photon (i.e., its energy level or wavelength) is retained after it has been absorbed. The probability of a photon's being absorbed is jointly a function of the wavelength of the light (photons at energy levels near the peak sensitivity of the receptor are more likely to be absorbed) and the intensity of the light (if more photons are present, the pigment is more likely to absorb one); but the receptor cannot detect these independently. For example, consider the L cone, the relative spectral absorption curve for which is shown in Figure 3.12. Let us assume that the absolute sensitivity of an L cone at its peak wavelength, 560 nm, is 0.5. If at a given time it gave a response corresponding to 500 photons absorbed, this could have resulted from 1,000 photons of 565 nm incident on the receptor, or 2,000 photons of either 617 or 503 nm, or 4,000 photons of either 638 or 472 nm, etc. It would thus be impossible, knowing just the output of this cone, to specify either the wavelength or the intensity of the light. The 500-photon absorption could have been produced by light of any wavelength within the visible spectrum and of any of a considerable range of intensities. One can thus see the absurdity of referring to the L and M cones as "color receptors": individually they tell essentially nothing about the color. The extent of this absurdity is even further heightened by referring to L cones as "red receptors" when they are in fact far more sensitive to green and yellow and even somewhat more sensitive to blue than to red light.

It can be seen that wavelength and intensity information are confounded at the first visual step. Separating these two variables to give at least partially separate spatial maps of luminance and color variations in the visual scene is one of the major tasks in the early visual processing.

Transduction

Virtually every neuron in the brain has both depolarizing and hyperpolarizing inputs onto its dendritic surface, resulting from the secretion by the various neurons synapsing onto it of either a depolarizing or a hyperpolarizing synaptic transmitter (the former increasing the Na^+ permeability and the latter the K^+ (or Cl^-) permeability). The moment-to-moment difference between these two opposing effects, conveyed to the effector end of the neuron either by graded potentials or by an intervening spike-carrying axon, determines the moment-by-moment amount of synaptic transmitter the neuron releases. The greater the depolarization, the more the synaptic release; the more hyperpolarization, the less synaptic release.

In these functional respects, the visual receptors are in every way similar to other neurons in the brain, except that the processes producing depolarization and hyperpolarization are not chemicals released by other neurons, but are reactions initiated inside the receptor outer segment itself by the momentary variations in the amount of light captured by the photopigments. The variations in potential generated by variations in light are conducted in a graded, decremental way to the synaptic region of the receptor where they produce variations in amount of synaptic chemical released: the more depolarization, the more the release.

The similarity between visual receptors and other neurons has been obscured for many visual physiologists by their tendency to think of the eye as a detector of light flashes (i.e., increments in light) rather than as a visual organ concerned with variations in amount of light across space and time. As it happens, in the vertebrate eye, light increments lead to hyperpolarization and decrements to depolarization (Toyoda, Nosaki, & Tomita, 1969), whereas in the invertebrate eye, it is the opposite. To one who conceives of the eye as just a detector of light flashes, this must be a puzzling situation indeed, since the response to a flash is a decrease in synaptic output! However, the visual system should not be thought of as a detector of flashes of light, but as a system concerned with detecting and analyzing *visual scenes,* which consist of both increments and decrements in light intensity, and of variations in wavelength as well. Since the visual system must be able to deal with both increments and decrements in light (and color changes in either spectral direction), it is presumably a matter of indifference whether increments lead to depolarization and decrements to hyperpolarization or vice versa.

How light is transduced into neural activity is still in dispute. Whatever the precise mechanism may be, it is clear that several critical processes take place: (1) An enormous amplification occurs. The absorption of one photon, or the decrease in absorption of one photon, can lead to a considerable polarization change under conditions of complete dark adaptation. (2) The process resulting from an increase or decrease in photon capture must extend over a considerable time period, thus allowing for the temporal integration of information. (3) The receptors must incorporate some adaptational mechanism such that the physiological consequence of a certain increment or decrement in photon capture can vary with the mean light level.

The first examination (Sjöstrand, 1953) of receptors with the greatly increased magnification provided by electron microscopy revealed the presence in receptor outer segments of stacks of disks that appeared to be separate from the outer membrane (see Figs. 3.6–8). Subsequent examination of this question (Cohen, 1970) has firmly established that the disks, which contain the photopigment, are totally isolated from the outer membranes in rods, and only attached at occasional points in cones. This poses an immediate physiological problem, for a current flow started on the receptor disk could not pass to the outer membrane, just as elsewhere in the nervous system it cannot cross from one neuron to an adjacent one.

The solution to this problem is chemical transmission from receptor disk to outer membrane. The breakdown of the photopigment molecule by the capture of a photon does not itself produce a potential change that spreads down the receptor. Rather, it starts a chemical process, which (after some time delay) in turn changes the potential across the outer membrane. There is thus a chemical mediator between the disk and the outer membrane.

How information is transmitted from the isomerized photopigment molecules to the outer plasma membrane is not completely understood. It was believed initially (Hagins, 1972; Hagins & Yoshikami, 1974) that Ca^{++} ions act as the chemical transmitter between receptor disk and outside membrane. The breakdown of a molecule of rhodopsin by light, by this theory, would open a pore in the disk membrane, releasing Ca^{++} which would diffuse to the outside membrane and close a Na^+ pore. It now appears more likely that there is instead a whole cascade of intervening chemical reactions.

The Na^+ pores in the receptor outside membrane appear to be kept open in the dark by phosphorylation of the membrane pore proteins by cyclic GMP. The isomerization of rhodopsin (or a cone pigment) in the receptor disk by light converts it to an activated molecule which then catalyzes the production of a number of molecules of transducin, which in turn activate many molecules of an enzyme, phosphodiesterase (PDE), which then by deactivating cGMP dephosphorylates the outer membrane protein and closes the Na^+ pores (Wheeler & Bitensky, 1977; Woodruff & Bownds, 1978; Liebman & Pugh, 1979). A decrement in light would cut down the amount of PDE and thus increase the amount of cGMP, which would phosphorylate and thus open the Na^+ pores. Ca^{++} may also play a role since injection of Ca^{++} into the outer segment not only mimics the effect of light (Yoshikami & Hagins, 1971), but also decreases drastically the amount of cGMP (Cohen, Hall, & Ferrendelli, 1978).

The effect of closing the Na^+ pores is to hyperpolarize the receptor outer membrane, but only for an instant. To maintain this level of hyperpolarization requires a steady bombardment with photons. Therefore a decrement in light, after a similar time delay, produces an increase in the number of Na^+ pores open and thus results in depolarization of the receptor membrane. The graded depolarization or hyperpolarization is then decrementally conducted down the receptor membrane to the synaptic region, where the level of polarization determines the amount of synaptic transmitter released by the receptor.

It can be seen that this chemical mediation process incorporates the possibility of great amplification, since one isomerized photopigment molecule can activate as many as 500 PDE molecules, and one molecule of PDE can inactivate many cGMP molecules. Since the interactions at the receptor outer membrane are very transient, responses to decrements in light are greatly amplified as well.

Temporal Filtering

An important consequence of this arrangement within the receptor outer segment is that it averages information over time. One instantaneous photon capture produces a gradually increasing and then decreasing polarization change which lasts several milliseconds; during this time interval the effects of other closely contiguous photon captures can add to it. The outer membrane potential at any given instant, then, is a weighted average of the events over a period of some milliseconds. This temporal smoothing attenuates high temporal frequencies, thus emphasizing low temporal frequency information.

How this process operates can be seen in Figure 3.13. A single photon capture is an instantaneous event, an impulse function (see Figure 3.13A). Its temporal frequency spectrum, then, will be very broad. The neural response of the receptor outer membrane is seen in Figure 3.13B. It can be seen that there is a considerable time delay to the response (what we see is not the world as it is now, but as it was a tenth to a twentieth of a second ago), but more importantly the response is enormously amplified and spread out over a considerable time period. In Figures 3.13C and D this is translated into the frequency domain. The physical stimulus and the photopigment response have a tiny amount of energy spread over a broad temporal frequency band; the temporal smearing and amplification inside the receptor produces a temporal response with a lot of energy at low temporal frequencies but little at high.

At the bottom in Figure 3.13 the same points are made with respect to a light whose intensity varies sinusoidally. The arrival of photons at the receptor will be periodic, but with superimposed high-frequency variations due to quantum fluctuations. There will also be high-frequency fluctuations due to the probabilistic nature of the photon capture, and of the whole process leading to synaptic release. The output as transformed by the receptor emphasizes the slow fluctuation and cuts out the high-frequency oscillations. The basic "assumption" on which the receptor operates (having learned its physics through evolution) is that the visual world is basically stable in time, varying only slowly: rapid changes are most likely quantum or physiological noise, to be ignored.

The illustrations in Figure 3.13 imply that the temporal filtering by the receptors is constant. Actually, as mentioned earlier, the system is more sophisticated than that and changes its temporal properties as a function of the background light level. The physiological mechanism by which this is accomplished has not yet been firmly established, but the existence of the process in the receptors has. The function subserved by such a change is clear. At low light levels there is not enough information available to resolve high temporal frequencies; the quantum noise would be very high relative to the signal. As light levels increase and there are a larger and larger number of photons per unit time, the signal/noise ratio at high temporal frequencies (as well as at low) would increase. It would thus be desirable for the system to filter out high temporal frequencies at low light levels, but to increase its high temporal frequency capability at higher light levels.

Adaptation

One of the major problems the visual system has to deal with is that of operating over an enormous intensity range, although the whole range does not have to be

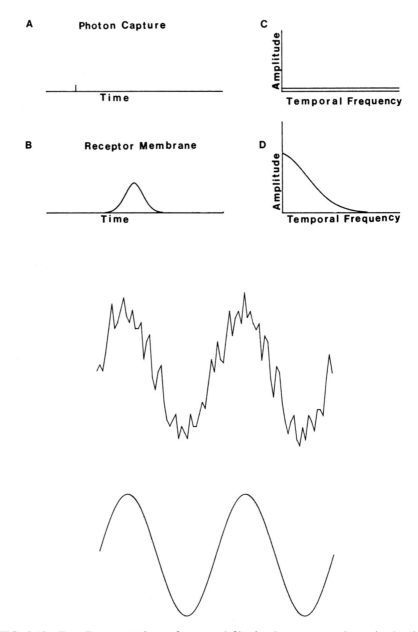

FIG. 3.13   Top: Representations of temporal filtering by receptors shown in the time domain (A and B) and the temporal frequency domain (C and D). See text for further explanation. Bottom: Diagrammatic representation of temporal filtering of an oscillating signal. The mean stimulus intensity varies sinusoidally, but noise due to quantum fluctuations is superimposed (upper trace). After low-pass temporal filtering by the receptors, the receptor output (bottom trace) follows the low temporal frequency variation in the signal but does not show the quantum noise.

covered at one time since the range of intensities at a given illumination level is usually moderate. It has long been clear from psychophysical studies that this problem is partially handled by a variable gain control mechanism (Craik, 1940), the system having high sensitivity at low light levels and progressively less sensitivity as background illumination increases. Early physiological studies showed that such a gain control mechanism is in fact present in the output of the retina (R.L. De Valois, Jacobs, & Jones, 1962; Jacobs, 1965). Lateral geniculate neurons give their full range of output over only about a 2-log-unit range of light intensities. When there is a sustained change in adaptation level, the cell may initially give a large response, but the firing rate soon returns to almost the same level as before, and the cell now signals intensity changes over about a 2-log-unit range around this new adaptation level. It has more recently been found that a large part of such an adaptational gain control occurs at the level of the receptors themselves (Norman & Werblin, 1974).

There are two adaptation changes that would be advantageous for the system: a decrease in sensitivity with increasing light levels, and a shift in the operating range such that the whole response range is utilized for a range of intensities about each adaptation level (see discussion in Chapter 5). Both rods and cones show sensitivity changes with variations in ambient light level; only cones shift their response range with adaptation.

Rods are about 10 times as sensitive as cones, for reasons which are not yet totally understood. Therefore at very low, scotopic, light levels, rods are the only functioning receptors. They then have both a high absolute sensitivity and a high differential sensitivity, that is, a certain increment or decrement in light intensity produces a large change in receptor polarization and thus in synaptic chemical release. As illustrated in Figure 3.14, increments and decrements of light around level A would produce larger changes in rod response than would those around B, where the intensity-response curve is flatter. Finally, as the mean light level increases still further, beyond C in this illustration, the rods become completely saturated. Under daylight, photopic, conditions, rods are hyperpolarized to a level where they release no synaptic chemicals and thus make no contribution to vision.

Cones, on the other hand, give no evidence of saturation when allowed to adapt for a few seconds to any given light level (short of fiercely high levels that would bleach out all the photopigment molecules). At a given mean light level, say, D in Figure 3.14, small increments and decrements of $\pm < 1.5$ log units would produce graded decrements and increments in synaptic chemical release. Increments or decrements of 2 or more log units (a 100-fold or more increase or decrease) would, however, produce maximum, saturating responses. So when a cone is adapted to C, lights D and E would be indistinguishably intense, each hyperpolarizing the cone to a level that blocks synaptic chemical release. But if allowed to adapt to level E, the cone will now depolarize to some extent and now give differential responses to small increments and decrements around this new level. Note that in this illustration the abscissa is *log* luminance: the sensitivity in terms of absolute changes in number of photons is thus much lower

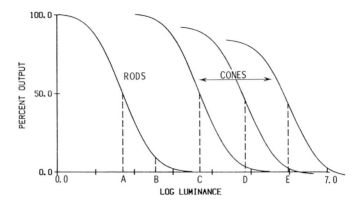

FIG. 3.14   Diagrammatic representation of rod and cone intensity-response functions at different adaptation levels over a 7 log range. At adaptation level A (about 1.7 log units on this scale), the rod output decreases or increases with high sensitivity as the light intensity varies about this level. When the adaptation level increases to B the rods do not compensate and therefore show a compressed intensity- response function. By adaptation level C rods are completely saturated and give no further response. The cones, in contrast, shift their intensity-response functions accordingly as the adaptation level changes from C to D to E, in the photopic range.

when the receptor is adapted to E than when it was adapted to C. Thus adaptation in cones involves both a change in operating range and a shift in sensitivity.

The presence of an "internal transmitter" in receptor outer segments provides a mechanism by which the receptor desensitization with increasing light levels could occur. There appears to be only about one PDE molecule for every 1,000 photopigment molecules. Nonetheless, there will be many PDE molecules available in the dark-adapted state, so the breakdown of a single photopigment molecule can activate many PDE molecules and have a high probability of closing a Na^+ pore in the outer membrane. At higher light levels, however, the PDE will increasingly be used up, so that it may now require some hundreds of photon captures to have the same probability of activating a PDE molecule to initiate the process as had a single photon capture at lower light levels. A second possible adaptational mechanism operating at this level is the limited number of Na^+ pores in the receptor outer membrane relative to the much larger number of photopigment molecules and intermediate transmitter chemicals (Ca^{++} or PDE). It has been estimated that there are but 6,000 Na^+ pores in a turtle cone (Baylor & Hodgkin, 1973), compared with millions of Ca^{++} ions or PDE molecules, and hundreds of millions of photopigment molecules. In complete dark adaptation, when all the disk membrane sites are closed, all 6,000 of the Na^+ pores might be open. The capture of a few photons under these circumstances would lead not only to a large amount of internal transmitter release, as discussed earlier, but also to a high probability of the transmitter's finding an open pore. Under photopic conditions, on the other hand, since most of the Na$^+$ pores would be closed, the probability of a certain amount of transmitter's producing a pore closure would be much less. It might now take a thousand photon captures to have the same probability of producing a threshold hyperpolarization of the membrane as did a single photon capture in complete dark adaptation. This leaves unexplained, however, the shift in the operating range of the cone system.

In summary, then, it may at first appear very strange that vertebrate receptors have evolved such a complex, indirect way of transducing light fluctuations into membrane polarization changes. Presumably it would have been possible for the breakdown of rhodopsin to have directly initiated a change in membrane polarization. What has been gained by interposing a whole series of chemical reactions between the photopigment breakdown and the conducted neural response? We can suggest at least three answers to this. One is that it allows for an enormous amplification of the responses to light changes, thus providing for extremely high sensitivity at dim light levels. A second is that it provides a low-pass temporal filtering that minimizes noise due to quantum and physiological fluctuations. Thirdly, it provides an adaptational mechanism, allowing for a modification of receptor sensitivity depending on the background illumination level.

Receptor Coupling

In a study of turtle cones, Baylor, Fuortes, and O'Bryan (1971) first established physiologically the presence of electrical coupling between receptors in a vertebrate retina. (Smith, Baumann, and Fuortes, 1965, had earlier found such coupling in the invertebrate *Limulus* eye.) They showed that a single cone showed summation of responses to lights as distant as 40 μm away, this being about the distance that lateral anatomical connections subsequently found between cones are seen to extend. Similar, even more pronounced summation is seen among turtle rods (E.A. Schwarz, 1975; Copenhagen & Owen, 1976), and the interactions are over considerably greater distances. The turtle has cones containing different pigments, and Baylor and Hodgkin (1973) showed that the coupling was restricted to receptors of the same photopigment type. Such receptor coupling is not a trivial process: it has been estimated by Fain, Gold, and Dowling (1976) that as much as 90% of the response of a given rod is due to its input from adjacent rods rather than to the light it itself absorbs.

For technical reasons, most studies of receptor coupling have been carried out on the turtle, rather than on primates. There are considerable anatomical and physiological differences between the visual systems of reptiles and primates, so one cannot immediately generalize from the studies of turtle to primates. However, lateral connections have been seen between cones in the human eye (Missotten & van den Dooren, 1966) and gap junctions at similar connections in the monkey retina (Raviola & Gilula, 1973). The best assumption, therefore, is that a similar organization probably exists in the primate retina. Such crucial questions as the lateral extent of the coupling for cones versus rods and for different cone types, how the lateral extent varies with retinal eccentricity, and how coupling varies with light level are matters to be settled in the future.

An important feature of receptor coupling is that the amount of coupling between receptors may be modified as a function of adaptation level. In locust, the receptors are electrotonically connected during dark adaptation, but become partially or even totally decoupled as light levels increase (Lillywhite, 1978). The mechanism for this may be the Ca^{++} level in the vicinity of the gap junction. It has been shown (Rose & Lowenstein, 1971) that the Ca^{++} level affects the junctional resistance between receptors, and the Ca^{++} level may itself very well fluctuate as a function of the ambient light level.

Spatial Filtering

One functional effect of receptor coupling is a spatial low-pass filtering of the retinal image. It is thus quite analogous in the spatial domain to the temporal filtering we discussed earlier, which takes place in the receptor outer segment. The effect of spreading the polarization change induced in one receptor to neighboring, coupled receptors is to attenuate high spatial frequencies while producing little effect on low spatial frequency information. The more extensive coupling found among rods than among cones would produce a greater attenuation of high spatial frequencies in rods and the extension of the attenuation to still lower spatial frequency regions. Similar lowering of the high spatial frequency cut would occur if, as seems likely, receptor coupling increases with retinal eccentricity.

Quantum noise limits high spatial frequency information, particularly at low light levels, just as was true for high temporal frequency information. Light scatter and optical aberrations also introduce spurious high spatial frequency inputs to the system. All of this "noise" would be attenuated by receptor coupling at low light levels.

At high light levels there is more "signal" present at high temporal frequencies; it therefore would be advantageous for the system to broaden its temporal passband to include higher frequencies under those circumstances. In the central fovea, the optic image also contains more "signal" at high spatial frequencies (because of a curtailment of the spectrum, minimizing chromatic aberration, and the pushing aside of the nuclear layers with their blood vessels, minimizing light scatter, as discussed in Chapter 2). It would thus be adaptive for the system to broaden its spatial passband to include higher spatial frequencies in this region by means of smaller cones and little, if any, lateral receptor coupling. But only at high brightness levels is there useful information at high temporal frequencies; and only at high light levels within the tiny part of the visual field subserved by the fovea is there meaningful information at high spatial frequencies. In almost all of the retina under most viewing conditions the most useful visual information is at lower spatial and temporal frequencies. Under these circumstances the extensive low-pass filtering in both the spatial and temporal domains carried out by the receptors maximizes the signal/noise ratio in the information.

In summary, the slow, prolonged internal conduction within the receptor outer segments, and the lateral electrotonic coupling of receptor synaptic areas, may appear to be strange malformations of the system if one thinks of the visual system's task as being the relaying of a precise point-by-point and instant-by-instant representation of the visual input to central regions. Considered, however, in terms of the temporally and spatially distributed nature of useful visual information, particularly as compared with the spatial and temporal distribution of noise (that which does not correspond to visual objects), these processes are eminently sensible and adaptive. The most reliable visual information is present at lower spatial and temporal frequencies, especially at low light levels. Extremely high spatiotemporal frequency information in the retinal image, except at the highest light levels in the foveal area, is mostly noise. Therefore a low-pass filtering in both the spatial and temporal domains at low light levels and in the peripheral retina considerably improves the signal-to-noise ratio, and thus the information about the "real" world.

RECEPTOR-HORIZONTAL CELL-BIPOLAR SYNAPSE

It will be recalled from the earlier anatomical discussion that bipolar cells make direct contact with anywhere from one to a large number of receptors, and that horizontal cells bring in an input to the receptor-bipolar synapse from the same retinal region plus a larger surrounding area.

Bipolar Responses

All vertebrate receptors appear to depolarize to decrements and hyperpolarize to increments of light, with the release of synaptic transmitter being proportional to the amount of depolarization. Bipolar cells, however, are clearly of two different varieties that respond in opposite directions to the receptor output. Some bipolars are depolarized by the receptor transmitter and are thus depolarized by light decrements and hyperpolarized by increments. Others are hyperpolarized by the receptor transmitter and are thus depolarized by increments and hyperpolarized by decrements. Let us abbreviate decrement by "D" and increment by "I" and refer to depolarization as "+" and hyperpolarization as "−". Then this situation can be summarized by characterizing all receptors as $+D-I$ in their response; half the bipolars are also $+D-I$, the other half $+I-D$. Since $+I-D$ bipolars do and $+D-I$ bipolars do not invert the sign of the receptor response, these two types are sometimes referred to as inverting and noninverting bipo lars, respectively.

It is very likely that receptors all secrete the same transmitter, and that the two bipolar types respond in opposite directions to this transmitter. This is the first of many bifurcations into parallel channels or paths that we shall see taking place in the course of the sequential processing of visual information.

Horizontal Cells

Receptors synapse onto both bipolars and horizontal cells within the receptor pouches and on the receptor surface as well. Horizontal cells, like the receptors and bipolars, show only graded, decrementally conducted potential changes, rather than firing all-or-none spikes as do many other neurons. Further, in most neurons the receptive (dendritic) region is at the opposite end of the cell from the effector region at which synaptic chemicals are released. At all their contacts with receptors and bipolars, however, horizontal cell processes appear to have sites that respond to the receptor transmitter immediately adjacent to regions containing vesicles for secreting transmitter chemicals. Thus the input to a horizontal cell from one receptor will affect the horizontal cell-bipolar synapse at that receptor itself, and will also be conducted laterally to affect neighboring receptor-bipolar synapses. Correspondingly, a given receptor-bipolar synapse will have horizontal cell input to it from a wide group of neighboring receptors, including that receptor itself (see Figure 3.9).

In animals that do not have the additional complication of different cone types and chromatic processing, horizontal cells are depolarized by receptor transmitters, and thus respond with depolarization to light decrements and hyperpolarization to increments. They are similar to other cells in that they release synaptic transmitters in proportion to the degree of depolarization. Thus receptors and horizontal cells show similar polarity of responses to variations in light. They must, however, secrete different transmitter chemicals, for bipolars respond in opposite ways to the receptor and the horizontal cell outputs.

At most of the connections in the outer plexiform layer, most notably within the receptor pouches, receptors, horizontal cells, and bipolars are all closely juxtaposed. The synaptic chemicals released by receptors must affect both bipolars and horizontal cells (they provide the only input to the horizontal cells). The transmitters released by horizontal cells, however, could conceivably affect only the bipolars, feed back onto the receptors, or do both. The evidence suggests that they do both. Recordings from both turtle receptors (Baylor & Fuortes, 1970) and those in gecko (Pinto & Pak, 1974) show that receptors respond in ways consonant with a horizontal cell feedback onto them. On the other hand, bipolars seem to be more affected by horizontal cell input than can be accounted for purely on the basis of this receptor feedback. It would thus appear that the horizontal cell output both feeds back onto receptors and feeds forward onto bipolars.

In this account of bipolar activity we have considered only the organization that is found in animals without color vision, or in components of visual systems (the scotopic, rod-dominated organization) based on just one receptor type. There are considerable complications, discussed below, when more than one cone type is present and the system is involved in separating color from luminance information. Unfortunately, most such studies have been on subprimate species such as goldfish and turtle which have notable anatomical and physiological differences from primates, at least at later levels. It is thus hard to judge the extent to which the early visual organization in such animals can be generalized to the primates, with which we are primarily concerned here.

R-H-B Circuit

There is thus a circuit made up of receptors, horizontal cells, and bipolars, the neural responses being graded potentials transmitted between cells by chemical synaptic transmitters. The bipolar cells carry the information to the next synaptic stage, and the easiest way of understanding this circuit is in terms of how bipolars respond to the various inputs. It is useful to think of there being two separate paths from receptors to bipolars: a direct path from receptors (R-B), and an indirect path from the receptors by way of horizontal cells (R-H-B) (see Figure 3.15). The critical fact in understanding this circuit is that the direct (R-B) input and the indirect (R-H-B) input produce opposite responses in the bipolars, this being true for both types of bipolars. Thus bipolars that are depolarized by the direct input are hyperpolarized by the indirect input, and vice versa.

It may seem nonsensical for a bipolar to be both depolarized and hyperpolarized by the receptors from which it receives input, since depolarization and hyperpolarization just cancel each other out. It would indeed make little sense were it not that somewhat different populations of receptors are sampled by the direct and indirect paths. A bipolar cell's direct input comes from the relatively small number of receptors with which it makes direct contact; its indirect input

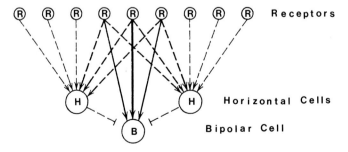

FIG. 3.15 Diagrammatic representation of the direct (solid lines) and indirect (dashed lines) inputs to a bipolar cell from receptors and horizontal cells. Note that the direct and indirect paths have opposite effects on the bipolar cell.

comes from these same receptors plus a large number of surrounding receptors. The bipolars thus perform a spatial differencing of two overlapping receptor populations of different spatial extent. There are also temporal differences between the direct and indirect paths, so bipolars temporally difference as well.

Bipolar Receptive Field

The receptive field (RF) of a sensory neuron is composed of the receptors from which it receives its input (Hartline, 1940). (One can also consider the RF to be those locations in the visual field which project to and thus activate these receptors.) Thus, all the receptors that feed into a bipolar cell, through either the direct or the indirect path, constitute the RF of the bipolar. By the organization of the RF of a neuron, one refers to the distribution of the polarity of the response (whether depolarization or hyperpolarization) across the RF. To specify this, however, one has to specify the nature of the stimulus. We have earlier alluded to and criticized the pervasive (albeit implicit) assumption that the visual system is a light detector (as opposed to a visual organ concerned with detecting objects that may be brighter, darker, or of a different color than their background). Because of this widespread assumption, virtually all RF maps in the vision literature describe the way a cell responds to light *increments.* It is equally important, however, to specify the RF organization of cells for light decrements, and for various color changes in the case of color-coded units. As we discuss in Chapter 7, for instance, a typical retinal cell has a very different RF organization for luminance changes than for color changes.

The RF organization of a $+I-D$ (or inverting) bipolar cell is shown in Figure 3.16. The response to a direct input from a circular area in the RF center is depolarization to increments; the indirect input produces hyperpolarization to increments, extends over a larger circular area, and is on the average less powerful than the direct input (see Figure 3.16A). These two depolarizing and hyperpolarizing areas of the RF have a common center, and each is strongest in the center. The drop with distance from the RF center can be accounted for by decremental conduction along the cell processes: the inputs from distant receptors, decrementally conducted for some distance, will be less powerful than those from nearby receptors. A bipolar may also make more connections in the central part of its RF than further laterally. Both of these factors would produce a quasi-gaussian distribution of input across the RF. Since depolarization and hyperpolarization sum algebraically, the cross section of the overall (incremental) RF profile is as shown in Figure 3.16B. A bipolar cell picks up from a two-dimensional retinal area, and is roughly radially symmetric. Thus its two-dimensional RF shape is as shown in Figure 3.16C. As can be seen, it has roughly the shape of a Mexican hat. A $+D-I$ bipolar cell's RF to incremental stimuli would, then, be like a Mexican hat turned upside down.

We have thus far been discussing the RF structure of $+I-D$ bipolars to increments in light. Let us now consider how such a cell responds to light decrements.

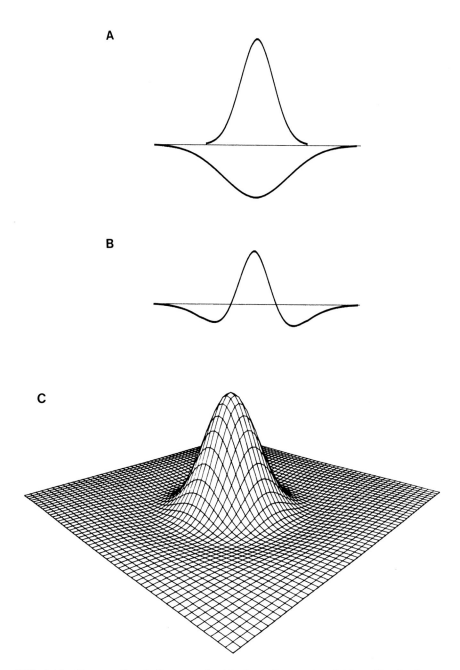

FIG. 3.16 Cross-sectional diagram of a bipolar cell receptive field profile. In the top drawing (A) the center and surround inputs are shown separately. Since they are opposite in sign and sum algebraically, the resultant combined RF profile is as shown in B. In C is a three-dimensional representation of the entire RF, showing its radial symmetry (after the receptive field model of Rodieck, 1965).

The direct path (R-B) produces a hyperpolarizing response to decrements, as discussed earlier. The indirect path (R-H-B) is opposite, producing a depolarizing response to decrements. Thus the RF structure of this type of bipolar to decrements is the mirror image of its RF to increments: − center and + surround.

Without having to go through the whole story in detail, we can see that the RF structure of a +D−I bipolar cell will be the mirror image in each case of that of the +I−D bipolar shown in Figure 3.16. It will thus have a + center and − surround RF to decrements (similar to that of the other cell to increments) and a − center and + surround RF to increments (like the other cell's RF to decrements).

Another way to examine and specify the response characteristics of a cell (and one which is useful in thinking about the system in terms of its functional organization) is to consider how it would respond to other types of stimuli, in particular what the optimal stimuli might be. If we consider the RF cross section of the +I−D bipolar (Figure 3.16B) we can see that an increment of light in the RF center will depolarize the cell; so will a decrement in the surround. If the cell shows even moderate linearity of summation (bipolars are in fact quite linear), a stronger depolarizing stimulus than either of these stimuli alone will be their combination: an increment in the RF center *and* a decrement in the surround. Correspondingly, the strongest hyperpolarizing stimulus would be a decrement in the RF center and an increment in the surround. Of course, in each case just the converse stimulus would be best for the +D−I bipolar, i.e., its optimal depolarizing stimulus would be a central decrement and a surround increment.

Insofar as bipolar cells show fairly linear summation of depolarizing and hyperpolarizing inputs within their RFs, one can informatively apply linear systems analysis to their responses. We will defer a discussion of that topic, however, until considering the very similar RF structure of certain ganglion cells, since the relevant experiments were first carried out at the ganglion cell level.

GANGLION AND GENICULATE CELLS

As discussed earlier, the bipolar-amacrine-ganglion cell synapse structurally resembles the receptor-horizontal cell-bipolar synapse at the earlier level. Amacrine cells are analogous in function to the horizontal cells in the outer plexiform layer in that they carry information laterally among various bipolar-ganglion cell synaptic regions. This is not to say that horizontal and amacrine cells modify the information in the same way.

The functional transformations that occur at the bipolar-amacrine-ganglion cell level are not well understood. The principal ganglion cell types found in the central retina greatly resemble bipolars in their functional properties. In the case of these cells, it is not clear what change has taken place at the bipolar-amacrine-ganglion cell synapse. At least one important new response type (Y cells, discussed below) is found first at the ganglion cell level, however, and its properties are thus doubtless due to interactions that take place here.

Both ganglion cells and LGN cells have been widely recorded from in both cat and monkey. There have been no consistent indications of any profound differences between ganglion and LGN cells in their responses to various stimuli. The functional role of the LGN is thus most obscure. It perhaps serves mainly as a site for interactions with, or gating by, inputs from other brain centers. In any case, in the absence of evidence for functional differences in visual responses, ganglion cells and LGN cells will be treated together in what follows.

With perhaps the partial exception of amacrine cells, all the neural activity in the retina prior to the ganglion cells takes place with graded, decrementally conducted potentials. Since only short distances are involved within the retina, there is no need for regenerative nerve impulses to intervene between the graded dendritic processes and the graded synaptic chemical release. At least some amacrine cells show small spike-like discharges, in addition to their large graded potentials (Werblin & Dowling, 1969). The significance of these is yet to be understood. Normal all-or-none spike discharges are first found in ganglion cell axons, serving to carry the outputs of the retinal calculations to distant central regions.

The occurrence of spike discharges in ganglion and LGN cells makes it possible to isolate the activity of individual cells with extracellular electrodes. They were thus studied before the development of the intracellular recording techniques required to study units at earlier levels, since these only show graded potentials. The existence of RFs with center-surround antagonism (similar to the center-surround opponency of bipolar cells we discussed above) was first found in recordings from cat ganglion cells by Kuffler (1953) and from rabbit ganglion cells by Barlow (1953). Both Kuffler and Barlow found that a stimulus that covered the whole of a cell's RF evoked a smaller response than one that just covered the RF center. Kuffler (1953), furthermore, mapped out the RF into separate excitatory and inhibitory areas (in terms of their responses to increments of light, the only type of stimulus he used), and found evidence for two ganglion cell types. These he termed on-center (because an increment in the center of the RF produced a discharge at light onset) and off-center cells (so named because an increment in the RF center in this type produced inhibition followed by an excitatory response at light offset).

The discovery of these two ganglion cell types and their RF organization was a major contribution to our understanding of visual processing. The classification of the units into on-center and off-center cells, however, carries two implicit assumptions with which we would disagree: that increments in luminance are of primary visual importance, and that only increases in cell firing carry important information. We would prefer to name such cells by the somewhat more inclusive terms $+I-D$ (fire to increment and inhibit to decrements), and $+D-I$, respectively. Neither this terminology nor that of on-center and off-center captures the important property of center-surround antagonism (for luminance-varying patterns).

Linear Analysis

A linear system's responses to any one-dimensional pattern would be predict-able from (1) its sensitivity to gratings of various spatial frequencies and (2) the extent to which these frequencies were present in the stimulus as determined by a Fourier analysis of the stimulus pattern. Any complex one-dimensional pat-tern can be broken down into the sum of sine waves of specified frequencies, amplitudes, and phases (see Chapter 1). If one knows how a cell responds to these individual sine waves, and if the cell shows linearity of summation within its RF, then its response to any pattern of any degree of complexity could be predicted just by adding up its responses to the individual sine wave components.

Such an analysis assumes linearity of spatial summation; whether such an assumption is justified is of course an empirical question. However, it should be noted that conventional RF mapping with spots of light makes quite the same linear assumptions, although not explicitly. That is to say, it would be of micro-scopically little interest how a cell responds to spots of light in different locations except insofar as such responses provide a guide as to how the cell would respond to other, more interesting and important patterns. But the conventional RF provides such a guide and thus has meaning only insofar as there is linearity of summation within the RF. A spatial frequency analysis thus only makes clear and explicit assumptions which are in fact implicit in conventional descriptions of the RFs of cells.

One can go one step further and point out that conventional RF mapping and spatial frequency analysis are mathematically equivalent, given linearity. In a linear system, one can operate equivalently in the space domain (i.e., RF) or in the frequency domain, and go back and forth between them. Thus a certain RF structure implies a certain spatial frequency selectivity, and vice versa. How-ever, their mathematical equivalence does not mean that they are equivalent in ease of use. In fact, we would argue that it is much easier and more rapid to determine the spatial frequency sensitivity of a cell than to do a *quantitative* RF mapping; in most cases it is also easier to see intuitively how a cell would respond to various stimuli from its spatial frequency sensitivity than from its RF map. These advantages to a frequency analysis will become even more pro-nounced when the properties of more complicated cell types are examined. For instance, as we discuss in Chapter 4, cortical complex cells' responses can be readily predicted from their spatial frequency tuning, but such cells cannot be mapped by conventional RF techniques.

Spatial Frequency Specificity

The responses of most ganglion cells to grating patterns are characterized by some degree of both spatial frequency and phase selectivity. Let us consider first the frequency selectivity, and discuss this with reference to a $+I-D$ ganglion cell with an RF like that of the bipolar cell diagrammed in Figure 3.16. Such a cell would give maximum depolarization to a grating of such a spatial frequency that the width of the light bar (a half cycle) coincides with the width of the RF center (see Figure 3.17 middle). The adjacent black bars of the grating would then fall on the RF flanks. Compared to its response to a uniform field of the same mean luminance, the cell's response to a grating of this frequency (in this phase) would consist of depolarization from the RF center, plus a decrease in hyperpolarization (which is equivalent to an increase in depolarization) from the surround. These would thus add to produce a large depolarization.

With gratings of lower spatial frequencies (Figure 3.17 top), the bright bar would not only cover the RF center, but encroach to some degree on the flanks as well, increasingly so the lower the spatial frequency. The depolarizing effect of center stimulation would thus be partially canceled by hyperpolarization produced by the bright bar on the flanks, and the cell's response would thus show some low spatial frequency attenuation.

Next consider the response of this $+I-D$ ganglion cell to a grating of too high a spatial frequency (Figure 3.17 bottom). The bright bar would cover only part of the RF center; the rest of the RF center, being stimulated by dark bars, would produce a canceling hyperpolarization. The same cancellation would also occur on the flanks, since they would be covered by both bright and dark bars. When the spatial frequency reaches twice the optimum, the RF center would be equally covered by a bright and a dark half cycle, so the output from the RF center would go to zero; so also would that of the flanks. Therefore the cell's response, maximum at some spatial frequency f (dependent on the RF size), would fall to zero at a stimulus spatial frequency of $2f$, and would be attenuated at frequencies below f.

Phase Specificity

For the $+I-D$ ganglion cell considered above, the maximum depolarizing response would occur when a grating of optimum frequency was aligned so that a bright half cycle coincided with the RF center. If this grating were now shifted 90° in phase in either direction, the RF center would be covered half by a white and half by a black half cycle. These would cancel to produce no output (given linearity of spatial summation). Correspondingly, the RF surround would give no output with the grating in this position. A further 90° phase shift from this null phase (altogether a 180° phase shift from the optimum position) would produce maximum hyperpolarization from this cell. Such a ganglion cell would thus be sensitive not only to the spatial frequency of a grating, but to its phase as well, the response changing from maximum depolarization to zero to maximum hyperpolarization with phase shifts of 90 and 180°, respectively.

The presence of a null phase position is of particular significance, because it indicates a high degree of linearity of summation within the RF: an increment in one half of the RF is precisely canceled by an equal-sized decrement in the

FIG. 3.17 Superposition of a ganglion cell RF on gratings of different spatial frequencies. In the middle figure the RF is superimposed on a grating whose light and dark bars are of such a width as to optimally stimulate both RF center and surround. In the top figure the same RF is shown on a grating of half optimal spatial frequency, and in the bottom, on one of twice optimal frequency. These latter patterns would produce little net excitation or inhibition from the cell whose RF is shown.

other half. The presence or absence of a null-phase position was used by Enroth-Cugell and Robson (1966) as the defining characteristic of X cells.

We have been discussing a $+I-D$ ganglion cell (commonly called an on-center cell), but the same arguments apply to a $+D-I$ ganglion cell (traditionally termed an off-center cell). Such a ganglion cell would also be somewhat selective for the spatial frequency of a grating (attenuating high spatial frequencies more sharply than low) and highly selective for the spatial phase of the pattern. The difference between these two ganglion (or LGN) cell types is that, given identical RF locations, one is phase shifted 180° with respect to the other. The phase that produces maximum depolarization in the one, produces maximum hyperpolarization in the other, and vice versa. Finally, it might be noted that both of these ganglion cell types have RFs that in cross section greatly resemble $1\frac{1}{2}$ cycles of a damped cosine wave. The RF, thus, is symmetrical about its center in cross section. The output of such a cell would thus be highly correlated with a sinusoidal grating of the appropriate frequency and in cosine phase with respect to the location of the RF center. The RF of a ganglion cell is of course two-dimensional in structure and is roughly radially symmetric about its center. It would thus respond well to a sinusoidal pattern of the right spatial frequency and phase regardless of its orientation. The X cells of Enroth-Cugell and Robson (1966) discussed above constitute a majority of the cells in cat and monkey retina, and project exclusively up the geniculostriate path (Dreher, Fukada, & Rodieck, 1976).

Y Cells

Enroth-Cugell and Robson (1966) found evidence in cat for another type of ganglion cell, which they termed Y cells, with quite different response properties from X cells. The critical distinction is that Y cells will respond to some extent (although not necessarily equally) to a grating at any phase angle. Thus no phase of the grating with respect to the RF will yield a null response. Typically, the higher the spatial frequency of the pattern the less phase specific the cell's responses become; at low spatial frequencies a Y cell tends to respond more like an X cell, although even at low frequencies it has no null phase. It thus shows quite nonlinear spatial summation within its RF. In responses to flashes of light, a $+I-D$ X cell shows an increment in firing at light onset and a decrement in firing at light offset. A Y cell, on the other hand, fires a burst at both the onset and the offset of the light. (In the traditional terminology it would be termed an on-off cell.)

The Y cell RF has been modeled (Hochstein & Shapley, 1976a, 1976b) as if the cell had two components to its input. A linear component tuned to a low spatial frequency (similar to the input to X cells) is postulated to feed into the RF center. Multiple nonlinear inputs tuned to higher spatial frequencies and widely distributed across the whole RF would constitute a surround mechanism. The form of the nonlinearity in the units making up the surround might be half-

or full-wave rectification. Such a model would account for the largely linear responses of Y-cells to low spatial frequency patterns, and the very nonlinear responses of these cells to high-frequency patterns.

It is worth pointing out here that retinal Y cells bear many similarities to cortical complex cells (R.L. De Valois, Albrecht, & Thorell, 1982). However, this does not imply that Y cells form the inputs to complex cells. The nonlinear subunits across which complex cells sum could be half-wave rectified outputs from cortical simple cells, somewhat as first suggested by Hubel and Wiesel (1962).

The retinal Y cells constitute about 5% of the ganglion cell population in cat. They project to the LGN, with collaterals to the colliculus. While Y cells form an important part of the collicular path, it is important to realize that in primates they constitute only a very small part of the geniculostriate path, almost all of which is made up of X cells.

In addition to X and Y cells, a number of other cell types have been described in cat retina. Such cells are often grouped together as W cells. We will not consider the properties of such cells here, since they seem to project mainly to the colliculus and other subcortical sites with which we shall not be concerned.

From a study of cat retinal ganglion cells, Cleland, Dubin, and Levick (1971) proposed that cells were dichotomous in their temporal properties, terming the two groups sustained and transient cells. The sustained cells were those which continued to respond to some extent to a long-lasting stationary stimulus, whereas transient cells gave only a brief response at stimulus onset and/or offset. This physiological categorization into sustained versus transient found a ready echo in psychophysiological theorizing which postulated separate sustained and transient channels. Furthermore, Cleland et al. (1971) argued for an identity between the X/Y spatial categorization and the sustained/transient temporal distinction, namely that X cells were sustained and Y cells transient. This relationship appears to hold quite well for ganglion cells, but not as tightly for LGN cells, and not at all at the level of the cortex. Nonetheless, the relationship was so widely accepted that many reports in the literature for a number of years used the X/Y terminology to designate cells that were experimentally distinguished purely on the basis of their temporal sustained/transient properties.

Different LGN Laminae

The LGN in primates consists of four layers of small cells (the parvocellular laminae) and two layers of large cells (magnocellular laminae). The parvocellular layer cells have a retinal input solely from X cells (Dreher et al., 1976; von Blanckensee, 1981; Kaplan & Shapley, 1982). The early reports from multiple-cell recordings that the outermost LGN layers (layers 6 and 5) showed most on-responses to incremental flashes of light (R.L. De Valois, Smith, Karoly, & Kitai, 1958) have been confirmed by recent single-cell recordings (Schiller & Malpeli, 1978). These cells contain mostly $+I-D$ cells, by our nomenclature, whereas parvocellular layers 4 and 3 contain mainly $+D-I$ cells. Most of the magnocellular cells (layers 2 and 1) are also X cells (von Blanckensee, 1981; Kaplan & Shapley, 1982; Derrington & Lennie, 1984), mingled with a certain number of Y cells. The early reports stating that all of the magnocellular cells were Y cells (Dreher et al., 1976; Schiller & Malpeli, 1978) may be attributed to their using temporal (sustained versus transient) rather than purely spatial criteria for classifying the cells. As we discussed above, there is an imperfect correlation at best between X cells and sustained cells. The temporal properties of the magnocellular X cells do in fact resemble those of the Y cells: they have shorter response latencies than the parvocellular cells, and are in general tuned to high temporal frequencies (Kaplan & Shapley, 1982; Derrington & Lennie, 1984). Most striking, however, are the differences in sensitivity for luminance patterns of parvocellular versus magnocellular cells. The latter are on the average about 10 times as sensitive at low spatial frequencies, with parvocellular cells showing little response to gratings of less than about 8% contrast (Kaplan & Shapley, 1982). By comparison, the human (and macaque) psychophysical contrast threshold over most of the spatial frequency range is near, or even well below, 1% contrast (see Chapter 5). One would expect, therefore, that the psychophysical threshold luminance contrast sensitivity function, particularly at low spatial and high temporal frequencies (that is, for patterns moving at high velocities), would largely reflect the activity of magnocellular units. A compensating factor that must be considered, however, is probability summation based on the much greater number of parvocellular units, particularly subserving the central retina (Derrington & Lennie, 1984).

RETINOGENICULATE COLOR ORGANIZATION

Most studies, both psychophysical and physiological, related to spatial vision have used only luminance-varying patterns, although in our opinion color-varying patterns are at least as important as luminance ones for spatial vision. This neglect of color in spatial vision studies has a number of origins. On the physiological side, it is partly due to the fact that many animals widely used in visual studies, e.g., *Limulus* and cat, have little if any color vision. On the psychophysical side, the neglect of color in spatial vision is partly attributable to the fact that many special issues that have occupied color vision theorists are largely unrelated to spatial vision, so color vision and spatial vision have tended to become separate specialties. Nonetheless, it is important to realize that much of our spatial vision is based on analyzing color variations in the environment, and how this is accomplished physiologically must be an integral part of any complete account of spatial vision. This we discuss in Chapter 7: to avoid duplication of treatment in this book, we have deferred a consideration of the special physiological problems involved with such color processing to that chapter.

4

Striate Cortex

The terminus of the projection originating in the eye is the enormous sheet of cells in the back of the brain known as the striate cortex. The retina is projected systematically onto the cortex, with hundreds of cells to process the output of each incoming fiber. Striate cells have several characteristics not seen earlier: binocularity, directional selectivity, and much more narrow orientation and spatial frequency selectivity. The nature of striate processing gives a number of clues to how the visual system functions in spatial vision.

ANATOMY OF STRIATE CORTEX

Projection to Striate Cortex

In the primate visual system, the projection from lateral geniculate to striate cortex (the first cortical visual area, and thus also called V1) follows the relatively straightforward pattern seen at earlier levels. All parts of the cerebral cortex are conventionally subdivided into 6 layers, with layer 1 at the cortical surface and layer 6 adjacent to the white matter. The primary destination of the axons of LGN projection cells is layer 4 of the striate (M.E. Wilson & Cragg, 1967), although there are also fibers that go to layers 1, 3, and 6. From V1 the path is much more complex and divergent, the cells in V1 projecting to multiple other cortical and subcortical visual areas. This complexity enters at an earlier level in subprimate mammals. In cat, for instance, geniculate cells project not just to V1, but to V2 and V3 (M.E. Wilson & Cragg, 1967) and to the Clare-Bishop area as well (Graybiel & Berson, 1981). The use of the cat visual system as a model for that of primates is thus considerably weakened at cortical levels.

The left LGN receives the fibers from the temporal portion of the retina of the left eye and the nasal portion of the retina of the right eye; both of these retinal areas are stimulated by light from the right visual field. Since the LGN fibers project only to the cortex on the same side, the projection onto the striate cortex is functionally a completely crossed one: the right visual field activates the left cortex and the left field the right cortex (see Figure 3.8). The cortical

94

regions receiving projections from near the vertical meridian are interconnected with the corresponding cortical regions in the other hemisphere through the corpus callosum (Myers, 1962; Hubel & Wiesel, 1967).

It was shown in early studies (Talbot & Marshall, 1941) using evoked-potential recordings that there is a systematic retinotopic mapping onto the cortex. That is, different retinal regions project to different cortical areas in a systematic fashion. In the macaque monkey, for instance, the fovea projects to the most lateral striate region, and increasingly peripheral retinal regions (up to about 7°) to more and more medial regions on the cortical surface. Still more peripheral areas project to cortical areas buried within sulci below the cortical surface (Daniel & Whitteridge, 1961). In humans, the whole striate area has migrated medially so that only the foveal projection is left on the outer surface of the cortex.

Retinal receptors are relatively uniformly distributed across the whole retina (considering both rods and cones), thus ensuring an initial faithful, relatively undistorted spatial transformation of the visual world into a physiological representation of it (except that the three-dimensional world is compressed into two dimensions). To a rough first approximation, the image of an object stimulates the same number of retinal receptors whether it is imaged on the fovea or on the periphery. However, under photopic conditions, with only cones active, there are many more central than peripheral units responsive to a given pattern. Beyond the receptors this relationship becomes even more grossly distorted: the image of an object projected to the fovea activates tens or hundreds of times as many ganglion cells as the same image falling on a peripheral region. Further topological transformations take place such that the central regions are further expanded at later neural levels, although neighboring retinal areas remain neighboring in the projection.

Much but not all of the topological transformation of the spatial representation takes place within the retina, from receptors to ganglion cells. It has been shown in cat (Fischer, 1973) that the ganglion cell density falls off in a logarithmic manner with retinal eccentricity. Thus there would be about the same number of ganglion cells in the annular strip between 1 and 2° peripheral as there are in the annulus between 10 and 20° peripheral. The area covered in the projection to the LGN and from there to the cortex was first thought to be about equal for every ganglion cell (Rolls & Cowey, 1970), but recent studies indicate that there is a large additional magnification of the foveal representation in the LGN and again in the cortical projection (Myerson, Manis, Miezin, & Allman, 1977; Connolly & Van Essen, 1984; Van Essen, Newsome, & Maunsell, 1984; Perry & Cowey, 1985). The increased central magnification from retina to LGN, at least, is only in the cells that project to the parvocellular layers (Perry & Cowey, 1985). The eventual cortical magnification of the central retina is such that about 25% of the striate cortex is devoted to processing the central 2.5° of the visual scene (an area roughly equal to that subtended by a 50-cent coin held at arm's length).

A very powerful procedure for studying functional anatomy is the activity-dependent 2-deoxyglucose (2-DG) technique (Sokolov et al., 1977). The rationale behind this approach is that since glucose is the metabolite of cortical cells, the more active the cell is, the more glucose it will take up and utilize. A closely related substance, 2DG, is taken up by cells as if it were glucose, but it cannot be metabolized and thus accumulates in the cells. When it is radioactively labeled, its location in the brain can subsequently be determined by autoradiography of the tissue sections. Therefore, if one injects radioactive 2-DG while presenting a particular visual pattern and then slices the brain and prepares it for autoradiography, the cells most responsive to the pattern presented will reveal themselves by their radioactivity.

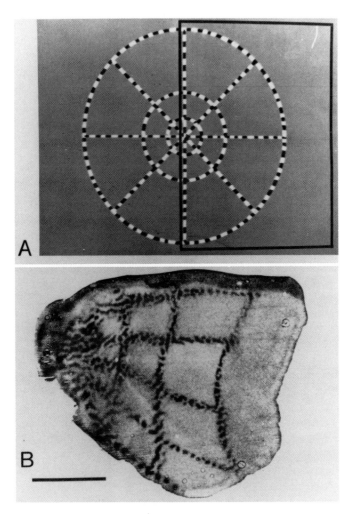

FIG. 4.1   (A) Stimulus used for mapping the retinotopic projection onto striate cortex. (B) pattern of 2-DG uptake in macaque striate cortex produced by this stimulus pattern. See text for details (from Tootell, Silverman, Switkes & R.L. De Valois, 1982a, *Science, 218,* 902-904. Copyright 1982, AAAS. Reprinted with permission).

Using this technique, Tootell, Silverman, Switkes, and R.L. De Valois (1982a) examined the retinotopic projection onto the cortex in macaque monkey. A ring-and-ray pattern was produced on a TV monitor. The rings and rays were made up of small, randomly sized rectangles that flickered in time, with the rings spaced logarithmically (see Figure 4.1A). The monkey was presented with that pattern centered on the fovea while being injected with radioactive 2-DG, and then the cortex was flattened, tangentially sectioned, and placed on X-ray film. An example of the resulting autoradiographs is shown in Figure 4.1B. The log-arithmically spaced rings can be seen to activate strips about equally spaced apart on the cortex, and regions stimulated by the rays making up the vertical, horizontal, and oblique meridians can be seen to form almost parallel strips across the cortex. Thus the cortical map reflects a roughly logarithmic transform of the retinal spatial mapping. The varying magnification of the retinal projection at different eccentricities, determined from such anatomical experiments or from electrophysiological recordings at different eccentricities, can be specified by the reciprocal of the cortical magnification factor (CMF). The CMF is defined as the number of mm on the cortex to which one degree on the retina projects, and thus its reciprocal is the number of degrees visual angle per mm of cortex. Note, however, that the retinal projection is overlapping, not point-to-point as a simple view of the CMF might lead one to expect. The CMF^{-1} increases lin-early with eccentricity, from about 0.15°/mm at the fovea to about 1.5°/mm some 20° peripheral (Hubel & Wiesel, 1974b; Van Essen et al., 1984; Tootell, 1985); see Figure 4.2.

It is to be noted that the fact that the various rays in Figure 4.1B are broken into segments is not related to the checks in the pattern presented. Rather, it reflects the nature of the projection of the two eyes onto the cortex. The ring-and-ray pattern in that experiment was presented to only one eye. Since the two

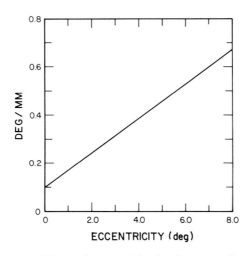

FIG. 4.2   The reciprocal of the cortical magnification factor as a function of eccentricity.

eyes project separately onto the cortex, in alternation over small distances (see discussion of cortical modules at the end of this chapter), what one sees in Figure 4.1B are just the segments related to the stimulated eye, individual ocular dominance columns. The gaps in the activated cortical strips would have been filled in to make continuous bands if both eyes had been stimulated in register by the ring-and-ray pattern. It can be seen that there are certain deviations from a complete log transform in the mapping: the rings in the pattern do not come out as straight lines, but bend increasingly with eccentricity. This is related to the directions taken by the ocular dominance columns in different cortical regions (Tootell et al., 1982a). Since the left-eye, right-eye projections lie side-by-side, the combined module is longer in that direction than in the other. The modules have their long dimension along the vertical meridian, making this then longer than the horizontal meridian.

Not the precise relationship discussed above, but the general expansion of the central retina in the cortical projection, has long been known. The enormous foveal representation relative to that of the periphery raises two questions. One is, how is the processing of information from retinal areas at different distances from the fovea affected by the vastly greater number of cortical cells receiving input from a patch of foveal receptors than from an equal-sized patch of peripheral receptors? The other, related question is, what consequences does this have for visual perception?

With respect to the second question, one extreme position has been stated by E.L. Schwartz (1980). He attributes to the logarithmic conformal mapping of retina onto cortex a major role in itself in the processing of spatial information. Thus, for instance, size constancy might be accounted for on the basis of the fact that as a centrally fixated pattern increases in retinal size (as one approaches it), its cortical projection would only shift laterally, not increase in size, given the logarithmic transform. For instance, the rings in Figure 4.1A can be thought of as a circle at each of 3 different distances; the cortical representations of these circles (see Figure 4.1B) are three roughly equal-length lines displaced laterally with respect to each other. However, Schwartz's model, based on the assumption that information in striate is coded primarily in terms of cortical distances, ignores or minimizes functional differences among neurons. There is by now, however, such an overwhelming amount of evidence for neuronal specificity, for each neuron's being responsive just to certain stimulus characteristics and not to others, that it seems unlikely that a proposal based on a lack of cortical specialization can adequately describe visual pattern analysis within the striate cortex. Schwartz's model has been criticized on other grounds as well (Cavanagh, 1982).

A clear possibility for the variation in physiological processing associated with the increased foveal representation at the cortex is that the RF size of foveally related neurons may be very small and that the RF size of units at increasing eccentricities may become larger and larger. If this were so, and if a constant overlap were maintained between neighboring RFs, then it would clearly require a large number of cells in the foveal area to cover the same region in visual space encompassed by the RF of a single peripheral ganglion or cortical cell. There is in fact much evidence at both the ganglion cell (Wiesel, 1960; Peichl & Wässle, 1979) and cortical levels (Hubel & Wiesel, 1974b; Dow, Snyder, Vautin, & Bauer, 1981; Van Essen et al., 1984) for an increase in RF size with eccentricity, and this is clearly the principal physiological change with eccentricity.

As an aside, it should be pointed out that the RF size of a cell is often considered to be directly related to its optimum bar width or to its peak spatial frequency tuning. In fact, there is not such a simple relationship. The overall RF size is a joint function of the spatial frequency tuning *and* the bandwidth of a cell—of the width of the RF center and of the number of sidebands. A narrowly tuned cell would have a larger number of sidebands (see Figure 4.18 below) and thus a larger overall RF size than a more broadly tuned cell that is tuned to the same spatial frequency. Since cells tuned to high spatial frequencies in general are more narrowly tuned (R.L. De Valois, Albrecht, & Thorell, 1982, and Figure 6.12 in this volume) than those responding best to low spatial frequencies, one would expect to find a smaller range of RF sizes than the range of peak spatial frequencies among cells in a given locus. One might also note that the optimum spatial frequency for a cell can be very precisely measured, but this is *not* true for RF size. Weak sidebands can be easily overlooked and the sensitivity at the edges of the RF falls off gradually, so the overall measured size of the RF can easily vary by a factor of 2:1, depending on the animal's excitability and the response criterion chosen.

Several lines of psychophysical and physiological evidence raise doubts that the differential cortical magnification is solely due to an increase in the RF size of cells (associated with a decrease in their spatial frequency peaks) with eccentricity. The strongest argument against attributing the foveal over-representation purely to peripheral cells' having large RFs and foveal cells' having only small RFs is that our highest sensitivity to almost every visual parameter appears to be highest in the fovea. Specifically, Robson (1975) and Robson and Graham (1981) have shown that one is most sensitive in the fovea not only to high spatial frequencies (which would presumably be detected by cells with small RFs), but to low spatial frequencies (which would be detected by cells with large RFs) as well. There is also both physiological and anatomical evidence, which we will discuss below, that cells with large as well as small RFs are to be found in foveally related parts of the cortex. On the other hand, D.H. Kelly (1984) has shown that if patterns are scaled with eccentricity according to the magnification factor, the whole contrast sensitivity function shifts to lower spatial frequencies, keeping about the same total bandwidth, with increasing eccentricity.

It is possible that some of the enormously magnified representation of the fovea in the cortex is due to a progressive drop in the range of cell peak spatial frequency tuning (and thus to some extent RF sizes) from fovea to periphery. Thus the portion of the cortex related to the fovea may have cells tuned to *all* spatial frequencies, low as well as high, but those tuned to the highest spatial frequencies may progressively disappear toward the periphery. Likewise, a full range of cells processing color, stereopsis, etc., may be present in the foveal projection but might become increasingly sparse toward the periphery. Such an arrangement would be consistent with the psychophysical evidence that almost all visual functions are optimal in the fovea.

It can be seen that such a schema is not really inconsistent with the evidence for a change in RF size with eccentricity, since the *average* RF size would indeed increase as cells with small RFs became fewer peripherally. But cells tuned to a wide range of spatial frequencies, with a wide range of RF sizes, should be found in central loci. Such indeed has been reported (R.L. De Valois, Albrecht, & Thorell, 1982), although more detailed studies of how cells vary with eccentricity would be desirable.

We are emphasizing the issue because the presence or absence of cells with a wide range of RF sizes at a given retinal locus bears not only on retinocortical mapping, but on the whole issue of multiple spatial channels (see Chapter 6).

Fine Anatomy of V1

When the geniculate fibers reach the cortex, they make synaptic contact, mainly with layer 4 cells, over a distance as long as 5,000 μm (Sholl, 1956). The fibers from the magnocellular and parvocellular LGN layers terminate in distinct subregions of cortical layer 4: the magnocellular fibers project to layer 4cα while the parvocellular LGN input terminates in layers 4a and 4cβ (Hubel & Wiesel, 1972). There is also a small input from the parvocellular LGN cells to the upper part of layer 6, and from the magnocellular cells to the lower part of layer 6. Finally, a small projection can be seen ending in layer 3; this perhaps originates in the few scattered interlaminar cells of the LGN.

The synaptic contacts made in both layers 4a and 4c are on the dendritic spines of spiny stellate and spiny pyramidal cells (J.S. Lund, 1973). A magnified view of this geniculostriate synapse reveals rounded synaptic vesicles and a thickened membrane structure, both of which have elsewhere been associated with excitatory synapses (Colonnier, 1968). However, the axosomatic endings on these same cells, from fibers that have an intracortical origin, have the flattened vesicles and distinctive membrane structure often associated with inhibitory synapses (Colonnier, 1968). The anatomical arrangement, then, suggests (but hardly proves) that the first cortical cells have an excitatory input from the geniculate combined with and modified by (lateral) intracortical inhibition. It thus appears quite similar in general plan to the arrangement seen at each of the three preceding synaptic levels, in retina and geniculate.

The stellate cells arborize mainly within layer 4 of the striate, but most of the rest of the interconnections are made predominantly in a direction at right angles to the cortical surface, i.e., vertical. In particular, the large pyramidal cells have dendritic trees that may extend up through all the overlying cortical layers. However, the direction of information flow through the circuitry within the striate cortex is no longer the relatively simple arrangement seen at earlier levels.

Although it is not possible at present to give an entirely satisfactory and clear picture of the intracortical circuitry, the outputs from the striate area appear fairly straightforward. A distinctive pattern of different projections has been found from each of the output layers (J.S. Lund et al., 1975).

Probably the most important output from the striate cortex, from the point of view of visual perception, is that to other, extrastriate visual areas. Much of this pathway comes from pyramidal cells whose cell bodies are in layers 2 and 3 of V1 (J.S. Lund, 1973), and whose axons go down through the underlying cortical layers to the white matter below layer 6. These cells project to V2, and perhaps to V3, V4, and other extrastriate areas as well.

Layer 4 of the striate cortex is mainly the region in which the LGN afferents terminate. There is, however, a projection from large cells in layer 4b as well as some cells in layer 5 to the middle temporal (MT) extrastriate area. This pathway, which originates in the magnocellular LGN layers, thus seems largely to bypass the main cortical machinery. To a considerable extent there appear to be two separate streams of information through these multiple levels. One goes from retinal α ganglion cells to magnocellular LGN cells to 4cα, 4b, and then to MT. The other goes from retinal β cells through the parvocellular LGN layers to 4cβ, to striate layers 3 and 2, and then to various prestriate regions. In addition to the MT output, the axons of many layer 5 pyramidal cells go to the superior colliculus, forming a major input to this region.

Perhaps 50% of the neurons whose bodies are in the deepest layer (layer 6) send their axons back down to the LGN. This feedback is by no means trivial in amount: there may well be more fibers going from cortex to LGN than there are in the "classical" path from LGN to cortex! This back-projection appears to be strictly retinotopic; that is, a cortical region feeds back to the same geniculate area that projects onto it. Furthermore, the region in layer 6 receiving parvocellular input projects back to the parvocellular LGN layers, and correspondingly for the magnocellular region (J.S. Lund et al., 1975). It is by no means obvious what function is subserved by this feedback.

The feedback from one level to the previous occurs not only from the striate cortex to LGN, but seems to be an almost universal feature of the visual path from this level on. Each of the areas to which V1 cells project sends fibers back to the striate. Even less is understood (if that is possible) about the function of these feedback connections than is understood about the striate-to-LGN feedback.

In addition to the extrastriate projections mentioned above, anatomical evidence (Gilbert & Wiesel, 1979) has been found for fibers going from one region of the striate down into the white matter only to end in another striate locus.

PHYSIOLOGY OF STRIATE CORTEX

Of principal concern to us in examining the physiology of the striate cortex in this book will be the different functional types of cells present at this level, and the spatial response characteristics of the cells, particularly in relation to those at earlier levels. We will discuss these two issues in sequence.

Functional Cell Types

The question of the classification of cells into different functional categories— how many different cell types are present, what the criteria for classification should be, etc.—is an issue that appears to receive much more heated discussion in the literature than is warranted by the problem. Doubtless every cortical cell differs from every other in some way, along some one of a vast number of dimensions. One might dichotomize cortical cells along any one of these dimensions, particularly if one did not ask for nor seek quantitative evidence as to whether the population was indeed dichotomous (or multimodal) along that dimension. In any case, which dimension is chosen as a basis for classifying cells should be to a large extent one of individual choice, in which a critical consideration is how well it fits in with a larger theoretical framework.

Simple and Complex Cells

From our point of view, the most fundamental difference seen among cortical cells is that first pointed out by Hubel and Wiesel (1962), namely between what they termed "simple" and "complex" cells. Not only does the distinction between these cell types have considerable theoretical importance (discussed below), but there is in fact objective evidence (R.L. De Valois, Albrecht, & Thorell, 1982) that it is truly a dichotomous distinction, not just two ends of a continuum.

Hubel and Wiesel (1959, 1962) categorized simple cells as those showing (1) distinct excitatory and inhibitory regions within their RFs (by which they meant excitation or inhibition to increments of light); (2) summation within the excitatory and within the inhibitory regions, so that a stimulus that covers all the excitatory region evokes a larger response than one covering only a portion of the excitatory region; (3) an antagonism between the excitatory and inhibitory areas, so that an increment in light that covers both an excitatory and an inhibitory area evokes less of a response that if it were restricted to the excitatory region alone (indeed, in most cases a stimulus covering both regions is totally ineffective in evoking a response); and (4) an orientation selectivity, that is, a response to a pattern of one orientation but not to one of some other orientation.

Complex cells (Hubel & Wiesel, 1962) were categorized as those showing (1) an absence of discrete excitatory and inhibitory subregions in their RFs (they give on-off responses to increments anywhere within the overall RF); (2) nonetheless, a large excitatory response to a bar of width some fraction (generally about one half to one third) of the total RF width, with no response to a bar covering the whole RF; (3) a response to such an optimal bar wherever it be placed within the RF; and (4) orientation selectivity.

It can be seen that both simple and complex cells have orientation selectivity, so that does not differentiate them. Furthermore, quantitative studies of orientation selectivity (Schiller, Finlay, & Volman, 1976b; R.L. De Valois, Yund, & Hepler, 1982) show there to be a continuum from nonoriented to very narrowly tuned cells. For these reasons, we will discard orientation selectivity as a criterion for distinguishing simple from complex cells. The other criteria, though, reflect basic functional differences between these cell types.

The distinction made by Enroth-Cugell and Robson (1966) between X and Y ganglion cells (see Chapter 3) can be seen to be functionally identical to the simple-complex distinction of Hubel and Wiesel (1962). The three main Hubel and Wiesel criteria for simple cells, listed above, are equivalent to saying that simple cells show linearity of spatial summation, Enroth-Cugell and Robson's criterion for X cells. The defining characteristics of complex cells are equivalent to their *not* showing linear summation, as is also the case for Y cells. The identity between these classifications would probably have been more readily apparent if the categorization of ganglion cells into X and Y cells had preceded rather than followed the classification of cortical units as simple and complex cells. It should be made clear that saying that X ganglion cells and simple cortical cells have similar summation characteristics, and that so do Y ganglion cells and complex cortical cells, should not be taken to imply that X cells feed into simple cells and Y cells into complex cells in a parallel arrangement, as against simple cells possibly feeding into complex cells in a serial, hierarchical fashion. That issue of the anatomical arrangements will be discussed below, but it is quite separate from the issue of functional characteristics, which is what we are concerned with here.

The basic operational distinction between X and simple cells, on the one hand, and Y and complex cells on the other, is sensitivity to spatial phase. Simple and complex cells are in general sensitive to the same types of stimuli, and in fact have quite similar spatial and orientation selectivities. But a simple cell fires to its optimal pattern when it is in one spatial phase or position, gives no response to it in some other phase, and will be inhibited by it in still another phase. A complex cell, on the other hand, responds to the optimal stimulus regardless of its spatial phase or position within its RF. A simple cell will fire to a white bar in some position; it will be inhibited by a black bar in the same location, and thus maximally distinguishes between increments and decrements (or white and black). A complex cell, on the other hand, will fire to either a white bar or a black bar in the same location, and thus is unable to distinguish between increments and decrements in luminance. Quite the same holds for those simple and complex cells which are also responsive to isoluminant red-green or yellow-blue patterns: simple cells give opposite responses to red and green, but complex cells, while responding to the *presence* of the pure color pattern, give much the same response to red as to green (Thorell, R.L. De Valois, & Albrecht, 1984); see Chapter 7.

Since cortical cells in general adapt quite rapidly to stationary stimuli, it is convenient to use moving or temporally modulated patterns to study their responses. To examine their contrast sensitivity, then, one can drift gratings of various spatial frequencies across the cell's RF and record the responses. In response to such a stimulus, a simple cell will give a modulated discharge at the same temporal frequency as the drift rate. When, say, the bright bar goes across the RF center and the dark bars are on the surround, the cell will fire; when, for this cell, the dark bar is on the RF center and the bright bars on the surround, it will be inhibited. Thus it will be excited during one half and inhibited during the other half of each drift cycle (see Figure 4.3A). The peristimulus time histogram (PSTH) of the responses, lined up with respect to the stimulus and averaged over several cycles, will be approximately sinusoidal, a sine wave stimulus producing a sine wave output. A Fourier analysis of the PSTH of the cell's responses will thus show most of the power to be at the fundamental, at the same frequency as the stimulus, as can be seen in Figure 4.3A. However, most simple cortical cells have little or no maintained firing rate in the absence of stimulation. Therefore, although the discharge rate can readily increase above the maintained rate in the excitatory phase, it cannot decrease much, if any, below the maintained rate during the inhibitory phase. There is therefore inevitably some DC component, some increase in the mean firing rate during stimulation. In the example shown in Figure 4.3A, for instance, the mean firing rate of the cell shifts from 0.0 to 40.0 spikes/sec. In a completely linear system, there would be no increase in mean rate, since the increases and decreases during the two phases would be equal and opposite. The half-wave rectification shown by simple cells

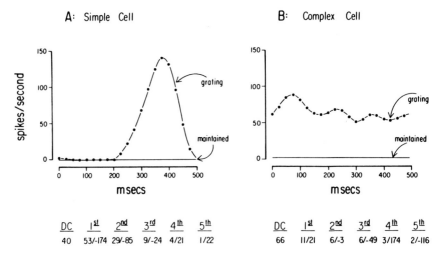

FIG. 4.3   Averaged response patterns of a simple cell (A) and a complex cell (B) to gratings of optimal spatial frequency drifted across their RFs. The figures below each graph display the results of a Fourier analysis of the peristimulus time histogram in each case, with the amplitude of the DC (mean firing rate), and the amplitude and phase of each of the first five harmonics. Note that the simple cell response shows the most power in the first harmonic (AC), while the complex cell response has its power concentrated in the DC (from R.L. De Valois, Albrecht, & Thorell, 1982, *Vision Res.*, 22, Copyright 1982, Pergamon Journals, Inc. Reprinted with permission).

as a result of their low maintained rates is thus an important nonlinearity in the functioning of the system (Albrecht & R.L. De Valois, 1981); see Chapter 11.

Complex cells give a quite different response to a drifting sine wave. Since a complex cell responds to this pattern (or other patterns) regardless of its position or spatial phase, it shows a continuous, largely unmodulated increase (or decrease) in firing rate while the pattern drifts across its RF (see Figure 4.3B). A Fourier analysis of the PSTH of a complex cell's responses, then, shows most of the power at the DC rather than at the first harmonic. A comparison of the response amplitude at the DC to that at the first harmonic (AC) should thus serve to distinguish a simple from a complex cell on an objective basis. Such a comparison, carried out on a large population of macaque monkey cells, indicates that although there are a few cells whose classification is ambiguous, the overall distribution is clearly bimodal (see Figure 4.4). It can also be seen from this graph that the AC/DC ratios for most simple cells cluster about the value expected from half-wave rectification (1.57).

Another variety of temporally changing stimulus that is useful for studying cortical cell responses is a counterphase flickering grating, that is, a stationary stimulus that is temporally modulated (a standing wave as opposed to a traveling wave). In a sinusoidal counterphase flicker, the pattern is gradually increased then decreased in amplitude, then increased and decreased in amplitude in opposite phase (see Figure 4.5). Thus at any point along the pattern, the light intensity (or the wavelength if it is a color pattern) varies sinusoidally in time.

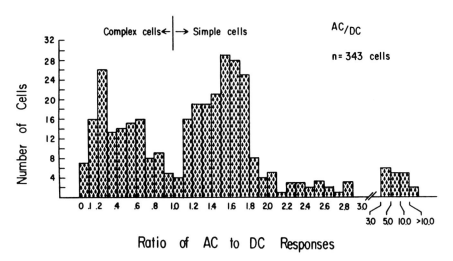

FIG. 4.4 Distribution of the modulated/unmodulated (AC/DC) response ratios for a large sample of macaque striate cortex cells. This distribution is clearly bimodal, thus indicating the presence of two distinct populations of cells. Those cells with ratios between 0 and 1 are complex cells; those with ratios greater than 1 are simple cells (from R.L. De Valois, Albrecht, & Thorell, 1982, *Vision Res., 22,* Copyright, 1982, Pergamon Journals, Inc. Reprinted with permission).

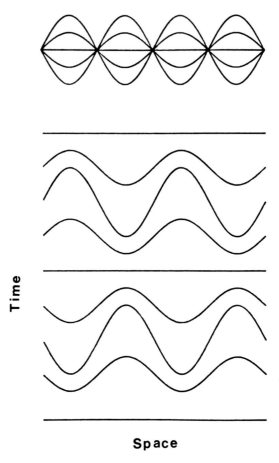

FIG. 4.5   Luminance at different points of a counterphase-modulated grating at different moments in time. The lower part of the figure shows the waveform across space at different instants. Space is represented on the *x* axis, and time on the *y* axis. The upper figure simply shows the superposition of these various waveforms to illustrate the fact that the luminance at the nodal points—the axis crossings—does not change.

The amplitude of the oscillation, however, varies along the pattern: it is 0 at the nodal points and maximum halfway between them.

In response to a counterphase flickering stimulus presented in different locations or spatial phases, a simple cell (like a retinal X cell) gives a response that varies with the spatial phase. Consider the case of a cell with a RF consisting of a center that is excitatory to increments and flanks that are excitatory to decrements (and inhibitory to increments), for instance. When the pattern is in a location at which the point of maximum modulation coincides with the RF center, the cell will first show an increase in firing as this part of the pattern is increased in luminance, and then will be inhibited during the second half cycle when the pattern there is being decreased in luminance (see Figure 4.6A, 225°). With a pattern of optimal spatial frequency, the flanking points of maximum modulation will coincide with the RF flanks. While the luminance is increasing on the RF center (producing excitation), the luminance is decreasing on each flank (also producing excitation), and vice versa during the second half cycle. The center and surround will thus sum to give a large excitatory response during the first half cycle, and inhibition during the second half cycle.

When the pattern is shifted 180° in phase the responses would of course be the same except that the cell is inhibited during the first half and fires to the second half cycle (see Figure 4.6A, 90°). Between these two locations, however, there is a position at which the luminance is increasing in one half of the RF center and in one half of each RF flank, while it is decreasing in the other half of the center and the surrounds throughout the cycle. If the cell shows linear summation of excitation and inhibition within its RF, then, it will give no response to the counterphase flickering pattern in this position or spatial phase. This is clearly the case for the cell whose responses are shown in Figure 4.6A, at 180°. In summary, a simple cell responds to one cycle of an optimally located counterphase flickering pattern of optimal spatial frequency with a sinusoidal output of the same temporal frequency as the stimulus (thus a Fourier analysis of its PSTH would show most of the power at the first harmonic). The amplitude of a simple cell's response varies with spatial phase, the cell giving no response to a counterphase modulation of the pattern in some (null-phase) location.

Shown in Figure 4.6B are the responses of a complex cortical cell to the same counterphase flickering pattern, presented in different locations with respect to its RF. Two differences from the responses of the simple cell are apparent, both of which show that complex cells are not phase specific. First, its responses are the same regardless of the absolute spatial phase of the pattern. Second, the cell responds at twice the temporal modulation frequency of the pattern: it fires when part of the pattern increases in luminance but also when that same part decreases in luminance. A Fourier analysis of the PSTH of a complex cell's responses to a counterphase flicker would show most of the power at the second harmonic, at twice the temporal frequency of the stimulus.

One aspect of counterphase flickering gratings should be mentioned, namely, that such a pattern is mathematically identical to two gratings of identical frequency and half the amplitude drifting in opposite directions. Indeed, observing a counterphase flickering pattern gives one just this visual impression: it is almost impossible to perceive it as flickering in place; rather, it appears to drift first in one direction then in the other. A considerable percentage of both simple and complex cortical cells are direction selective, responding to patterns moving in one direction but not in the opposite direction (Hubel & Wiesel, 1962; Henry & Bishop, 1972; R.L. De Valois, Yund, & Hepler, 1982). Many such cells are actively inhibited by movement in the nonexcitatory direction. From this, one would predict that a strongly direction-selective cell should be rather insensitive to counterphase flickering gratings compared to its response to a grating drifting in the preferred direction, whereas a nondirectional cell should show no such

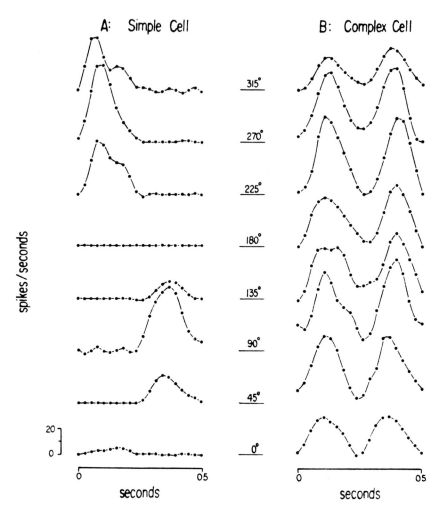

A: Simple Cell   B: Complex Cell

spikes/seconds

315°

270°

225°

180°

135°

90°

45°

0°

20

0

0   05

0   05

seconds   seconds

FIG. 4.6   Responses of a typical simple cell (A) and complex cell (B) to a stationary, counterphase-modulated grating presented at different spatial positions (phase) with respect to the cell's RF. The numbers in the central column represent the displacement (in degrees of phase angle) of each stimulus. Note that the simple cell response shows two distinct peaks, separated in time with respect to the stimulus onset (the stimulus waveforms at various instants are shown in Figure 4.5) and stimulus phase (with maxima separated by 180°), and intermediate null phase. It thus shows linear spatial summation. The complex cell response has two peaks for each stimulus position, with no null phase. It thus responds at twice the temporal frequency of the stimulus modulation and shows very nonlinear spatial summation.

differences. This prediction has been at least partially verified (Cooper & Robson, 1968).

Although we have been emphasizing phase-specificity (in simple cells) and the lack thereof (in complex cells) as the principal defining characteristic of these cell types, it is important to realize that it is absolute phase of patterns (with respect to the cell's RF) which is being referred to, not the relative position or phase of different parts of the pattern. The fact that complex cells have orientation selectivity for grating patterns indicates that they are sensitive to the relative position or phase of different portions of the grating. Consider a vertical sine wave grating on a TV monitor. If the phase of this pattern were shifted each successive horizontal line of the display by a certain amount, one would have an oblique, not a vertical, grating. A narrowly tuned complex cell that responds to the vertical grating would not respond to the oblique pattern, so it must be sensitive to the position of the pattern at various vertical locations.

Even- and Odd-Symmetric Receptive Fields
The cell whose responses were shown in Figure 4.6A is one whose classical RF would consist of an excitatory center (to light increments) and antagonistic flanks (see Figure 4.7A). Some cells of this type also have additional excitatory and inhibitory flanks. Found equally frequently are cells with just the reverse RF structure: their RF to increments would have an inhibitory center and excitatory flanks (see Figure 4.7B). To a counterphase flicker such a cell would give

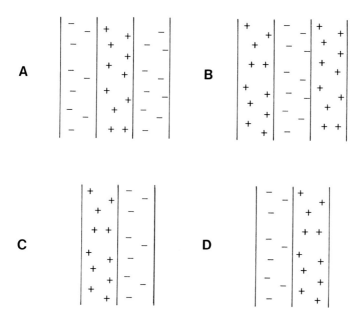

FIG. 4.7   Typical simple cell receptive fields as described by Hubel and Wiesel. Cells A and B have even-symmetric receptive fields, with excitatory and inhibitory centers, respectively. Cells C and D have odd-symmetric receptive fields.

responses identical to that of the cell in Figure 4.6A except that they would be shifted 180° in phase. The cell would inhibit to the first half cycle and fire to the second half cycle. The RFs of both of these cell types are symmetrical about their center (or even-symmetric), and are similar in shape to $1\frac{1}{2}$ or more cycles of a cosine wave that is damped out with a gaussian fall-off. These cells are thus similar in general symmetrical shape (in one dimension) to the RFs of the X ganglion cells we discussed earlier.

Hubel and Wiesel (1962) also reported the presence of simple cells with a somewhat different RF structure, in which one half of the RF was excitatory and the other half inhibitory (to increments), or vice versa (see Figures 4.7C and D). It can be seen that the RFs of these cells are asymmetric (sometimes termed odd-symmetric), and resemble damped sine rather than damped cosine waves. On close examination, some of these cells also have additional flanks, but the RF is nonetheless asymmetric. The optimal grating positions for such a cell would be shifted 90° in phase relative to that for the cell shown in Figure 4.6A.

In recording from pairs of simple cells isolated at the same time with the same electrode, Pollen and Ronner (1981) found that such pairs often consisted of one even- and one odd-symmetric cell: the responses of these cells to a drifting grating were always 90° out of phase with each other. Since this relationship held despite changes in the spatial frequency of the grating (within the range of frequencies to which the cells were responsive), it must be that the two cells had exactly the same RF location but were of different RF symmetries, rather than being simply two similar cells shifted in RF position with respect to each other.

The resemblance of even- and odd-symmetric RFs to damped cosine and sine waves, respectively, suggests the possibility that cells with such RFs could be analyzing for the cosine and sine components of the waveforms of complex stimuli, acting as localized spatial frequency filters, as we discuss further in Chapters 6 and 8.

X/Y and Sustained/Transient

The distinction between simple and complex cells, and between retinal X and Y cells, is in terms of their spatial characteristics. Cells also differ in their temporal characteristics, e.g., in the optimal rate of temporal modulation of a counterphase flicker, or optimal drift rate of a drifting pattern, and have been categorized as sustained or transient (see Chapter 3). The sustained/transient distinction is fairly well correlated with the X/Y spatial difference in the case of retinal ganglion cells and LGN cells, but it does not appear to be among cortical cells. It is not in fact clear that there is a dichotomy in the temporal dimension among cortical cells at all. "Sustained" cells respond well to long-duration stimuli, and should thus be sensitive to low temporal frequencies; "transient" cells, on the other hand, should be maximally sensitive to more rapidly changing stimuli, that is, to high temporal frequencies. A quantitative examination of the temporal frequency characteristics of a large sample of cortical cells in monkey (Albrecht, 1978) shows that most cortical cells are quite broadly tuned for different temporal frequencies: they have much broader bandwidths in the temporal than in the spatial frequency domain. Furthermore, it is clear that there is a continuum of temporal frequency sensitivity, ranging from cells maximally sensitive to quite low temporal frequencies, e.g., 1 Hz or less, to those tuned to more than 10 Hz, with the majority being maximally sensitive in the 2–8 Hz range. There is no evidence, either within the simple cell population or within the complex cells or within the population as a whole, for a bimodal distribution of temporal properties such as would justify a dichotomy into sustained versus transient cell types. Furthermore, a comparison of the temporal properties of simple versus complex cells also indicates little evidence for any significant temporal differences between these two classes of cells, which differ so drastically in their spatial properties.

Hypercomplex Cells
In their first reports of the properties of cells in cat cortex, Hubel and Wiesel (1959, 1962) reported two functional varieties of cells: simple and complex, as we have been discussing. Later (Hubel & Wiesel, 1965) they reported the presence of an additional cell type, which they termed hypercomplex cells. These cells were reported to resemble complex cells except that the *length* of the optimal oriented line was also a critical factor in determining their response. If the bar was too long at either one or both ends, the response of the cell would be drastically reduced, perhaps even to zero. These cells were thus described as being end-stopped at either one or both ends. Hypercomplex cells, then, respond not to extended bars but to bar segments; not only must the width and orientation of the bar be appropriate, but its length as well.

More recent, quantitative examinations of this type of cell (Schiller, Finlay, & Volman, 1976a; Gilbert, 1977; Kato, Bishop, & Orban, 1978) have forced some modifications of this picture. One is that some so-called hypercomplex cells resemble simple cells in all but their end-stopping; others resemble complex cells. The other is that most cells that would be classified as simple or complex on other grounds in fact show end-stopping to some degree. Although there is some contrary evidence in cat (e.g., Kato et al., 1978), it appears from the data of Schiller et al. (1976a) and from our monkey striate recording that hypercomplex cells are just at one extreme of a continuum of amount of end-inhibition rather than being a discrete cell type.

We have examined the responses of cortical cells to grating patterns of various numbers of cycles, centered on the cells' RFs (R.L. De Valois, Thorell, & Albrecht, 1985). As one increases the number of cycles of the optimal-frequency grating, a cell's response increases up to some point, as we will discuss later. However, a still further increase in number of cycles often produces a decrement in response; on occasion the response will go completely to zero for, say, a grating of 7 or more periods. Thus it appears that many cells are not only end-stopped, but side-stopped as well (a property one would not observe, of course, if the RF were explored solely with bars or edges). It might be better to consider that these "hypercomplex" properties reflect the presence of inhibition which extends around the whole RF. In some cells such surround inhibition is relatively weak; in others it is sufficiently strong to completely inhibit the cell if the stimulus pattern encroaches on the surround either by being too long or by having too many cycles (see Figure 4.8). Cortical cells, then, respond optimally to a delimited patch of grating (of some particular orientation and spatial frequency, as discussed below).

Temporal Frequency Versus Velocity

While receptors and neurons early in the visual path respond best to changing visual stimuli, most also respond well, for some seconds, to a static stimulus as well. Cortical neurons, however, give almost no sustained response to a stationary, unchanging pattern. Therefore their properties are usually examined by

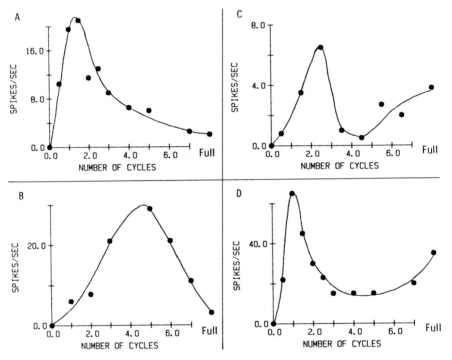

FIG. 4.8   Responses of four striate cortex cells to gratings of optimal spatial frequency and varying numbers of cycles. Note that each of these side-stopped cells responds best to a grating patch made up of only a few cycles. In each case, increasing the number of cycles (and thus the width of the overall stimulus pattern) produces some diminution of the response. On occasion (cells C and D) increasing the number of cycles still further leads to a secondary increase in the response, suggesting possible disinhibition. Not all cells show side stopping; see Figure. 4.15 for counterexamples (from R.L. De Valois, Thorell, & Albrecht, 1985, *J. Opt. Soc. Am. A,2,* 1115–1123. Reprinted with permission).

moving a pattern back and forth across the cell's RF. In early studies, in which the typical pattern was a light or dark bar, the temporal properties of the stimulus were specified in terms of its velocity (amount of movement per unit time; for visual stimuli the number of degrees of visual angle per second). Some cells were found to respond best to rapidly moving bars, others to slowly moving bars, so cells were characterized by their velocity tuning properties. However, there are two confounded variables in such a stimulus presentation: rate of movement, and rate of change in luminance or color. It is not clear from such studies whether movement or temporal change is the crucial variable for continued activity of the cell, or along which dimension cortical cells are selective.

It is of course possible to separate the movement versus temporal change variables by comparing responses to moving patterns versus ones flickered on and off in place, the latter producing only temporal change whereas the former have both movement and temporal change. It is also possible to assess which is the crucial variable for the cells' selectivity by using moving grating patterns of different spatial frequencies. Consider two gratings of 1 and 2 c/deg. If the 1-c/deg black-white grating is moved constantly at a particular rate, it will have a velocity of 1 deg/s (each bar moving 1 deg visual angle per second); at each point in the field there will also be a temporal luminance change at 1 c/s (1 Hz). If one now moves the 2-c/deg grating at a velocity of 1 deg/s, each point in the visual field will have a temporal modulation of not 1 but 2 Hz, twice the temporal frequency of the 1-c/deg grating moved at the same velocity. Correspondingly, of course, if the two gratings have the same temporal frequency, the lower spatial frequency pattern will have twice the velocity of movement as the other. Thus, temporal frequency = (velocity) × (spatial frequency).

Using either of these techniques (flicker versus movement; moving gratings of different spatial frequency), one can ask the question of whether temporal frequency or velocity is the crucial variable for cortical cells. The answer is quite clear: for almost all striate cells, it is temporal frequency, not velocity. Most cells do not require a moving stimulus, but respond well to a stationary flickering pattern; and they are tuned to a particular temporal frequency range, not to a certain range of velocities. Thus a cell tuned spatially to, say, 1.4 c/deg might give equal (but smaller) responses to each of the two patterns of 1 and 2 c/deg discussed above. When tested with a 1-c/deg grating moving at various rates and temporal frequencies, it might respond best to a 3-Hz pattern, and not respond to the grating when it has a temporal frequency of less than 1 or more than 8 Hz (as discussed above, this can of course be restated to say that it responds best to a 3-deg/s movement and cuts off at 1 and 8 deg/s velocities). When tested with moving 2-c/deg gratings, however, it will be found to again respond best to 3 Hz and cut off at 1 and 8 Hz, although these are now of course quite different velocities. It is thus apparent that it is tuned to a certain range of temporal frequencies, not to a certain velocity range.

Considered in terms of naturalistic stimuli, these properties of striate neurons are rather paradoxical. When a pattern such as a branch moves, the broad range of different spatial frequency components of which it is composed all move at the same velocity, but at very different temporal frequencies. One would there-fore think that a system concerned with detecting movement, or utilizing move-ment information for form vision, would be velocity tuned. Some velocity-tuned cells have in fact been found (Movshon, Adelson, Gizzi, & Newsome, 1985) in areas V2 and MT, leading to the supposition that these regions, but not most of the striate cortex, may be specifically involved with movement analysis. Whether such velocity tuning is found among the subclass of striate cells that form the V2-MT projection (e.g., layer 4b of striate), or whether it is an emergent characteristic of processing past the striate is at present unknown.

Ocular Dominance and Binocularity

The ipsilateral and contralateral inputs to the cortex in monkey are totally dis-crete, and the initial cortical cells in layer 4 are largely monocular (Hubel & Wiesel, 1968). The separate projection of the eyes, in ocular dominance columns arranged in strips across the cortex, can be seen in Figures 4.1B and 4.22, and is discussed more extensively below. The remainder of the cortical cells in the upper and lower cortical layers are largely binocular, responding to stimulation of the appropriate region in either eye. Overall, about 80% of cortical neurons in both monkey and cat are binocular, the most common type being equally responsive to either eye (Hubel & Wiesel, 1962, 1968). It should be noted that the usual tests of binocularity—whether a cell can be driven by either eye alone—may considerably underestimate the true extent (and nature) of binoc-ularity. Many cells cannot be driven by stimulation of, say, the left eye alone, but their responses to stimulation of the right eye are significantly modified by concurrent patterns in the apparently nonresponsive eye (von der Heydt, Ador-jani, & Hänny, 1977; Poggio & Fischer, 1977).

The joining of the inputs from the two eyes onto one cell within the cortex clearly provides a mechanism by which we can see a single visual world despite having two separate eyes. It can potentially do more than that: since each eye gets a slightly different view of three-dimensional objects, it is possible to gain information about depth from an appropriate comparison of the activity in the two eyes. Such a process (termed stereopsis) is known from psychophysical experiments to be an important source of depth information.

The image of a fixated point will fall on the fovea of each eye; other points that are at roughly the same depth will fall on corresponding points in the two eyes, e.g., 2.3° away from the fovea in each eye, etc. Objects nearer or farther than the fixation depth, however, will fall on disparate retinal points, the amount of the disparity between the two eyes being proportional to the distance away from the fixation plane, and the sign of the disparity indicating nearer or farther depths.

If various cortical binocular cells received inputs from the two eyes that sys-tematically varied, from cell to cell, in relative disparity, these various units would be activated by objects at various depths. For instance, a unit that received inputs from exactly corresponding points would be activated by an object on the fixation plane; one that received inputs from just slightly disparate points would be activated by objects just slightly in front of or behind the fixation plane, etc.

That such a cortical organization exists in cat striate cortex was first proposed by Barlow, Blakemore, and Pettigrew (1967) and Nikara, Bishop, and Pettigrew (1968). They plotted the RFs of binocular cortical cells in one eye and then the other and found a considerable scatter between the RF loci in the two cases. From this they concluded that each of these cells could be involved in signaling about patterns at slightly different depths; that is, that there were a large number of different depth channels for each retinal locus.

The validity of physiological studies of stereopsis depends on control of eye position. If the eyes moved differentially in the course of a recording experiment, the RFs in the two eyes would appear scattered even if they all in fact came from corresponding points in the two eyes. Hubel and Wiesel (1970) suggested that such was the case, since with careful monitoring of eye position they found the binocular cells in both cat and monkey to have corresponding RFs with negligible disparity. A recent study (Poggio & Fischer, 1977), in which eye movements were controlled by training the monkey to fixate the target, found results that partially agreed with both these opposing positions. They report that most binocular cells have zero disparity between their inputs from the two eyes, but are very sensitive to disparity differences. Such cells, then, would signal about objects in the fixation plane, and would give very precise depth information at that depth. In addition, Poggio and Fischer report cells that are much more broadly tuned, one group tuned to depths in front of and another group to depths behind the fixation plane. This study then agrees with that of Hubel and Wiesel in finding coincident RFs for most binocular striate cells, rather than the variety of disparities reported earlier, but they agree with Pettigrew and collaborators (Barlow et al., 1967; Nikara et al., 1968) in finding that most striate cells in fact appear to be concerned with signaling binocular depth.

Spatial Properties of Cortical Cells

Orientation Selectivity

The most striking finding of Hubel and Wiesel's (1959) study of cortical cells was that the vast majority of cells were selective for patterns of a specific orientation, the particular optimum orientation varying from cell to cell. This was an important finding because it was so unexpected, and also because it made clear that the cortical cells were doing something quite different from those cells which came before. The RFs of cells from receptors through the LGN are characterized by radial symmetry—the very antithesis of an orientation-specific structure. This finding of cortical cell orientation selectivity therefore produced a considerable change in thought about cortical functioning.

Hubel and Wiesel (1962) not only discovered that most cortical cells have orientation selectivity, but they also postulated an influential model of how the cells might acquire such selectivity—namely, by summing the outputs of LGN cells whose RFs were in different but aligned spatial locations. This model is discussed more extensively below.

The early studies of orientation selectivity of cortical cells involved a qualitative assessment of their properties; more recently there have been several quantitative studies of large samples of cortical cells in both cat (Henry, Dreher, & Bishop, 1974) and monkey (Schiller et al., 1976b; R.L. De Valois, Yund, & Hepler, 1982). These studies make it clear that the degree of orientation selectivity varies considerably from cell to cell, between the two extremes of orientationally nonselective units (see Figure 4.9B) to very narrowly tuned ones (see

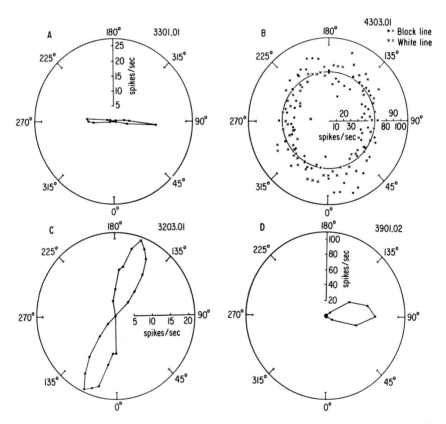

FIG. 4.9   Responses of four striate cortical cells as a function of the orientation of a moving line. The angle in the polar plot represents line orientation; distance from the center reflects response amplitude. The line always moves in a direction orthogonal to its orientation. Cell A is an extremely narrowly tuned simple cell. Cell B is a nonoriented complex cell. Cell C is a simple cell with about average orientation bandwidth and no directional selectivity. Cell D is a complex cell with average orientation tuning and complete directional selectivity (from R.L. De Valois, Yund, & Hepler, 1982, *Vision Res., 22,* 531–544. Copyright 1982, Pergamon Journals, Inc. Reprinted with permission).

Figure 4.9A). Shown in Figure 4.9C is a cortical cell with average (median) narrowness of tuning (R.L. De Valois, Yund, & Hepler, 1982). It can be seen that this cell is not direction selective: it responds about equally well to movement in either direction of a grating of optimal orientation. The cell whose responses are plotted in Figure 4.9D, on the other hand, responds to a pattern at 90°, but only if it moves to the right; the cell is unresponsive to a leftward moving pattern (which would be plotted at 270°).

The cells whose responses are plotted in Figs. 4.9A, C, and D appear to have a response minimum at 90° away from the optimum orientation. However, the minimum response is actually at the "flanks" of the excitatory orientations. In the case of a broadly tuned cell, this would be about 90° away, but in the case of many narrowly tuned cells the minimum is considerably closer to the peak than that, with the response slightly increasing 90° away (see Figure 4.10). It can be

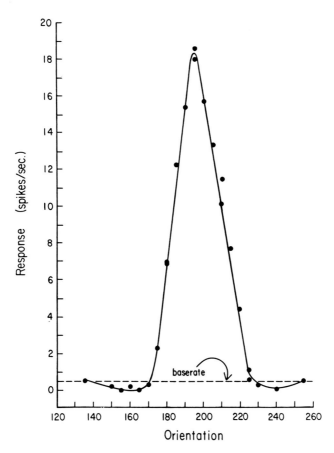

FIG. 4.10 Orientation tuning function for a cell which shows inhibition of the maintained discharge to orientations just outside its excitatory passband region (from R.L. De Valois, Yund, & Hepler, 1982, *Vision Res., 22,* 531–544. Copyright 1982, Pergamon Journals, Inc. Reprinted with permission).

shown for cells that have a maintained discharge that there is not just an absence of response at off-orientations, but active inhibition. It appears, then, that the orientation tuning involves not just a summation across cells with different RF locations, as in the Hubel and Wiesel (1962) model, but an active inhibitory process which may be maximum between cells tuned to neighboring orientations. This question, along with more direct evidence bearing on it, is discussed further below.

The selectivity of a cell along a particular dimension is conventionally quantified by its bandwidth: the distance between the points to either side of the peak at which the response falls to half its maximum peak response. Thus a cell that gave its maximum response of 100 spikes to a pattern at 90° and dropped to 50 spikes at 70 and 110° would have an orientation bandwidth of 40°.

In Figure 4.9 examples are given of cells with varying orientation bandwidths. In Figure 4.11 are presented distributions of bandwidths for four samples of macaque cells: simple and complex cells from foveal and from near nonfoveal cortical regions. It is clear that there is a wide range of orientation tuning among cortical cells, with the median bandwidth being about 45°. It can also be seen that there is little or no difference in bandwidths between foveal and parafoveal cells, but that simple cells are on the average slightly more narrowly tuned than complex cells. These results agree well with most other quantitative studies of orientation tuning of cortical cells in monkey (Schiller et al., 1976b) and cat (Henry, Bishop, & Dreher, 1974). It appears that cat cortical cells on the average are a little more narrowly tuned than those in monkey.

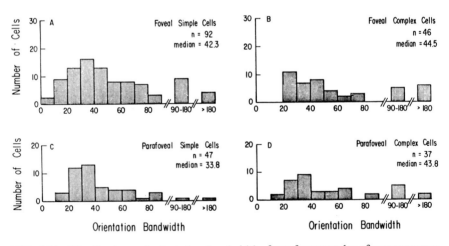

FIG. 4.11   Distributions of orientation bandwidths from four samples of macaque monkey striate cortex cells. A represents foveal simple cells; B, foveal complex cells; C, parafoveal simple cells; D, parafoveal complex cells. Note that there are no striking differences between simple and complex cells, or between foveal and parafoveal samples (from R.L. De Valois, Yund, & Hepler, 1982, *Vision Res., 22,* 531–544: Copyright 1982, Pergamon Journals, Inc. Reprinted with permission).

Cortical cells are found tuned to every orientation around the clock, cells with these various peak sensitivities being arranged in systematic order within the cortex. In the foveal projection area of monkey cortex, there are somewhat more cells tuned to vertical and horizontal than to oblique orientations (Mansfield, 1974; R.L. De Valois, Yund, & Hepler, 1982). This provides a likely basis for our slightly greater sensitivity to vertical-horizontal patterns than to oblique ones (Campbell, Kulikowski, & Levinson, 1966).

Spatial Frequency Selectivity

In their first recordings from cat cortex, Hubel and Wiesel (1959, 1962) reported that cortical cells were somewhat more selective for the width of patterns than were ganglion cells. In particular, they noted that striate cells would give no response to a bar covering the whole RF, whereas at earlier levels a cell will typically give an attenuated "center" response to such a pattern. However, these differences in spatial characteristics were not very dramatic with the bar and edge stimuli Hubel and Wiesel used, much less striking than the differences in orientation tuning of cortical versus retinal cells. As discussed further in Chapter 6, though, this apparent absence of a large difference in spatial tuning was due to the fact that the cells were only tested with bars and edges—stimuli which have broad spatial frequency spectra. If cells are examined with spatially narrow-band stimuli, the differences in spatial tuning between cortical and retinal cells are as dramatic as are their differences in orientation tuning.

Retinal ganglion cells and LGN cells are rather broadly tuned for spatial frequency (see Chapter 3). The first studies of the spatial frequency tuning of cat (Campbell, Cooper & Enroth-Cugell, 1969; Maffei & Fiorentini, 1973) and monkey cortex (R.L. De Valois, K.K. De Valois, Ready & von Blanckensee, 1975; Schiller, Finlay, & Volman, 1976c; R.L. De Valois, Albrecht, & Thorell, 1977; Albrecht, 1978) found many cells to be much more narrowly tuned. Cells at subcortical levels have sharp high spatial frequency cuts, but only gentle decreases in sensitivity to low spatial frequencies; most cortical cells, on the other hand, have fairly sharp attenuation at both low and high spatial frequencies (see Figure 4.12). Cortical cells thus have a distinctly band-pass spatial frequency characteristic, as opposed to the almost low-pass characteristic of LGN and ganglion cells' spatial frequency tuning.

Spatial frequency selectivity, like orientation selectivity, can be quantitatively specified by the cell's bandwidth, the spatial frequency distance between the points to either side of the cell's peak frequency at which the response falls to half maximum. The spatial frequency bandwidths of cortical cells tuned to different spatial frequency ranges have bandwidths which are roughly constant on a ratio, or logarithmic, scale. Thus a typical narrowly tuned cell may have high and low spatial frequency half maxima which are in a 2:1 ratio, regardless of whether a cell is tuned to 1 c/deg, in which case the low and high cuts would be, say, 0.7 and 1.4 c/deg, or tuned to 10 c/deg with low and high cuts of 7 and 14 c/deg. This is in fact what one would expect from a constant RF *shape* (in terms of the number of oscillations in the RF) regardless of the RF size. Therefore it

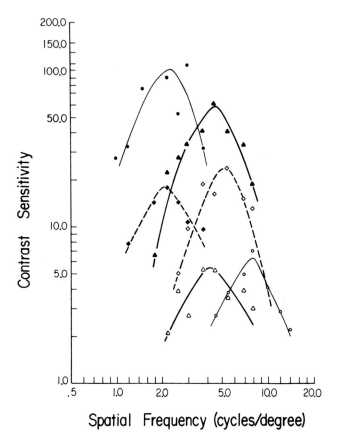

FIG. 4.12   Contrast sensitivity functions for six macaque striate cortex cells. Note that each cell shows fairly sharp attenuation to both low and high spatial frequencies (from R.L. De Valois, Albrecht, & Thorell, 1982, *Vision Res., 22,* 545–559. Copyright 1982, Pergamon Journals, Inc. Reprinted with permission).

is customary to specify spatial frequency bandwidths on a logarithmic scale, in terms of octaves (a term taken over, of course, from music where it refers to a 2:1 ratio of frequency). Formally, the bandwidth is

$$(\log F_h - \log F_l) / \log 2$$

where F_h and F_l are the high- and low-frequency half-amplitude points, respectively.

In Figure 4.13 is shown the distribution of spatial frequency bandwidths for a population of macaque cortical cells (R.L. De Valois, Albrecht, & Thorell, 1982). It can be seen that a small subsample has broad spatial tuning similar to LGN cells, but that most are much more narrowly tuned, the median spatial frequency bandwidth being about 1.4 octaves. A sizable fraction (about one third) of the cells have bandwidths between 0.5 and 1.2 octaves, quite narrowly

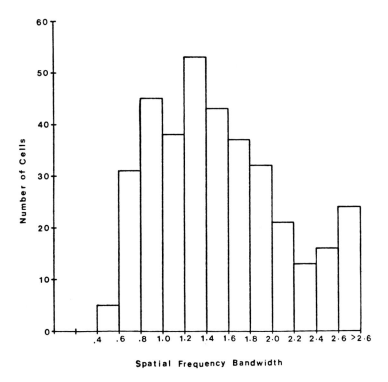

FIG. 4.13   Distribution of spatial frequency bandwidths for a large sample of macaque striate cortex cells (from R.L. De Valois, Albrecht, & Thorell, 1982, *Vision Res., 22,* 545–559. Copyright 1982, Pergamon Journals, Inc. Reprinted with permission).

tuned indeed, given the overall range of more than 8 octaves to which we are sensitive. Similar distributions of bandwidths have been reported in other quantitative studies of cortical cells in both cat (Movshon, Thompson, & Tolhurst, 1978c) and monkey (Schiller et al., 1976c; Albrecht, 1978; Kulikowski & Bishop, 1981).

Hubel and Wiesel (1962) described the RF of one common type of cortical simple cell as having an excitatory center (to an increment) and antagonistic flanks. Qualitative RF maps such as those they presented (see Figure 4.7) are incomplete in giving no indication of the relative strength of excitation and of inhibition to increments in various subregions (and in fact making the excitation appear to be uniform across the center and the inhibition uniform across the surround). Quantitative measures of the RF of a typical broadly tuned simple cell, however, reveal a cross-sectional profile that oscillates smoothly from excitation to inhibition (see Figure 4.14C). It can be seen that a cross section through the center of the RF of such a broadly tuned cell has a shape similar to that of the X ganglion or bipolar cell diagrammed in Figure 3.16 except that the surround is much stronger in the case of the cortical cell, so that uniform stimulation across the RF gives little if any response.

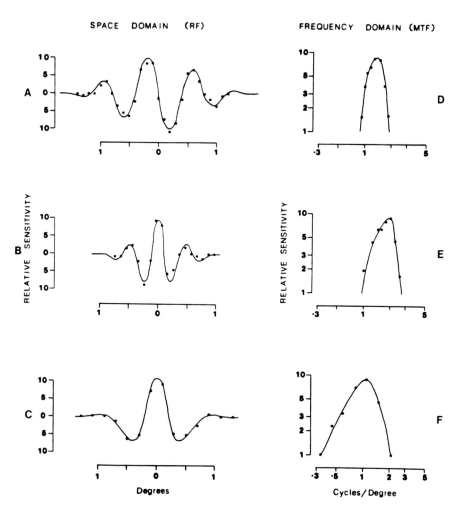

SPACE   DOMAIN   (RF)

FREQUENCY   DOMAIN (MTF)

FIG. 4.14   Quantitative simple cell receptive field profile (space domain) and corresponding spatial frequency tuning function. The RF profile was measured by recording
the responses (*y* axis) to a narrow, flickering black-white bar in different spatial positions
(*x* axis). The solid lines in the column on the left represent the RF profiles predicted by
measuring the response to gratings of different spatial frequencies (right). The data points
are actual responses (from Albrecht, 1978. Reprinted by permission).

Insofar as the visual system is linear, one can go from the space domain to
the spatial frequency domain by the Fourier transform, and predict from the RF
shape of cells what their spatial frequency tuning should be, or vice versa by the
inverse Fourier transform. There have been several reports of success in making
such predictions for both cat and monkey simple cells (R.L. De Valois, Albrecht,
& Thorell, 1978; Movshon, Thompson, & Tolhurst, 1978a; Albrecht, 1978;

Kulikowski & Bishop, 1981). On the other hand, Schiller et al. (1976c) failed to confirm this for the cells they tested. Linear summation across RF profiles such as those shown in Figure 4.7 would give bandpass spatial frequency tuning functions with bandwidths of roughly 1.2 to 2 octaves, depending on the weighting of center and surround. One such cell, shown in Figure 4.14C, was found to have a spatial frequency bandwidth of 1.3 octaves. Such RFs, then, can account for the more broadly tuned half of the cortical population. It would not, however, account for those numerous cells with bandwidths of less than one octave. The linear prediction for such cells (Albrecht, 1978; R.L. De Valois et al., 1978; Kulikowski, Marcelja, & Bishop, 1982) is of an RF with additional excitatory and inhibitory regions, that is, with multiple oscillations in the RF, rather than just $1\frac{1}{2}$ as in the classic Hubel and Wiesel model.

There are two types of evidence that cortical cells with such multiple-oscillatory RFs exist, and that they are those cells with narrow spatial frequency bandwidths. One is that direct RF mapping with a small spot or bar has revealed additional sidebands in the case of many cortical cells (R.L. De Valois et al., 1978; Movshon, Thompson, & Tolhurst, 1978b; Andrews & Pollen, 1979; Mullikin, Jones, & Palmer, 1984). The results from such an experiment (Albrecht, 1978) are shown in Figure 4.14. From the spatial frequency tuning of each of these three cells (see right hand columns), RF profiles were predicted by the reverse Fourier transform (see lines in left hand column). The actual determinations of the RF profiles by mapping with a thin flickering line (data points in left column) are seen to fit the predicted curves quite well. The cells shown in Figures 4.14A and B have quite narrow spatial frequency tuning, with bandwidths of 0.8 and 0.9 octaves, respectively (see Figures 4.14D and E). The cross sections of their RFs are seen to have additional oscillatory sidebands.

A second type of evidence for multiple-oscillatory RFs for narrowly tuned cells comes from determining the number of cycles of a grating that produce the largest response from a cell. If a cell has a classic RF with one excitatory and two inhibitory regions, such as that shown in Figure 4.14C, increasing the number of cycles of a grating above $1\frac{1}{2}$ cycles should produce no further increase in response. However, if there are additional sidebands, such as shown by those cells in Figures 4.14A and B, the response of the cell should continue to rise as additional numbers of cycles are added to a grating.

We (R.L. De Valois et al., 1985) find that such is usually the case (see Figure 4.15), and that cells that prefer more than 2 cycles of grating are more narrowly tuned than those that respond maximally to less than 2 cycles, as would be predicted. If one considers just the 30% subpopulation of simple and complex cells that are narrowly tuned, with spatial frequency bandwidths less than 1.2 octaves, the average number of cycles in the optimum grating is 3.3, considerably more oscillatory than the classic 1.5-cycle RF.

We might note that if it makes little sense, as is discussed in Chapter 6, to consider even classic simple cells as bar detectors (as opposed to spatial frequency filters), it makes even less sense to so characterize a cell with a multiple-lobed, oscillating RF.

Cortical cells have been found to be tuned to a wide range of spatial frequen-

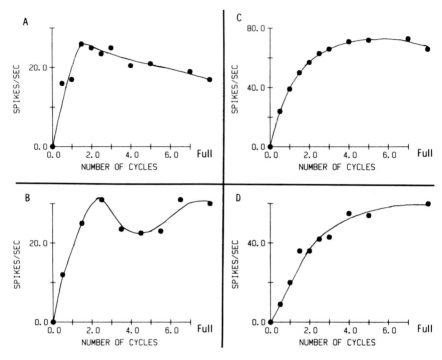

FIG. 4.15   Responses of four macaque striate cortex cells to gratings of optimal spatial frequency and varying numbers of cycles. Note that only cell A responds maximally to a grating of as little as 1.5 cycles. For each of the other cells the response increases somewhat as more cycles are added. Cells A and B also show inhibition to patterns of still greater numbers of cycles, as was also shown in Figure 4.7 (from R.L. De Valois, Thorell, & Albrecht, 1985, *J. Opt. Soc. Am A2*, 1115–1123. Reprinted by permission).

cies. As discussed earlier, there are two possible bases for such a range, with entirely different implications. One is that these differences in peak tuning might reflect a foveal-peripheral gradient in spatial frequency tuning. Foveal cells might be sensitive to high spatial frequencies (and, on the average, have small RFs), whereas cells located increasingly peripherally might be tuned to increasingly lower spatial frequencies (having generally larger and larger RFs). The other possibility is that there are cells tuned to each of a wide range of spatial frequencies present at each cortical locus (just as there are cells tuned to the complete range of orientations at each locus).

These two possibilities have quite different consequences for vision. Variations in spatial frequency tuning related just to eccentricity would account for the progressive loss of acuity with increasingly peripheral fixation, but would not provide a mechanism for processing complex visual stimuli by using multiple spatial frequency channels for each retinal locus. On the other hand, if cells with a wide range of peak spatial frequencies were all located in each cortical region, the substrate for multiple spatial channels would be present.

Hubel and Wiesel (1974b) indicate that the RF size of cortical units varies considerably with eccentricity, although their data also show some degree of variation in RF size at a given locus. As discussed earlier, RF size is also partially related to spatial frequency tuning. Quantitative measures of the spatial tuning characteristics of a large population of foveally related cells in monkey (R.L. De Valois, Albrecht, & Thorell, 1982) have clearly shown that cells tuned to each of a very wide range of spatial frequencies (over at least a 5-octave range), are all present in this one cortical locus. It is notable that cells tuned to very low spatial frequencies (as low as 0.5 c/deg) are found in the foveal projection region. The same was found to hold for a somewhat more peripheral site, except that cells tuned to the highest spatial frequencies were far fewer here (see Figure 4.16). With the progressive elimination of high spatial frequency cells with increasing eccentricity, the *average* RF size would increase with eccentricity, thus perhaps accounting for Hubel and Wiesel's (1974b) results, although more data would be desirable from far peripheral sites. But it is very clear that the cells in any one region do in fact encompass a wide range of peak spatial frequencies.

This point is supported also by 2-DG studies of spatial frequency organization in cat (Tootell, Silverman, & R.L. De Valois, 1981). The pattern of uptake seen with stimulation by a high spatial frequency pattern extends from the central region only part of the way to the peripheral cortex, not as far peripherally as the stimulus itself actually extends. A low spatial frequency pattern, on the other hand, produces columns extending over the whole stimulated area, including specifically the very central projection region. Thus both low and high spatial frequencies stimulate the foveally related cortex, but only low spatial frequencies the far periphery.

An anatomical characteristic which may be related to this progressive narrowing of the spatial frequency range with eccentricity is the progressive thinning of the peripheral cortex. In the far periphery it may only be about 40% as thick as it is in the central projection region. This could reflect a decrease in the total number of cells due to the elimination of cells tuned to high spatial frequencies.The distribution of peak spatial frequencies shown in Figure 4.16 indicates that most cells in the foveal area are tuned to the mid spatial frequency range at a photopic testing luminance. The distribution of cells can be seen to approximate the shape of the CSF at this luminance, with its maximum sensitivity at 1 to 6 c/deg and lower sensitivity to both low and high spatial frequencies.

The spatial frequency bandwidth of cortical cells is consistently related to their peak spatial frequency (Kulikowski & Bishop, 1981; R.L. De Valois, Albrecht, & Thorell, 1982): cells tuned to high spatial frequencies have on the average a somewhat narrower octave bandwidth than those tuned to lower spatial frequencies (see Figure 6.11). On an absolute frequency scale, of course, quite the reverse is true: the bandwidth in c/deg of cells tuned to low spatial frequencies is much narrower.

Simple and complex cells have very similar spatial frequency bandwidths, with simple cells slightly more narrowly tuned on the average than complex

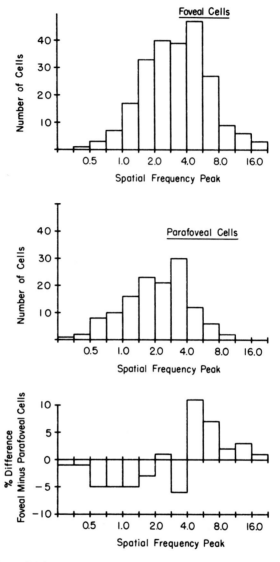

FIG. 4.16 Peak spatial frequency tuning for samples of foveal and parafoveal cells in macaque striate cortex. The top panel shows the distribution of peak frequencies for the foveal sample. The middle panel has corresponding data for a parafoveal sample. The lower panel illustrates the difference between the two distributions. Note that the foveal sample has a higher proportion of cells tuned to high spatial frequencies (from R.L. De Valois, Albrecht, & Thorell, 1982, *Vision Res., 22,* 545–559. Copyright 1982, Pergamon Journals, Inc. Reprinted by permission).

cells. The distributions overlap almost completely. These results are in agreement with other quantitative studies of cat (Movshon et al., 1978c) and monkey cortical cells (Schiller et al., 1976c).

Finally, the peak spatial frequency sensitivities of simple and complex cells are also similar (R.L. De Valois, Albrecht, & Thorell, 1982); see Figure 4.17.

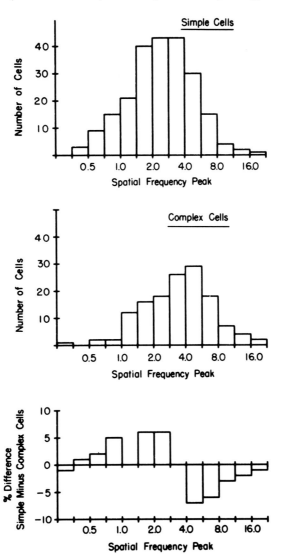

FIG. 4.17   Distributions of peak spatial frequency sensitivities for samples of simple and complex cells. Note that while there are both simple and complex cells tuned to all spatial frequency regions, the cells tuned to the highest frequencies are most often complex cells (from R.L. De Valois, Albrecht, & Thorell, 1982, *Vision Res., 22,* 545–559. Copyright 1982, Pergamon Journals, Inc. Reprinted by permission).

There are both simple and complex cells in the foveal projection area that are tuned to low, middle, and high spatial frequencies. Overall, however, complex cells are tuned to slightly *higher* spatial frequencies than are simple cells. It can be seen in the lower panel of Figure 4.17 that at high spatial frequencies the percentage of complex cells exceeds that of simple cells, so that, for instance, 10% of the complex cells in the sample collected by De Valois, Albrecht and Thorell, 1982, had spatial frequency peaks over 8 c/deg, whereas only 3% of simple cells were tuned to these very high spatial frequencies. This finding is consistent with the relative phase insensitivity of vision at high spatial frequencies (see Chapter 8), but it is surprising considering the fact that at subcortical levels the cells comparable to complex cells (the Y cells) have large RFs and are tuned to lower spatial frequencies than are X cells. However, it is by no means clear what the relation is between retinal and cortical cell types, as is discussed below.

Relation Between Spatial Frequency and Orientation

Spatial frequency and orientation are closely related to each other in terms of two-dimensional spatial frequency analysis (see Chapter 9). It is thus of particular interest to consider the relationship between the tuning of cells along these two parameters. There have been two studies (Movshon et al., 1978c; R.L. De Valois, Albrecht, & Thorell, 1982) which have quantitatively measured both the orientation and the spatial frequency tuning of a large sample of cells (in cat and monkey cortex, respectively). Both studies found a strong positive correlation between narrowness of tuning of cells along these two dimensions. Cells that are narrowly tuned for orientation tend likewise to be narrowly tuned for spatial frequency. Cells with very broad spatial frequency tuning, e.g.,>2 octaves, tend to be nonoriented.

Putting together the outputs of the two eyes into a binocular organization is certainly one major feature of striate cortical processing. The other main accomplishments at this level appear to be that of developing orientation and spatial frequency selectivity (which together constitute two-dimensional spatial frequency selectivity) in multiple channels. Since there are multiple synaptic levels within the striate, it is possible that the cells with differing narrowness of two-dimensional spatial frequency tuning may be at different stages in this process. Indeed, Hubel and Wiesel (1968) have shown that most of the nonoriented cells are in layer 4, the input layer of the cortex. On the other hand, it is conceivable that there is some functional benefit to the system to have cells with varying narrowness of tuning: the cells with narrow and those with broad spatial tuning may subserve different visual roles.

A two-dimensional spatial frequency filtering would require some degree of independence between spatial frequency and orientation tuning. To encode faithfully the presence of a certain range of spatial frequencies in the local stimulus, a cell should show the same spatial frequency tuning regardless of the orientation of the test grating, and vice versa. As pointed out by Daugman (1980), the classic Hubel and Wiesel (1959, 1962) model of a cortical simple cell RF (made by summing the outputs of an aligned group of LGN cells) would be expected to show very different spatial frequency tuning at off-orientations, compared to those shown at the peak orientation. Therefore, a cell with this "classic" RF shape would not have any single two-dimensional spatial frequency range to which it would confine its responses. This is obviously not at all what would be desired for a two-dimensional spatial filter. On the other hand, a two-dimensional Gabor function RF (a sinusoid tapered by a gaussian in both x and y) would show fairly constant spatial frequency tuning regardless of orientation.

Tests of the responses of cells to gratings of a wide range of spatial frequencies and orientations (Webster & R.L. De Valois, 1985) show that actual striate cells behave much as would be predicted if the RFs approximated a two-dimensional Gabor function: they show some but only slight change in spatial frequency tuning with variations in orientation. From these measures of cells' responses to various spatial frequencies at multiple orientations, and vice versa, one can determine the precise response characteristic in the frequency domain, and the space RF by the inverse Fourier transform of this. An example of such a two-dimensional RF is given in Figure 4.18. It can be seen in Figure 4.19 that the RF shape of a typical cell closely approximates a Gabor function in both x and y.

Variations With Eccentricity

The characteristics of cells at different visual eccentricities unfortunately have not been as extensively studied as one would like. We have already mentioned that the average peak spatial frequency of cells shifts to lower frequencies with increasing eccentricity (and thus the RF size in general goes up), but that this most likely results from a progressive loss of cells tuned to high spatial frequencies, low-frequency cells being found in all cortical areas. The orientation peaks also change somewhat with eccentricity (Mansfield, 1974; R.L. De Valois, Yund, & Hepler, 1982), with an even balance between vertical and horizontal cells versus oblique ones found peripherally, and an imbalance toward the former found in the foveal projection regions.

Although the peak spatial frequency and orientation tuning of cells changes with eccentricity, the narrowness of tuning does not appear to do so, at least within the fovea and near parafovea (R.L. De Valois, Yund, & Hepler, 1982). Parafoveal cells appear to be performing as precise an analysis of stimuli as foveal cells, although over a more restricted (and lower, on the average) spatial frequency range.

In an extensive study of cat striate cortical cells at different eccentricities, J.B. Wilson and Sherman (1976) found that the proportion of simple cells to complex cells falls off drastically with eccentricity (although one study has failed to confirm this finding; Berman & Payne, 1982). If this is so, the central (equivalent to the foveal) cortex has mainly simple cells and the far periphery almost exclusively complex cells. As Wilson and Sherman point out, the same relationship holds in the retina between X and Y cells, which are functionally similar to cortical simple and complex cells, respectively. The possible relevance of this to color and phase specificity of vision at different eccentricities is discussed in Chapters 7 and 8.

SPACE DOMAIN

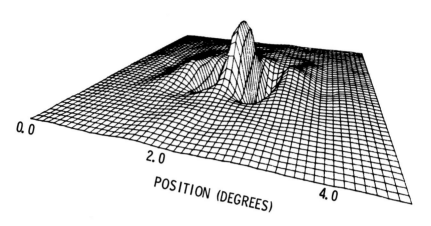

FREQUENCY DOMAIN

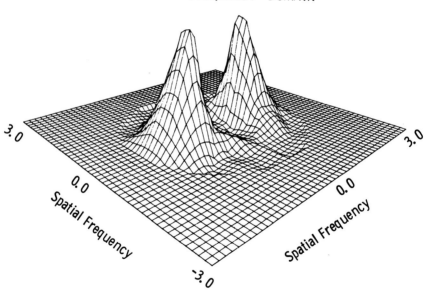

FIG. 4.18   Three-dimensional representations of the RF profiles (in both space and frequency domains) of a fairly narrowly tuned cat simple cell. In the frequency domain plot
it can be seen that the cell responds to a delimited, compact range of spatial frequencies.
Note in the space domain plot that this cell has an oscillatory RF with multiple lobes
along the x axis and is elongated in the y direction (from Webster & R.L. De Valois, 1985,
J. Opt. Soc. Am. A,2, 1124–1132. Reprinted by permission).

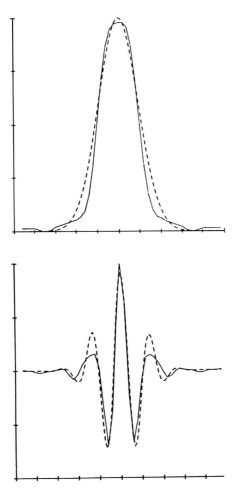

FIG. 4.19   Cross section through the RF profile shown in Figure 4.18 (solid lines) and the best-fitting Gabor function (dashed lines). In A is the RF profile of the oscillating excitatory and inhibitory regions; in B is the RF profile along its length (from Webster & R.L. De Valois, 1985, *J. Opt. Soc. Am. A2* 1124–1132. Reprinted by permission).

Functional Architecture

Interrelation of Functional Cell Types

The manner in which cortical cells are interconnected is a major question for cortical physiology and anatomy, but is of somewhat lesser concern with respect to the topics we are covering here. Hubel and Wiesel (1959, 1962) first suggested what is now the classical model of interrelations among cortical cell types. We will briefly discuss this model and the evidence for and against it.

The Hubel and Wiesel model (which, we should note, they have repeatedly emphasized was put forth only as a tentative working hypothesis) is that there is a systematic, hierarchical order of cells in the cortex, as is present in the retina with receptors→bipolars→ganglion cells. In cortex, they propose that simple cells are formed by ordered arrays of LGN cell inputs and in turn form the input to complex cells. The complex cells then feed together to produce hypercomplex cells, which presumably are the output cells that project to other levels. Since many nonoriented cells were found in monkey cortex, Hubel and Wiesel amended this description (which was initially based on their recordings in cat cortex) to add a fourth level in primate, consisting of nonoriented cells, between LGN and simple cells, (Hubel & Wiesel, 1968). Since in recent formulations they have questioned, as have others (Schiller et al., 1976a), whether hypercomplex cells constitute a separate category of cell, the central tenet of their proposal is that of a hierarchical relationship between simple and complex cells.

A second aspect of Hubel and Wiesel's (1962) model of cortical organization is that each of these cell types receives only excitatory inputs from the preceding level, and that the critical response characteristics of both simple and complex cells are determined by the RF locations of the cells providing these excitatory inputs. Thus simple cells produce their orientation selectivity by summing inputs from a number of LGN cells (or nonoriented cortical cells) whose RFs are systematically displaced spatially with respect to each other in a row at a particular orientation. The RF of the simple cell, then, would be the sum of the RFs of the input cells. A similar arrangement is envisioned in which complex cells sum together the outputs of simple cells whose RFs are displaced laterally with respect to each other.

Much evidence has been brought to bear, pro and con, on each of these aspects of the influential Hubel and Wiesel model of cortical architecture. It is at present not clear to what extent the basic hierarchical model must be modified or discarded (D. Rose, 1979); the weight of evidence clearly supports a major modification of the purely excitatory aspect of the model, however.

Hubel and Wiesel (1959, 1962) described and differentiated simple from complex cortical cells before Enroth-Cugell and Robson (1966) distinguished between retinal X and Y cells. If the order had been reversed it would perhaps have been more apparent that simple cells are functionally similar to X cells in terms of spatial summation, and complex cells to Y cells. The possibility of simple and complex cells being arranged in parallel rather than serially might have therefore been given more serious consideration. There is considerable evidence for at least a partially parallel arrangement. It has often been shown (e.g., Hoffman & Stone, 1971; Stone, 1972; Bullier & Henry, 1979a, 1979b, 1979c; Henry, Harvey, & J.S. Lund, 1979) that many complex cells, as well as many simple cells, receive a direct monosynaptic input from the LGN. But Bullier and Henry found that both X and Y geniculate cells feed into both simple and complex cortical cells, so the cortical dichotomy is not just an extension of the earlier X–Y separation. Further evidence for parallel processing in the cortex is the finding by Gilbert (1977) that as many as 40% of the cells in the main striate input layer,

layer 4c, are complex cells. Furthermore, some complex cells have response properties that are not seen in simple cells and that cannot readily be derived from a summation of simple cell inputs: they respond to random dot patterns and other complex textures to which simple cells do not respond (Hammond & MacKay, 1975); some complex cells respond to higher velocities of stimulus movement than any simple cells do (Movshon, 1975); few complex cells show inhibition by off spatial frequencies, although virtually all simple cells do (K.K. De Valois & Tootell, 1983). All of this rather convincingly argues that at least some, if not all, complex cells must have a direct input that does not come solely from simple cells.

There is also convincing evidence that simple as well as complex cells must feed on to later centers, counter to the hierarchical model in which only complex (or hypercomplex) cells project out of striate cortex. The most compelling evidence is that we certainly have absolute phase-specificity in our visual perception, and ability to distinguish black from white (and red from green and blue from yellow); see Chapters 7 and 8. Since only simple cells are phase specific, however, their output must go on to later centers, not just end on complex cells, which have no phase specificity in this sense. The same argument holds with respect to cells in V4 or elsewhere with color specificity (Zeki, 1973), which they could not have if their input were purely from complex cells.

We can thus safely conclude that the phase-specific simple cells and non-phase-specific complex cells must to some degree be in parallel in the striate, both in their inputs and in their outputs. As we argue elsewhere in this book, each of these cell types is carrying useful, and quite different, kinds of visual information. The presence of both of their distinctive characteristics is evident in the ultimate visual percept. One need not conclude, however, that simple and complex cells form totally parallel paths from retinal and geniculate X and Y cells, respectively. It is entirely possible that some complex cells are constructed from simple cell inputs, as Hubel and Wiesel suggest, while others receive a direct Y-cell input from the LGN; or both simple cells and LGN Y cells might feed into complex cells in general. A detailed discussion of various possible models is to be found in D. Rose (1979).

There are a number of observations which suggest that complex cells are at least partially constructed within the cortex, as Hubel and Wiesel proposed, rather than just being the cortical component of the Y-cell path. One is that whereas Y cells are very rare in the retina (perhaps 3% in cat retina), complex cells constitute approximately 50% of the cortical population. Another is the fact (discussed earlier) that complex cells are tuned on the average to higher spatial frequencies than are simple cells (R.L. De Valois, Albrecht, & Thorell, 1982), whereas retinal Y cells are tuned to lower spatial frequencies on the average than are retinal X cells. Finally, complex cells have certain properties, e.g., sensitivity to binocular disparity and to the two-dimensional Fourier spectral components of patterns (K.K. De Valois, R.L. De Valois, & Yund, 1979), which would not be expected if they received input only from LGN Y cells, but would be if they were built up at least partially from cortical simple cells.

Although these are important questions of physiological and anatomical organization, they are secondary from our point of emphasis here on functional properties. The critical consideration with respect to spatial vision is that there are two different cortical systems, however constructed, one with and one without spatial phase specificity.

A second aspect of the Hubel and Wiesel (1962) hierarchical model is its postulate that cortical cells gain their response properties from the precise architectural arrangement of RFs of cells at the preceding stage. For instance, the orientation selectivity of simple cells is assumed to arise from excitatory inputs from specific LGN cells whose RFs are systematically displaced with respect to each other. An alternative possibility is that much if not all of the orientation and spatial frequency tuning is produced by intracortical inhibitory interactions.

One strong bit of evidence for a prominent role for cortical inhibition is the great prevalence of inhibitory synapses of intracortical origin on all cortical cells. Recording intracellularly from cortical cells, Creutzfeldt, Kuhnt, and Benevento (1974) found large inhibitory as well as excitatory postsynaptic potentials. Lee, Cleland, and Creutzfeldt (1977) also found that the excitatory RF region of striate cells is essentially circular, not elongated, so that the orientation tuning must be a result of inhibitory inputs. In cells with sufficient maintained discharge for a decrease in firing to be seen, strong inhibitory responses are found to stimuli of off-orientations in both simple and complex cells (R.L. De Valois, Yund, & Hepler, 1982). The same is true for spatial frequency: frequencies off the peak of a cell's preferred spatial frequency (particularly higher spatial frequencies) are often found to profoundly inhibit the cell (K.K. De Valois, 1978; K.K. De Valois & Tootell, 1983).

The strongest direct evidence for a prominent role for intracortical inhibition in producing orientation and direction selectivity comes from observing the effects of blocking the presumed inhibitory transmitters (Sillito, 1975; Sillito, Kemp, Milson, & Berardi, 1980). There is good evidence that GABA serves as an inhibitory transmitter in the cortex; if an agent (bicuculine) that blocks GABA is injected in the vicinity of the recording electrode, most cells soon show a greatly decreased direction and orientation selectivity. Some become completely nonoriented. Since the excitatory inputs are presumably not affected by bicuculine, they must not be providing the orientation tuning.

One of the attractions of the idea that striate cells gain their selectivities by intracortical interactions rather than by a very precise set of inputs from earlier levels is that the neural connections involved (and thus the requirements for genetically specifying them) would be greatly simplified (Swindale, 1979). It would also provide a good rationale for the systematic arrangement of cortical cells by orientation and spatial frequency, with cells tuned to neighboring regions along these dimensions being located next to each other. To sharpen their tuning, cells would require inhibitory inputs from other cells with slightly different selectivities. This would be simplified with systematic columnar arrangements.

Modular Structure and Columnar Organization

A modular organization of the striate cortex was first found by Hubel and Wiesel (1962, 1974a) in single-cell recording experiments in both cat and monkey. In recording with an electrode penetration at right angles to the cortical surface, they found that successive cells had certain response characteristics in common. Specifically, the peak orientation tuning and the laterality of the cells (whether the cells were responsive just to the contralateral eye, just to the ipsilateral eye, or to both) in a "column" through the cortex would all be nearly the same. A probe through an adjacent region would encounter cells with RFs that overlapped with those of the cells in the first column, but that had a quite different orientation peak and/or laterality of response (these being the two variables on which they concentrated). The cortical arrangement was most clearly delineated with the use of oblique or tangential probes, more parallel to the cortical surface. Figure 4.20 shows the results from one such experiment (Hubel & Wiesel, 1974a) in which each successive cell in an oblique traverse had a slightly different peak orientation. It can be seen that the peak orientations repeat after about 0.8 mm across the cortex. This cortical expanse, which contains cells tuned to the full range of orientations, was termed by Hubel and Wiesel an orientation hypercolumn.

In recordings made from layer 4 cells, Hubel and Wiesel (1974a) also found evidence for ocular dominance hypercolumns. The cells along a tangential probe for about 0.5 mm might have an ipsilateral eye preference, then for the next 0.5 mm the contralateral eye would be dominant. Such an ocular dominance orga-

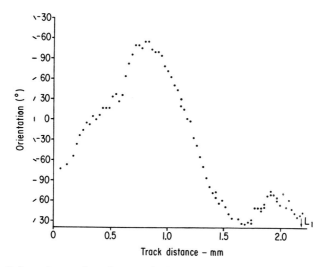

FIG. 4.20 Orientation tuning of successively encountered cells during an oblique electrode penetration of monkey striate cortex. Note the systematic variation of orientation tuning with distance as the electrode traverses cortical columns (from Hubel & Wiesel, 1974a. Reprinted by permission).

nization is present in both cat and monkey, but it is clearer in the latter. In the approximately 1-mm extent across the cortex of such an ocular dominance hypercolumn, there would be two orientation hypercolumns, one for each eye. Hubel and Wiesel also reported that the cells within such hypercolumns have overlapping RFs; going still further across the cortex one would encounter the same sequence of orientation and laterality changes again, but with the RF location of the cells shifted to a neighboring (though partially overlapping) region of the visual field. There is also anatomical evidence for such ocular dominance columns in the human visual cortex (Hitchcock & Hickey, 1980).

Although ocular dominance and orientation hypercolumns were first found in recording experiments, the organization across the whole cortex can be more readily established in anatomical experiments. The ocular dominance organization was clearly revealed in an experiment in which radioactive proline was injected into one eye of a monkey (Wiesel, Hubel, & Lam, 1974). Proline is transneuronally transported to the cortex. Autoradiography of the cortex then reveals the regions where the inputs from the labeled eye project. It was also shown by a reduced silver staining of the cortex (Le Vay, Hubel, & Wiesel, 1974); see Figure 4.21. Seen in cross section the ocular dominance organization is columnar (although only pronounced in layer 4). In tangential sections of the cortex, however, these columns form strips across the cortex of a constant width, but taking fairly random directions. The ocular dominance organization can also be seen in 2-DG studies. If only one eye is stimulated, the cortical cells and processes responsive to that eye will take up the radioactive 2-DG and be revealed by autoradiography. This can be seen in the retinotopic study illustrated in Figure 4.1. Only one eye was stimulated by the ring-and-ray pattern in

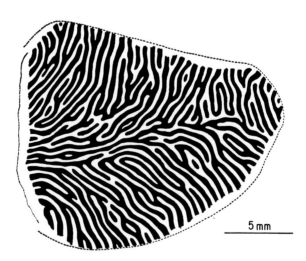

5 mm

FIG. 4.21   Ocular dominance slabs in monkey striate cortex reconstructed from tangential sections, using a reduced silver stain (from Le Vay, Hubel & Wiesel, 1975. Reprinted by permission).

that experiment. The small dark square within each module is the ocular dominance column related to the stimulated eye; the adjacent nonradioactive region is that connected with the unstimulated eye.

Hubel, Wiesel, and Stryker (1978) used this 2-DG technique to examine the orientation arrangement across the cortex. Stimulation with a pattern of a single orientation was found to produce a columnar pattern of 2-DG uptake in a cross section through the cortex. In a tangential section through the cortex, these columns were seen to combine into strips across the cortical surface. By combining proline injection into one eye and the 2-DG technique with a single-orientation stimulus pattern during injection, it is possible to see the relationship between the ocular dominance and the orientation slabs. These slabs appear to intersect at random angles rather than in a simple systematic way that would make it conceptually easy to visualize. Nonetheless, the arrangement is such that nearby regions related to each eye would include cells tuned to every orientation.

The picture thus far in cat cortex is of a block of cells about 0.5 mm on a side related to one eye and consisting of strips of cells of common orientation selectivity so that across one edge of the block there would be cells tuned to each orientation in turn. Adjacent to this in some direction would be a corresponding block related to the other eye. These two orientation hypercolumns and one ocular dominance hypercolumn together would constitute what we shall term a cortical module (CM), since it appears to consist of all the cortical cells with different functional properties and selectivities that are processing information from one general area of the visual world.

What about the other dimension across the cortical surface? Are all the cells in a given orientation slab within an ocular dominance column alike in other characteristics, or is another dimension arranged in columnar strips at right angles to orientation? There is evidence that another dimension, namely, spatial frequency, is in fact laid out across the cortex in a manner similar to that found for orientation. If, using the 2-DG technique, one presents a cat with a pattern consisting of every orientation (presented sequentially) but only a single spatial frequency, a cortical pattern very similar to that seen with presentation of just a single orientation at every spatial frequency is obtained (Tootell, Silverman, & R.L. De Valois, 1981; Silverman, 1984). In cross section, columns of 2-DG uptake are seen going through all cortical layers, indicating a columnar spatial frequency organization (see Figure 4.22). The distance between spatial frequency columns (a spatial frequency hypercolumn) is roughly 1 mm, about the same as an orientation hypercolumn. In tangential sections, it can be seen that the cells tuned to a single spatial frequency are arranged in slabs or bands across the cortical surface, again similar to the pattern seen for orientation. However, the directions of the orientation and spatial frequency slabs differ from each other (Silverman, 1984). The orientation slabs in cat appear to run at right angles to the vertical meridian at the V1–V2 border, but the spatial frequency slabs appear to radiate out more from the area centralis projection region. Such an arrangement would produce a regular intersection of spatial frequency and orientation slabs. Such a model is diagrammed in Figure 4.23. When an animal is presented

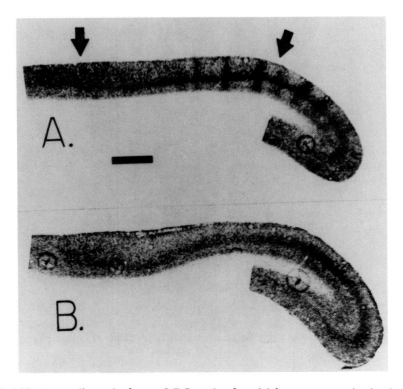

FIG. 4.22   Autoradiographs from a 2-DG study of spatial frequency organization in cat striate cortex. In A is a cross section through the cortex of an animal exposed to a pattern of all orientations but only a single spatial frequency, 1.8 c/deg (a high spatial frequency for a cat). Columns of high 2-DG uptake can be seen around the right-hand arrow, which indicates the cortical representation of the center of the retina. The visual pattern extended all the way out to the peripheral region indicated by the left-hand arrow, but columnar uptake to this high spatial frequency pattern is seen only in the region of the area centralis. In B is a cross section through the cortex of a control animal that was shown a pattern of all spatial frequencies at all orientations. Note the absence of columns. In both A and B continuous high 2-DG uptake can be seen in the cortical input layer, layer 4. The calibration bar is 2 mm. The bubbles in both A and B are histological artifacts (from Tootell et al., 1981, *Science, 214,* 813–815. Copyright 1981, AAAS. Reprinted by permission).

with a single spatial frequency at a single orientation, only those cells sensitive to that particular spatial frequency *and* that particular orientation should be activated, and thus just the intersections between these two cortical organizations should be seen. Such is the case. In tangential sections of the cortex of a cat exposed to one spatial frequency at one orientation one sees a leopard-like dot pattern rather than the zebra-like stripe pattern seen with either of these variables alone. That the spatial frequency and orientation organizations are sys-

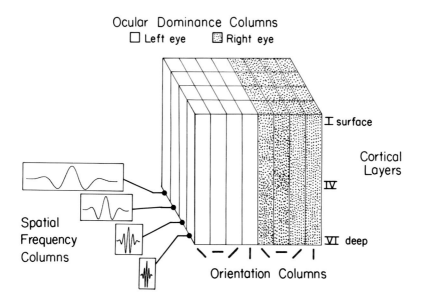

Ocular Dominance Columns
□ Left eye   ▨ Right eye

I surface

Cortical
Layers

IV

Spatial
Frequency
Columns

VI deep

Orientation Columns

Model of Striate Module in Cats

FIG. 4.23 Schematic model of the columnar organization of cat striate cortex. Within each ocular dominance region are orthogonally arranged columns of cells tuned to different spatial frequencies and different orientations such that all spatial frequency/orientation combinations occur within each module.

tematically related to each other is indicated by the regularity of the intersection points seen in such a section.

In macaque monkey cortex, there also appears to be a systematic modular arrangement of ocular dominance, orientation, and spatial frequency, but with a somewhat different pattern from that in cat. One striking peculiarity of the primate striate cortex, as opposed to that of the cat, is that there is a very non-uniform distribution of cytochrome oxidase (cyt-ox), a metabolic enzyme found in the mitochondria of cells (Horton & Hubel, 1981; Horton & Hedley-White, 1984). If a tangential slice through the cortex is stained for cyt-ox, numerous spots or blobs are seen (see Figure 4.24). These cyt-ox-rich blobs are most prominent in layer 3, but they are also apparent in the other cortical layers, with the possible exception of layer 4 (Horton, 1984). They are associated with a fine LGN projection, which can be seen in fiber stains of layer 3 of the flattened cortex (Tootell, Silverman, R.L. De Valois, & Jacobs, 1983). The cyt-ox blobs are fairly regularly spaced at ca. 0.5 mm separation, and there are a total of about 5,000 of them across the whole striate cortex.

Although the cyt-ox blobs associated with one eye disappear with long-term enucleation, their appearance does not depend on the short-term nature or level

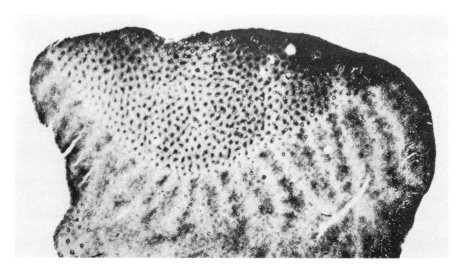

FIG. 4.24   Tangential section through the visual cortex of a squirrel monkey, stained for cytochrome-oxidase (cyt-ox). Primary visual cortex (V1) can be seen to be dotted with numerous cyt-ox blobs (from Tootell et al., 1983, *Science, 220,* 737–739. Copyright 1983, AAAS. Reprinted by permission).

of visual activity. They can thus be used as landmarks on the otherwise uniform-appearing striate cortex, to help in the elucidation of the cortical functional architecture. With the 2-DG technique, the orientation organization can be seen in one animal and the spatial frequency in another, but in the absence of cortical landmarks one cannot tell how these are related to each other. However, since one can combine 2-DG autoradiography and cyt-ox staining on the same brain section (Silverman & Tootell, in preparation) the interrelations among the various types of functional organization can be obtained by seeing how each in turn is related to the cyt-ox blobs.

In one such experiment, a pattern of all spatial frequencies at all orientations was presented to one eye, to activate all the cells in one set of ocular dominance columns. An autoradiographic section was then computer processed and dichotomized into low-uptake and high-uptake regions. The results were ocular dominance stripes across the cortex that had the appearance of zebra stripes. When the cyt-ox uptake pattern from this same brain section was similarly treated, the result was the pattern of cyt-ox blobs scattered across the striate. When these two patterns were superimposed, it could be seen that the cyt-ox blobs are located right in the middle of the ocular dominance columns, either in the middle of the ocular dominance strips from the unactivated eye or that from the activated eye (Switkes, Tootell, Silverman, & R.L. De Valois, 1986). There thus are two blobs for each ocular dominance hypercolumn, and two or four for each CM, depending on one's model.

What about the relationship between the blobs and other functional groupings? The evidence is clearest in the case of spatial frequency (Tootell, Silverman, Switkes & R.L. De Valois, 1982b). A stimulus containing all spatial frequencies at all orientations produces an almost uniform cortical uptake pattern in a 2-DG experiment, with just slight inhomogeneities due to the cyt-ox blobs to be seen in tangential sections. A pattern of just a low spatial frequency (e.g., 1 c/deg) at all orientations, on the other hand, produces a very dot-like 2-DG uptake pattern extending across the whole stimulated cortex. The low spatial frequency 2-DG dots are superimposed on the cyt-ox blobs when the 2-DG and cyt-ox patterns from the same section are superimposed. When a high spatial frequency, e.g., 8 c/deg, is used, the cortical pattern is very different. First of all, the high spatial frequency pattern only extends out a small distance into the periphery, rather than covering the whole cortex related to the retinal areas stimulated. Second, the pattern seen in tangential sections is also very different from the low-frequency pattern: it looks like an array of doughnuts. When superimposed on the cyt-ox blobs from the same section, the high spatial frequency doughnut pattern is seen to lie all around the blobs, which coincide with the holes in the doughnuts. Most interesting is the pattern seen with an intermediate spatial frequency of 3 c/deg. Stimulation in a 2-DG experiment with that spatial frequency produces uptake in the whole 6° stimulated area, but the pattern varies with eccentricity. In the foveally related cortex it is dotty (like a low spatial frequency pattern), whereas in the peripheral cortex it is like doughnuts (like a high spatial frequency pattern). It thus appears that the spatial frequency organization in the CM is a radial one, with low spatial frequencies (low frequencies for that eccentricity) in the center of the module, coinciding with the cyt-ox blob, and high spatial frequencies increasingly farther out.

The orientation organization in monkey is quite different from that for spatial frequency. In cross section through the cortex both are columnar, but stimulation with one orientation at all spatial frequencies produces stripes in tangential sections that skirt but do not go through the cyt-ox blobs. The patterns for different orientations presumably go in different directions within a CM. The overall two-dimensional spatial frequency (spatial frequency by orientation) pattern within a CM, then, bears some resemblance to a two-dimensional spectral polar plot, with orientation at different axes and spatial frequency increasing radially out from the center (see Figure 4.25).

Livingstone and Hubel (1984) report that the basic organization with respect to the cyt-ox blobs is related to color, with color-selective cells in the blobs and not outside. Their color experiments are confounded with spatial frequency, however, since they have used low spatial frequency chromatic patterns to test for color selectivity. A low spatial frequency color pattern does indeed produce 2-DG uptake on the blobs, but so does a low spatial frequency isochromatic luminance-varying pattern. And a high spatial frequency color grating of 6 c/deg activates cortical regions *outside* the blobs (Tootell et al., in preparation).

One problem that is not completely understood is the relationship between the functional organization of the cortex (ocular dominance, orientation, and spatial frequency hypercolumns) and the retinotopic mapping onto the cortex.

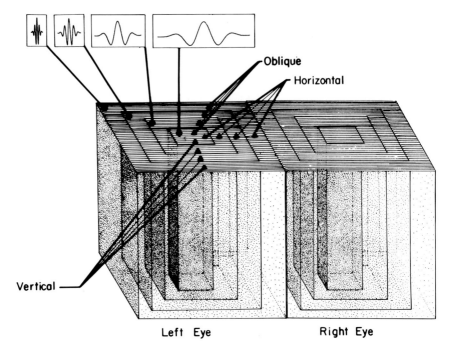

Model of Striate Module in Monkeys

FIG. 4.25 Schematic model of the columnar organization of primate striate cortex. The various two-dimensional spatial frequencies are postulated to be in a polar arrangement, with spatial frequency increasing from the center (coincident with the cyt-ox blob for that half module) out and orientation being represented at various angles.

Retinotopic mapping implies that neighboring cortical areas represent neighboring retinal locations, but the functional mapping indicates that a neighboring cortical area may contain cells with a different orientation, spatial frequency, or ocular dominance selectivity. How does the brain avoid being able to see only one orientation at one location, and another orientation at a neighboring location, etc.? This may not be that much of a problem, for several reasons. One is that it is not clear to what extent the retinotopic mapping extends down to small cortical distances. There is some evidence for a shift in RF location with small displacements in cortical recording loci, particularly in layer 4, but there are also reports of considerable scatter in RF center locations within a given column (Hubel & Wiesel, 1974b). It may be that the retinotopic mapping only provides relatively coarse positional information, finer localization (other than in layer 4) being encoded in other ways, e.g., in terms of phase (see Chapter 8).

Another reason that there may not be a conflict between retinotopic and functional mapping in the cortex is that the cortical modules are very small with respect to the RFs of most cells. In the foveal center, for instance, the distance between neighboring CMs may correspond to only 0.15° visual angle (see earlier discussion of cortical magnification factor). This corresponds to the RF diameter of a cell tuned to about 20 c/deg (with an oscillating RF consisting of 2 or more cycles of excitation and inhibition). There are very few cortical cells tuned to higher spatial frequencies than that; the RFs of all the 99+% of cells tuned to lower spatial frequencies would extend not only over neighboring orientation columns but also across whole neighboring CMs. In fact, a foveal cell tuned to some low spatial frequency, say 0.5 c/deg, will have an RF covering the regions of visual space analyzed by dozens, if not hundreds, of neighboring CMs. In the periphery, each CM covers a larger retinal area, but the RFs of the highest frequency cells would be correspondingly larger. There would not, then, be any gaps in the visual field for certain classes of stimuli.

The overall model we have arrived at suggests that the primate striate cortex is divided up into perhaps 2,000 to 3,000 CMs, each about 0.5 by 0.7 mm, across the cortical surface. Each CM processes information from a particular, different locus in the visual field, to a considerable degree overlapping with that represented in the neighboring CMs. The RFs of cells tuned to the very highest spatial frequencies within a CM may overlap minimally with those in the neighboring CMs, but the vast majority of cells, those tuned to middle and low spatial frequencies, will have RFs that overlap many neighboring CMs. The size of the CMs is fairly constant across the cortex (slightly smaller in the periphery), but the distance across the visual field between adjacent CM centers varies greatly with retinal eccentricity, from about 0.1° visual angle in the case of foveally related CMs, to several degrees for those related to far peripheral regions. Each CM contains perhaps 100,000 to 200,000 cells, and consists of an arrangement of orientation columns intersecting with spatial frequency columns. Since orientation by spatial frequency is the same as two-dimensional spatial frequency (see Chapter 9), this means that within each CM are cells tuned to each of the many regions in two-dimensional spatial frequency space. Those tuned to a given two-dimensional spatial frequency region at a given location in space are all arranged in a column through all six cortical layers. This whole array is duplicated within the CM, once for each eye, the separation of the inputs from the eyes being considerable in layer 4, but much less in upper and lower layers, thus providing for the possibility of extracting information about the third dimension as well (see Chapter 10).

Color in Cortex

We are not concerned in this book with color processing per se: that deserves and has received volumes devoted to it alone. Rather, we consider color only in relation to spatial vision. However, since we believe color to play an important role in spatial vision, we need to examine the spatial processing of color-varying, as well as luminance-varying, stimuli. Almost all studies of the cortical processing of spatial information have used just luminance-varying patterns (understandably so, of course, in studies of cat cortex). Thus relatively little is known about color-spatial processing.

The cells in the macaque LGN (see Chapter 7) have a low-pass spatial frequency characteristic in response to pure color stimuli. LGN cells, which show a modest low spatial frequency drop to luminance-varying patterns, show no low-frequency attenuation at all to color-varying stimuli (R.L. De Valois, Snodderly, Yund, & Hepler, 1977). Most cortical cells, on the other hand, show a band-pass spatial frequency characteristic both to luminance-varying and to color-varying gratings (Thorell, 1981; Thorell et al., 1984). A given cell may respond optimally to a red-green grating of 2 c/deg, with considerably less sensitivity to red-green gratings of either higher or lower spatial frequency, giving no response at all to patterns above, say, 4 or below 1 c/deg.

To a first approximation the tuning characteristics of cortical cells to pure color-varying patterns are the same as those to pure luminance-varying patterns we have been considering up to now. Most cells have fairly narrow spatial frequency bandwidths, and cells tuned to a variety of spatial frequencies are to be found in a CM (Thorell et al., 1984). The cells also show orientation selectivity to pure color patterns, with about the same orientation bandwidths as are shown to luminance patterns. Within a cortical region, cells are found with peak sensitivities to each of the various orientations for color patterns, as was found for luminance-varying patterns.

As discussed earlier, stimulation with luminance-varying patterns reveals two fundamentally different varieties of cortical cells: simple and complex cells. Both of these cell types are also to be found among those responsive to pure color patterns. For instance, some (simple) cells will fire to red on green and inhibit to green on red at the same RF location (the red and green being equated for luminance). Other (complex) cells will fire both to red on green *and* to green on red at the same RF location (R.L. De Valois, 1972; Thorell et al., 1984). The distinctions made earlier between the responses of simple and complex cells to drifting and to counterphase-flickering luminance gratings also apply to their responses to isoluminant color gratings.

There have been reports that there is a dichotomy among cortical cells, some responding to color stimuli and others to luminance patterns (Gouras, 1974; Michael, 1978a, 1978b, 1978c). We find, on the contrary, that most of the same cells respond to both color and luminance patterns, as was true also for the LGN. Specifically, about 80% of foveal macaque cortical cells respond both to luminance-varying and to color-varying patterns, and show much the same responses to each (Thorell et al., 1984). Smaller percentages respond to only one or the other.

Although, as we have been pointing out, cortical cells to a first approximation show similar responses to pure color as to pure luminance patterns, there are certain differences. Although most cells have similar color and luminance spatial frequency bandwidths, when they differ it is almost always in the direction of a broader color tuning resulting from less low-frequency attenuation (Thorell et al., 1984). Furthermore, fewer of the cells tuned to the highest spatial frequencies are color responsive. The net effect of these two differences is that the color sensitivity averaged across all cells is shifted to lower spatial frequencies and shows little decrease in sensitivity to low spatial frequencies, compared with the overall responses to luminance patterns (Thorell et al., 1984). This is in agreement with the difference between the color and luminance behavioral contrast sensitivity function (see Chapter 7).

Later Cortical Areas

Our discussion so far has been restricted to the striate cortex, to only the first of at least a half dozen cortical regions that have been anatomically and physiologically identified as being involved with the processing of visual information. It would clearly be desirable to understand the anatomy and physiology of these later centers and how they further process visual information. We believe, however, that it is premature for that endeavor, since not enough is understood either of the detailed physiology of these later centers or of the likely functional processes, relevant to spatial vision, that operate at those levels.

One issue with respect to post-striate physiology that seems worth raising, however, is the evidence for or against a progressive hierarchical arrangement of cells in subsequent visual areas. That is, is visual information processed serially through the striate, then successively through cells in V2, V3, . . . , or are the later areas more in parallel, each dealing with a different subset of the total? A serial arrangement was rather suggested by the early results of Hubel and Wiesel in which they found mainly simple and complex cells in V1, but mainly complex and hypercomplex cells in V2 and V3 of cat (Hubel & Wiesel, 1965). Since they were arguing for a serial arrangement of simple to complex to hypercomplex cells, these findings supported a serial arrangement in later levels. This position was built upon by others to construct perceptual models of increasingly specific feature detectors (Neisser, 1967; Lindsay & Norman, 1972). The actual increases in specificity of units in V2 and V3 compared with V1, however, did not seem to be nearly as great as demanded by these models.

Recent studies of the anatomical connections among the various poststriate areas indicate a combination of serial and parallel processing, with an emphasis on the latter. Cells in V1 project to a number of other regions, in a parallel fashion, with many of these outputs coming from different laminae of V1. The best worked out of these are the projections from layer 2 and 3 cells of V1 to V2; from layer 4b and 5 cells to MT; from other layer 5 cells to the superior colliculus; and from layer 6 cells to the LGN (J.S. Lund et al., 1975). There have also been reports of V1 projections to V3 and V4 (Zeki, 1978). In addition, the various poststriate regions appear to differ considerably in the retinal regions represented (Allman, Baker, Newsome, & Petersen, 1981). In MT different retinal eccentricities are more uniformly represented than is the case with V1 (which, as we have noted, has a great magnification of the foveal retina), whereas another poststriate region, DL (dorsolateral), is largely restricted to processing input just from the central retina. All of this suggests a parallel organization, of different poststriate (and subcortical) regions receiving and further analyzing different aspects of the information in V1. On the other hand, there are also projections from V2 to MT, which in turn projects to the inferotemporal cortex (IT), to form a serial series V1 to V2 to MT to IT; there is also a serial path from V1 to V2 to V4 to IT.

Physiological studies also suggest that poststriate areas are specialized for dealing with subportions of the total visual information, in a combined serial and parallel arrangement (Zeki, 1973, 1978; Allman et al., 1981; Van Essen & Maunsell, 1983). Specifically, cells in MT (also termed the superior temporal sulcus movement area, and V5, by Zeki, 1978) appear to be particularly involved with the analysis of stimulus movement. Virtually all the cells here are direction sensitive, and they appear to be selective for movements in particular directions in the frontoparallel plane or in depth (Zeki, 1974, 1978). Furthermore, some at least appear to be putting together information about the movement direction of various spatial frequency components of an object into a response to the overall pattern movement direction (Movshon et al., 1985). Cells in V2, on the other hand, have been reported to be selective for stereoscopic depth (Hubel & Wiesel, 1970; Poggio & Fischer, 1977). Finally, the cells in V4 have been reported to be concerned with color processing by Zeki (1973): he reported not only that almost all the cells in this area are color-selective, but also that they are arranged in color columns. Although these reports on V4 have been disputed (Schein, Marrocco, & de Monasterio, 1982), no one questions that there are great differences in the functional characteristics of the cells located in the various poststriate areas.

The physiological evidence, then, along with the nature of the anatomical projections, suggests that the visual information after V1 is processed more in a parallel than in a serial arrangement. From the point of view of spatial vision, however, there is a paucity of physiological information from poststriate areas to indicate the nature of these later processing steps. The generally parallel anatomical organization, however, suggests that there may be a limited number of synaptic levels beyond V1 for the processing of spatial information.

5

Contrast Sensitivity and Acuity

In previous chapters we have discussed the current status of our knowledge of the anatomy and physiology of the visual system. We shall now consider various aspects of visual behavior. In each case we will attempt to relate the psychophysical phenomena under consideration to physiological processes that may underlie those characteristics of visual perception.

In this chapter we consider the overall sensitivity of human observers to spatially varying patterns. We first examine the luminance contrast sensitivity function (CSF), the sensitivity of observers to luminance-varying sinusoidal gratings of different spatial frequencies. Next, we discuss the implications of the human CSF for certain aspects of everyday visual perception. Finally, we shall attempt to relate the CSF to certain more classical measures of human spatial vision, the acuity tests. In this chapter we shall only consider CSFs for isochromatic, luminance-varying, one-dimensional gratings. We shall later (Chapter 7) turn to a discussion of color-varying patterns, and then (Chapter 9) to two-dimensional patterns.

SPATIAL CONTRAST SENSITIVITY FUNCTIONS

Any complex waveform can be analyzed into (or, conversely, synthesized from) a series of sine and cosine waves (see Chapter 1 on linear systems analysis). The luminance of a sine wave grating is constant along the axis parallel to the stripes and varies sinusoidally along an orthogonal axis. If the visual system were a linear system, knowing the observer's sensitivity to sinusoidal gratings of various spatial frequencies would allow one to predict the detectability of any other one-dimensional pattern. This is, of course, the great power of a linear systems approach and one reason for using sinusoidal gratings as visual stimuli.

As is discussed in Chapter 2, the manner in which a lens or optical system will pass spatial information can be determined by measuring its modulation transfer function (MTF). To do this, one measures the amplitude of the output for each spatial frequency, given an input of known amplitude. If, say, the output amplitude were 70% of the input amplitude for a given spatial frequency, then the contribution of that frequency to the response to any complex pattern could be precisely calculated as 70% of the input amplitude at that frequency. If a system operated linearly, it would only be necessary to measure its response to one input amplitude for each frequency in order to calculate its response to any complex input.

In recordings from single cells in the visual system one can determine an MTF, since a cell's discharge rate can be quantitatively measured for a range of spatial frequencies of constant contrast (although we do not wish to imply that the input-output characteristic of a single cell is necessarily linear). When the whole organism is the device being studied, however, the problem of determining a transfer characteristic is more difficult for lack of a reliable, objective, quantitative measure of the magnitude of the organism's response to various spatial frequencies and contrasts. The requisite psychophysical experiment would be to present different spatial frequencies at a variety of fixed contrasts and require the subject to give a contrast-dependent response. While this can be done by having the subject estimate the contrast magnitude (e.g., Cannon, 1979) or match the apparent contrast of the test grating with that of a grating of standard spatial frequency, it is less than an ideal solution at best. One solution to this problem is to use a constant-response criterion and measure the stimulus amplitude necessary to produce it. In practice, the response chosen is usually absolute contrast threshold for the detection of the pattern. The resulting function is termed the contrast sensitivity function (CSF), contrast sensitivity being expressed as the reciprocal of the contrast required for detection. This measure is not directly comparable to a lens modulation transfer function, and the assumptions that underlie its use are many and shaky. The uninitiated and, perhaps even more so, the true believer should be wary indeed. Despite the obvious limitations of a technique that represents a system with many known nonlinearities by a single set of points, however, the measurement of contrast sensitivity has proven to be quite useful. Its predictive ability suggests that under many conditions the treatment of the visual system as a quasilinear system is not unreasonable.

Shape of the Luminance Contrast Sensitivity Function

In Figure 5.1 is a typical CSF for a normal human observer, obtained for static, luminance-varying gratings with central fixation at a photopic light level. It can be seen that the highest sensitivity is in the mid spatial frequency range, around 2-6 c/deg, with a sharp drop in sensitivity to high spatial frequencies, and a gentler but still pronounced loss in sensitivity at low spatial frequencies, as well, when frequency is plotted on a logarithmic scale. (If spatial frequency is plotted on a linear scale, however—as is customarily the case for a true MTF—quite the converse is true: the low-frequency drop is sharper by far than the high-frequency fall-off.) The corresponding CSF for macaque monkey is shown for comparison, since much of the relevant physiology comes from studies of macaques.

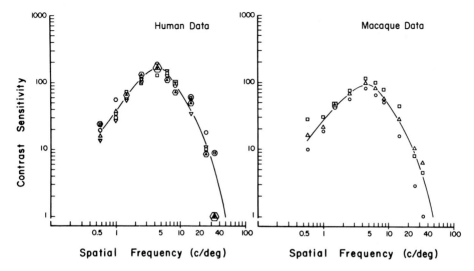

FIG. 5.1 Photopic luminance CSFs for human and macaque observers. Contrast sensitivity is the reciprocal of the contrast necessary to detect a pattern at threshold. Here it is plotted as a function of test spatial frequency (from R.L. De Valois et al., 1974, *Vision Res., 14,* 75–81. Copyright 1974, Pergamon Journals, Inc. Reprinted by permission).

Behavioral contrast sensitivity functions for luminance patterns have been measured for a variety of species: humans, macaques, squirrel monkeys, owl monkeys, cats, falcons, and goldfish, to name a few. Figure 5.2 illustrates CSFs for several species, all collected at photopic light levels (although by no means under totally comparable conditions). It is interesting to note that the general shape of the function on a log frequency scale is quite similar for all these species, the differences consisting largely of simple translations along the spatial frequency axis. (There may also be significant interspecies differences in absolute sensitivity, but this is the aspect most affected by such variables as the precise experimental testing conditions, etc. The absolute sensitivity has been ignored in Figure 5.2, by normalizing the data.) The typical CSF for each of these species is an asymmetric inverted U-shaped function, with greatest sensitivity at some middle range of spatial frequencies. Sensitivity decreases for both higher and lower frequencies, with the high-frequency fall-off generally somewhat sharper than the low-frequency fall-off.

It is apparent from Figure 5.2 that the CSFs for these various species cover quite different spatial frequency ranges. There is virtually no overlap, for instance, between the ranges of spatial frequencies to which cats and falcons are sensitive. Any narrow-band stimulus (of reasonably low contrast) which the cat could see would be invisible to the falcon if viewed from the same distance, and vice versa. There is an obvious relationship between the spatial frequency ranges of these various animals and the spatial dimensions of the visual objects with which they are mainly concerned in their everyday life. The spatial frequency

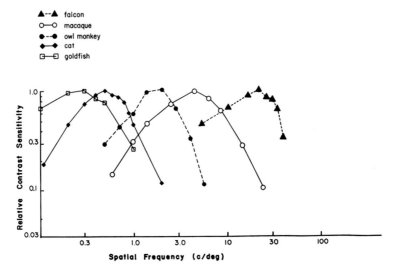

FIG. 5.2   CSFs for several different species. The data are all normalized relative to the point of maximum sensitivity for each function. Note the qualitative similarity in shape of the various functions despite their displacement along the log spatial frequency axis (data redrawn from Northmore & Dvorak, 1979 [goldfish]; Blake et al., 1974 [cat]; Jacobs, 1977 [owl monkey]; R.L. De Valois et al., 1974 [macaque monkey]; Fox et al., 1976, and Fox & Lehmkuhle, personal communication [falcon]. *Vision Res.,* Copyright 1974, 1977, 1979, Pergamon Journals, Inc. Reprinted by permission).

content of the image of a small animal on the ground would be concentrated at very high spatial frequencies for a falcon soaring at a great height. The predominant frequencies might be as high as 50 c/deg (a spatial frequency range to which the falcon is very sensitive, but a range which we can barely resolve) for a falcon flying at 100–200 m. For a short-legged, ground-dwelling cat looking at the same stimulus from a distance of 1–2 m, the pattern would have its peak energy at about 0.5 c/deg, where the cat's visual system is most sensitive.

It is important to note that most animals tested so far have been found to show low spatial frequency attenuation, which as we shall see has major behavioral advantages. (The very different shape of the color CSF will be discussed in Chapter 7.) Perhaps because of limitations in the total capacity of the visual path, each species has also been found to have significant sensitivity to an overall spatial frequency range of no more than about 6 to 8 octaves.

Variation of Spatial CSF With Luminance

Contrast sensitivity varies with both luminance level and retinal location. For high photopic luminances, the human CSF may peak at 5–6 c/deg, and spatial frequencies of 50–60 c/deg can be detected with high contrast under optimal conditions (Campbell & Green, 1965). It is under these conditions that the bowed shape of the contrast sensitivity function is most evident. Regardless of light level, the high frequency end of the curve always shows a sharp fall-off (again assuming that frequency is plotted on a logarithmic axis), but the low-frequency attenuation is most obvious under photopic conditions.

As the luminance level is progressively reduced, the point of greatest sensitivity shifts to lower and lower spatial frequencies (Patel, 1966; Daitch & Green, 1969; R.L. De Valois, Morgan, & Snodderly, 1974). Thus the transition from a photopic to a mesopic luminance level might produce a shift in the peak spatial sensitivity from 6 to 2 c/deg (Figure 5.3). This shift in peak sensitivity results from a much greater loss in contrast sensitivity to high than to low spatial frequencies as luminance levels decrease, although contrast sensitivity to low frequencies declines somewhat as well. At low scotopic light levels little or no low-frequency attenuation is apparent. It is possible that some attenuation still occurs, but at spatial frequencies lower than those which can conveniently be measured.

At this point we should interject some cautionary notes. One is that the spatial CSF depends on the temporal properties of the stimulus presentation, particularly at low spatial frequencies, as discussed further below. Under the usual testing conditions, this is a poorly controlled variable, due to eye movements. The

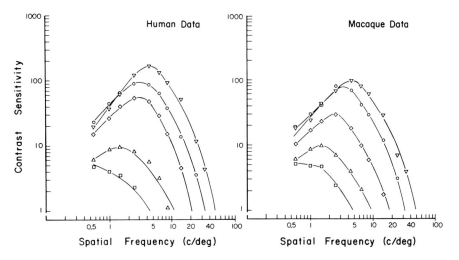

FIG. 5.3. The luminance CSF as a function of absolute luminance level. Contrast sensitivity was measured for both human and macaque observers for a range of spatial frequencies at each of five adaptation levels (5, 0.5, 0.05, 0.005, and 0.0005 foot Lamberts, respectively). Note that the peak sensitivity shifts to lower spatial frequencies as luminance is reduced. At the same time, the low-frequency attenuation becomes less prominent, finally disappearing at the lowest luminance level (from R.L. De Valois et al., 1974, *Vision Res., 14,* 75–81. Copyright 1974, Pergamon Journals, Inc. Reprinted by permission).

data we have been discussing were collected with a stationary pattern and uncontrolled eye movements. The measurement of contrast sensitivity to very low spatial frequencies presents some additional special problems. We speak of a sinusoidal grating of some particular spatial frequency as though all the power in the stimulus were at that frequency. For that to be strictly true, the grating would have to be of infinite extent. In practice, of course, no such stimulus exists. The best one can hope to do is to make an extended grating in which most of the power is concentrated at or very near the nominal spatial frequency. The greater the extent of the grating (the greater the number of cycles it contains), the more nearly will that be the case. Since any stimulus is of limited extent, and since for any given field size the number of cycles present will be a direct function of the spatial frequency, the problem will always be more severe for low frequencies.

In practice, if a "sinusoidal" grating is to have a reasonable concentration of power at its purported frequency, there should be several cycles of the grating present. Otherwise, the power in the stimulus spectrum will be spread over a broad range of frequencies (D.H. Kelly, 1975). The practical difficulties that can result from this fact will be illustrated in our subsequent discussion of spatial frequency specific adaptation (Chapter 6).

With the commonly used oscilloscope displays there are two opposing considerations. The first is due to the oscilloscope raster. If a subject is too close to the display, the individual raster lines can be resolved, thus unavoidably complicating the stimulus by introducing unintended spatial frequencies in the region to which the subject is sensitive. The curvature of the screen can also become a problem. On the other hand, if the subject is far enough away that he cannot resolve the raster lines, the display will cover too small a visual angle to produce several cycles of a very low-frequency stimulus. This problem has been alleviated somewhat as such displays have become larger and have higher resolution. Of course, the raster also introduces a limit to the fineness of the grain of the pattern that can be produced (and thus the high spatial frequencies), but that can be simply overcome by increasing the viewing distance.

Variation of Spatial CSF With Retinal Locus

Contrast sensitivity varies not only as a function of light level, but also with retinal locus of the pattern being detected. As a pattern is shifted from the fovea into the periphery, the changes in its detectability are very similar to those produced by lowering the luminance level. The overall contrast sensitivity decreases, peak sensitivity occurs at progressively lower spatial frequencies, the high-frequency fall-off moves to lower frequency regions, and the low-frequency attenuation becomes less apparent (Rovamo, Virsu, & Nasanen, 1978). The precise nature of the sensitivity changes with eccentricity, however, and whether the fovea or periphery is more sensitive to various spatial frequencies are difficult questions because the answers depend very much on the testing conditions.

If the same size patch of grating is used for each spatial frequency at each eccentricity, sensitivity falls drastically with eccentricity (Hilz & Cavonius, 1974), whereas if the peripheral patterns are made increasingly large, compensating for the presumed cortical magnification factor, the peak spatial frequency shifts to lower frequencies with eccentricity while the contrast sensitivity to low spatial frequencies shows an absolute increase (Rovamo et al., 1978; D.H. Kelly, 1984). In this case, however, probability summation (see Chapter 6) could operate to increase the apparent peripheral sensitivity, since the stimulus extent increases greatly with eccentricity. (Note that some of the early studies used the ganglion cell variation with eccentricity as the basis for their estimates of the "cortical magnification factor," assuming that they were the same. As discussed in Chapter 4, this may not be so.) One reasonable approach to this question is that used by Robson and Graham (1981), in which patches of gratings of a constant number of cycles were used in all cases. With such constant stimuli, they found that sensitivity to every spatial frequency was greatest in the fovea, and that high spatial frequency sensitivity fell relative to low as eccentricity increased. This issue, which has considerable theoretical importance with relevance to the question of multiple spatial frequency channels, will be discussed further in Chapter 6.

Luminance Sensitivity Versus Contrast Sensitivity

In the above sections, we have been considering the contrast sensitivity of observers and the way in which it varies with luminance level and retinal locus. It is important here to distinguish between contrast sensitivity and sensitivity to luminance differences. Contrast is a relative measure: the amplitude of a waveform relative to its mean. At a mean luminance level of 0.5 cd/m^2, a sinusoidal grating of 50% contrast would have a peak of 0.75 and a trough of 0.25 cd/m^2; at a mean luminance of 500 cd/m^2, a similar 50% contrast grating would have a peak of 750 and a trough of 250 cd/m^2. An observer with constant contrast threshold (of 50%) at these two light levels, then, would be just able to detect a peak-to-trough difference of 0.5 cd/m^2 at the low light level and a difference of 500 cd/m^2 at the high. Thus he would be 1,000 times as sensitive to luminance differences at the low as at the high light level. Conversely, of course, an observer with a constant sensitivity to luminance increments or decrements between peaks and troughs of the grating would show a contrast sensitivity that varied with the mean light level, being 1,000 times as sensitive at the high light level, in the example above, as at the low.

With this in mind, it is of interest to replot the data in Figure 5.3 against absolute luminance sensitivity (see Figure 5.4). It can be seen that at high spatial frequencies, absolute luminance sensitivity measures roughly converge to the same curve, whereas at low spatial frequencies the absolute sensitivity dramatically increases as light levels are decreased (so that contrast sensitivity is more nearly constant). Note that the Weber fraction would describe the latter, not the former, case.

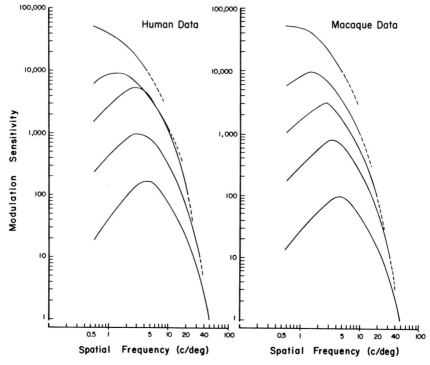

FIG. 5.4   Absolute modulation sensitivity as a function of luminance level. Here the data from the preceding figure have been replotted to show the sensitivity to absolute luminance differences rather than to contrast (a relative measure). See text for discussion (from R.L. De Valois et al., 1974, *Vision Res., 14,* 75–81. Copyright 1974, Pergamon Journals, Inc. Reprinted by permission).

TEMPORAL AND SPATIOTEMPORAL CSF

Temporal CSF

We are principally concerned in this book with the way in which the visual system deals with spatial rather than temporal variations. Nonetheless, in examining the implications of the spatial CSF for visual perception, it is necessary to give some consideration also to how our sensitivity to changes in luminance varies with temporal frequency.

A temporal CSF can be obtained by sinusoidally flickering a large, spatially uniform field at different temporal frequencies, the task of the observer being to detect the presence of flicker. Early attempts to systematically measure a temporal CSF using sinusoidal flicker were made by Ives (1922) and de Lange (1952). In Figure 5.5 is shown a typical temporal CSF obtained under photopic luminance conditions (D.H. Kelly, 1961). It can be seen that it resembles the

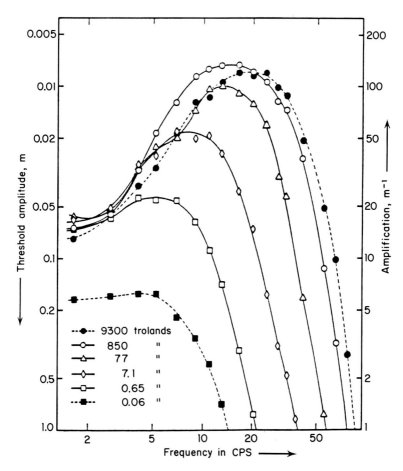

FIG. 5.5 Photopic temporal CSF. The task of the observer here is to detect the sinusoidal flickering of a spatially uniform field. Note the general similarity of the function to the spatial CSF shown in Figure 5.3 (from D.H. Kelly, 1961, *J. Opt. Soc. Am., 51,* 422–429. Reprinted by permission).

spatial CSF in showing both high- and low-frequency attenuation. As discussed in Chapter 3, the high temporal frequency attenuation can be largely (but not entirely) accounted for by the variable-duration process intervening between photon capture by the photopigments and the initiation of polarization changes in the receptor outer membrane. The low temporal frequency attenuation can be partially attributed to the slight time delay in the surround response within antagonistic center-surround RFs. At low temporal frequencies the center and surround responses largely coincide and thus cancel. At middle temporal frequencies the longer surround latency might even put center and surround out of phase so they would add rather than subtract from each other. In Chapter 7 we discuss the very different temporal CSF for color-varying patterns. Like the spatial CSF, the temporal luminance CSF peaks at lower frequencies as the luminance level is progressively reduced (D.H. Kelly, 1961). The high temporal frequency fall-off occurs sooner, and the low-frequency fall-off becomes less pronounced.

Variation of Spatial CSF With Temporal Frequency

Under normal circumstances the eyes are never truly still. The image of a stationary object will move on the retina even when the subject attempts to fixate steadily on a point. It should perhaps come as no surprise, then, that movement of the retinal image is an important factor in human vision.

Although the eye cannot be voluntarily held steady, it is now possible to stabilize the retinal image by monitoring eye movements and moving the stimulus an exactly compensatory amount. When this is done, the now-stabilized image rapidly fades and may even disappear within a few seconds (Ditchburn & Ginsborg, 1952; Riggs et al., 1953). Even though the contrast of the image may be quite high, it will no longer be visible. If the pattern is composed of luminance variations, it may be possible to make it reappear by greatly increasing the contrast. If it is composed of a pure chromatic variation, however, it may not be possible to raise the contrast enough to make the pattern become visible again (D.H. Kelly, 1979a, 1983).

We can think of the stabilized image as representing one end of a continuum of temporal modulation of a spatial pattern—one with a temporal frequency of 0 Hz. By first stabilizing a spatial pattern, e.g., a grating of a particular spatial frequency, and then moving it at a controlled rate, it is possible to produce image motion of known and precisely controlled temporal frequency, something which is not possible with an unstabilized pattern in the presence of normal eye movements. One can then measure contrast sensitivity for various spatial frequencies at each of a range of temporal frequencies. Robson (1966) and van Nes, Koenderink, Nas, and Bouman (1967) were the first to measure such a combined spatiotemporal contrast sensitivity function, but without the precise control of temporal frequency provided by modern stabilization techniques. D.H. Kelly (1983, 1984) has repeated these measurements by stabilizing the retinal image and then moving it at known speeds, as discussed above. He found a bandpass spatial CSF, similar to that seen in the usual unstabilized determinations, when luminance-varying gratings were moved at moderate to low temporal frequencies. When the temporal frequency was increased, however, sensitivity to high spatial frequencies decreased slightly while sensitivity to low spatial frequencies showed a large increase. At these high temporal frequencies the *spatial* CSF becomes low-pass, not band-pass, since low spatial frequency attenuation disappears. On the other hand, at very low temporal frequencies, below those possible with unstabilized vision, the low spatial frequency attenuation is profound. These data are summarized in Figure 5.6, which shows a combined spatiotemporal contrast sensitivity surface.

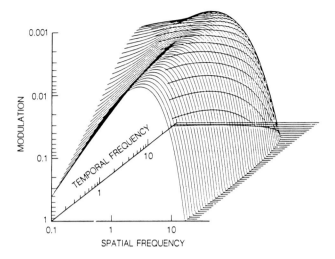

FIG. 5.6 Combined spatiotemporal CSF. This surface represents luminance contrast sensitivity measured for each of several spatial frequencies at each of several temporal frequencies. Precise temporal control was obtained by first stabilizing the image and then temporally modulating it under computer control (from D.H. Kelly, 1979b, *J. Opt. Soc. Am., 69,* 1340–1349. Reprinted by permission).

ORIGIN OF BAND-PASS FILTER PROPERTIES

Although an MTF (or, by somewhat tenuous extension, a CSF) allows one to predict the response of a linear device to any complex input, it does not specify how that device is constructed. The attenuation in the human contrast sensitivity to high spatial frequencies, in particular, may be produced by a variety of optical and neural processes. Prominent among these are such optical factors as imperfections in the cornea and lens, diffraction by the pupil, scattered light in the eye, and incorrect shape of the eyeball (see Chapter 2).

The retina itself can also be considered as an optical system, as well as a neural system. The inner parts of the retina act as a diffuser, and the receptors themselves, because of their finite size and spacing, also act to attenuate high spatial frequencies (see Chapter 2). Direct measurements of the optical transmission characteristics of the freshly excised retina have been made by Ohzu, Enoch, and O'Hair (1972) in rat and by Ohzu and Enoch (1972) in humans. They show that the optical attenuation by the retina, like that produced by the cornea-lens combination, is minimal at low spatial frequencies but becomes a significant factor at high spatial frequencies.

One way to estimate the attenuation produced by optical factors is to measure the CSF using gratings produced directly on the retina by laser interferometry (e.g., Campbell & Green, 1965). As expected, such experiments demonstrate that the resolution of the eye is somewhat higher with the eye's optics largely bypassed. The attenuation produced by the optics of the eye is minimal at low spatial frequencies and increases with increasing spatial frequency. These measurements indicate that the optical imperfections do not completely account for the high frequency fall-off of the CSF, there being significant high spatial frequency attenuation in the absence of any optical limitations. As discussed in Chapters 2 and 3, the spatial sampling by the receptors sets an upper limit to the extent to which the nervous system can transmit high spatial frequency information. This thus contributes to the attenuation of the high spatial frequency end of the CSF.

The attenuation of contrast sensitivity to high spatial frequencies in the retinal periphery can be partially but not entirely accounted for on optical grounds. The optical quality of the eye does fall to some extent with increasing eccentricity, but considerably less than does the change in contrast sensitivity to high spatial frequencies. For instance, the optical resolution of the eye drops to about 60% of the foveal value at 20° eccentricity (Jennings & Charman, 1981), but the photopic acuity out this far is only about 20% of that at the fovea. Nonoptical factors must thus play an important role in loss of high spatial frequency information with eccentricity.

The change in receptor density per se across the retina is also insufficient to account completely for the loss of high spatial frequency contrast sensitivity with increasing eccentricity. The density of cones in the foveal area is about the same as that of rods in the 18–20° peripheral region where they are most prevalent (Østerberg, 1935), but the sensitivity to high spatial frequencies in foveal cone vision is obviously far better than in peripheral rod vision. However, if only cone spacing is considered, some considerable drop in contrast sensitivity with eccentricity is to be expected, since peripheral cones are larger than those in the fovea and are increasingly separated from each other by interspersed rods. It is not clear, though, that this entirely accounts for the lower peripheral high spatial frequency sensitivity.

Two additional aspects of retinal physiology appear to be among the neural factors that may underlie the loss in high spatial frequency sensitivity with increasing retinal eccentricity and with decreasing luminance levels. The first is the increase in the size of ganglion cell RFs in the periphery. There is of course no one-to-one transmission from receptor to bipolar to ganglion cell in any part of the retina, given receptor coupling and lateral inputs from horizontal and amacrine cells. In fact, the interplay among these various retinal cells is undoubtedly the single most important factor in determining the spatial analysis carried out by the retina. However, ganglion cells integrate over significantly different extents at various eccentricities. Most foveal ganglion cells receive their input only over quite restricted retinal regions, in many—perhaps most—cases the RF centers being only a single cone. But as the distance from the fovea increases, the average size of the summation area for a single ganglion cell increases correspondingly, so that in the periphery ganglion cell RF centers are quite large (Wiesel, 1960; Enroth-Cugell & Robson, 1966; Fischer, 1973).

The other factor is the difference between rod and cone summation pools, their relative distributions and sensitivities. Rods are coupled together over larger distances than are cones, and bipolars and ganglion cells that pick up from cones tend to have smaller RFs than do rod bipolars and ganglion cells. This, in conjunction with the fact that rods are more sensitive at low light levels (at least at low temporal frequencies) than are cones, produces a system that has decreasing sensitivity to high spatial frequencies with increasing retinal eccentricity and with decreasing luminance levels.

Understanding the origin of the low-frequency attenuation of the CSF at first seems to present a greater problem. Optical imperfections of the eye selectively attenuate only high spatial frequencies and cannot account for low spatial frequency attenuation. Variations in receptor spacing would also be largely irrelevant. The initial low spatial frequency attenuation is almost surely the consequence of the neural inhibitory interactions between center and surround of retinal RFs, as discussed in Chapter 3. Every cell with an antagonistic center-surround receptive field will operate to some extent as a spatial frequency band-pass filter. The degree of low spatial frequency attenuation will depend on the relative strengths of the center and surround inputs, but there will always be some. From the very earliest postreceptoral levels in the neural analysis of visual information, most cells operate as band-pass spatial frequency filters for luminance-varying patterns, showing not only the insensitivity to high frequencies that one expects on optical and neural sampling grounds, but also a decreased sensitivity to low spatial frequencies. The visual system does not just transmit intact whatever information is passed by its optical system; rather, it begins immediately to process that information in ways that exaggerate some kinds of information and filter out others. It is an information-processing device, not just a passive transmittal system.

It is apparent that the general shape of the CSF, with both low- and high-frequency attenuation, can be accounted for on the basis of the eye's optics, receptor spacing, and neural interactions discussed above and earlier in this book. However, the evidence so far considered does not answer the question of the relation between the response properties of individual neurons in a given retinal region and our overall contrast sensitivity at that eccentricity. Do all foveal ganglion or LGN cells have (approximately) the same CSF, a broad one that matches the overall perceptual foveal CSF? Or, alternatively, do the different ganglion and LGN cells have narrower spatial frequency tuning, with the behavioral sensitivity being some sort of envelope of the differing sensitivities of the individual units? The answer to these questions is very clear for striate cells, as we shall discuss further in the next chapter (most striate cells are much more narrowly tuned than the behavioral CSF), but the answer is not so certain for units at earlier levels. Although there is not adequate information about the CSF of large populations of individual ganglion or LGN cells at different eccentricities, the available evidence (von Blanckensee, 1981; Kaplan & Shapley, 1982; Hicks, Lee, & Vidyasagar, 1983) indicates that to a first approximation many individual cells have almost as broad a spatial frequency tuning range as the overall organism.

An interesting and important complication in this question of the relationship between the sensitivity of individual retinal and LGN cells and that of the whole organism is the presence of different types of cells with very different absolute sensitivities. The psychophysical studies of the CSF we have been discussing examine *threshold* sensitivity; presumably only the most sensitive retinal ganglion or LGN cells would contribute to such detection. But while most studies of the properties of LGN cells (and most models, including ours, of vision based on cell properties) have concentrated on the mass of parvocellular LGN cells, Kaplan & Shapley (1982) have shown that, with medium temporal frequencies, the cells in the two small magnocellular layers are some ten times more sensitive at low to medium spatial frequencies. This would lead one to expect that threshold psychophysics might be mainly related to the properties of these as yet ill-understood magnocellular units and the cortical cells that derive their input from them.

IMPLICATIONS OF THE CSF FOR VISION

One reason we have been giving such emphasis to the CSF is that a number of classical visual problems can be understood, at least to a first approximation, from a consideration of the CSF. Many situations that have long been treated as isolated problems in vision can now be subsumed into one and can be given a unified treatment in terms of the properties of the CSF.

Detecting Objects Versus the Illuminant

It is a paradox that the stimulus to vision is the amount of light coming from different parts of the visual world, but this quantity—the absolute amount of light—is almost totally irrelevant to the main task of the visual system, that of detecting and identifying objects. The reason for this is that the differences in the amounts of light reflected by different objects are insignificant compared to the differences in the amount of light due to changes in the illuminant. The same object will reflect a small or a large amount of light, depending not so much on the characteristics of the object as on the time of day. A white object under dim illumination may reflect only a thousandth (or even only a millionth) as much light as a dark object under high illumination. The whitest objects rarely reflect more than about 80% of whatever light strikes them; the blackest objects, about 4%. There is thus at most about a 20:1 ratio of light levels due to the visually relevant properties of objects. However, differences in illumination level between a dark night and a bright snowy day can be greater than 1,000,000,000:1! Thus, almost all the variation in light level is due to the illuminant rather than to the object. The visually relevant information is a small fluctuation riding on a huge waveform produced by the illuminant. One can see how foolish it would be for the retinal network to relay up to the brain information about absolute light levels, for that information is almost completely irrelevant. Furthermore, it is far beyond the capability of the nervous system, with its limited capacity for transmitting information, to signal such vast changes with great precision.

To solve this problem, the visual system clearly must transform the receptor output in ways that minimize the contribution of the illuminant and capture and emphasize the tiny variations due to objects. There are two main differences between the characteristics of the illuminant and those of objects which make this a solvable problem. One is the spatial frequency band at which most of the power (in the frequency domain) lies for the illuminant as opposed to the object. It is clear that most visually interesting objects tend to be quite nonuniform; instead, they show much spatial variation across a section of the visual field. The illuminant, on the other hand, is spatially much more uniform: on a dark night the whole visual world is dark; on a sunny day it is bright everywhere except in the deepest shadows. By attenuating zero and near-zero spatial frequencies while amplifying higher spatial frequencies, then, the visual system is minimizing the contribution of the illuminant and emphasizing the contribution of objects. The attenuation of very low spatial frequencies is clearly not complete—it is in fact useful to be able to distinguish noon from midnight—but sufficiently so as to make it possible to pull out the more relevant information.

Second, it can be seen that attenuating very low temporal frequencies (adaptation) has a similar utility in minimizing the contribution of the illuminant. Changes in light due to the passage of the sun across the sky are very slow. (We should note that there is a rumor that it is actually the earth which rotates in this situation.) The temporal changes due to objects, however, are usually relatively rapid, given either movement of the observer through the environment or head and eye movements. So again, by selectively attenuating very low temporal frequencies, the visual system minimizes the contribution from the illuminant relative to that from objects. A side effect of this is that if steady fixation were maintained, objects should disappear from vision. In fact they do. It has long been known that with steady fixation small objects in the periphery disappear (Troxler's effect). The same can be seen with larger blurred patterns (see Figure 5.7). Fine, centrally fixated patterns do not disappear with steady fixation, but that is because "steady fixation" is not really steady. If all head and eye movements (relative to the pattern) are eliminated by optical means (Riggs et al., 1953; Ditchburn & Ginsborg, 1952), virtually the whole visual world does in fact disappear.

Filtering out low temporal frequencies has one additional virtue for the visual system, namely that of minimizing afterimages. An intense pulse of light to the receptors produces receptor activity that does not end with the cessation of the light; some neural activity apparently continues for half an hour or more, perhaps until the bleached photopigment molecules are all regenerated. This is reflected in adaptational aftereffects. If they were readily seen, such prolonged

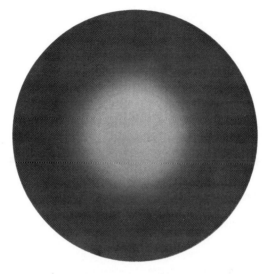

FIG. 5.7   Disappearance of a centrally fixated pattern. Observe this pattern from a distance of about 10 inches and steadily fixate the center for several seconds. If you succeed in maintaining steady fixation, the inner disk will disappear and the entire circle will appear equally bright. It may even be possible to make the perimeter of the outer circle disappear so that the entire figure appears uniform.

aftereffects could produce major interference with vision: our percept at any given moment would reflect a melange of present and past stimuli. However, afterimages do not move on the retina with eye movements, and they thus constitute very low, almost zero temporal frequency information. By filtering out very low temporal frequencies, then, the visual system not only eliminates irrelevant information about the illuminant, but greatly reduces the effects of afterimages (and shadows of retinal blood vessels) as well.

The images of objects against a background have a constant contrast, not a constant luminance amplitude. Contrast, not luminance, is therefore the visually important parameter. The difference in *luminance* between black and white objects is small at low luminance levels, but at high luminance levels it is very large. The ratio of the two, or the *contrast*, however, remains constant. What is clearly needed to maintain object constancy, then, is a luminance gain-control mechanism driven by the mean luminance level, such that at low light levels the gain would be high, and it would progressively decrease with increasing luminance to maintain constant contrast sensitivity. The decreasing probability of a small number of photon captures' having an effect on the polarization of the receptor outer membrane as light levels increase (as discussed in Chapter 3) would produce a change in sensitivity in the desired direction. So too would the direct feedback from horizontal cells onto receptors, desensitizing the receptors increasingly as the mean luminance level rises.

It is apparent from Figure 5.3 that the visual system does not maintain constant contrast sensitivity with changes in luminance (or eccentricity) at all spatial frequencies. Only at low spatial frequencies does it even approximate this. The high spatial frequency information about objects which is transmitted by the visual system, therefore, will change with luminance and eccentricity. Insofar as our detection and characterization of objects is based on high spatial frequencies, then, objects will change their appearance with luminance changes. However, insofar as the visual system bases its detection and identification of objects on lower spatial frequencies, object constancy will be approximately maintained. This book will still be identifiable as a book under scotopic luminance conditions or when viewed in the periphery. Such identification does not depend on high spatial frequency information. Reading the print, however, will of course not be possible in either case since that depends on resolving high spatial frequency information.

We have been writing as if the illumination level were always constant across the visual field. Often, however, some parts of the field are in sunlight and other parts in shadow from clouds or large objects. In fact, the luminance contrast across a border formed by shadowing may exceed 90% on a sunny day. To handle this, the visual system needs to adjust its gain not from an estimate of the mean luminance across the whole field but from a more localized region. There are mechanisms which do this. The horizontal cells have a considerable lateral extent, and coupling between neighboring horizontal cells would extend the sampling region still more, but the lateral spread falls far short of the total extent of the retina. Thus a gain control mechanism from horizontal cell feedback onto receptors would be setting the gain on the basis of the regional mean luminance level, thereby accommodating regional variation in illumination produced by shadows. There probably are multiple sites at which such gain control mechanisms operate, and the lateral extent of the adaptation may vary considerably with the different levels. Another way of reducing the effects of changes in mean luminance levels produced by shadowing is to base one's visual judgments less on luminance differences and more on chromaticity.This will be discussed at some length in Chapter 7.

Relation to Brightness Contrast and Similitude

A popular visual illusion illustrates the phenomenon of brightness contrast: a gray patch on a black background appears lighter than a physically identical gray on a white background. The grays are shifted perceptually away from the background and thus contrast with it. There are other circumstances in which the converse of contrast, which we (R.L. De Valois and K.K. De Valois, 1975) have termed similitude, operates: a gray on a black background appears darker than the same gray figure on white. (Similitude is also known as assimilation or the spreading effect of von Bezold.) Helson (1963) showed that similitude rather than contrast operates when very fine gray test lines are used.

Both the existence of contrast and similitude and the situations in which one

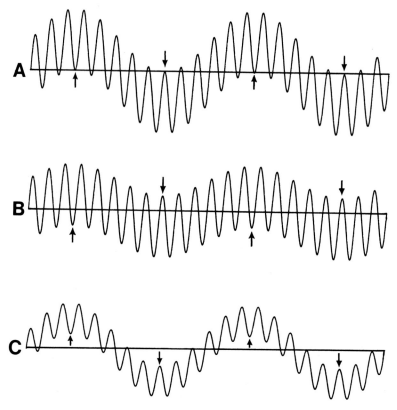

FIG. 5.8   (A) The luminance profile of a grating composed of two components, *f* and 11*f*, of equal amplitude. (B) Profile of the *f* + 11*f* pattern in which *f* is reduced in amplitude. (C) Profile of the *f* + 11*f* pattern in which 11*f* is reduced in amplitude. The arrows indicate the points to be compared.

or the other occurs can to some extent be predicted from the spatial CSF. Consider a pattern whose luminance profile is as shown in Figure 5.8A, a low spatial frequency, plus a much higher spatial frequency (*f* + 11*f*). The trough of the middle wave of the high-frequency pattern in the middle of the bright half of the low-frequency wave is identical in luminance with the peak of the middle wave of the dark half cycle of the low frequency (see arrows). In the absence of any contrast or similitude effects, then, these two points should appear identical in brightness. But if the sensitivity to the low frequency is attenuated (and if the apparent contrast of the low frequency is reduced relative to that of the high frequency), the gray on the white part of the low frequency wave will appear darker than the gray on the dark part, a change in the brightness contrast direction (see Figure 5.8B). So brightness contrast in this situation can be seen as a manifestation of our higher sensitivity to middle than to low spatial frequencies (for luminance-varying patterns).

What about similitude? If the pattern in Figure 5.8A were shifted to a higher spatial frequency range, our greatest sensitivity would now be to the carrier frequency (the lower spatial frequency). The higher frequency pattern would now be on the part of the CSF showing severe attenuation. One's sensitivity to the fine variations would therefore be reduced relative to that to the lower carrier frequency. Now the gray on white would appear whiter and the gray on black blacker (see Figure 5.8C). This would thus be in the similitude direction.

A stimulus pattern such as that diagrammed in Figure 5.8A is shown in Figure 5.9. The two bars to be compared are indicated by arrows. If this pattern is seen from close up, clear contrast effects will be seen; if looked at from some greater distance, say 3 m, a change in the similitude direction will occur. It is somewhat difficult in looking at the pattern in Figure 5.9 to compare just the two bars indicated in the presence of all the others. A modified version of this pattern is

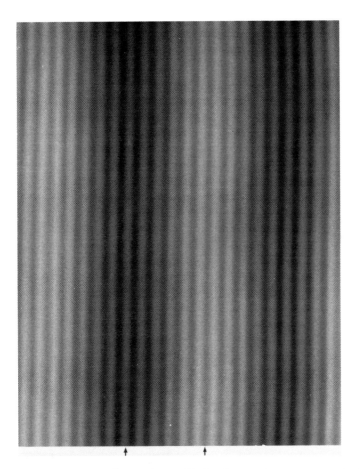

FIG. 5.9 Pattern corresponding to the profile in Figure 5.8A. The arrows indicate the two bars to be compared. See text for explanation.

FIG. 5.10   A modified version of the pattern shown in Figure 5.9. Here just the two bars to be compared are shown superimposed on the carrier wave. The two bars have the same luminance.

shown in Figure 5.10, in which just two bars are shown on the carrier wave. Here very clear contrast effects are seen. However, since these bars have a very broad spatial frequency spectrum, it is not possible to get a clear similitude effect from viewing this pattern at 3 m (even at that distance one is more sensitive to the middle frequencies in the bar pattern than to the carrier).

We have discussed above a number of ways in which the initial visual processing stages contribute to the solution of detecting "object" properties in the presence of irrelevant variations due to the illuminant. One should not conclude, however, that brightness contrast and constancy can be completely accounted for on the basis of the characteristics of cells at these early levels. In fact, there are good reasons to believe that significant poststriate processes are also involved. One is that brightness contrast (and the computations involved in brightness constancy) involve spatial interactions that extend over much longer distances than any interactions found at or before the striate cortex. As we have pointed out (Yund, Snodderly, Hepler, & R.L. De Valois, 1977), although contrast effects can extend up to 10° or more (Yund & Armington, 1975), surround interactions at LGN (and striate cortex) levels are much more restricted in extent. The temporal properties of long-distance brightness (and color) contrast effects also do not correspond to those of cells at striate or earlier levels. We have found that these long-distance contrast effects cannot follow temporal changes above about 2 Hz (R.L. De Valois, Webster, K.K. De Valois, & Lingelbach, 1986), whereas such surround interactions as are to be seen in cells at earlier levels extend up to much higher temporal frequencies. Furthermore, direct evidence has been reported of units in V4 that do exhibit some of the extended interactions involved in perceptual contrast and constancy effects (Zeki, 1985). The nature of the neural transformations that take place within V4 has yet to be determined, however.

Suprathreshold Contrast Responses

Throughout this section we have been discussing the *threshold* CSF and explaining various visual phenomena on the basis of low- and high-frequency attenuation relative to the middle spatial and temporal frequencies. But, it might legitimately be argued, most of our everyday vision is at suprathreshold levels, to which the shape of the threshold CSF might not apply. There are in fact some data which suggest that at suprathreshold levels, the contrast response function is almost flat rather than bowed at high and low spatial frequencies.

It was first noted by Georgeson and Sullivan (1975) that high (and also to some extent low) spatial frequency gratings never appear as faint and fuzzy as low-contrast gratings of the middle spatial frequencies do. Instead, if they are seen at all, high-frequency gratings appear to be of relatively high contrast. This has been quantified by having subjects match the apparent contrast of gratings of different spatial frequencies against the contrast of a standard middle-frequency grating. Subjects in fact see a 20-c/deg grating of, say, 20% contrast as having about the same contrast as a 5-c/deg grating of the same physical contrast, despite the fact that the lower frequency pattern is far above its contrast threshold and the higher frequency just slightly so (see Figure 5.11). One does not see any obvious correlate of this phenomenon in the responses of striate cortex cells. Cells tuned to high spatial frequencies give graded numbers of spikes to patterns of increasing contrast, just as do units tuned to lower spatial frequencies, with no obvious differences in their intensity-response slopes. It may thus be that any perceptual enhancement of high spatial frequency contrast reflects poststriate processes.

While these contrast-matching experiments are very interesting, we do not feel that one is justified in considering the bowed CSF function to be just a threshold epiphenomenon. For one thing, contrast matching is a quite different procedure

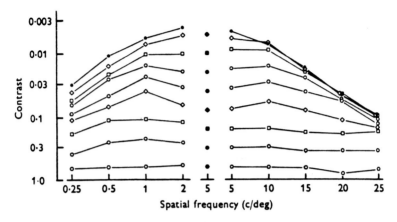

FIG. 5.11   Contrast matching. Subjects were asked to determine the contrast of test gratings of various spatial frequencies which perceptually matched the contrast of a 5-c/deg
reference grating. The lines connect the test grating contrasts which appear to match the
corresponding reference grating. Note that once each test grating is well above its own
threshold the functions become virtually flat. Thus although the threshold at 20 c/deg is
much higher than that for 5 c/deg (top line), when both gratings have a physical contrast
of 20% or more, their perceptual contrasts are also equal (bottom lines) (from Georgeson
& Sullivan, 1975. Reprinted by permission).

than a sensitivity measurement, and one should not conclude from such experiments what the suprathreshold contrast-response function is for different spatial frequencies. For another, other measures, such as magnitude estimation
(Cannon, 1979), indicate that the bowed shape of the CSF is maintained for
suprathreshold contrasts, rather than completely flattening out.

Two other considerations should also make us hesitate to conclude that the
classic CSF is of limited importance and only applies to the rare occasions when
we are perceiving threshold patterns. One is that while many visual patterns are
indeed of fairly high contrast, we believe that the more critical variable is not
the overall pattern contrast but rather the contrasts or power within the rather
narrow bandwidths of the individual spatial frequency channels (see Chapter 6).
The other consideration is that of inhibitory interactions among spatial frequency channels. Many psychophysical tests, under both threshold and suprathreshold conditions, have been carried out with simple single grating patterns
of very restricted spatial frequency spectra. When multiple spatial frequencies
are present in the field, however, powerful inhibitory interactions can be seen
(see Chapter 11). Under most normal visual conditions, the stimuli in all parts
of the visual field are quite complex. Mutual inhibitory interactions among the
many stimulated channels might cut down the sensitivity of each, so that the
system may under normal circumstances be operating much closer to threshold
than one might conclude just from the single sine wave sensitivity data.

CLASSICAL ACUITY MEASURES

Although spatial CSF measurements are now widely used in vision research, they are of relatively recent vintage. The first attempts at measuring contrast sensitivity across a broad range of spatial frequencies were those of Schade (1956). Historically, the study of spatial vision has emphasized measurements of acuity, the finest resolvable detail in a pattern of very high contrast. Clinically, acuity measures are still generally used to assess spatial vision.

The most familiar clinically used acuity test is the Snellen chart. Several rows of letters, of steadily decreasing size, are shown to the subject at a constant viewing distance. The size of the smallest letters that can be read gives a measure of acuity. This is commonly expressed as a fraction relating the distance at which a subject can discriminate a standard pattern to the distance at which a "normal" subject can perform the same task. Thus a person whose Snellen acuity is 20/40 can read at 20 ft what the prototypical normal subject can read at 40 ft. At the 20/20 acuity level, the discriminative features (e.g., the separation between the bars of the letter E) are separated by 1' arc. A grating with the same separation between its bars would be 30 c/deg.

There are some obvious problems with the use of the Snellen chart to measure acuity. Not all letters are equally discriminable from each other, even though they may be of the same height and feature width. It is much easier to discriminate a B from an I, for instance, than a B from an R. In the first case, the overall shapes of the letters are sufficiently different that the letters can be discriminated solely on that basis even when the fine details cannot be resolved. (Some Snellen charts compensate for this by using only letters of approximately equal discriminability.) The Snellen letter chart also has the obvious fault of being restricted to use with people who can read the alphabet, thus limiting its use among small children and those who are illiterate. Another problem associated with the use of Snellen charts is that if the number of letters per line is inversely proportional to the size of the letters, as it often is when line length is kept constant, one may obtain quite a different estimate of acuity than if the number of letters and their relative spacing are kept constant (Bailey & Lovie, 1976). Some of these problems can be simply solved by the use of either of two other common variations of the eye chart. One is the Landolt C test, in which all the forms to be discriminated are annuli with one section cut out, similar to the letter C. In this version of an acuity test the stimulus can be oriented with the gap at top, bottom, left, or right, the subject's task being to tell where the gap lies. This requires neither letter recognition nor sophisticated verbal ability. A similar variation uses a standardized stimulus similar to the capital letter E. Again, it can be oriented in any of the four directions, and the subject's task is to identify the direction in which it points. This, like the Landolt C, overcomes two of the major objections to the Snellen chart. In clinical practice these are commonly used measures of acuity. In the laboratory, however, there have been many others, e.g., subjects are asked to see how close two dots or two lines can be brought and still discriminated as two rather than one.

We do not wish to present a long discussion of common clinical acuity measures here, but merely to remark that acuity tests such as those discussed above are, to a first approximation, measures of the high spatial frequency cut-off point in the CSF. (For a more complete discussion of acuity measures see Westheimer's chapter in Adler's *Physiology of the Eye*, 1965.) In most acuity tests, the major experimental manipulation of the test pattern is a reduction in the size of the feature to be discriminated, e.g., the gap between two bars, until it can no longer be resolved. The effect of this is to push the relevant portion of the pattern's spatial frequency spectrum to higher spatial frequency ranges. Thus, in essence, such acuity tests measure the highest spatial frequencies discriminable at a given contrast (usually approaching 100%). The contrast sensitivity function, on the other hand, measures the lowest contrast detectable at a given spatial frequency. For the highest visible spatial frequencies, these two kinds of tests must be measuring the same thing, since threshold contrast at the least detectable spatial frequencies would also approach 100%.

In the case of the Snellen letters, the situation is somewhat more complex in that the letters contain a broad spectrum of spatial frequency components, and the discrimination is not necessarily based on the highest frequencies involved. The general shape of a letter or other stimulus may be defined by the low spatial frequency components contained in it, while the finer details (which are those that the test is intended to measure) are related to higher spatial frequency components. Thus in the case of the Snellen letters one can have poor sensitivity for very high spatial frequencies and still identify certain letters by their overall shapes. This is one reason that the use of a simple Snellen chart can be problematical.

Given the relationship between contrast sensitivity to high spatial frequencies and standard acuity measures, it should come as no surprise to find that they vary in much the same manner with luminance and with retinal eccentricity. Acuity falls off dramatically with either a reduction in luminance (try reading this book under very dim light for an example) or with an increase in retinal eccentricity (focus on the page number and see how many lines you are able to read). This correlates, of course, with the fact that the high frequency fall-off of the CSF occurs at lower and lower spatial frequencies as luminance is lowered or retinal eccentricity increased. The CSF measures the sensitivity of the visual system to spatial variations in luminance across the whole visible range of spatial frequencies. Acuity tests, on the other hand, assess only one point, usually the highest point in that range, and are thus very limited measures. It may seem strange, then, that nearly all optometrists and ophthalmologists use only acuity measures and thus get a very limited assessment of spatial vision. There are three reasons that this is so, one theoretical and two practical. The first is the widespread belief that object recognition and pattern perception depend almost exclusively on the perception of fine detail—sharp edges, for example—which is formed by high spatial frequency components. This belief is buttressed by the observation that we can easily recognize figures in simple line drawings, and it is particularly prevalent among those of us who spend a great deal of time reading, where the perception of fine details is in fact crucial. However, at many points in this book, we take issue with this point of view. We believe that low spatial frequency information is at least as important as high frequency information for object detection and recognition, and for many other aspects of vision. For clinical data relevant to this question see Marron and Bailey (1982).

The other reasons for the use of acuity tests rather than complete measures of contrast sensitivity in most clinical settings are somewhat more compelling. The first is the technical difficulty of measuring the CSF as compared to the ease of using the standard acuity tests. The latter require only readily available printed test charts or slide projectors and an appropriately lighted test chamber. Contrast sensitivity measurements, on the other hand, require the generation of sinusoidal gratings of many different spatial frequencies, each of variable contrast. This is most readily done on a display oscilloscope with electronic control circuitry, using equipment not available in most clinical settings. There have been attempts to produce simpler printed test gratings which could be used to assess contrast sensitivity, but to date none is widely used.

As an addendum, we note that low-contrast versions of standard letter charts have been developed (e.g., Regan & Neima, 1983) and are being tested and used in some clinics. When the overall contrast is reduced, the spectral power in each spatial frequency band is correspondingly reduced. If the contrast is pushed low enough, the power in the high spatial frequencies will be reduced below threshold levels. In that case, the letters could only be detected and identified by the use of the lower spatial frequency components. This in effect allows one to measure not just sensitivity to the highest spatial frequencies, but the (possibly more relevant) lower frequencies as well.

The remaining reason for primarily using standard acuity measures in a clinical setting is perhaps the most telling. Many causes of high spatial frequency sensitivity loss are optical, and if so, can often be alleviated by the use of corrective spectacle lenses. Low spatial frequency losses in sensitivity, however, cannot be corrected by such simple measures, since they generally do not have an optical origin. Purely on practical grounds, then, standard acuity measures reveal the major correctable optical defects, while the additional deficits that might be shown by determining the full CSF are probably intractable. It makes sense, then, for clinicians to expend their limited time and resources on those problems which can be alleviated rather than on others which may be equally or more serious but which cannot be treated.

There are some situations, however, in which the measurement of the complete CSF would be of great use to a clinician. We shall mention two. The more common of these two concerns cataract patients. Hess and Woo (1978) have measured the CSFs of a population of patients with cataracts (a clouding of the lens that can eventually produce functional blindness). They found two distinct types of visual loss that occurred with cataract. The first was a high-frequency loss with little deficit in the low spatial frequencies. The second was an overall loss in contrast sensitivity affecting the low frequencies as well as the high. This, they reported, was by far the more disabling problem. Patients with such low-frequency losses reported much more severe visual problems than did patients with only high-frequency loss. Both sets of patients, however, gave similar measures on a classical acuity test. Thus, a patient might, from acuity measures alone, appear to have too slight a defect to demand treatment when in fact he was suffering from an extreme loss of vision. If an ophthalmologist needed information on the severity of the visual deficit to help make a decision about the appropriate time for surgery, it would obviously be much more useful to know whether the loss was restricted to high spatial frequencies than just to know an acuity score.

The other situation in which it would be extremely useful to measure the entire contrast sensitivity function is in diagnosing certain types of visual/neurological problems. It is not uncommon to have patients complain of rather ill-defined visual losses. If no deficits appear on standard acuity and visual field tests, it is easy to conclude that a patient is malingering. Repeated complaints would certainly try the patience of the most conscientious practitioner. But consider the following possibility. Suppose a patient should develop a neurological problem that was reflected in a contrast sensitivity loss restricted to the middle spatial frequency range. His performance on acuity tests would be unchanged, since those tests depend only on the integrity of the high spatial frequency system. The effects of the loss on his visual behavior might be catastrophic, though. Although it might be very difficult for him to describe his difficulties, they would be very real indeed. And the only way the loss could readily be detected and identified would be by measuring his complete CSF. This is not just a hypothetical situation, but has in fact been reported for patients in the early stages of multiple sclerosis (Regan, Bartol, Murray, & Beverley, 1982). They may complain of vague, poorly defined visual losses; on testing, they are found to have a selective sensitivity loss in the middle spatial frequency range. Thus, a neurologist or ophthalmologist who has patients appear with such devastating but undefined visual losses might be wise to consider measuring the entire CSF, not just the high end of it that is reflected in acuity tests.

In summary, then, it can be seen that classical acuity measures are largely a rather imprecise means of determining just one point on the spatial CSF. Acuity can be deduced (though not always perfectly) from the CSF, but the total spatial CSF contains much important additional information about the spatial capabilities of the individual. In extolling the virtues of the CSF, we do not want to imply that it measures all the variables relevant to visual perception. There are many complexities in the whole problem of visual pattern recognition that go far beyond the elementary tasks measured in the CSF (or in the classical acuity tasks). But considering, as we do in this treatment of spatial vision, only the initial, rather elementary stages of the process, we would argue that the whole CSF is much more informative than are classical acuity tests alone.

Hyperacuity

There is a third kind of measure of sensitivity to spatial variations, which bears a superficial resemblance to the measures of sensitivity to spatial separation (such as the two-point threshold) just described. However, since in these tests the resolution is some 10 to 30 times finer than in standard acuity tests, they have been termed hyperacuity measures. Of the many types of hyperacuity, two of particular interest are Vernier acuity and stereoacuity. In Vernier acuity a subject is asked to judge whether or not two line segments, end to end with a gap between them, would, if extended, form a continuous line. One can do almost as well with a variant of the task consisting of just two dots, which are to be judged to be lined up vertically or not. A lateral offset between the lines or dots as small as 2 to 5″ of arc has been found to be detectable, as against 1′ of arc between the finest resolvable bars in a classical acuity test (Westheimer & McKee, 1977). The same threshold is found in stereoacuity, in which the precision with which an observer can align two lines in depth is measured in binocular vision. Similar results are also found for the detection of a sudden lateral jump of a line (Westheimer, 1979).

The similarity of the terms acuity and hyperacuity is unfortunate, because it suggests that similar processes are involved—which is not the case, as pointed out by Westheimer (1979). In the classical acuity tests the fundamental nature of the task is to discriminate between two different figures—to tell whether one or two lines are present. In terms of the CSF, acuity is related to the highest spatial frequency detectable. On the other hand, the hyperacuity tests measure the observer's ability to determine the *location* of the relevant stimulus characteristics. Hyperacuity could thus be related to the determination of the *phase* of the sine wave components involved (although Westheimer, 1977, deems it unlikely).

In principle, localization, or determination of phase, can be carried out to any degree of precision, limited only by noise, given a sufficient amount of information. This is not true for acuity. Hyperacuity is not limited by the spacing of the spatial samples in the same way as is two-point resolution. As discussed in Chapter 2, the spatial separation of foveal receptors would by itself determine the high spatial frequency limit of the CSF and thus acuity (even if optical factors did not). However, the receptor separation does *not* set the limit for the localization of some feature, or the determination of the phases of detectable (lower) frequencies in the pattern, which is the basic capability required for so-called hyperacuity. A simple linear model of visual processing would predict that hyperacuity would be far superior, by a factor of 10 or more, to two-point or grating acuity limits (Geisler, 1984). One thus need not postulate some complex, higher-order visual processing capability to account for fine hyperacuity thresholds.

As an example of the way in which one could localize a point of light to a far greater precision than the interreceptor spacing, consider the upper portion of Figure 5.12. Here two receptors, A and B, feed into some later unit that differ-

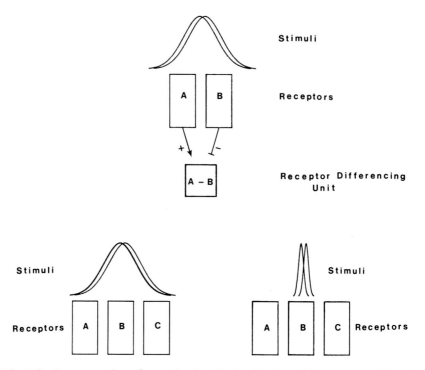

FIG. 5.12   Demonstration of a mechanism for localization with greater precision than the interreceptor spacing. Note that such a mechanism would only work with a blurred point spread function.

ences their outputs. When the point spread function of the spot is centered slightly closer to A than to B, A would give, say, a response of 55 and B of 45. The unit differencing their output would thus give a response of 10. A slight displacement to position 2 (much less than the interreceptor distance) would now give outputs of 45 and 55 from A and B, respectively, and a difference of −10. If the output of this differencing unit could be read accurately, even smaller displacements than this would be detectable. Rather than one differencing unit giving a variable output, one might have an array of later elements, each of which is maximally activated by a different proportion of output from A and B. Thus these later units would by interpolation detect displacements of the pattern far smaller than the A to B receptor spacing. Barlow (1979) has suggested, in fact, that the numerous small neurons in layer 4c of the striate cortex might be involved in something like this sort of interpolation. Such models do not account, however, for many of the most intriguing aspects of hyperacuity, such as the fact that the two lines in a Vernier task can be separated by a considerable amount (indeed, a small separation *improves* performance), or even replaced by just two dots defining imaginary vertical lines; or that one has good hyperacuity for patterns which are rapidly moving across the field (Westheimer & McKee,

1975, 1978). These obviously demand more sophisticated models than any so far offered.

It is important to note that the detection of a spatial position difference, as discussed above, would only be possible if the light distributions from the two patterns were sufficiently broad to extend across more than one receptor (see the lower portion of Figure 5.12). This suggests that it may not even be the highest detectable spatial frequencies which are crucial for hyperacuity, contrary to the situation with other types of acuity. We know from psychophysical studies (see Chapter 8) that our ability to localize or discriminate the phase of high spatial frequency patterns is very poor. This is consistent with our finding (R.L. De Valois, Albrecht, & Thorell, 1982) that complex cells, which are not phase specific, are on the average tuned to higher spatial frequencies than are phase-specific simple cells. Thus on these grounds also we would expect that detection of the highest spatial frequencies, which determines acuity, would not be involved in hyperacuity. In fact, it is not. Westheimer (1979) has shown that considerable defocus (which demodulates high spatial frequencies) leads to little loss in Vernier (hyper)acuity. The highest spatial frequencies are thus apparently not required; it is likely that middle spatial frequency information, to which we are most sensitive, is mainly utilized in making such judgments. The factors that limit hyperacuity are those which limit brightness discrimination and the overall CSF, not those which limit acuity or detection of the very highest spatial frequencies.

6

Multiple Spatial Frequency Channels

In Chapter 5, we described the CSF, discussed the manner in which both high and low spatial frequency attenuation might occur in the visual system, and pointed out some consequences for visual perception of the shape of the CSF. In this chapter we address the question of whether a single broadly tuned mechanism underlies the CSF. Until the late 1960s, visual scientists had implicitly assumed that to be the case: the low frequency attenuation was attributed to center-surround antagonism in the RFs of ganglion cells, and all ganglion cells (and implicitly later cells as well) were assumed to have the same broad sensitivity profile as the CSF. In 1968, however, Campbell and Robson made the then revolutionary suggestion that the visual system might contain something like groups of independent, quasilinear band-pass filters, each of which was more narrowly tuned for spatial frequency than the overall CSF. The CSF would then reflect not the sensitivity of a single typical visual channel or cell, but some envelope of the sensitivities of all these multiple filters, or channels. Somewhat similar proposals were also put forth by Pantle and Sekuler (1968) and by Thomas (1970). These ideas had a large impact on vision because they provided a model of how the visual system might be analyzing spatial patterns which was quite different from the mechanisms previous workers had considered. In this new model, the visual system was considered to be operating not purely in the space domain, analyzing the amounts of light at different points in space or edges where the amount of light abruptly changes, but rather operating at least partially in the spatial frequency domain, responding to patterns on the basis of their underlying frequency content.

One of many attractions of this suggestion is its similarity to generally accepted ideas about the manner in which the auditory system operates. There is great appeal in (and some sound scientific grounds for) assuming that the nervous system solves analogous problems in similar ways. Thanks to more than a century of diligent work by auditory scientists, there is a large and impressive body of knowledge and highly developed theory about the ways in which the auditory nervous system might carry out a quasilinear frequency analysis in the temporal domain. If the visual system should be performing a similar analysis in the spatial domain, many of the ideas first developed by auditory theorists might be relevant to the visual system. (See Chapter 12 for a more extensive discussion of many reasons why the visual system might be performing a local spatial frequency filtering of visual information.)

In the initial formulations of ideas about multiple channels, and in almost all the early tests of the ideas, only one-dimensional stimulus patterns were used and the possible operation of one-dimensional filters considered. In this chapter, therefore, we confine our attention to such simple patterns. Two-dimensional channels will be considered in Chapter 9.

DEFINITION OF "CHANNEL"

There is now a considerable body of psychophysical, physiological, and anatomical evidence supporting the suggestion that the CSF represents the envelope of many more narrowly tuned channels. We shall consider several types of experiments bearing on this issue in turn, but we need first to address the question of what is meant by a "channel." The generalized notion of a channel refers to a filtering mechanism, something which passes some, but not all, of the information that may impinge upon it. Spatial or temporal frequency filters may transmit whatever input is present above a particular frequency (high-pass), below a particular frequency (low-pass), or within a restricted frequency region, with rejection at both ends (band-pass). A system that filters with multiple channels, then, would be one with a number of different band-pass channels tuned to different frequency ranges, plus possibly low-pass and high-pass channels at either end of the range. We can see that the concept has two essential components. One is that of spatial frequency filters sufficiently narrowly tuned that each is responsive to only some fraction of the total range encompassed by the organism's CSF (see Figure 6.1). The second is that of parallel processing of information, in which the pattern within a given limited spatial region is not analyzed on the basis of the point-by-point luminance level, but rather is simultaneously analyzed by multiple spatial frequency filters, each responding insofar as the spectrum of this spatial pattern contains energy within its particular spatial frequency band (see Figure 6.2).

Certain difficulties arise when one attempts to specify more precisely than we have above what constitutes a psychophysical "channel," or when one considers exactly what the physiological underpinnings may be of the hypothesized channels. One widely recognized definition of a "channel" is that it is composed of all those cells with receptive fields that are identical in every respect save retinal location (cf. Graham, 1980). A group of cells, each with a certain RF periodicity (giving it a particular spatial frequency bandwidth) and optimally sensitive to, say, 2 c/deg, would constitute the 2-c/deg "channel" which would detect the presence of energy at that spatial frequency in the stimulus pattern. Another group of cells similar except for being tuned, say, to 3 c/deg would be another, 3-c/deg channel. Representatives of each of these channels would have RFs located in each region of at least the central visual field. All of these spatially dispersed 2-c/deg units would together, then, form the 2-c/deg channel.

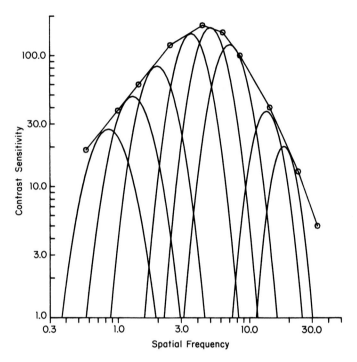

FIG. 6.1   Spatial contrast sensitivity function as the envelope of many more narrowly tuned spatial frequency selective channels.

It can be seen that this definition introduces still a third aspect of the channel concept, in addition to those of multiple parallel units and narrow spatial frequency tuning that we discussed earlier. This is that the underlying units have spatially restricted RFs and are somehow related to similar units with RFs in different spatial locations. Most psychophysical studies related to multiple channels—all the earlier ones and most still done today—used large, redundant stimulus displays, e.g., gratings covering a large part of the visual field, and they considered only the detection or appearance of the overall pattern. Given this, it was easy to think of the process as a global one, although few theorists (e.g., Kabrisky, 1966) explicitly proposed that the visual system might be doing a global frequency analysis. It is immediately obvious to anyone who has examined the properties of striate units that cells at this level have restricted RFs, as do those at earlier levels; any spatial filtering they do must be on a quite local basis. So a spatially extended 2-c/deg grating will be responded to by many units tuned to this frequency, but with RFs scattered across the visual field. Graham's (1980) definition of channel raises the important issue of how these spatially displaced units of similar tuning properties are related to each other. The implication is that their outputs may be combined in some more global 2-c/deg detector.

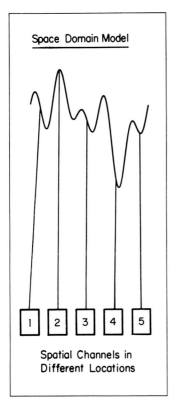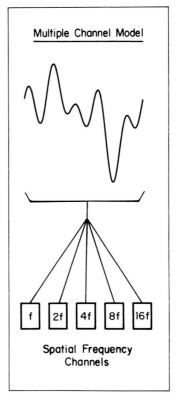

FIG. 6.2   Two simplified models of spatial analysis. In the space domain model (left), each point in space is analyzed by a separate filter which responds to the average luminance in a small region around that point. In the multiple spatial frequency channel model (right), a somewhat larger but still delimited region of space is analyzed by each of several fairly narrowly tuned spatial frequency filters, each of which responds to the power in the pattern which falls within its frequency band. In the space domain model the analysis is carried out serially across space on a point-by-point basis. In the multiple spatial frequency channel model the analysis over the same restricted region is carried out in parallel by different spatial frequency filters.

While this aspect of multiple channels is an important issue, we would like to restrict our discussion of it here, because it takes us beyond our present knowledge of probable physiological substrates. Some complex striate cells show increased responses to increasing numbers of cycles of a grating of their optimal spatial frequency, but yet have quite broad spatial frequency bandwidths (Webster & R.L. De Valois, 1985). This suggests that these cells are integrating the outputs of more spatially restricted units (ones tuned to this spatial frequency) whose RFs are scattered over some distance. However, the total extent of the RFs of even such complex cells is only a small part of the whole visual field. If more global spatial frequency channels exist, we can with considerable certainty state that they are not at or before the striate cortex. Cells at later levels, however, have increasingly extensive RFs, and it is possible that some poststriate cells may respond to the amount of energy at, say, 2 c/deg over a whole large part of the visual field. However, since at the present time evidence on this question is lacking, we would like to concentrate on questions on which physiological and psychophysical evidence converge.

The main problem we see with most definitions of "channel" is that they imply a limited set of properties, e.g., bandwidths, in the underlying units, and a static character to the channel properties. Such assumptions may be useful for modeling purposes, but they do not seem to us to be in accord with either the physiological or the psychophysical evidence. Striate cortex recordings (e.g., R.L. De Valois, Albrecht, & Thorell, 1982) have shown that the various cells that are maximally sensitive to a grating of, say, 2 c/deg vary greatly in the breadth of their spatial frequency tuning (and thus, by implication, in their RF profiles). It seems to us reasonable to assume that many if not all of those cells will be contributing to the detection of a 2-c/deg grating (or the amount of energy at 2 c/deg in a more complex pattern), rather than just a small subset of units with a particular RF shape. Also, as the contrast of a 2-c/deg pattern is raised many more units will be activated, some of which may have different properties than those responsive at a lower contrast level, e.g., a unit tuned optimally to 2.5 c/deg may now be responsive as well. With practice in detecting a particular pattern, one may learn to attend to some subset of the whole population initially involved, thus accounting for increases in sensitivity and narrower bandwidths over time (K.K. De Valois, 1977b). There are also inhibitory interactions among units (see Chapter 11). In some situations, such as masking, there may be more inhibitory activity than in other situations, thus different populations of units may be involved, and perhaps the individual properties of underlying units may change as well.

This heterogeneity among neurons and the variability in their properties are bothersome only if one considers that "channels" are discrete structural entities which are invariant with any stimulus parameter other than spatial frequency. While it is certainly easier to think in terms of models of channel behavior if one assumes channels that are cast in concrete, it seems very unlikely that this is in fact the case! We are thus led to the position that spatial frequency channels are composed of whatever cells are contributing to the transmission of information about a stimulus with power at particular spatial frequency at any given moment. They are thus not rigidly defined and certainly cannot be described under any and all circumstances by the specification of one or two parameters.

Some (e.g., Westheimer, 1981) have questioned whether the channel concept in spatial vision has been useful at all. Surely its success in the prediction of the detectability of complex visual patterns (e.g., Campbell & Robson, 1968; Campbell, Carpenter, & Levinson, 1969; Graham & Nachmias, 1971), or the explanation of perceptual changes with adaptation (e.g., Blakemore & Sutton, 1969) is sufficient justification. Another is that the notion of spatial frequency channels and quasilinear frequency filtering has prompted a salutary reexamination of ill-specified but widely accepted models which assumed that the visual system performed a naturalistic feature analysis of spatial patterns. Such ideas, which have great intuitive appeal, can often blind one to considering other possibilities that may more accurately reflect the real characteristics of the system. Whether or not a frequency filtering model is eventually superseded by other ideas (as virtually any scientific model will be as our understanding increases), it will have played an important role in forcing us to reconsider readily accepted but perhaps ill-founded assumptions about how the visual system functions.

A final justification for the use of channel models in general is that they are in accord with much physiological evidence. Whether or not we understand completely why the visual system might choose to use multiple channels which are selective along the domain of spatial frequency (however, see the discussion in Chapter 12), the fact is that such selectivity is prominent in striate cortex cells. Whatever its function, spatial frequency filtering is something which the visual system seems indubitably to be doing. It behooves us to note and try to understand, not to ignore this.

Psychophysical Evidence for Multiple Spatial Frequency Channels

The initial ideas with respect to multiple spatial frequency channels, and most of the early evidence for the notions, came from psychophysical experiments of various sorts. These experiments bear on both of the related but distinct fundamental issues mentioned earlier: whether there are multiple (versus single) parallel spatial channels, and whether these channels are selective for spatial frequency (as opposed, for instance, to size or pattern width).

Detection of Patterns Based on Amplitude Spectra

In the initial paper that raised the possibility that the visual system spatial frequency filters patterns, Campbell and Robson (1968) measured the detection threshold for various complex patterns and related the detectability of these to their amplitude spectra and the observer's sine wave CSF. If detection depends on the activation of one (or more) independent narrow-band filters, a pattern should first be visible when (and only when) any one of its frequency components reaches its own threshold contrast. An alternative possibility, which was the dominant theoretical view earlier, is that the overall contrast of a pattern is the critical factor in determining its threshold. It will be remembered from Chapter 1 that contrast can be defined as $L_{max} - L_{min}/L_{max} + L_{min}$. Two different patterns, e.g., a square wave grating and a sine wave grating, can have equal contrasts—equal peaks and troughs—but very different amplitudes of the underlying frequency components. Only if the visual system were filtering patterns into multiple spatial frequency components would one expect the detection of various patterns to be related to their spatial frequency amplitude spectra rather than to their overall contrast, when these differ.

Campbell and Robson found that for a variety of periodic complex waveforms (square and rectangular wave gratings, sawtooth waveforms, etc.) the amplitudes of the individual spatial frequency components, not the overall contrasts of the patterns, determined threshold detection. Consider, for instance, the detectability of sine wave and square wave gratings. The fundamental component of a square wave (see Chapter 1) is a sine wave of the same frequency but of $4/\pi$ (= 1.27) times the amplitude of the square wave. If the overall contrast of the pattern is the crucial variable, a sine wave and a square wave grating should be detected at the same contrast; if the patterns are being detected on the basis of the outputs of various parallel, narrow-band spatial frequency channels, on the other hand, the square wave grating should be detectable at a lower pattern contrast. Campbell and Robson found the square wave grating in fact to be more detectable by precisely the ratio predicted from a consideration of the relative amplitudes of the square and sine wave fundamentals for all gratings except those of very low spatial frequencies (see below).

Another important observation that Campbell and Robson reported was that at threshold a sine wave and a square wave of the same fundamental frequency are perceptually indiscriminable. Only when the third harmonic of the square wave reaches its own (independent) threshold do the two patterns become discriminably different perceptually. This indicates that at threshold only the fundamental component of the square wave (which is of course of the largest amplitude) is being responded to by the visual system, as one would predict if the square wave were being broken down into its separate frequency components in multiple spatial frequency channels.

Campbell and Robson found the linear predictions to hold quite precisely when square waves of moderate to high spatial frequencies were studied. The human CSF shows marked attenuation at low spatial frequencies, however, which would lead to quite different predictions for low-frequency square waves. Since sensitivity to low spatial frequencies drops rapidly, it should be possible to find a frequency range in which the visual system would be more sensitive to the third harmonic of a square wave (which has only one third the amplitude of the fundamental) than to the fundamental frequency itself. At that point the $4/\pi$ relationship between threshold contrasts for sine and square waves should break down, with the square wave becoming progressively more detectable relative to the sine wave as the fundamental frequency is reduced, since the sine wave, of course, has no higher harmonics. Campbell and Robson found this to hold, as well, thus buttressing their argument.

Another demonstration that the amplitude of the individual spatial frequency components, not the overall contrast of the pattern, determines detection thresholds was presented by Graham and Nachmias (1971), who examined the detectability of a grating composed of two frequency components, f and $3f$, as a function of the relative phase of the two gratings. When the two gratings are combined in such a relative phase angle that their peaks coincide (peaks-add), the contrast of the pattern is much greater than when they are combined so that their peaks are out of phase (peaks-subtract). Figure 6.3 shows the luminance profiles of two such patterns and their appearance. If the overall pattern contrast determines detection, the peaks-add grating should be far more detectable since it has greater overall contrast. However, Graham and Nachmias found that the patterns were equally detectable: the amplitudes of the individual spatial frequency components, not the overall contrast, determine detectability.

Frequency-Specific Adaptation

Perhaps the single most convincing psychophysical demonstration that the visual system contains multiple channels, each of which operates more or less as a band-pass spatial frequency filter, is spatial frequency specific adaptation. When, by selective adaptation, one can differentially affect either the sensitivity to or the appearance of two different patterns, then it may be assumed that the two patterns are processed by nonidentical underlying structures. If adaptation to pattern A reduces sensitivity to A but does not affect sensitivity to B, then there is the strong implication that the neural elements that were affected by the adaptation subserve the detection of A but not of B. Note that this does not carry any implication about the type of neural change that might underlie it, whether fatigue, prolonged inhibition, gain control, or whatever, although that is an interesting question in its own right.

Pattern-specific adaptation has provided a compelling argument for the existence of multiple spatial frequency channels. Spatial frequency specific adaptation was demonstrated initially by Pantle and Sekuler (1968) and by Blakemore and Campbell (1969). The former used square wave patterns, while the latter used sinusoidal gratings. Since square waves are more complex (i.e., they have more frequency components), the experiment using sine waves is more straightforward. We will therefore consider sine wave adaptation as in the Blakemore and Campbell experiment in more detail.

In order to produce a baseline against which to measure possible adaptation effects, contrast sensitivity is first measured for a variety of different spatial frequencies, thus defining an unadapted CSF. The subject then adapts to a high contrast grating of a single spatial frequency, following which the CSF is measured again. During the retest period the subject must periodically readapt for a short period in order to maintain a high, constant level of adaptation.

Before adaptation, the CSF typically has an inverted U shape, with highest sensitivity to middle spatial frequencies. If there were a single channel underlying the CSF, as was implicitly assumed by early investigators, the effect of adaptation should be to lower the overall CSF uniformly. On the other hand, if the overall sensitivity were some envelope of the sensitivities of multiple channels tuned to different spatial frequency ranges, adaptation to some one spatial frequency might produce a loss in contrast sensitivity over a restricted range of spatial frequencies. This is what Blakemore and Campbell in fact found, as did

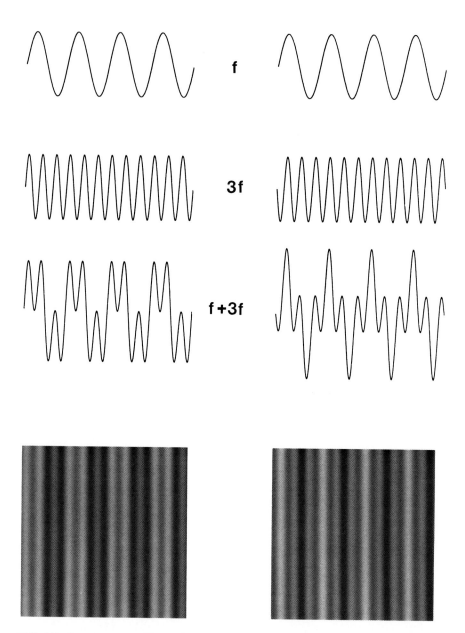

FIG. 6.3   Luminance profiles and patterns produced by adding f and $3f$. The addition of equal-amplitude components at f and $3f$ in either peaks-subtract (left) or peaks-add (right) phase produces the luminance profiles shown above. Below each profile is a photograph of the corresponding pattern.

Pantle and Sekuler; see Figure 6.4. If the subject adapts to a middle-range spatial frequency, say, 5 c/deg, the CSF will show a band-limited depression centered at the adaptation frequency, with a loss at the adaptation frequency of as much as 1 log unit. According to Blakemore and Campbell, spatial frequencies on either side of the adaptation frequency will show a smaller loss, decreasing as the test frequency is further removed from the adaptation frequency. The loss generally falls to zero, the postadaptation contrast sensitivity being the same as the preadaptation contrast sensitivity, when the test frequency is about an octave (different by a factor of 2) on either side of the adaptation frequency, and frequencies further removed are not affected. Blakemore and Campbell reported that the function describing the adaptational loss is asymmetric, having a steeper high-frequency fall-off, with a full bandwidth at half amplitude of about 1.2 octaves. They found the effect to be centered on the adaptation frequency for all frequencies above 3 c/deg. Below that, the loss remained centered at 3 c/deg. They also reported that adaptation to high spatial frequencies produced slightly narrower adaptation functions than did adaptation to low frequencies.

It is also interesting to note that the apparent contrast of a suprathreshold grating may also be affected by adaptation to a high-contrast grating of similar spatial frequency (Blakemore, Muncey, & Ridley, 1971, 1973). Following adaptation to a grating of 2 c/deg, for example, subsequently viewed gratings of 2 c/deg, even though clearly suprathreshold, will appear to be of reduced contrast. The magnitude of the reduction in apparent contrast is a function of the similarity of test and adaptation gratings along the dimensions of spatial frequency and orientation and of the contrast of the adaptation grating. Thus the effects of

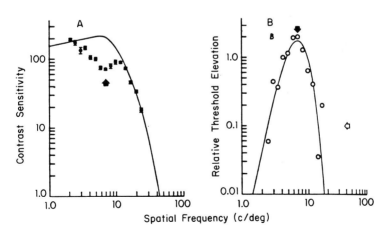

FIG. 6.4 (A) CSF before (solid line) and after (data points) adaptation to a grating of a single spatial frequency. (B) Threshold elevation at different spatial frequencies produced by the adaptation . Note the band-pass loss in contrast sensitivity around the adaptation frequency (indicated by arrows) (from Blakemore & Campbell, 1969. Reprinted by permission).

spatial frequency adaptation are not restricted to the detection of near-threshold patterns but can be seen in the appearance of high-contrast patterns, as well.

Several subsequent investigations have modified the description of one or more of the characteristics of the spatial frequency specific adaptation described by Blakemore and Campbell, as discussed below, but none of them has challenged the central finding—namely, that adaptation to a single spatial frequency produces a band-limited loss in contrast sensitivity centered at that frequency rather than depressing the entire CSF. The fact that adaptation produces a loss so profound yet so restricted indicates that the CSF does *not* describe the filtering characteristics of a single, broadly tuned analyzer. That any given part of the function can be selectively depressed demonstrates that the different spatial frequency regions are subserved by different structural elements with some considerable degree of independence.

One of the most puzzling aspects of the Blakemore and Campbell report was the finding that adaptation to frequencies lower than 3 c/deg produced a loss centered on 3 c/deg. It seems unlikely that there should be no low-frequency channels, given the fact that we can discriminate among various low frequencies with reasonable ease. If there were only one detector responding to all low frequencies, then such patterns should be indiscriminable if properly matched for contrast above threshold. Jones and Tulunay-Keesey (1975) showed that this finding of Blakemore and Campbell's was an artifact resulting from the small size of the grating display they used. If the display is sufficiently large, the adaptational loss follows the adapting frequency down to much lower spatial frequencies (see Figure 6.5). They pointed out that in a restricted stimulus display, with too few cycles, the power spectrum is spread over a broad range. For instance, an adaptation pattern with a nominal frequency of 1 c/deg on such a small display would have considerable power even beyond 3 c/deg. Since one is considerably more sensitive to 3 than to 1 c/deg, the maximum adaptation might well occur at 3 rather than at 1 c/deg.

There have been several other amendments and corrections to Blakemore and Campbell's original findings. Their results suggested completely independent channels: adaptation to one spatial frequency appeared to have no effect on contrast sensitivity to frequencies farther than one octave away from the adaptation frequency. Careful measurements have revealed, however, that contrast sensitivity to frequencies farther away may actually be increased by spatial frequency adaptation (K.K. De Valois, 1977b; Tolhurst & Barfield, 1978); see Figures 6.5 and 6.6. This suggests that spatial frequency channels are not truly independent, but rather may be mutually inhibitory. If so, reducing the activity of one channel would reduce the inhibition it exerts on channels tuned to other spatial frequencies, thus increasing their sensitivity. Similar suggestions of inhibitory interactions among different spatial frequency channels come from studies that have examined the effect of simultaneously adapting to more than one spatial frequency (e.g., Nachmias, Sansbury, Vassilev, & Weber, 1973; Stecher, Sigal, & Lange, 1973; Tolhurst, 1972b; K.K. De Valois & Switkes, 1980). The general finding is that adaptation to a pattern containing more than one spatial fre-

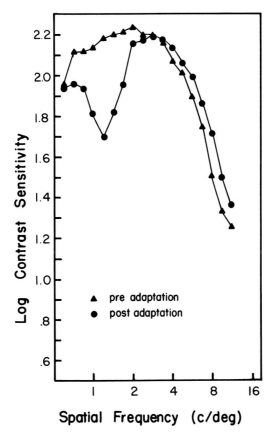

FIG. 6.5   Spatial frequency adaptation effect following adaptation to a low spatial frequency. Note that when a large display is used the loss in contrast sensitivity remains centered on the adaptation frequency (from K.K. De Valois, 1977b, *Vision Res., 17,* 1057-1065. Copyright 1977, Pergamon Journals, Inc. Reprinted by permission).

quency produces a smaller loss in contrast sensitivity than one would predict from a similar model that posited independent channels. The apparent inhibitory interactions revealed by such studies, however, are clearly relatively minor compared to the large loss of sensitivity at and around the adaptation frequency. These findings are important, though, in allowing us to understand better the physiological interactions (e.g., K.K. De Valois & Tootell, 1983) and organization underlying spatial frequency specific channels.

Other criticisms of the Blakemore and Campbell (1969) study deal with either psychophysical techniques or other aspects of the experimental methodology. For example, the method of adjustment, which they used, is often roundly condemned for being subject to criterion effects. While this certainly is true, replications of the study using more sophisticated forced-choice methods produce

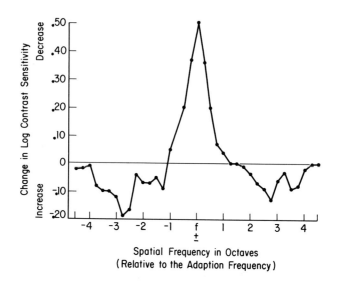

FIG. 6.6   Change in contrast sensitivity produced by spatial frequency specific adaptation. Note that in addition to the loss in contrast sensitivity for frequencies near the adaptation frequency, there is also an enhancement in contrast sensitivity for frequencies further removed (from K.K. De Valois, 1977b, *Vision Res., 17,* 1057–1065. Copyright 1977, Pergamon Journals, Inc. Reprinted by permission).

very similar results. The central finding of a band-limited, frequency-specific loss in contrast sensitivity following adaptation remains unchanged. Similarly, the free-scan viewing of a stationary grating has been shown to produce a small amount of patterned retinal adaptation, which might lead to retinal afterimages (Arend & Skavenski, 1979). However, the use of steady fixation and either drifting or phase-reversing (counterphase-flickering) adaptation gratings does not materially alter the findings of the experiment; nor does stabilization of the pattern on the retina combined with controlled modulation significantly change the effect (Jones & Tulunay-Keesey, 1975).

Spatial Frequency Specific Aftereffects

If, in a selective adaptation experiment such as those we have been discussing, prolonged inspection of a grating selectively depresses the sensitivity of just that restricted population of cortical cells tuned to the adaptation frequency (thus selectively inactivating one channel), there should also be measurable effects on the perceptual character of patterns seen later. (By perceptual character we mean to imply more than just the apparent contrast of a pattern, which, as we discussed above, also changes.) Blakemore and Sutton (1969) first noticed that there is a striking change in the appearance of certain grating patterns following adaptation: gratings of other nearby spatial frequencies were shifted in apparent spatial frequency. Specifically, gratings of a spatial frequency lower than the adaptation frequency appeared perceptually to be lower still after adaptation; higher frequencies appeared shifted still higher in spatial frequency after adaptation. This effect can be observed by inspecting the patterns in Figure 6.7. Note that the two gratings to the right are identical. Now adapt for a minute or two to the patterns on the left by staring at the fixation line, being careful to move your eyes constantly back and forth along the fixation line to reduce selective retinal adaptation and the formation of afterimages. Then glance briefly at the fixation point between the two gratings at right. Do they still appear identical? Most people readily see that the top grating, which now stimulates a region that had been adapted to a low spatial frequency; appears to be of a higher spatial frequency than the physically identical pattern at bottom right, which stimulates a region that had been adapted to a high frequency.

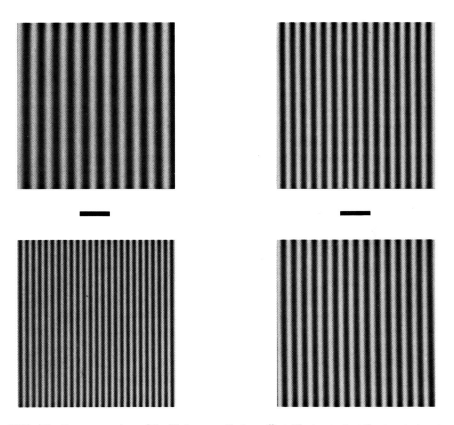

FIG. 6.7   Demonstration of the Blakemore-Sutton effect. First note that the two test gratings on the right are identical. Now adapt for about 1 min while scanning back and forth along the fixation bar between the two gratings on the left, then quickly shift your gaze to the fixation line between the test gratings on the right. They should now appear different in spatial frequency, each one being shifted away from the frequency of the adaptation grating that occupied the same retinal area.

This aftereffect, examined in further quantitative experiments by Blakemore, Nachmias, & Sutton (1970), can readily be explained on the basis of multiple spatial frequency channels. If, as shown in Figure 6.8, our perception of a pattern as having a particular spatial frequency is based on the relative activity rate in overlapping spatial channels, and if the effect of adaptation is to selectively depress the sensitivity (and responsiveness) of the channel(s) activated by the adaptation stimulus, the predicted shift in the apparent frequency of gratings away from that of the adaptation grating can be predicted. Note that this involves an important additional assumption—namely, that the outputs of the various spatial frequency channels are somehow labeled. In other words, it assumes that activity within a given mechanism does not just signal the presence of some contrast in the stimulus, but rather that it also signals a specific spatial frequency. Thus, one could unambiguously conclude that the stimulus contained energy at or near 2 c/deg if the 2-c/deg channel was active. Such an assumption is not required to explain the results of most of the detection experiments. As applied to the Blakemore and Sutton experiment, it requires some additional assumption about the way in which one interprets the outputs of multiple, simultaneously active detectors. A high-contrast pattern of a particular spatial frequency will activate many cells, only some of which are maximally sensitive at that spatial frequency (see our earlier discussion about the makeup

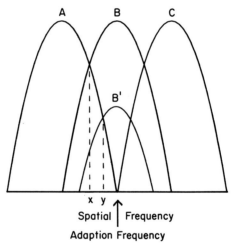

FIG. 6.8   A model of spatial frequency channels and the effects of adaptation, to account for the Blakemore-Sutton apparent spatial frequency shift. Three spatial frequency channels (A, B, and C) are presumed to signal the apparent spatial frequency in this region by their relative activity rates. For instance, *x* will have a certain apparent spatial frequency because it equally stimulates channels A and B. Following adaptation to a grating of the middle frequency, the sensitivity of channel B is reduced to B'. Now, a grating of frequency *y* will equally stimulate channels A and B (now B'), and thus will look the same as *x* had looked before adaptation.

of channels). In order to assign a spatial frequency to such a pattern, based on the output of a large, varied collection of cells, one might assume either that the frequency of the stimulus was the peak spatial frequency of the most active cell, or that the stimulus frequency was reflected by some central tendency of the distribution of peak frequencies of the active cells. In either case, the underlying assumption is that cells (or perhaps very small cortical regions) are tagged in such a way that activity in a given cell somehow signals a particular spatial frequency (or perhaps a narrow range of spatial frequencies). Some such assumption is necessary to explain the Blakemore and Sutton experiment, but any of a number of similar models would suffice.

Blakemore and Nachmias (1971) also measured both the loss in contrast sensitivity and the apparent spatial frequency shift produced by grating adaptation as a function of the orientation of the test grating relative to that of the adaptation grating. They found that when the test grating was tilted about $6\frac{3}{4}°$ with respect to the adaptation grating, the decline in the magnitude of *both* effects could be matched by a reduction in contrast (of the adaptation grating) by a factor of two. This quantitative similarity strongly suggests that a common underlying mechanism is responsible for both of these phenomena.

A similar shift in the apparent spatial frequency of a grating was demonstrated by Klein, Stromeyer, and Ganz (1974), using two simultaneously presented gratings rather than an adaptation pattern and a subsequent test pattern. They showed that the apparent spatial frequency of a grating within a small central test region depends, to some extent, upon the spatial frequency of a grating seen in a surrounding (but not overlapping) annulus. Gratings which are higher in frequency than the surrounding pattern appear to be still higher. Those which are lower in frequency than the surrounding pattern appear to be lower yet. The shifts in apparent spatial frequency as a function of the frequency of a surrounding grating section are similar to those seen in the Blakemore and Sutton adaptation experiment.

It is important to distinguish between these experiments and the earlier figural aftereffect demonstrations of Kohler and Wallach (1944). In the latter case, the subject steadily fixates an adaptation pattern, without (intended) eye movement, and then inspects a test pattern. The contours of the test pattern now appear to be displaced away from those of the adaptation pattern. It can be seen that the figural aftereffects of Kohler and Wallach consist of changes in the apparent position of contours after adaptation to nearby contours, but such a phenomenon cannot explain the Blakemore and Sutton aftereffect. Since the eyes are moving back and forth during adaptation to the pattern in Figure 6.7, the contours of the grating will stimulate all retinal areas approximately equally. There is no selective adaptation of certain discrete *spatial locations*, as there is in figural aftereffects (although the adaptation is restricted to a general retinal region). Rather, the selective adaptation is in the *spatial frequency domain*. Insofar as striate units have both spatially localized RFs and have spatial frequency selectivity, however, the same essential mechanism could be involved in each case.

It is well known that if one stares for a time at a bright light and then looks away, various aftereffects of the stimulation are seen for several seconds. Such afterimages can be partly attributed to selective bleaching of receptor photopigments or gain control changes in the receptors, and partly to the afterdischarge of receptors or later neural elements. Some afterimages (e.g., negative color afterimages) can most readily be accounted for on the basis of neural rebound (see R.L. De Valois & K.K. De Valois, 1975). After prolonged excitation a neuron tends to exhibit a refractory period when it is less likely to fire; after prolonged inhibition it may rebound into excitation. If similar postadaptation processes occur in cortical neurons activated by various spatial patterns, one might expect to see patterned afterimages on blank surfaces after prolonged inspection of certain figures. Georgeson (1976) has reported seeing such spatial afterimages, which he called "hallucinations." He reported that after looking at a pattern of one orientation, one spontaneously sees gratings of slightly different orientations when staring at a blank field. He also reported that "hallucinatory" gratings of slightly different spatial frequencies appear after inspecting a grating of a particular spatial frequency. It should be emphasized that in this situation, as in the Blakemore and Sutton aftereffect tests, the adaptation patterns were inspected with moving fixation, so the aftereffects cannot be attributed to luminance adaptation in certain spatial locations. They occur within the spatial frequency domain.

These spatial afterimages find a ready explanation in multiple spatial frequency and orientation channels. We presumably can identify the orientation and spatial frequency of a grating because units tuned to that particular frequency and orientation are more active than are those units tuned to other spatial frequencies and orientations. A uniform or blank field, correspondingly, would normally appear uniform because all channels are equally active (or inactive). But after prolonged exposure to a particular spatial frequency and/or orientation of pattern, the various channels would no longer be equally sensitive, so that uniform, broad-band stimulation might well produce more activation in some spatial frequency and/or orientation channels than in others. Alternatively, if some spatial frequency and orientation channels had been inhibited by the cells most responsive to the inspection pattern, rebound excitation would result in these units' firing more rapidly, even in the absence of subsequent stimulation, thus producing "hallucinatory" gratings of other orientations and frequencies. The fact that the patterns seen are slightly off in orientation and spatial frequency from the inspection pattern is consistent with the nature of cortical inhibitory interactions (see Chapter 11).

An explanation for such spatial afterimages is fairly straightforward. What is not obvious, however, is an explanation for the paucity and faintness of these afterimages. When compared to retinal afterimages (negative color afterimages, for example), they are poor fare indeed. The reason may lie in the much lower levels of spontaneous activity found in the cortex as compared to retinal ganglion cells and LGN cells. Indeed, the sharp reduction in spontaneous neural activity is among the most noticeable differences between cells in the striate cortex and those at earlier neural levels. Suppose now that in the cortex the identity of a visual stimulus is signaled by the relative firing rates of various neurons. If the effect of adaptation is to hyperpolarize some cells and concomitantly depolarize others, the relative firing rates of the two groups will now differ significantly if both groups of cells have unadapted spontaneous activity rates greater than zero. The cells that were excited by the stimulus will now show an abnormally low spontaneous rate, and those that were inhibited will rebound to a higher-than-normal spontaneous rate.

Consider what the result would be, however, if these same groups of cells were strongly hyperpolarized in the resting state so that they showed no spontaneous firing. Their spontaneous rates can be considered as being below zero. Their resting levels would have to be raised considerably before random fluctuations in ionic currents would produce action potentials. Thus, even if these cells were depolarized to some extent following prolonged inhibition, the rebound effect might not be sufficient to raise the resting level enough to allow random fluctuations to produce frequent action potentials. Sensitivity to subsequent stimulation (measured in terms of stimulus amplitude necessary to produce firing) would be increased, but afterimages that depended on rebound firing in the absence of stimulation would not be seen.

Spatial Frequency Selective Masking

Psychophysical evidence for the existence of multiple spatial frequency selective channels also comes from masking studies, in which the detectability of a particular pattern is measured alone and then in the presence of another, masking pattern. If the presence of the mask has no effect on the detectability of the test pattern, then one can assume that mask and test are detected by independent mechanisms. The interpretation of the condition in which a significant masking effect is seen, however, is rather more complicated. There are at least two straightforward ways in which such a result could be produced. The most commonly assumed one is that both the mask and test stimuli excite some of the same units. The detectability of a 2-c/deg grating, for instance, presumably measures the activity of a channel centered at 2 c/deg. Suppose that a grating of 3 c/deg also excites that channel to some extent. If the contrast-response function for that channel is compressive (e.g., it shows a Weber fraction relationship), then the presence of one suprathreshold excitatory input (here the 3-c/deg mask) would increase its threshold for detection of an additional input (the 2-c/deg test grating). The "mask" grating here acts as a stimulus pedestal upon which the test increment must be detected. By measuring the spatial frequency range over which masking interactions are found, one can derive an estimate of channel bandwidth and shape. Since we know that similar relationships do hold for very many neural systems, this is not an unreasonable assumption.

There is another, perhaps equally likely, possibility, however. Assume now that there are mechanisms centered at 2 and 3 c/deg, respectively, which have nonoverlapping excitatory ranges but which are mutually inhibitory such that activity in one directly inhibits the other, thus effectively increasing the threshold of the second mechanism. The presence of a masking grating of 3 c/deg, whether or not it excited the mechanism centered at 2 c/deg, would increase the threshold for detecting the simultaneous presence of a 2-c/deg grating by virtue of the increased inhibition it produces. Thus, the existence of spatial frequency specific masking does not provide unambiguous information about the shape or bandwidth of the detection channel under consideration. The fact that masking extends only over a limited spatial frequency range, however, does imply the presence of multiple channels that are considerably more narrowly tuned than the overall CSF.

Several investigators have found evidence for spatial frequency specific masking effects. Carter and Henning (1971), Stromeyer and Julesz (1972), and Henning, Hertz, and Hinton (1981) examined the detectability of grating patterns in the presence and absence of band-limited noise patterns. These experiments are similar in logic and design to critical band masking experiments in audition, in which one determines the width of the band of frequencies around the test frequency that can mask it. They found evidence for spatial frequency selective masking, in that the detectability of a grating pattern of a particular spatial frequency was severely degraded by a noise pattern of the same or nearby spatial frequency range, but little affected by the presence of noise patterns that were an octave or more distant in spatial frequency.

The use of a noise mask allows one readily to derive an estimate of the critical band. Masking by a single spatial frequency grating, however, allows a more precise determination of interactions between individual frequencies. If the mask is, say, a 1-octave-wide noise band, it is not clear whether the masking is due to the power present in a narrower band, to the interactions among the various frequencies present in the noise band, or to something like the integrated power over the entire masking bandwidth.

Several experiments (e.g., Pantle, 1974; Legge & Foley, 1980; K.K. De Valois & Switkes, 1983; Switkes & K.K. De Valois, 1983; H.R. Wilson, McFarlane, & Phillips, 1983) have measured masking of a single spatial frequency grating by another single frequency grating. Figure 6.9 presents data from one such experiment (K.K. De Valois & Switkes, 1983), in which both test and masking gratings were luminance-varying patterns of identical space-averaged luminance and chromaticity. It can be seen that masking—i.e., the decrease in contrast sensitivity—is profound when test and mask are identical or very near in spatial frequency and the mask is of high contrast. Masking decreases as mask and test frequencies diverge, falling to zero by about $f +/- 2$ octaves. The function is peaked, centered at f, and asymmetric, with higher frequencies masking a given test frequency more effectively than do lower frequency masks.

These masking results might be attributed to a pedestal mechanism, in which the added contrast is less effective by being superimposed on an existing contrast, its effectiveness being decreased because of a compressive contrast-response relationship. Alternatively, it could be due to direct inhibitory interactions. Whatever the mechanism, band-limited masking functions such as that

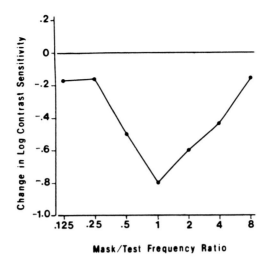

FIG. 6.9 Spatial frequency specific masking. A high-contrast mask of a given frequency selectively reduces contrast sensitivity to gratings of nearby spatial frequencies but has little effect on those which are further removed. The data plotted here show the change in log contrast sensitivity at a given spatial frequency as a function of the mask/test frequency ratio (redrawn after Switkes & K.K. De Valois, 1983. Reprinted by permission).

shown in Figure 6.9 imply multiple spatial frequency channels of finite bandwidth.

Subthreshold Summation

A paradigm methodologically similar to suprathreshold masking is one which measures subthreshold summation. The logic and procedure are as follows. Suppose that there exists a channel with a linear input-response relationship and two or more different excitatory stimuli. The output of that channel will be detected if and only if its response reaches some criterion level, but a subthreshold stimulus might still produce a small response even though it does not reach the detection threshold. Now assume that the input-response function for the first stimulus is known, such that one can produce a stimulus of half threshold contrast. Add to that a second stimulus which is also of half threshold contrast. Neither alone would be detected (since the response to neither would reach the criterion level), but one might well expect their combination to be detected. If the channel only needs n response units to reach threshold, and if it makes no difference to the channel whether those n units came from the same or different stimuli, then two stimuli, each of half threshold contrast, should combine to produce a threshold response.

This is easiest to imagine in the case of two identical gratings which are added together in phase, where the procedure reduces to one of merely increasing the contrast from a subthreshold to a threshold level. The same logic may be applied, however, to the case in which the two gratings differ in spatial frequency. If the channel shows linear summation within its passband, then two excitatory stimuli, each of which is of 0.5 times threshold contrast, should sum to produce a threshold response. Thus, by measuring the frequency range over which subthreshold summation occurs, one can derive an estimate of channel bandwidth.

In a subthreshold summation experiment similar to that described above, Sachs, Nachmias, and Robson (1971) did indeed find subthreshold summation between gratings of closely spaced spatial frequencies but not between more widely spaced ones. This again implies the existence of multiple channels, each of which is more narrowly tuned than the overall contrast sensitivity function. In a later section we will consider the actual estimates of bandwidth that are derived from these various types of experiments.

Retinal Inhomogeneity

Almost all of the experiments we have been discussing above have used stimulus patterns that covered a considerable portion of the central retina. This raises a problem for the evaluation of the evidence discussed above for multiple channels. It is well known that our sensitivity to high spatial frequencies or very fine detail is greatest in the central fovea and decreases drastically with increasing retinal eccentricity. Given this progression, it is conceivable that the supposed high spatial frequency channels just reflect foveally related activity, that the near periphery is the site of detection of medium spatial frequencies, and that low frequencies are detected only in the far periphery (van Doorn, Koenderink, & Bouman, 1972). Much of the classical discussion of acuity, as well as many accounts of variation in RF size as a function of eccentricity (e.g., Hubel & Wiesel, 1974b), suggests such an organization. An arrangement like that, however, would produce a strange visual system indeed. Large (blurry) objects, for example, would only be perceived, or at least would be detected best, in the periphery. If such a suggestion were correct, it would compromise the interpretation of the psychophysical evidence for multiple spatial frequency channels. Analyzing complex patterns into their individual spatial frequency components in a spatially local frequency analysis would demand that these multiple channels all be processing information from the same retinal region. Thus establishing whether there are multiple channels all located within a given retinal region is an important question.

Robson (1975b); Graham, Robson, and Nachmias (1978); Watson and Nachmias (1980); Robson and Graham (1981); and Watson (1982) attempted to determine whether different spatial frequency channels are present in a given location or whether they merely correspond to different retinal eccentricities. Robson and Graham examined the detectability of spatially delimited grating patterns of a constant number of cycles, of various spatial frequencies, presented at various eccentricities. Thus the size of the stimulus patch was inversely related to its spatial frequency. Their evidence suggests that every small region in visual space is in fact analyzed by channels tuned to a variety of spatial frequencies. The high spatial frequency channels do tend to drop out with increasing eccentricity, but the entire range of visible spatial frequencies is detected within the foveal projection itself, and smaller, but still broad ranges of spatial frequency are detected more peripherally. Furthermore, they found sensitivity to all spatial frequencies, low as well as high, to be greatest in the fovea.

This approach seems a reasonable one. There are, however, other methods that yield quite different answers. In particular, if the extent of the stimulus is increased with increasing retinal eccentricity (to compensate for the presumed CMF), the retinal region of greatest contrast sensitivity depends on the test spatial frequency (Rovamo et al., 1978; D.H. Kelly, 1984). See our earlier discussion of the variation of the spatial CSF with retinal locus (Chapter 5).

Physiological and Anatomical Substrates of Spatial Frequency Channels

Although spatial frequency channels are described on the basis of psychophysical experiments, they must, of course, have some physiological substrate. It is useful to consider the characteristics of psychophysically measured channels in relation to what is known about the properties of cells at various levels in the visual system. While the functioning of the system is specified by psychophysical experiments, the relevant physiology puts limitations on the types of models that can reasonably be suggested to explain the psychophysical findings. Much of the evidence relating to cell characteristics at the retinal, geniculate, and cortical levels has been summarized in the preceding chapters. Here we will consider only those findings which are directly relevant to the psychophysically measured spatial frequency channels.

Neural Level

Consider first the question of the neural level that is reflected in psychophysical "channel" experiments. It is generally accepted that psychophysically measured spatial frequency channels are cortical in origin. There are several reasons for this assumption. First, the channels are orientation selective. Adaptation to a grating of one spatial frequency at one orientation produces a temporary loss in contrast sensitivity for gratings of that and nearby frequencies only if they are at the same or similar orientations. Gilinsky (1968), in an early paper that led to much subsequent work with pattern-specific adaptation, demonstrated an orientation-specific loss in sensitivity to a low-contrast vertical grating following adaptation to a similar high-contrast grating. Adaptation to a horizontal grating had no effect on the detection of a vertical grating. Blakemore and Nachmias (1971) found that both the contrast sensitivity loss and the apparent frequency shift with adaptation were sharply orientation specific. Sekuler, Rubin, and Cushman (1968) found a similar dependence on the relative adaptation and test orientations for the threshold elevation produced by adaptation. Since, as Hubel and Wiesel (1959, 1962) first showed, neurons in the striate cortex are the first in the geniculostriate pathway to show narrow orientation tuning, the orientation specificity of these processes implicates units at this level, or possibly still later levels.

A second reason for assuming that spatial frequency channels are of cortical origin is that there is considerable interocular transfer of spatial frequency adaptation effects. Blakemore and Campbell (1969) found interocular transfer of about 60%. It has been well established (e.g. R.L. De Valois, 1965; Wiesel & Hubel, 1966) that there is very little, if any, binocular interaction in LGN cells in primates. Indeed, the first cortical units may also be largely monocular (see Chapter 4). Thus the presence of significant interocular transfer implies a cortical locus for the effect being studied.

The third reason for concluding that psychophysical channels reflect the cortical, rather than retinal or LGN, organization is the narrowness of the spatial frequency tuning of cells at these various levels. The cells in striate cortex are the first in the path to show reasonably narrow spatial frequency tuning, as well as fairly narrow orientation tuning (see Chapters 3 and 4 and further discussion below).

Still another reason for attributing the characteristics of multiple spatial frequency channels as revealed in some of these psychophysical experiments to striate cortex cells is that cells at this level, but not at earlier levels, appear to show the appropriate adaptational changes. As we discussed in Chapter 3, LGN cells have very broad spatial frequency tuning. Since one might have thought a priori that both LGN and cortical cells could be subject to adaptation in the Blakemore and Campbell experiment, it is rather puzzling that one finds only narrow, spatial frequency specific (and orientation-specific) adaptation effects. If both broadly tuned geniculate units and narrowly tuned cortical units were adapted by the stimulus conditions in that experiment, one would expect to find a selective sensitivity loss around the adaptation frequency (due to cortical cells) superimposed on a general overall depression in the CSF (due to LGN cells). Nothing like this is in fact seen. Rather, at off spatial frequencies one can see an actual enhancement of sensitivity (K.K. De Valois, 1977b). The physiological basis for this appears to be that cortical cells show adaptation with prolonged presentation of an appropriate stimulus pattern (Maffei, Fiorentini, & Bisti, 1973; Vautin & Berkley, 1977; Movshon & Lennie, 1979a; Albrecht, Farrar, & Hamilton, 1984), but LGN cells do not (Movshon & Lennie, 1979b). The cortical evoked potential has also been found to show selective spatial frequency adaptation (Bonds, 1984).

The "adaptation" of cortical cells is often thought of as some sort of fatigue process resulting from overstimulation. The general assumption is that adapted cells are in a refractory state similar to that demonstrated in other neurons following repetitive stimulation. This is a simple and attractive hypothesis, both because of its similarity to processes known to occur elsewhere in the nervous system and because it is easy to "explain" in terms of such relatively simple factors as transmitter depletion. (There is, however, some contrary evidence from both psychophysical [Dealy & Tolhurst, 1977] and physiological [Movshon, Bonds, & Lennie, 1980] experiments.)

Another possibility is that adaptation may reflect the contrast gain control process found to operate at striate levels among many cells. Ohzawa, Sclar, and Freeman (1982) showed that many cortical units adjust their sensitivity to the average contrast of test patterns present within their RFs. Such cells increase their sensitivity when presented with only low-contrast patterns, but decrease their sensitivity in the presence of high-contrast patterns (such as those used in the typical Blakemore and Campbell adaptation experiment). Such a mechanism has the clear functional advantage of extending the contrast range over which a cell can give useful information.

Narrow Spatial Frequency Tuning

The first study of the spatial frequency tuning of striate cells (Campbell, Cooper, & Enroth-Cugell, 1969) found most cortical units to be relatively broadly tuned (although more narrowly tuned than ganglion cells). However, recent studies (e.g., Maffei & Fiorentini, 1973; R.L. De Valois, K.K. De Valois, Ready, & von Blanckensee, 1975; R.L. De Valois, Albrecht, & Thorell, 1978; Movshon et al., 1978c; Kulikowski & Bishop, 1981; R.L. De Valois, Albrecht, & Thorell, 1982) based on many more cells (and perhaps with improved recording techniques) have found large numbers of more narrowly tuned units. (One might note parenthetically that the Campbell et al., 1969, study is one of the rare occasions in the history of science on which an investigator published data that appear to be biased *against* rather than in favor of his theory.)

The most relevant data are those from recordings made of the responses of cells in monkey striate cortex, in which (as discussed in Chapter 4) we find the average spatial frequency bandwidths of both simple and complex cortical cells to be about 1.4 octaves, with a significant number of units having a bandwidth of 1 octave or less. The most narrowly tuned striate cells have a bandwidth at half amplitude of about 0.6 octaves (R.L. De Valois, Albrecht, & Thorell, 1982). Other studies of monkey (Kulikowski & Vidyasagar, 1982; Foster, Gaska, & Pollen, 1983) and cat (Glezer, Ivanoff, & Tscherbach, 1973; Glezer & Cooperman, 1977; Movshon et al., 1978c) striate cells have reported similar tuning properties. The bandwidth of an average cell covers only a fraction of the total range of spatial frequencies to which the organism is sensitive (see Figure 6.10). In the fovea, the total CSF covers at least 6 to 8 octaves; the typical cell has a bandwidth of less than a quarter of that range. (We might note that this is actually somewhat less than the proportion of the total orientation range covered by the orientation bandwidth of a typical cortical cell.) In the periphery, the CSF may narrow, due to an absence of cells tuned to the highest spatial frequencies, and

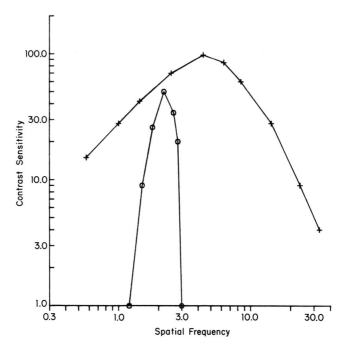

FIG. 6.10   Macaque behavioral CSF (crosses) and the CSF of a single macaque striate cortex cell (circles). Note that the cell's CSF has a very much narrower bandwidth than that of the overall behavioral CSF. The latter presumably reflects the activity of many more narrowly tuned individual cells, as depicted in Figure 6.1.

the cells there would cover a larger proportion of the total CSF if their band-widths are no narrower than those in the fovea.

Studies of the functional anatomy of the striate cortex also provide support for there being units tuned to limited spatial frequency ranges. As discussed in Chapter 4, if radioactively labeled 2-DG is injected into a cat while it binocularly observes a pattern containing all orientations (over time) but just a single spatial frequency, autoradiography on cortical sections reveals a clear columnar pattern of increased glucose uptake (Tootell et al., 1981); see Figure 4.24. Within a cortical region of about 1 mm x 1 mm, one group of cells has greatly increased activity and thus takes up a lot of the labeled 2-DG, whereas the other cells within the region do not. This indicates that only a subpopulation within the module is responsive to that particular spatial frequency: if each cell had the sensitivity of the overall CSF, each would respond to the pattern and uniform glucose uptake would result. When a binocular pattern made up of all spatial frequencies and all orientations is presented, just such a uniform pattern of uptake is in fact seen (Tootell et al., 1981). The same selective activation of the striate cortex by a pattern of just one spatial frequency is also found in monkey cortex (Tootell et al., 1982b). Although the overall anatomical arrangement of spatial frequency columns is different in monkey cortex from that seen in cat, one finds again that patterns of a given single spatial frequency activate only a subpopulation of the cortical units.

Multiple Channels in a Given Region

Electrophysiological data are also available that are directly relevant to the question of whether there are cells tuned to multiple spatial frequencies within a given cortical area (the other possibility being that cells tuned to different spatial frequencies occur at different eccentricities). Here there are certain apparent contradictions in the physiological evidence. Two classic studies of the RF size of cells at different eccentricities (Hubel & Wiesel, 1974b; Albus, 1975a) both reported arrangements of cells within the striate cortex that are somewhat contrary to the requirements for multiple spatial frequency channels. Since these studies are widely accepted, the skepticism of many physiologists about spatial frequency models can be understood. Both of these studies reported that cells in the foveal (or central) projection region of cortex have small RFs, with RF size increasing with eccentricity. Some variability in RF size was found in each region, but much less than the variation with eccentricity. Thus some monkey foveally related striate cells were reported to have tiny RFs and others 2 or 3 times as large, but none to have nearly as large RFs as those seen in peripheral cells (Hubel & Wiesel, 1974b). Insofar as RF size, as measured in these experiments, is directly related to spatial frequency tuning (a very questionable jump, as we shall see), such findings clearly pose a problem for models of multiple spatial frequency channels processing information from a given retinal region.

On the other hand, two studies that specifically measured the optimal spatial frequency tuning of cells (as opposed to some measure of the overall RF size) reported quite different results. These studies in cat (Movshon et al., 1978c) and monkey (R.L. De Valois, Albrecht, & Thorell, 1982) found a wide range of spatial frequency peaks among foveally (or centrally) related units. In cat, the situation is complicated by the dual projection from the LGN to both areas 17 and 18. Movshon et al. (1978c) found that area 17 cells are tuned to a higher spatial frequency range than those in area 18, but within each of these areas the cell tunings cover considerably more than the 1-octave range of RF sizes reported by Albus (1975a). In our study of monkey striate cells (R.L. De Valois, Albrecht, & Thorell, 1982), we found an even wider range (ca. 4 to 5 octaves) of peak spatial frequency tuning among units in the near-foveal cortex, with the cells peaking everywhere from about 0.5 c/deg up to as high as 16 c/deg (see Figures 4.16 and 4.17). One might note in passing that there appears to be a continuous distribution of peak frequencies within this range, with no evidence for grouping into, for example, four distinct classes as the model of H.R. Wilson and Bergen (1979) would suggest.

Clearly those studies directly examining the spatial tuning of cells (Movshon et al., 1978c; R.L. De Valois, Albrecht, & Thorell, 1982) are the most relevant to questions of multiple spatial frequency channels, and they provide unequivocal evidence for cells within a given cortical region being tuned to each of a wide range of different spatial frequencies. Nonetheless, one would like to understand the apparent discrepancy between these studies and the others which measured RF size. Although the overall RF size of a cell should be somewhat related to its spatial frequency tuning (see Chapter 4), there is no reason to expect a one-to-one relationship. The width of the RF center of a simple cell should be equal to a half period of the optimal spatial frequency grating, but how each of these is related to the *overall RF size* is a more complex matter. It is important to note that Hubel and Wiesel (1974b) measured RF size not in terms of the optimal width bar, but by marking the locations at which a response was first elicited when a bar was moved towards the RF center from each side in turn. The resulting rectangle was taken as the RF size. For complex cells, the overall width of the RF is some amount greater than the optimum bar width, a relationship that varies from cell to cell and that may also vary with eccentricity. Many simple cells have periodic RFs, with multiple sidebands of decreasing sensitivity. If a rough RF mapping detected only the central excitatory region, one would conclude that the RF was a quite different size than one would if some of the sidebands were strong enough to be noticed. This could produce a very large difference indeed. Furthermore, the true RF size is a joint function of the optimum spatial frequency and the bandwidth (more narrowly tuned cells have more sidebands and thus larger total RF size than do broadly tuned cells with the same spatial frequency peak). Since cells tuned to high spatial frequencies are more narrowly tuned than low-frequency cells (see Chapter 4), the range in total RF size should be at least an octave less than the range in spatial frequency peak. These factors make reports of only a small range of RF sizes in foveal cortex less of a problem than they first seem. In addition, as stated initially, the crucial data are the actual spatial frequency tuning characteristics of cells.

Very clear anatomical evidence for a range of different spatial frequency tuning peaks within the central striate cortex has also been obtained in 2-DG studies of cat and monkey. When the 2-DG single spatial frequency experiment described above was repeated with single spatial frequencies ranging, in different animals, from 0.25 up to 2 c/deg (which cover a range from low to high spatial frequencies for the cat), columnar groupings of cells within each cortical module were found in each case (Tootell et al., 1981; Silverman, 1984). The columns of cells tuned to low spatial frequencies were found in all striate regions stimulated, including specifically the projection of the area centralis (which is homologous to the foveal projection in primate). When high spatial frequencies were used, however, columns were seen only in the central projection area. In studies of macaque monkey cortex (Tootell et al., 1982a), similar evidence was found for a grouping of striate cells by spatial frequency. Here again, it is clear that low spatial frequency patterns do *not* just activate peripheral cortex, but rather produce uptake all the way up to and including the foveal input region. High spatial frequency patterns produce uptake in these foveal regions as well, but the activation they produce falls off at some eccentricity, depending on how high a spatial frequency was used.

In summary, then, direct physiological and anatomical data support the psychophysical evidence that the overall behavioral CSF is made up of multiple subunits or channels with fairly narrow spatial frequency tuning. These studies indicate that each cortical module, which processes information from a given limited part of the visual world, has within it cells tuned to each of many spatial frequency ranges. These cells tuned to different spatial frequencies appear to be very systematically arranged in both cat and monkey cortex, in a columnar organization similar to that seen for cells tuned to different orientations.

CHANNEL TUNING CHARACTERISTICS

Any description of a system in terms of band-pass channels (along any dimension) raises questions concerning the tuning of those channels. A perfect, global, Fourier analyzing device, for example, would be composed of a set of band-pass filters, each of which was infinitely narrow. Activity in any one channel would unambiguously signal the presence of energy at one particular spectral point (in the case of spatial frequency analysis, at one particular spatial frequency). In practice, however, there is no truly ideal Fourier analyzer, and the visual system is certainly doing something far different from this: it does not do the global analysis required for extremely narrow channels at all. The nature of the analysis that can be carried out depends, among other things, upon the narrowness of the filters that transmit the necessary information. Thus, the question of the narrowness of tuning of visual spatial frequency channels is one of some importance.

Channel Bandwidth

There are two precautions that should be borne in mind in considering the bandwidth of spatial frequency channels. The first is that the precision with which one can measure such a function with a psychophysical experiment such as adaptation is not very great. A given subject may show considerable variability from day to day or even from session to session within the same day. This is true for criterion-free experimental paradigms (such as forced-choice methods), as well as for the faster method-of-adjustment paradigms. While long-term, repeated measures should allow one to converge on a reasonably accurate estimate, it is a mistake to assume a greater precision than one's psychophysical method (or even the visual system) allows. Extended practice and repeated measures can lead to greatly decreased fluctuations, but systematic changes (in sensitivity or bandwidth, for example) may result (K.K. De Valois, 1977b; McKee & Westheimer, 1978).

A second, more difficult problem with psychophysical estimates of spatial frequency bandwidths is that different types of experiments may lead to significantly different values. Quite different estimates of channel bandwidth come from studies of subthreshold summation as opposed to masking experiments, for instance. Subthreshold summation studies typically produce very narrow bandwidth figures (e.g., Sachs, Nachmias, & Robson, 1971); masking experiments generally yield broader estimates (e.g., Legge & Foley, 1980). Does this mean that one set of estimates is right and others, wrong? That, of course, depends in part on one's model of spatial frequency channels. We would argue that different experimental techniques could simply be tapping different types of channels or different levels of interactions. Such differences should not be distressing unless one assumes that channels are fixed and immutable physiological entities, sculpted perhaps in dendrites, and unchanging, regardless of the conditions.

It is also possible (perhaps even likely) that the logic applied to some of the experimental paradigms is in error, and that the measurements therefore do not reflect channel bandwidth directly, but perhaps something like the bandwidth of inhibitory interactions, or probability summation. Such suggestions have been made by Dealy and Tolhurst (1977) concerning adaptation experiments, and by Graham et al., (1978) with respect to grating summation experiments. One should thus be cautious about interpreting such experiments.

With these caveats in mind, it is of interest to look at the bandwidth estimates derived from different types of psychophysical experiments, and to compare these with the physiological data. In Table 6.1 are summarized the full bandwidths at half amplitude of the spatial frequency channels as estimated from a selection of various types of experiments. It can be seen that with the exception of the subthreshold summation experiment, most of the studies come to a rough agreement on a spatial frequency bandwidth of about 1 to 1.4 octaves. With the sensitivity of each channel falling to half amplitude about 0.6 octaves to either side of its peak, stimuli about 1 octave away to either side would be almost totally ineffective.

Shown also in Table 6.1 are results from a physiological study of macaque striate cortical cells (R.L. De Valois, Albrecht, & Thorell, 1982). It can be seen that the mean bandwidth of striate cells, both simple and complex, is somewhat larger than the psychophysical estimates of channel bandwidths, reflecting perhaps the inclusion of the considerable proportion of cortical cells with rather geniculate-like spatial frequency tuning (and often little or no orientation tuning). Since the bandwidth distributions are skewed, the medians give a better estimate of the central tendency, but they are also slightly larger than the psychophysical estimates. However, the cortical population (see Figure 4.12) includes a sizable proportion of cells that are tuned as narrowly as, or more narrowly than, the psychophysical estimates.

Single-unit recording and 2-DG studies in the striate cortex can provide very powerful evidence as to the total population of cell properties to be found, e.g., the total range and distribution of spatial frequency and orientation bandwidths. This sets distinct limits to plausible psychophysical models: theories postulating cells extremely narrowly tuned for orientation or spatial frequency would be untenable (at least at the level of the striate cortex), as would theories postulating

TABLE 6.1. Channel bandwidth estimates (in octaves)

Technique	Psychophysical Measures	
	Study	Bandwidth
Adaptation	Blakemore & Campbell (1969)	1.3
	K. K. De Valois (1977b)	0.7
Masking: high-contrast gratings	Pantle (1974)	2.4
	Legge & Foley (1980)	1.8
	Wilson, McFarlane, & Phillips (1983)	1.2 to 2.4 (frequency dependent)
Masking: low-contrast gratings	Sachs, Nachmias & Robson (1971)	0.4
	Legge & Foley (1980)	0.5
	Watson (1982)	0.5
Masking: noise	Stromeyer & Julesz (1972)	1.0 to 1.5

Animal	Electrophysiology: Bandwidths of striate cortex cells	
	Study	Bandwidth
Macaque	De Valois, Albrecht, & Thorell (1982)	1.4 (0.5 to 3.0)
Macaque	Foster, Gaska, & Pollen (1983)	(0.7 to 2.8)
Cat	Movshon, Thompson, & Tolhurst (1978c)	1.3 (0.7 to 3.2)

a single very broadly tuned cell type whose sensitivity approximated the behavioral CSF. What the physiological evidence cannot do as well, however, is to tell us which cells within this overall population are involved in a particular task—e.g., those being tapped in the psychophysical studies discussed earlier in this chapter. Indeed, one cannot even say with confidence whether a particular behavioral response reflects the activity of one, or thousands, of cortical cells. What we can say, however, is that there is clearly no contradiction between the psychophysical and physiological data in indicating the presence of multiple mechanisms with spatial frequency bandwidths of about 1 octave tuned to each of many spatial frequencies across the spatial spectrum.

Bandwidths at Different Spatial Frequencies

Blakemore and Campbell (1969) estimated channel bandwidths by adapting to each of a number of spatial frequencies and measuring the resulting loss of contrast sensitivity. They concluded that bandwidths were somewhat narrower at high than at low spatial frequencies. Interpretation of this result is difficult, since with the small overall size of their stimulus pattern (1.5°), the bandwidth of the stimulus would be broader at low spatial frequencies (since only a few cycles of the stimulus would be present across the small oscilloscope face). It is a finding that would be worth examining with better experimental techniques. It is of interest, however, that physiological data from units in monkey striate (R.L. De Valois, Albrecht, & Thorell, 1982) confirm a narrowing of the tuning with

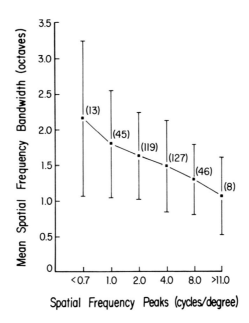

FIG. 6.11   Bandwidth distribution of macaque striate cortical cells as a function of their peak spatial frequencies. Plotted are the means ($\pm$ 1 SD) of the spatial frequency bandwidths of a large group of cells. The numbers in parentheses show the number of cells in each group (from R.L. De Valois, Albrecht, & Thorell, 1982, *Vision Res., 22*, 545–559. Copyright 1982, Pergamon Journals, Inc. Reprinted by permission).

increasing spatial frequency (see Figure 6.11). Cells tuned to the very highest spatial frequencies are almost twice as narrowly tuned (on an octave scale) as those tuned to the lowest spatial frequencies. (Similar bandwidth narrowing at high spatial frequency has been found in cat striate cells by Kulikowski & Bishop, 1981.) However, it should be remembered that the bandwidths in Figure 6.11 are plotted on an octave, or logarithmic, scale. On a linear scale of spatial frequency, cells tuned to low spatial frequencies would be much more narrowly tuned than those with high spatial frequency peaks. Thus a cell with peak sensitivity to 0.5 c/deg and a 2-octave bandwidth would respond to gratings from about 0.25 to 1.0 c/deg, a 0.75-cycle linear range. A cell peaking at 10 c/deg and with only a 1-octave bandwidth would respond from 7 to 14 cycles, a 7.0-cycle linear range, almost 10 times as large as the lower frequency cell, which had double the octave bandwidth.

SPATIAL FREQUENCY OR SIZE?

We have been assuming throughout this chapter that the spatial dimension along which the visual system filters spatial information is (local) spatial frequency, but some of the experiments discussed above could be interpreted as providing evidence for local size-tuned channels rather than spatial frequency channels. We will consider psychophysical, physiological, and anatomical experiments that bear directly on the issue of whether size or spatial frequency is the better description of the relevant visual spatial dimension. The infinity of possible spatial functions would seem to preclude the possibility of ever making an absolute determination of the most critical single spatial variable, but certainly it is possible to compare two reasonably well-defined variables.

A grating may be considered not as a pattern of a particular spatial frequency, but rather as a series of bars of some particular specifiable width, of some edge-to-edge distance. The adaptation experiments of Blakemore and Campbell (1969), for instance, could then be interpreted as showing the existence of size-tuned channels, mechanisms tuned to respond to bars of a particular width, rather than to particular spatial frequencies. Experiments can be, and have been, done to discriminate between these two possibilities. If a grating is considered as a series of bars of a particular width, the adaptational loss in contrast sensitivity produced by adapting to a single bar moved back and forth across the field should be equivalent in spatial tuning (though probably not in amplitude) to that produced by adapting to a drifting grating. From the point of view of its Fourier spectrum, however, a bar is quite different from a grating, particularly from a sinusoidal grating. A single bar has an extremely broad spectrum, with power at nearly all visible spatial frequencies (see Figure 6.12). If the visual system analyzes spatial patterns in terms of spatial frequencies, then, a single bar should excite virtually all the spatial frequency channels of the appropriate orientation and retinal locus, and adaptation to a single bar should reduce contrast

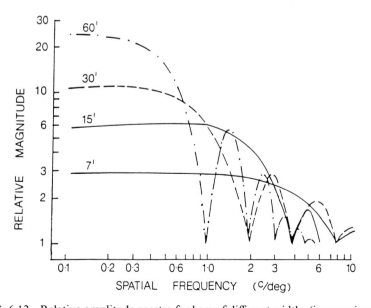

FIG. 6.12   Relative amplitude spectra for bars of different widths (in arc minutes).

sensitivity to a broad range of spatial frequencies (although that effect would presumably be rather small, since the absolute amplitude in any one restricted frequency region would be small). By the same argument, a sinusoidal grating patch, which has a much more restricted power spectrum, would be expected to produce adaptation only in a similarly restricted spatial frequency range.

Sullivan, Georgeson, and Oatley (1972) measured the effect of adapting to gratings on the detection of bars and vice versa. Adaptation to a grating of 5 c/deg produced a small decrease in contrast sensitivity for bars of a wide range of widths, not just bars of a width equivalent to one half cycle of a 5-c/deg grating. In addition, adaptation to bars of any of a wide variety of widths produced a small loss in contrast sensitivity to gratings of 5 c/deg. In other words, there was much less selectivity when a bar was used as either test or adaptation stimulus than when gratings were used for both. This result is readily predicted from a consideration of the spatial frequency spectra of bars and gratings, but not from a consideration of bar width and the equivalent bar widths of gratings. It suggests that the channels are not size channels, but spatial frequency channels, as we have been referring to them.

The same comparison between bars and gratings can be made at the physiological level. If cortical cells are bar detectors, analyzing complex patterns into bars of various widths, they should be very selective for bar width. If a grating is treated as a series of bars, then cells should show similar selectivity for bars and gratings. On the other hand, if cortical cells are analyzing the (local) visual scene into its spatial frequency components, one would expect them to be very selective for gratings but quite unselective for single bars, given the broad spatial frequency spectrum of bars, as discussed above.

R.L. De Valois et al. (1978) and Albrecht, R.L. De Valois, and Thorell (1980) directly compared the narrowness of tuning of the same cortical cells for sinusoidal gratings of various spatial frequencies and for bars of various widths, matched in contrast. Both simple and complex cells showed considerably nar-

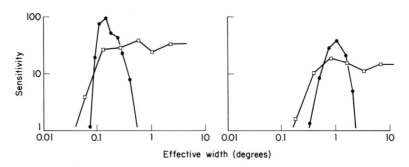

FIG. 6.13   Tuning functions for two representative striate cortex cells. Plotted are the sensitivity functions for bars of various widths (squares) and sinusoidal gratings of various spatial frequencies (circles). Note that both cells are much more narrowly tuned for grating frequency than for bar width (from Albrecht et al., 1980, *Science, 207,* 88–90. Copyright 1980, AAAS. Reprinted by permission).

rower tuning for sinusoidal gratings than for bars of various widths; not a single cell was found that was less selective for gratings than for bars (see Figure 6.13). Similar results were also reported by Schiller et al. (1976c) in comparing selectivity for sine versus square wave gratings.

The physiological data, then, agree with the psychophysical results that a grating is best considered *not* just as a series of bars of a particular width, being detected by cells tuned to a particular bar width. Rather, cells are more selective along the dimension of spatial frequency, and the responses of cells to bars (as well as to other stimuli) can be predicted to a first approximation from the local Fourier spectra of the patterns and the contrast sensitivity of the cell.

DO CELLS RESPOND TO SPATIAL FREQUENCY COMPONENTS?

The physiological and anatomical experiments discussed above address the general question of whether the essential machinery is present in the cortex for patterns to be filtered into multiple spatial frequency channels. The preponderance of the evidence, as we have indicated, supports this. What such physiological experiments do *not* answer, however, is the crucial question of whether the system functions sufficiently linearly to actually analyze patterns into their separate frequency components. This question was addressed at the psychophysical level by such experiments as those of Campbell and Robson (1968) and Graham and Nachmias (1971) discussed earlier. The question can also be posed—even more directly—at the physiological level. Such experiments have been carried out by K.K. De Valois et al. (1979); Maffei, Morrone, Pirchio, and Sandini (1979); and Pollen and Ronner (1982).

Consider a square-wave grating. The Fourier spectrum of a square wave (see Figure 1.3) consists of a fundamental with an amplitude of $4/\pi$ ($= 1.27$), with respect to a sine wave of the same contrast, plus odd harmonics in decreasing amplitudes. If contrast were the crucial determinant of a cell's responses, sine and square wave gratings of optimal frequency and equal contrast should produce equal responses. On the other hand, if the cell were responding to the individual frequency components in the patterns, it should give 1.27 times as large a response to the square wave as to the sine wave. Another way to address the same question would be to compare responses to a square wave grating of a particular contrast and a sine wave grating of 1.27 times as high contrast; these have identical fundamental components. Pollen and Ronner (1982), recording the overall amplitudes of the responses of striate cells to such patterns, found that they behave as expected from the amplitudes of the Fourier fundamentals, not from the overall pattern contrasts.

We have confirmed the results of Pollen and Ronner. We have also examined the peristimulus time histogram for possible responses to higher harmonics of the square wave grating, as well. A square wave of one third the optimum spatial frequency for a cell has a third harmonic which would be at the cell's optimum frequency. One would thus expect a simple cell to fire three times to each passage of such a low spatial frequency square wave grating across its RF (note that the cell would *not* respond to a sine wave grating of this frequency). This is what we found (see Figure 6.14). Similar results have also been reported by Maffei et al. (1979). Furthermore, the amplitudes of the responses to the third harmonic were

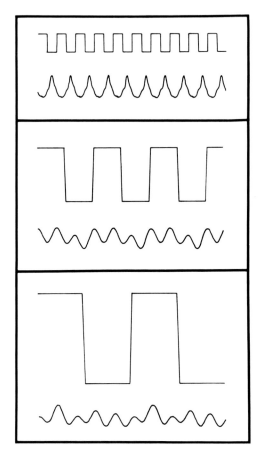

FIG. 6.14   Responses of a macaque striate cortex cell to square wave gratings of three different spatial frequencies drifted across its RF. The square wave in the upper box has its fundamental component at the cell's "best" spatial frequency. Note that the cell shows one response peak per stimulus cycle. In the middle box the square wave fundamental frequency is reduced by a factor of three. The third harmonic of the waveform is now in the cell's band-pass, and there are correspondingly three response peaks per cycle. In the lower box the stimulus fundamental is one fifth of the cell's "best" frequency. To this pattern the cell shows five response peaks which correspond to the fifth harmonic of the square wave—that component which is now the dominant stimulus for this cell. Note that the square wave amplitude has been systematically increased to keep the amplitude of the relevant stimulus component constant as its fundamental frequency varies.

precisely those predicted from the amplitude of this Fourier component (i.e., one third as large as the response to the fundamental). Many narrowly tuned striate cells also respond to the fifth harmonic of a square wave grating (when the square wave is of such a low base frequency that its fifth harmonic is at the optimum spatial frequency for the cell); see Figure 6.14 bottom.

Such results are totally unpredictable from our phenomenological impression of a square wave—we can perceive no third or fifth harmonic lurking within the pattern. It is also not at all what one would predict from striate cells which are supposedly responsive to edges: there are not three—to say nothing of five— edges in one cycle of a square wave. But it is just what would be predicted if the striate network were indeed filtering patterns into their local spatial frequency components.

7

Sensitivity to Color Variations

The study of the visual system is often arbitrarily divided into topics which are then treated as discrete fields. Two of these are spatial vision and color vision. Such an arbitrary division leads one to overlook the very important areas of intersections between fields. In this chapter we shall consider one of these intersections, that between color vision and spatial vision.

Outside of the artificial conditions of the laboratory, the printed page, and black-white photography, most visual scenes vary across their extent in both chromaticity and luminance. Sometimes color and luminance covary spatially, as in the case of a uniformly bright red object upon a uniformly dark green background. More often, however, their distributions are only partially correlated. Most objects are visible only because they reflect incident light from some distant source. Whether the light comes from the sun or from an artificial source, it usually emanates primarily from a restricted area and thus casts shadows in a three-dimensional world. The major effect of shadowing is the introduction of luminance discontinuities in a scene, for there is relatively little effect on the wavelength distribution. In a sunlit scene, for example, objects are both directly illuminated by the sun and indirectly illuminated from many directions by scattered light. In general, the spectral distributions of the direct and indirect light vary much less than the intensity distributions produced by shadows.

In the case of sunlight, light scatter produced by the atmosphere will indirectly illuminate the scene with light that is somewhat more skewed toward the short wavelengths than the unscattered light that comes directly from the sun, due to the wavelength differential of Rayleigh scattering. Thus, objects in the shade tend to have a slightly more bluish cast than objects seen in the sunlight, but this color difference is quite minor. The *intensity* of light reflected by an object, however, may vary drastically, depending on whether the object is illuminated directly by the source or indirectly by scattered light. In a sunlit scene on a clear day, for instance, the intensity of the light incident upon a directly illuminated object may be 30 times as great as the intensity of the light incident upon an object in shade. If a uniform object is half in sunlight and half in shade, then, the luminance contrast between the two halves may be greater than 90%, even though both halves reflect the same proportion of the incident light. The color contrast produced by the slight differences in the wavelength composition of the direct and scattered light in the same scene would be trivial. If an early task of the visual system is to segregate the different parts of the visual image into objects preparatory to identifying those objects, then in situations like that described above the spatial distribution of wavelength differences would give a more veridical representation of the real world than would the spatial distribution of intensity differences.

Color vision, though quite useful, is very expensive neurally. A large proportion of the visual system of Old World primates, for instance, is dedicated to processing information about wavelength differences. It is not surprising, then, that animals (e.g., many of the carnivores) that depend predominantly on nonvisual senses, and many nocturnal species, should not have evolved very good color vision. Similarly, the ungulates and other grass eaters, which can easily find food, may not require very fine visual systems. But for animals such as primates, birds, and insects, whose nonvisual senses are often not particularly acute and whose food sources (e.g., fruit or flowers) may be more easily differentiated from their surrounds by color than by brightness differences, it is extremely important to be able to use color vision to make spatial discriminations.

Consider the problem of finding the ripe cherries in a cherry tree. Without color vision, one would find that the irrelevant contours produced by shadowing effectively mask the regularity of form and brightness of the fruit. With color vision, however, the problem is readily solved. The color contrast produced by red cherries against the green leaves is quite obvious, despite the irregular and imperfectly correlated luminance contours.

In our earlier discussions of luminance contrast sensitivity we have referred to physiological data from both cats and monkeys. This is reasonable because we have the appropriate psychophysical data from those species and know that their sensitivity to luminance contrast is very similar to our own. Although the cat CSF function is displaced along the spatial frequency axis relative to ours, its form and the manner in which it varies with other parameters are very similar to ours.

In the case of color vision, however, one must be much more cautious. It is well known that many of the commonly used experimental animals (cat, for example) have vanishingly small color vision capability in comparison with our exquisite color vision. It would clearly be inappropriate to use an animal that is nearly color-blind as a physiological model for human color vision. There are many other animals with good color vision (some fish, birds, and insects, for example) which are anatomically and physiologically so dissimilar to mammals that they are also inappropriate models for human color vision. Certain of the primates, however, specifically the Old World monkeys, have color vision which is nearly identical to ours (R.L. De Valois & Jacobs, 1968; R.L. De Valois, Morgan, Polson, Mead, & Hull, 1974; R.L. De Valois, Morgan, & Snodderly, 1974), and they are anatomically and physiologically quite similar to humans. Therefore, when we refer to physiological results bearing on the topic of spatial color vision, we will largely restrict our discussion to experiments on Old World monkeys.

COLOR SPATIAL CONTRAST SENSITIVITY FUNCTION

Pure Color Gratings

In a pure color grating, the dominant wavelength (and thus the hue) varies sinusoidally between two extremes across the width of the pattern (across the stripes of the grating). The various wavelengths are equated for luminance, so the pattern varies *only* in chrominance. Along an orthogonal axis (along the length of one stripe of the grating), there is no variation in either color or luminance. Thus, for a red-green sinusoidal grating, dominant wavelength (thus hue) changes continuously along the grating from a red through various red-green mixtures to a green and back. The spatial frequency of the grating is the number of complete red-green cycles per degree visual angle.

The amplitude, or contrast, of a color grating is more difficult to define, since it requires the selection of a somewhat arbitrary unit of magnitude. A luminance scale has an absolute zero: no light. A 100% contrast sinusoidal luminance grating varies in amplitude from twice the mean to zero. In the case of a pure color grating, however, there is no absolute physical limit to the corresponding scale (in this case, wavelength). Nonetheless, there is a perceptual limit to a color difference, just as there is to a luminance difference. In one possible metric, the contrast of a color grating might reflect the magnitude of the color difference in the grating with respect to the most extreme colors possible along a particular color axis. If the different colors are represented in a scaling of color space such as the CIE chromaticity diagram (see Boynton, 1979), 100% contrast might be taken as the longest possible distance in this space or, alternatively, the longest possible distance along a particular axis. Such a specification, of course, suggests that this is an optimal model of color space and raises additional problems of how to relate the scale along various axes. It also does not answer the question of how to relate color contrast to luminance contrast. These questions are not trivial, and the best solution is not apparent.

It is difficult technically to produce a pattern that varies spatially as a continuous sequence of different monochromatic wavelengths, but such is not required, given the laws of color mixture. By mixing a red and a green, all the intermediate colors can be produced. An isoluminant red-green grating can thus be made by summing two out-of-phase isochromatic luminance gratings that are properly matched in luminance. If a red sinusoidal luminance grating is added 180° out of phase to a green luminance grating of the same spatial frequency, amplitude, space-average luminance, and luminance contrast, the result will be a red-green grating of the same spatial frequency in which hue varies sinusoidally and luminance is invariant with position. (This assumes that heterochromatic luminances add linearly. Unfortunately, this assumption, known as Abney's law [Abney & Festing, 1886; Abney, 1913] is not always confirmed by rigorous experiment [e.g., Ives, 1912; Pieron, 1939; Guth, Donley, & Marrocco, 1969].) To produce such a grating, one may feed a sinusoidally varying signal

FIG. 7.1 Red-green pure color grating. In this pattern the chromaticity varies sinusoidally from red through various red-green mixtures to green and back. If the color reproduction processes were perfect, there would be no associated variations in luminance.

 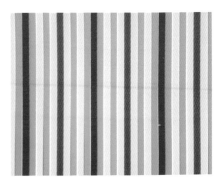

FIG. 7.10 Examples of color similitude (also known as assimilation and the spreading effect of von Bezold). In the upper left figure, the green bars are all identical, whether surrounded by yellow or blue. Note that they appear similar to their surrounding color and thus different from each other. In the top right figure, the reddish-orange bars are also identical. Similarly, in the lower pattern the green (left) and red (right) squares are the same in the upper and lower halves of the figure.

into the *z*-axis of the red gun of a color television monitor and a corresponding (but out-of-phase) signal to the green gun. With such patterns of various spatial frequencies, the color contrast sensitivity of observers can be measured. Figure 7.1 shows an example of a pure color grating, and Figure 7.2 its construction and cross section in color versus distance coordinates.

There is ample evidence (see R.L. De Valois & K.K. De Valois, 1975; Boynton, 1979; Hurvich, 1981) that the visual system analyzes color along three dimensions. These may be called the luminance or black-white axis, the red-green axis, and the yellow-blue axis. (One can argue from various kinds of evidence that the appropriate third axis is a tritan axis, i.e., one which is defined solely by variations in S-cone activity, with absorption by the L and M cones held constant. It appears that early in the pathway, the information is in fact so encoded. Perceptually, however, the third axis is clearly the yellow-blue axis. It appears that some late transformation must occur in this regard in visual processing.) Consequently, most of the relatively few studies of color contrast sensitivity have used either red-green patterns or blue-yellow patterns. There is little information about contrast sensitivity to patterns that vary along both red-green and blue-yellow axes (e.g., red-blue). Contrast sensitivity functions for red-green and for blue-yellow gratings differ both from each other and from the comparable function for luminance. Before discussing these differences, however, we shall consider some technical problems that arise in determining the color spatial CSF, and that complicate the interpretation of the results.

Van der Horst, de Weert, and Bouman (1967) and van der Horst and Bouman (1969) made some of the first and most comprehensive measures of color contrast sensitivity. They presented pure color gratings to subjects who were asked to identify the contrast at which they could just detect the hue variation in either a red-green grating or a blue-yellow grating of a particular spatial frequency. Note that this is not an absolute pattern-detection but a hue-detection criterion. This may appear at first to be a meaningless distinction, since the pattern can presumably not be perceived at all except on the basis of its hue variation. However, van der Horst et al., like many other investigators who have worked with pure color gratings, had noticed a peculiar fact. With isoluminant red-green gratings of low spatial frequencies, brightness appears to be relatively constant across the extent of the grating, whereas its hue changes in a regular progression from red to green and back. With a high spatial frequency, however, the grating no longer has the appearance one would expect of an isoluminant color pattern. Rather, it looks like a monochromatic luminance grating whose color is the mixture color of the two extremes. For instance, a high spatial frequency (say, 10 c/deg) red-green grating appears to be a yellow-black luminance grating. A blue-yellow grating loses its chromatic appearance at even lower spatial frequencies.

One possible conclusion about this unexpected phenomenon is that it reveals a very interesting characteristic of the visual system. The other and much more worrisome possibility is that appearances, in this instance, do not deceive. The apparent luminance grating might, in fact, be a real luminance grating produced

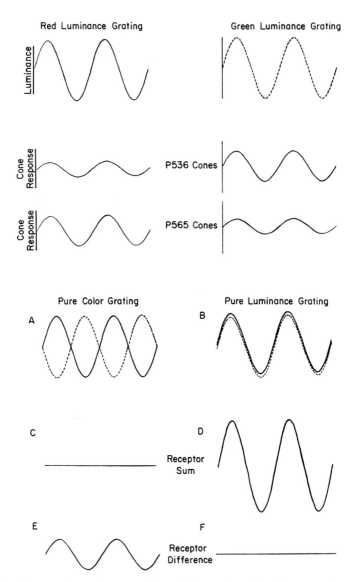

FIG. 7.2   Construction and cross sections of chromatic and luminance gratings. The top row of the figure shows two luminance grating cross sections, one red and one green. In each case, luminance varies sinusoidally across space. The next set of functions illustrates the relative responses of arrays of middle or M (P530) and long or L (P560) wavelength cones to each of the individual gratings. Note that both cone types would respond to both gratings, but with different amplitudes. In A, the red and green luminance gratings have been added *out of phase* to produce a pattern which varies in chromaticity but which is constant in luminance across its extent. This corresponds to the pattern shown in Figure 7.1. In B, the two components have been added *in phase* to produce a luminance grating of the same contrast (but twice the mean luminance as the individual components). In C and D are reflected the *sums* of the cone responses to each of the component patterns. In E and F are shown the *differences* in the cone responses to the same patterns. Note that the receptor sums vary with luminance contrast, whereas the receptor differences vary with color contrast (from R.L. De Valois & Jacobs, 1984. Reprinted by permission).

as an optical artifact. The latter is the conclusion of van der Horst et al. (1967) and the reason for their definition of the psychophysical task. They reasoned that if the grating appeared to be luminance varying, it probably was. Their interest, however, was not in luminance contrast sensitivity, but rather in color contrast sensitivity. Hence they considered detection on the basis of color to have occurred only when the subjects could actually perceive the difference in hue. Careful study of this curious—and we believe important—phenomenon suggests to us that it may not be due to luminance artifacts. Let us consider the various factors that might account for the effect.

There are three optical factors that could produce a regular luminance variation on the retina from a presumably isoluminant, pure color grating: axial chromatic aberration, radial chromatic aberration, and diffraction. As we discussed in Chapter 2, axial chromatic aberration refers to the fact that lights of different wavelengths are imaged at different depths in the eye, and thus are differentially in or out of focus at the level of the receptors. If the stimulus of interest is a sine wave, defocusing it will not change its spatial frequency or its phase but will reduce its amplitude. Suppose then that a subject views a red-green grating produced by interleaving two sinusoidal luminance gratings of 630 and 520 nm, respectively. If the two are properly matched in amplitude for equal luminance, the resultant grating should be an isoluminant, pure color grating. Since the eye cannot be in focus for both of these wavelengths simultaneously, however, the two component gratings cannot both be in focus on the retina. If the eye is in focus for the 630-nm component, the 520-nm component will be partially demodulated. The result will be a grating that varies in luminance as well as in chromaticity. Axial chromatic aberration can be virtually eliminated (in an experimental arrangement) with the use of a small artificial pupil, which increases the depth of focus for both component gratings, and with an achromatizing lens placed in front of the eye.

Diffraction by the pupil could also artifactually induce a small luminance grating from a pure color grating, and this would be increased, not lessened, by the use of a small artificial pupil. Both such a diffraction artifact and any residual artifact from axial chromatic aberration would have the effect of demodulating one of the component gratings with respect to the other.

The third possible artifact, radial chromatic aberration, refers to the fact that patterns produced by lights of two different wavelengths will be slightly differentially magnified at the retina. Thus, in the case mentioned above, the retinal images of identical gratings of 630 and 520 nm would have slightly different spatial frequencies. For an extended pattern, the two images would be periodically in and out of register, producing beats (which would be luminance artifacts) across its extent.

There are a variety of methods that either eliminate or compensate for these different potential sources of luminance artifacts. Their use may restore the chromatic appearance of gratings over a middle range of spatial frequencies (suggesting that luminance artifacts are at least partially responsible), but generally fails to eliminate the effect completely. We shall discuss what we believe to be a possible explanation below.

Spatial Color Contrast Sensitivity Function

The spatial contrast sensitivity for pure color patterns differs from luminance contrast sensitivity in two important respects (van der Horst & Bouman, 1969; Granger, 1973; Granger & Heurtley, 1973). First, sensitivity to pure color patterns falls off sooner on the high-frequency end when hue perception is the criterion. Secondly, there is little if any attenuation of sensitivity to low spatial frequencies for color gratings. Thus, while the luminance CSF has a band-pass characteristic at photopic levels, the color CSF is low-pass.

Van der Horst and Bouman (1969) used spatial frequencies as low as 0.7 c/deg, and found no loss in sensitivity up to that point. However, Watanabe, Sakara, and Isono (1976), using a very large screen, were able to measure sensitivity to extremely low spatial frequencies. They report some low-frequency attenuation, but at spatial frequencies very much lower than the comparable points for luminance gratings. Over most of the spatial range, then, our spatial color CSF can be thought of as low-pass.

Figure 7.3 shows typical spatial CSFs for red-green gratings measured with both pattern detection criteria (seeing any pattern at all, irrespective of hue appearance) or hue detection criteria (perception of color differences). The general shape of the functions is similar in both cases. The high-frequency fall-off is fairly sharp, with an absence of low- frequency attenuation in both color CSFs.

When the chromatic grating to be detected varies along a blue-yellow hue axis, results are similar. Most reports, however, note that the CSF for blue-yellow shows high-frequency attenuation at much lower spatial frequencies than does

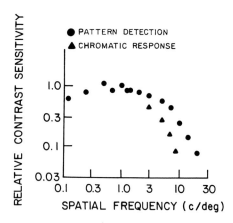

FIG. 7.3   Contrast sensitivity functions for isoluminant red-green patterns. In the function marked by triangles, the criterion was the detection of color differences, not just of pattern. In the function marked by circles, the task was detection of a pattern, whether or not it appeared of a different color. Note that the functions are similar except that at high spatial frequencies one can detect isoluminant gratings even though they do not appear colored (data redrawn from Granger & Heurtley, 1973, *J. Opt. Soc. Am., 63,* 1173–1174. Reprinted with permission).

that for red-green (van der Horst & Bouman, 1969; Granger & Heurtley, 1973). This is widely assumed to result from the sparse retinal distribution of S cones. A recent paper by Mullen (1985), however, reports no difference between the high-frequency cut-off for red-green and blue-yellow. She attributed the earlier results to the effects of chromatic aberration; such aberrations are difficult to eliminate and would affect the blue-yellow CSF more than the red-green. It should be noted that none of the studies cited has measured sensitivity to spatial variations in chromaticity along a tritanopic confusion axis (rather than a true blue-yellow axis). Only with stimuli lying along a tritan axis should the distribution of S cones be a strong determinant of the CSF.

Temporal Color Contrast Sensitivity Function

With a large, uniform patch of light that changes in wavelength at various temporal frequencies, it is possible to determine a temporal CSF. As with measurements of spatial color CSFs, it is critical that the wavelengths be equated in luminance, but the optical aberrations that become problems at high spatial frequencies of course do not arise.

Various experimenters (e.g., Regan & Tyler, 1971; D.H. Kelly, 1974, 1975) who have determined the color temporal CSF generally agree in finding that the color functions differ from the comparable luminance temporal CSFs in showing no low temporal frequency attenuation and in having a lower high temporal frequency cut. Thus, the results obtained with temporal modulation parallel those obtained with spatial modulation. Figure 7.4 shows a typical set of color and luminance temporal CSFs. D.H. Kelly (1983) has also obtained a combined spatiotemporal CSF for color-varying patterns. The complex resultant surface shows that one has highest sensitivity to low spatial frequencies at low temporal modulation rates.

Physiological Bases for Color CSFs

There are a number of physiological studies that are relevant to the topic of the color spatial and temporal CSFs. We shall not review here the psychophysical evidence for the analysis of color information by separate red-green and blue-yellow opponent-color systems (see R.L. De Valois & K.K. De Valois, 1975; Boynton, 1979; Hurvich, 1981). We shall briefly describe the spatial analysis carried out by ganglion and LGN cells and attempt to show how this is related to the psychophysics of color spatial vision.

It seems very likely that in primates, as in goldfish, some of the most crucial neural interactions underlying color vision take place at the receptor-horizontal cell-bipolar cell synapse. Nonetheless, we shall discuss this topic only at the level of the ganglion and LGN cells because there is very little experimental evidence in primate from the earlier neural levels. Almost all the relevant physiological

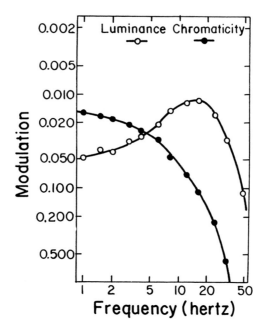

FIG. 7.4 Temporal CSFs for luminance and for red-green chromatic modulation. The task in this case is to detect the flicker of a large, spatially uniform test field. These data would provide one plane in a combined spatiotemporal contrast sensitivity surface (from D.H. Kelly, 1975, *Science, 188,* 371–372. Copyright 1975, AAAS. Reprinted with permission).

studies were carried out first at the LGN and then later in studies of ganglion cells.

The great majority of the cells in the primate retinogeniculate pathway, which projects to the striate cortex, are X cells—all of the numerous cells in the four parvocellular layers and most of the fewer cells in the two magnocellular layers of the LGN (von Blanckensee, 1981; Kaplan & Shapley, 1982). We shall thus be primarily concerned with the characteristics of different varieties of retinogeniculate X cells.

One of the most striking characteristics of most ganglion and geniculate cells in macaque monkeys (and presumably humans) is that they show chromatically opponent responses. To large spots or to low spatial frequency patterns, at least 70 to 80% of geniculate cells show excitation to luminance increments of some wavelengths of light and inhibition to others; see Figure 7.5 (R.L. De Valois, Smith, Kitai, & Karoly, 1958; R.L. De Valois, 1965; R.L. De Valois et al., 1966; Wiesel & Hubel, 1966; Derrington, Krauskopf, & Lennie, 1984). Such cells clearly are involved in color processing, since their responses are very much a function of the wavelength of the light. It is clear (see Figure 7.2) that while luminance information is carried by the summed output of different receptor types, color information is present in receptor differences. Opponent cells are

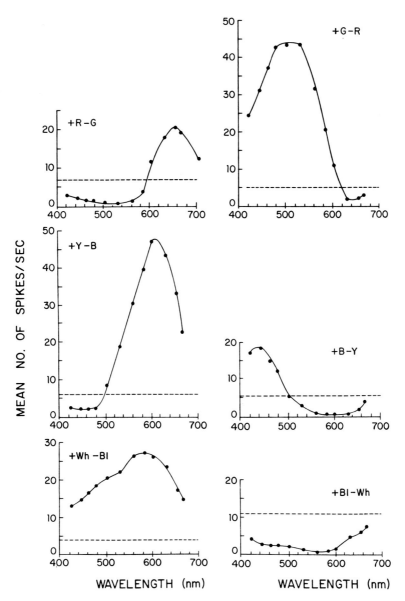

FIG. 7.5   Responses of typical LGN cells to incremental flashes of various wavelengths. The top four response functions show representative examples of the four basic color opponent cell types. The lower two illustrate the responses of cells that are sensitive primarily to luminance contrast, rather than color contrast (from R.L. De Valois, Abramov, & Jacobs, 1966, *J. Opt. Soc. Am.*, *56*, 966–977. Reprinted with permission).

clearly extracting such color information. Several reports (e.g. R.L. De Valois, 1965; R.L. De Valois et al., 1966; Wiesel & Hubel, 1966; Lennie, Derrington, & Krauskopf, 1982; Zrenner, 1983) also described a class of spectrally nonopponent cells that fire to luminance increments of any wavelength, or to decrements of any wavelength. Other studies (e.g., Patmos & van Norren, 1975) have shown, however, that with various techniques such as chromatic adaptation opponent interactions can be demonstrated in most of these cells as well.

The location of the spectral regions that produce excitation and inhibition varies from one opponent cell to the next. One important question is whether there are a limited number of different opponent cell types, and if so what their characteristics are. Merely classifying LGN cells by, say, their peak excitatory wavelength, would produce a very large number of categories, since virtually every cell differs from every other. The relevant issue is whether there is some grouping of the cells, in addition to the extensive random variability characteristic of biological systems. It should be noted that this is not the same question as that of the underlying cone inputs, although these issues have often been confused with each other in the literature.

Mainly on the basis of the wavelength at which the responses for a given cell cross from excitation to inhibition, we reported that LGN opponent cells can be grouped into four categories (R.L. De Valois et al., 1966). These we termed + R−G (cells that fire to red and inhibit to green, shifting from excitation to inhibition above 560 nm under a state of neutral chromatic adaptation with luminance increments in the stimuli), their mirror-image variety, the +G−R cells; +B−Y cells (which fire to blue and inhibit to yellow, shifting from excitation to inhibition at wavelengths shorter than 560 nm); and finally their mirror-image cells, +Y−B. From quite different experimental procedures (measuring responses to equiluminant chromatic stimuli modulated in different directions through color space), Derrington, Krauskopf, and Lennie (1984) also concluded that there were four opponent cell types (although the YB cells were found to lie along a tritanopic axis rather than along a yellow-blue axis. Their experimental techniques, which involved shifting from a white adaptation light to a chromatic stimulus of equal luminance, also produced a shorter wavelength cross over point dividing RG and BY cell types). The earlier evidence for only four basic opponent cell types had been disputed (e.g., de Monasterio, Gouras, & Tolhurst, 1975a, 1975b) on the basis of studies of the receptive field organization of opponent cells and of their presumed cone inputs. Neither of those types of experiments, however, bears directly on the issue of the number of functional classes of color cells.

The fact that the majority of macaque ganglion and LGN cells have chromatic-coding properties adds considerably to the complexity of the RF structure. There has been much confusion in the literature concerning the RF organization of these cells and the way in which it relates to their processing of color and of luminance. Much of this confusion derives from a tendency to confuse cone input maps with RF maps. An RF map, as initially defined and as used currently in other areas of vision, is an indication of the way in which a cell responds to a particular kind of stimulation at different locations in the visual field. It implies nothing about what receptor types the cell may be receiving inputs from, and it should not be confused with a map of presumed cone inputs. This is of particular importance in a consideration of these chromatically opponent ganglion and LGN cells, because such have cells have quite different RFs for color-varying and for luminance-varying patterns. This point is effectively masked by treating a presumed cone input map as if it were an RF map.

As discussed in Chapter 3, luminance and wavelength variations are completely confounded at the receptor level. An increase in photon capture, leading to hyperpolarization, can result from either an increase in the number of incident photons with no change in wavelength or from a shift to a more favorable wavelength with no change in the number of photons—or, of course, from some combination of the two. It should be noted, however, that a luminance increment (of any wavelength) hyperpolarizes *all* receptor types, whereas a given wavelength change (with no associated change in luminance) may hyperpolarize one receptor type, shifting the light toward its peak sensitivity, but depolarize another receptor type, by shifting the light away from its peak sensitivity. Thus, for pure luminance changes all receptors respond alike, but for pure wavelength changes, they may differ.

Primate color-opponent ganglion and geniculate cells receive an excitatory input from one cone type and an inhibitory input from another (or possibly from both others). The majority of these also have a different spatial distribution of these two opposite inputs (Wiesel & Hubel, 1966), such that for a $+G-R$ cell, for instance, the excitatory M cone input might be concentrated in the RF center and the inhibitory input from L cones would cover a larger, shallow, disk-shaped region centered at the same point. If one were to map the RF of such a cell with a spot of light (either white or monochromatic) that was a luminance increment with respect to the background, both cone types would be activated. But since the excitatory (M cone) input predominates in the RF center, and the inhibitory (L cone) input in the surround, the cell would have an antagonistic center-surround RF (see Figure 7.6). However, mapping the same cell with a small spot of light that was not a luminance increment but an equiluminant wavelength shift from, say, 570 to 540 nm, would produce a quite different RF map (R.L. De Valois & K.K. De Valois, 1975; R.L. De Valois, Snodderly, Yund, & Hepler, 1977). Such a pure color stimulus would have opposite effects on the two underlying cone types, producing more activation of M cones and less of L cones. Such a stimulus in the RF center would thus produce an increase in excitatory (M cone) input. It would also, contrary to the situation with a luminance increment, produce an increase in net excitation when it was presented in the surround, by decreasing the inhibitory (L cone) input; see Figure 7.6.

The visual consequences of these very different RF structures for color and for luminance-varying patterns can be seen in the very different responses spectrally opponent LGN cells give to luminance and to color patterns of different sizes or spatial frequencies (R.L. De Valois, Snodderly, Yund, & Hepler, 1977). As a luminance-varying pattern centered on a cell's RF is increased in width,

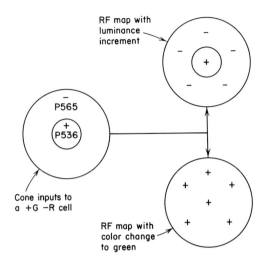

FIG. 7.6   Cone input map for a single + G−R LGN cell (left), and RFs of such a cell for luminance increments and for color changes. Note that there is a center-surround antagonism for luminance but not for color. See text for further discussion (from R.L. De Valois & K.K. De Valois, 1975. Reprinted with permission).

the response increases up to a point, then decreases for still wider bars, as the antagonistic RF surround is invaded (see Figure 7.7). For a color-varying pattern, however, the response does not decrease, but rather continues to increase to very wide bars, since RF center and surround are synergistic for color.

If the stimulus is not a circular spot of light, but rather a grating, this same difference will be reflected in the cell's CSF to color and to luminance. It will be remembered from our earlier discussion that the high spatial frequency cut is related to the RF center size, the sensitivity dropping to zero at a frequency that corresponds to one cycle across the RF center. But the effective "center" size of an LGN cell's RF is different for luminance-varying and for color-varying patterns, in the latter case covering the whole RF since center and surround inputs act synergistically. Thus the high spatial frequency fall-off for LGN cells occurs at lower spatial frequencies for color-varying than for luminance-varying patterns (see Figure 7.8). The low-frequency attenuation seen to luminance patterns is attributable to center-surround antagonism. Since for LGN cells color center and surround are synergistic, not antagonistic, as pointed out in Figure 7.6, one sees low-frequency attenuation in the MTF of LGN cells for luminance-varying but not for color-varying gratings.

Consider now the temporal color CSF in relation to LGN cell responses. Our statements above to the effect that LGN RF center and surround are antagonistic for luminance and synergistic for color is correct if one tests with long-lasting stationary stimuli. To consider the temporal properties of these cells, however, one must examine their dynamic characteristics. The essential property that accounts for the differing luminance and color temporal CSFs is a latency dif-

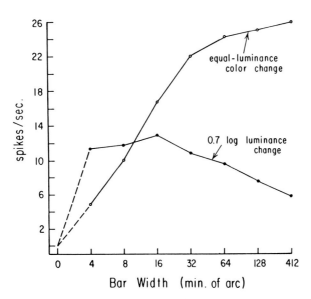

FIG. 7.7 Responses of a color-opponent LGN cell to bars of various widths. The bars, which were centered on the RF and flashed on, differed from the background either in luminance or in color. The color patterns contained no luminance change (from R.L. De Valois, Snodderly, Yund, & Hepler, 1977. Reprinted with permission).

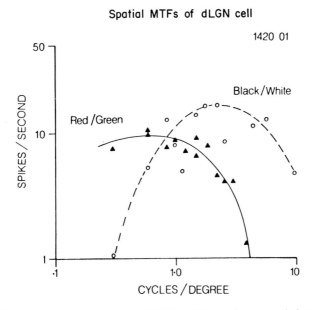

FIG. 7.8 Responses of a color-opponent LGN cell to luminance and chromatic gratings of various spatial frequencies. Note that the response to luminance patterns shows low spatial frequency attenuation, but that to chromatic patterns does not (from von Blanckensee, 1981. Reprinted with permission).

ference between center and surround responses. If the information to bipolars coming down the indirect path were delayed relative to that down the direct receptor-bipolar path, the surround response would slightly lag the center response. This would be expected due to the longer path (through horizontal cells) and an extra synapse. Such has been found in comparable systems in other (non-primate) animals (Ratliff, Knight, Toyoda, & Hartline, 1967).

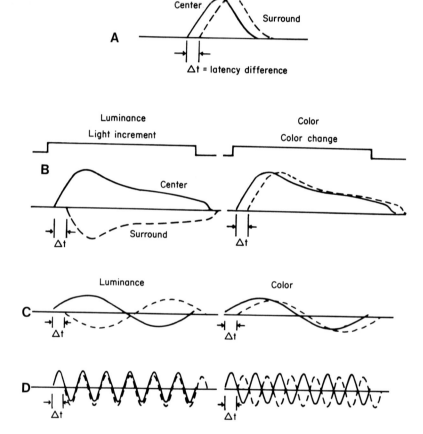

FIG. 7.9   Effects of a constant latency difference between center and surround mechanisms. A fixed center-surround latency difference such as that illustrated at the top (A) would have quite different consequences at different temporal frequencies, and for color versus luminance flicker. Note that for a single long-duration stimulus (B), the effect of the latency difference is minimal. For such patterns, center and surround are thus largely antagonistic for luminance and synergistic for color. The same is true for low temporal frequency modulation (C). With rapid temporal modulation (D), however, the same small latency difference will produce a 180° phase shift, making the center and surround inputs synergistic for luminance and antagonistic for color.

With a long-duration stimulus, this surround delay would have minimal effects, but as the flicker rate of a stimulus is increased, there would be an increasing phase lag, till at some rate center and surround would respond in antiphase (see Figure 7.9). For luminance-varying stimuli, this 180° phase shift would make center and surround not antagonistic, but *synergistic.* There should be increased sensitivity to such temporal frequencies, as indeed there is. But if, at these temporal frequencies, center and surround are synergistic for luminance, they should be antagonistic for color. So color sensitivity should fall as luminance sensitivity rises; D.H. Kelly (1975) found just that to occur. At still higher temporal frequencies, of course, a further phase shift would make center and surround again antagonistic for luminance, and sensitivity should drop.

We earlier postulated this explanation for the differences between color and luminance temporal CSFs (R.L. De Valois, Snodderly, Yund, & Hepler, 1977). Recent evidence from a study of monkey opponent-color ganglion cells (Gouras & Zrenner, 1979) gives experimental support to the notion.

SIGNIFICANCE OF COLOR CSFS FOR VISION

As we have been discussing, the spatial and temporal CSFs for color differ from those for luminance in two respects. Color sensitivity is relatively higher at low spatial frequencies, there being little or no low-frequency attenuation in either the spatial or the temporal domain (except to extremely low frequencies: a ganzfeld, or totally uniform field, looked at for a long time has been reported to lose color). Second, color sensitivity drops off earlier as spatial and temporal frequencies increase, relative to sensitivity to luminance variations. With both spatial and temporal variations, blue-yellow sensitivity is generally found to fall off earlier at high frequencies than does sensitivity along a red-green axis (although a recent study by Mullen, 1985, showed essentially the same high spatial frequency fall-off for red-green and blue-yellow). A number of deductions can be made from these sensitivity functions.

Different Frequency Bands

Intensity and wavelength changes in the environment form two different, physically independent sources of information about the world. Animals lacking color vision get a single map of the world in which wavelength and intensity variations are confounded (objects reflecting only wavelengths to which the animal is very insensitive and those reflecting very little light of any wavelength would both be seen as dark). Those animals with color vision, however, get two separate versions of the nature of the visual world. The shape of the color and luminance CSFs indicate that these two versions of the world are quite different from each other. To a first approximation, the luminance version gives us a middle and high spatial (and temporal) frequency representation of the visual world, emphasizing fine detail, and rapidly changing or moving patterns. The color version covers low and middle spatial (and temporal) frequencies, giving us more information about large objects and extensive areas.

The rough division of the spatial frequency range between luminance and color makes sense from several points of view, when one considers both the optical and physiological limitations of the eye and the nature of visual objects. It is reasonable that high spatial frequency information be attenuated because diffraction and chromatic aberrations of the eye would render much of the high spatial frequency color information spurious, particularly that related to variations along a blue-yellow axis. The relatively greater sensitivity to color than to luminance at the low spatial frequency end of the spatial spectrum appears adaptive when certain aspects of visual patterns are considered. We argued earlier (Chapter 5) that since very low spatial and temporal frequency luminance information tells one more about the illuminant than about the object, filtering out low frequencies only eliminates irrelevant information. However, low- frequency color information is quite different. The apparent color of the world (which depends more on the reflectances of objects than on the characteristics of the illuminant) changes little through the day or across the visual field with cloud cover, etc. The salience of color at low spatial frequencies would in particular appear very useful in dealing with shadows. On sunny days, in almost any environment except perhaps a flat desert, there are numerous shadows cutting across the shapes of objects. These form very powerful and deceptive contours in the field, which must surely make the detection, characterization, and localization of objects more difficult. Low spatial frequency color information would be very useful here, since the color of an object is little affected by the presence or absence of a shadow. If the shadow of a branch were to fall across a person's body, the additional luminance contours introduced could make it more difficult to identify the shape as being that of a person. The colors involved, however, would extend across and beyond the shadow, being much less affected by it. Thus the low-frequency color version of the image would be a more veridical representation of the object than would the luminance version.

At this point we must interject a cautionary note. The discussion should not be read as implying that luminance variations produced by a directional light source are always, of necessity, detrimental. There are algorithms by which one can derive information about three-dimensional shape from shading, for instance.

Color Contrast and Similitude

We suggested in Chapter 5 that large brightness contrast effects would be seen over much of the spatial frequency range because of our greater sensitivity to middle than to very low spatial frequency luminance variations. In the case of color-varying stimuli, however, the situation is quite different: our sensitivity drops very little down to even quite low spatial frequencies. We should thus expect color contrast to be much less powerful than brightness contrast, as it in fact is when measured under comparable conditions.

We earlier also suggested that over that spatial frequency range at which sensitivity is less than to very low frequency patterns, one should predict a change not in the direction of contrast but in the direction of similitude (assimilation). The pattern should appear more similar to its background, rather than more different. In the case of luminance-varying patterns, the range of spatial frequencies at which one would expect similitude effects is quite restricted, namely, at only very high spatial frequencies. With color-varying patterns, however, one might expect similitude effects over most of the visible spatial frequency range, since sensitivity to color variations increases almost monotonically as spatial frequency decreases. Specifically, color similitude effects might appear at mid-spatial frequencies, where there are powerful brightness contrast effects. That appears to be the case. An example is shown in Figure 7.10, in which a pattern is presented in roughly equiluminant color (assuming fidelity in the color printing). One of the same patterns presented in color in Figure 7.10 is shown in black-white in Figure 7.11. In the black-white pattern one sees contrast effects: the same gray appears lighter on a black background than on a white background. However, the various colored squares of the same dimensions (Figure 7.10) appear changed in color in the similitude direction, not away from the background color, but toward it. These effects can be simply predicted from the differing luminance and color spatial CSFs.

It is curious that color contrast has been emphasized so much in the percep-

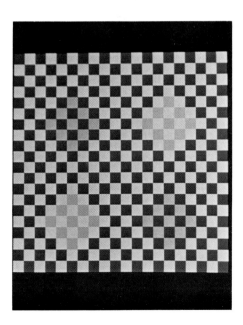

FIG. 7.11 A pattern similar to the bottom pattern in Figure 7.10, except that it is composed of black-white luminance variations.

tion and vision literature and color similitude virtually ignored, for it seems that the latter is by far the more important phenomenon. Color similitude is the rule in color interactions; color contrast is relatively rare.

Minimally Distinct Borders

Edges and borders have been widely discussed in the classic vision literature. One of the reasons for this emphasis is the widespread belief that objects are perceived by virtue of their edges, and that the first task in identifying an object is to locate its edges (perhaps by means of detecting the zero-crossings in spatially filtered versions of the image, Marr, 1982). This notion, which has some intuitive appeal, is strengthened by the ease with which we can perceive figures in line drawings, where only sharp edges are present.

In an extensive series of experiments, Boynton and his colleagues have examined the relative roles of luminance and color differences in determining the sharpness of borders. They have shown that when two patches of light of different colors are present side by side, a sharp border is usually seen between them. If subjects are allowed to adjust the intensity of the light on one side until the border becomes minimally distinct, the colors will be set to equal luminance (Boynton & Kaiser, 1968). That is to say, when only chromatic differences are present, the border is quite indistinct; making one side of higher luminance than the other immediately produces a sharper border. Furthermore, if borders between equiluminant red-green and equiluminant blue-yellow patches are compared, it is clear that the border in the latter case is very much more blurred. So luminance differences are more effective in producing sharp borders than red-green color differences, and blue-yellow color differences are less effective still.

The direction of these results is predictable from the differences in the luminance and color CSFs. Recall that high spatial frequencies are responsible for sharp borders. (Consider a sine wave grating, which is extremely blurred; adding successive higher odd harmonic frequencies to it makes the edges increasingly sharp until a square wave grating with sharp edges finally results.) Since our sensitivity to high spatial frequencies is high for luminance variations, less for red-green pure color variations, and least for blue-yellow color variations, it is clear that the minimum border data are exactly what one might expect. The studies of the minimally distinct border in effect confirm the differences in sensitivity to high spatial frequencies for color versus pure luminance gratings.

It is important to realize that high spatial frequencies represent only one end of the CSF. Even though we are relatively insensitive to high spatial frequency color patterns, middle and especially low spatial frequencies are perceived quite well. Only if one believes that pattern vision (or object perception) depends solely on the high-frequency information contained in sharp edges would this be grounds to eliminate color differences as a possible (or partial) basis for spatial vision. In fact, the contrast sensitivity function for pure color patterns is itself sufficient evidence that color differences can subserve some pattern vision. Otherwise, of course, one would be unable to detect at any contrast the pure color gratings used to measure the function.

The color interactions we have been discussing here are all fairly local phenomena, in which the appearance of an area is affected by the stimuli in neighboring regions. Color and lightness contrast, however, can operate over very long distances in the visual field (Yund & Armington, 1975). Such long-distance interactions find no counterpart in the responses of LGN (Yund et al., 1977) or striate cells. Up through the striate cortex, visual processing is fairly local. One of the main roles of later, poststriate cortical regions must be to put together information from various local regions. Such is obviously required for pattern detection, since the images of many objects are far larger than the extent of any striate RFs or the subtense of any striate module. It must also be true, for instance, for movement perception, since whether a given object is seen as stationary or moving depends on its displacement relative to that of objects elsewhere in the visual field. It also must be the case for color vision since color and lightness contrast and constancies all involve long-distance interactions. Evidence for such long-distance color interactions in post-striate areas has been reported (Zeki, 1985). These processes, while very important, are beyond the scope of what we are attempting to cover in this book.

Color Vision Without Color Knowledge

We presented data in Figure 4.17 indicating a difference in peak spatial frequency distributions for simple and complex cells in monkey striate cortex. Cells tuned to the highest spatial frequencies are more often complex cells than simple cells. As we have seen, many simple and complex cells respond to pure color patterns, but they do so in quite different ways (differences related to their differing responses to luminance-varying patterns). Simple cells, like LGN spectrally opponent cells, respond in an opposite manner to different spectral regions. Simple cells, then, are color selective as well as being color sensitive. Complex cells can also be very sensitive to color variations, but they respond to them in ways very different from those of LGN opponent cells. A typical complex cell will respond, for instance, to an equiluminant red-green grating drifted across its RF, to a counterphase-flickered red-green grating, or to an equiluminant color shift from a red field to a green bar on the red background. But complex cells are not color selective. They respond in the same way to a red bar on a green background as to a green bar on a red background. To a counterphase flicker, they give the same response regardless of the position of the grating with respect to the RF. This is of course similar to their lack of specificity with respect to black-white patterns, as illustrated in Figure 4.6. This lack of color specificity for either black-white or red-green or blue-yellow patterns can be seen to be equivalent to a lack of phase specificity (K.K. De Valois, 1973): to be able to pick out which is the red and which the green in a red-green grating requires knowledge of the phase of the pattern. In most respects complex cells behave exactly the same to color differences as to luminance differences. The spatial frequency and orientation of the pattern determine the cell's response, but pattern phase is completely irrelevant. To say that a complex cell is not color sensitive because it responds in the same manner to red and to green is equivalent to saying it is not sensitive to luminance because it responds in the same way to black and to white—and no one would suggest the latter.

Insofar as the cells sensitive to the highest spatial frequencies are complex cells, one would be able to detect pure color patterns at high spatial frequencies without being able to specify the particular colors involved, or even to say whether there were color rather than luminance patterns present. In fact, we find that on the average complex cells responding to pure color patterns are tuned to higher spatial frequencies than are color-responsive simple cells (see Figure 7.12B). We believe that detection by complex cells, rather than optical artifacts, could account for our ability to detect high spatial frequency pure-color patterns although their chromaticity can not be made out (see Figure 7.12A). It could also account for the curious appearance of high spatial frequency pure color gratings discussed earlier. One need only assume that, faced with an ambiguity as to whether a given pattern consists of color or luminance variations, the visual system treats it as a luminance pattern.

The clinical syndrome of color agnosia is relevant in this regard. There have been numerous reports in the neurological literature for over 100 years of occasional patients, suffering from some cortical lesions which appear to be post-

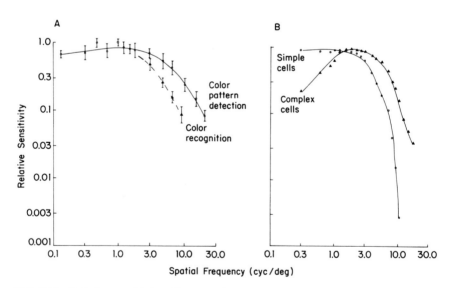

FIG. 7.12   Relative sensitivity of human observers (A) and of the two classes of macaque cortical cells (B) to isoluminant color-varying patterns. See text for discussion (from Thorell et al., 1984; psychophysical data redrawn from Granger & Heurtley, 1973, *J. Opt. Soc. Am., 63,* 1173–1174. Reprinted by permission).

striate, who report rather odd problems with their color perception. These individuals are unable to name the colors of various colored objects, but they are not color blind. In one well-studied case (Kinsbourne & Harrington, 1964), the patient was found to perform perfectly normally on various color vision tests (such as being able to discriminate figures in the Ishihara plates, or to sort equiluminant colors in spectral order) but was quite unable to correctly name the colors involved. The problem was not merely a verbal one: the patient could be taught to use color names to identify various geometrical shapes, for instance. Such a color agnosia patient behaves exactly as we would expect from one whose color vision was entirely dependent on the activity of complex cells rather than simple cells. In other words, he behaves across the whole spatial frequency range somewhat as a normal observer does at very high spatial frequencies, being able to discriminate pure color patterns, but not to identify the particular colors involved.

MULTIPLE COLOR SPATIAL FREQUENCY CHANNELS?

As with sensitivity to luminance-varying patterns, the appropriate next question is whether the observed color contrast sensitivity function reflects the filter characteristic of a single channel or the envelope of the sensitivities of multiple channels. The evidence is more limited than for luminance-varying patterns, but what evidence there is suggests that there are multiple color sensitive spatial frequency channels which are, in general, somewhat less finely tuned for spatial frequency than are the comparable luminance channels.

Psychophysical Evidence

The most compelling bit of psychophysical evidence for multiple frequency specific luminance channels comes from selective adaptation studies (e.g., Blakemore & Campbell, 1969). There have been two brief reports (K.K. De Valois, 1978; Bradley, Switkes, & K.K. De Valois, 1985) of a similar spatial frequency specific loss resulting from adaptation to isoluminant red-green gratings. Adaptation to a grating that varies sinusoidally in hue (red-green) produces a reduction in sensitivity to gratings of the same color (i.e., red-green) and similar spatial frequency. As with luminance gratings, the loss in color contrast sensitivity is band limited and centered on the adaptation frequency, although somewhat broader in bandwidth than the comparable luminance functions. One can thus conclude that there are multiple spatial frequency channels that are sensitive to pure color patterns.

Another kind of psychophysical evidence for multiple channels comes from masking studies. If a subject is asked to detect the presence of an isoluminant red-green grating superimposed on another suprathreshold isoluminant red-green grating of identical space-average luminance and the same or different spatial frequency, a spatial frequency masking function can be obtained (K.K. De Valois & Switkes, 1983; Switkes & K.K. De Valois, 1983). Such a function is quite similar in character to the equivalent functions obtained with luminance gratings (e.g., Pantle, 1974; Foley & Legge, 1981). The color-color masking functions tend to be somewhat broader and flatter, however. This evidence, too, implies the existence of multiple spatial frequency selective channels that are sensitive to pure color patterns.

Physiological Evidence

It would be difficult to argue for multiple spatial frequency channels for pure color stimuli on the basis of LGN cell properties. Although different cells do have different high frequency cut-off points (and could thus subserve discrimination among high spatial frequencies), they are virtually all low-pass for isoluminant color stimuli. There is no physiological evidence for even moderately narrow spatial frequency band-pass mechanisms for pure color stimuli at the

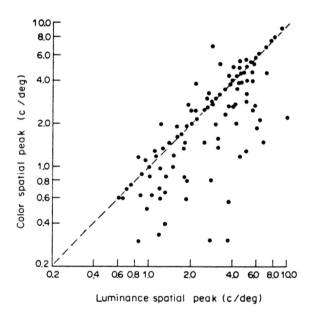

FIG. 7.13 Comparison of peak spatial frequency for color and luminance for a large sample of macaque cortical cells. Note that although most cells show similar tuning for color and for luminance, those which do not are most likely to respond to higher frequency luminance patterns and lower frequency color patterns (from Thorell et al., 1984, *Vision Res., 24,* 751–769. Copyright 1984, Pergamon Journals, Inc. Reprinted with permission).

LGN. The attenuation of low spatial frequency luminance patterns that is produced by center-surround antagonism does not occur for color because of the effective center-surround synergism in this case.

In striate cortex cells, however, the spatial filtering characteristics for color and for luminance are much more similar. Just as there is a continuum of spatial frequency bandwidths of cortical cells for luminance gratings, for instance, there is a similar continuum of bandwidths for pure color gratings. For any given cell, the spatial tuning function for pure color is likely to be very similar, often identical, to its spatial tuning function for luminance. When a cell has nonidentical tuning functions for color and for luminance, however, the bandwidth for color is likely to be broader than the bandwidth for luminance (Thorell, 1981; Thorell et al., 1984). Cortical cells, like LGN cells, are more likely to act as low-pass spatial frequency filters for pure color stimuli than for luminance stimuli; and if the peak spatial frequency (i.e., that spatial frequency to which the cell is most sensitive) differs, the color peak is likely to be lower than the luminance peak (see Figure 7.13).

There is, thus, both psychophysical and physiological evidence for multiple spatial frequency channels in the pure color domain. This suggests not only that color differences alone can subserve spatial vision, but that color-based spatial vision also operates very much like luminance-based spatial vision.

LUMINANCE-COLOR INTERACTIONS

In Chapter 6 we discussed spatial frequency masking data for luminance gratings, and earlier in this chapter we described comparable data for pure color gratings. The question we would like to raise here is what sort of interactions take place when luminance-varying and color-varying patterns are simultaneously present. We have seen that either luminance alone or color alone can be a sufficient basis for some pattern vision, but in the real world it is rare to find a scene in which either luminance or color varies alone (except, perhaps, for such artificially created scenes as black print on a white page). So while it may be a necessary first step to study sensitivity to each in isolation, one must examine the interaction of color and luminance in order eventually to have any real understanding of spatial vision.

There are many studies in the literature that examine the effect of spatial variables on chromatic discriminations. In many cases the stimuli used vary in both chromaticity and luminance (e.g., Hilz & Cavonius, 1970; Boynton, Hayhoe, & MacLeod, 1977), making it difficult to disentangle the observed effects. For example, one such set of experiments concerns what Boynton et al. have termed the "gap effect." Subjects were asked to discriminate a chromaticity difference between two subfields that were matched in luminance. The two fields were either exactly juxtaposed with no border other than that formed by the chromatic difference or separated by a dividing line (or gap) of various widths. Depending on the conditions, interposing a gap was found sometimes to decrease discriminability, sometimes to increase discriminability, or sometimes to have no effect. The gap effect may also depend on the color and size of the subfields, as well as many other variables which have not been systematically investigated. In the particular case of the gap effect (unlike many other such phenomena) there has been an attempt to understand and categorize the relevant variables (Boynton et al., 1977). Even so, the resulting explanation only allows a qualitative understanding and cannot provide predictions for novel stimulus configurations. With the very fractional understanding we have of most color-luminance-spatial variable interactions we are even less able to make quantitative predictions. We would suggest that what is needed is some unifying theoretical structure based on empirical data that would encompass many stimulus configurations and experimental paradigms, allowing quantitative predictions in a wide variety of situations.

We have studied color-luminance interactions by examining the simultaneous interactions of luminance and pure color gratings (K.K. De Valois & Switkes, 1983; Switkes & K.K. De Valois, 1983). An interesting and profoundly asymmetric pattern of interactions appeared. As can be seen in Figure 7.14, both the luminance-luminance and the color-color masking functions are band-pass and centered on the test frequency. They are steeper on the low-frequency side (indicating that high frequencies mask low to a greater extent than low frequencies mask high). The color-color masking is often somewhat less peaked and broader in bandwidth than the luminance functions. (The difference in magnitude of the masking effect, and perhaps to some extent the difference in shape as well, is due

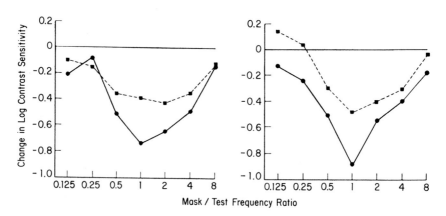

FIG. 7.14 Spatial frequency masking functions for isoluminant red-green gratings (dashed lines) and for isochromatic luminance gratings (solid lines) for two subjects. The masking effect (change in log contrast sensitivity) is plotted as a function of mask/test frequency ratio (from K.K. De Valois & Switkes, 1983, *J. Opt. Soc. Am., 73,* 11-18. Reprinted with permission).

in these data to the arbitrarily chosen mask contrasts.) What is of particular interest, however, are the cross-masking conditions. It was found that a pure color grating has a profound masking effect on a luminance grating, masking luminance about as effectively as a luminance grating does. However, in the converse experiment, the masking of a pure color test pattern by a luminance grating, masking is much less profound, with a significant loss in sensitivity only when mask and test gratings are of the same frequency.

There are several points of interest in these data. First, although the masking is quite frequency specific in all cases, for the two crossed conditions (luminance test-color mask and color test-luminance mask) there appears to be no phase specificity. The lack of effect of relative phase in the crossed conditions implicates a higher level process than a simple point-by-point interaction. It also allows one to rule out one kind of mechanism postulated by Boynton et al. (1977), namely, that introducing luminance contours into an otherwise pure-color pattern should improve discrimination by delineating the subregions over which a chromatic averaging process takes place. Using a square wave luminance mask of the same frequency as the sinusoidal color test grating did not improve detection, regardless of the relative mask-test phases, although in one phase angle the square wave perfectly delineated the subregions over which color averaging should occur, whereas with a 90° phase shift the average color difference between two adjacent bars of the square wave would be zero. That no difference occurred despite the fact that all other conditions remained constant implies that in this experiment either there is no such averaging process at work or its influence is minimal at best.

The most significant conclusion to be drawn from this study concerns the relative weighting of color and luminance information in the analysis of a pattern in which both are present. To the extent that color and luminance interact (and that interaction is quite substantial), color seems to be by far the dominant stimulus characteristic (at least in the kinds of patterns used here). Not only does color mask a luminance stimulus of the same spatial frequency much more efficiently than the converse, but it produces masking over a much greater range of spatial frequencies. Luminance masks color a relatively small amount under the most propitious circumstances and may even increase the detectability of a superimposed pure color stimulus under some circumstances. This suggests that the study of spatial vision using only luminance-varying stimuli is neglecting some of the dominant factors involved. Any real understanding of pattern vision will require first understanding the way in which luminance and color interact.

Color and luminance information may interact in pattern vision in at least two different ways. One is simply due to the fact that there appears to be multiplexing of color and luminance within the same cells at early levels of the visual system. The second is a more active gating process by which color information can selectively interfere with the analysis of luminance information. For the former there is ample physiological evidence; for the latter, very little. We do know that the responses of color-opponent cells in the LGN are dictated by the color attributes of the stimulus up to luminance mismatches of ± 0.5 log unit (R.L. De Valois, Jacobs, & Abramov, 1964).

In summary, the visual system can utilize chromatic information to analyze patterns, it apparently does so in a manner very similar to that used for analyzing luminance information (i.e., by multiple spatial frequency channels), and color and luminance can and do interact in ways that cannot be deduced from their independent attributes. The apparent predominance of color in a stimulus containing both chromatic and luminance variations can be attested to by anyone who has ever attempted heterochromatic brightness matching. The importance of color for spatial vision should not be overlooked, and any attempt to understand spatial vision without considering the role played by color must surely fail.

8

Spatial Localization: Phase and Position

In this chapter we raise the general question of how the visual system knows where something is. How does the system gain, maintain, and process information about spatial coordinates? Such information is of course present at the level of the receptors, since each receptor is stimulated by light from a different visual direction. If the subsequent visual processing were merely a remapping of the receptors onto the cortex, there would be no problem of localization—but of course such a process would accomplish nothing toward the most critical visual task, that of determining what objects in the visual field produced the particular pattern of receptor activity present at a given moment. As we have seen, such a point-by-point remapping is not what occurs in the retinal and striate processing. But since each later neural element is integrating information over some spatial region, it necessarily loses some degree of the spatial localization present in the receptors. This makes more interesting the question of how the system as a whole maintains localization information, and we address that question in this chapter. We also raise the question of whether under all circumstances positional information in fact *is* maintained.

We have been discussing the visual system in terms of spatial frequency filtering, arguing that describing the early stages of the system as a bank of local spatial frequency filters is both reasonable and meaningful. However, it will be remembered from our discussion of Fourier analysis (Chapter 1) that to describe a complex waveform fully, not only must the frequency and amplitude be specified, but the phase of each component also. Phase is the localization component in a Fourier analysis: e.g., a sine and a cosine wave of the same frequency have the same shape, but one is shifted in location with respect to the other. The question of how the visual system deals with phase is thus relevant to the question raised above of spatial localization.

Many of the early discussions of spatial frequency analysis by the visual system ignored spatial phase, and experiments even showed that phase was irrelevant in some tasks (e.g., Graham & Nachmias, 1971). However, it is clear that the visual system is sensitive to the spatial phase of patterns under some conditions, and that in many of the situations in which spatial frequency channels have been studied, the phase as well as the spatial frequency of the patterns is critical (Tolhurst, 1972a; K.K. De Valois, 1973, 1977a; Stromeyer, Lange, & Ganz, 1973). We will discuss some of the evidence for phase specificity in this chapter, but we will also present evidence that under some circumstances phase sensitivity does not seem to be present.

ABSOLUTE VERSUS RELATIVE PHASE

We shall not consider phase as a property of temporal waveforms but will only deal with spatial phase. Even when so restricted, phase is an ambiguous term with respect to visual stimuli. If one considers a grating of a single spatial frequency, phase becomes a location term. The phase of a grating is specified with respect to some specific arbitrary point in space. Changing the spatial phase would be equivalent to sliding the grating along an axis perpendicular to its bars and in the same plane. The appearance of the entire grating would not change—it would still appear to be a grating of the same spatial frequency—but the intensity at any given point in the visual field might be different (depending, of course, on the spatial frequency of the grating and the extent of the translation). Under some circumstances this would be perceived; under others, it might not. We will refer to this aspect of phase as *absolute phase*.

Absolute spatial phase has to do with the localization of visual patterns or of components of visual patterns. This raises the general question of how it is that spatial localization is accomplished. If one considers the system to be performing a spatially localized frequency analysis of visual stimuli, with phase-sensitive units, there are potentially two quite different possible ways the system could gain information about location. One, which we will term a phase mechanism, involves decoding the phases of the various frequency components in the local area being analyzed. The other, which we term a positional mechanism, would involve an analysis of *which* local area is activated. With respect to the presumed underlying cortical mechanisms, these two processes would reflect in the first case the relative activation of different phase-selective units tuned to each frequency range within a cortical module, and in the other case which particular cortical module (or subdivision thereof) is involved. Both of these potential mechanisms may be involved in spatial localization, but they have not been clearly distinguished in the literature.

With extended, repetitive, sinusoidal gratings, of course, only a phase mechanism could be operative to detect a difference between a grating at two different phase angles, since all cortical areas would be stimulated by each grating. With a spatially delimited pattern, however, these two potentially operative systems could be distinguished. Consider, as an example, an extended grating, a small patch of which is seen through a window. One could keep the window in constant position and shift the grating, producing a phase shift in the pattern but no change in its overall position. Or one could keep the grating stationary but move the window, producing a positional change but no phase shift in the grating pattern. Shifting only the grating should hypothetically not change which cortical area or module is stimulated, but would change which subgroups of phase-sensitive units within these modules are activated. Shifting the window without moving the grating, on the other hand, would move the pattern to a new cortical region, but would not change the functional sub-population of cells activated.

Our discussion above of absolute phase is of course predicated on the visual system's performing a spatial frequency filtering into multiple channels. If one does not accept that possibility, localization of a pattern would perhaps be thought to be accomplished purely in the space domain, that is, by the spatial localization of some such features as bars, edges, or zero crossings.

The second use of the phase concept is with respect to the positional relationships between two or more spatial frequencies in the same region. Regardless of the absolute position or phase of either grating, two gratings may have some particular *relative phase*. For instance, if at some arbitrary point of origin gratings of f and $2f$ both have positive-going axis crossings, then they have a relative phase angle of $0°$. In this example, they are both in sine phase. If, on the other hand, f were in sine phase, and $2f$ in cosine phase, then the two gratings would have a relative phase of $90°$. Relative phase is thus important in the consideration of complex waveforms. Consider a pattern composed of f and $3f$. If the two gratings are added in cosine phase a peak of the $3f$ grating will coincide with each peak of the f grating, and so also for the troughs. When added together in sine phase, however, each peak of the f grating will occur at the same point as a trough of the $3f$ grating. Therefore, the overall contrast of the patterns being added together in cosine phase will be greater than in the sine phase case, and the appearance of the two patterns will be quite different. So, the overall shape of an $f + 3f$ pattern will remain constant regardless of its absolute position in the visual field (or absolute phase), but if the relative phases of the two components are changed, one being shifted with respect to the other, the appearance of the pattern will change correspondingly, insofar as the system is sensitive to relative phase.

IS THE VISUAL SYSTEM SELECTIVE FOR SPATIAL PHASE AS WELL AS FREQUENCY?

In looking at the visual system from the point of view of linear systems analysis one is struck by the many points of similarity between visual and auditory function. We suggest that the way in which the visual system processes spatial information is similar in many respects to the way in which the auditory system processes temporal information. It is in this context that we raise the question of the utilization of phase information. It is well known that the auditory system can perform extremely fine discriminations of auditory frequency, but it makes minimal use of phase information, except in the binaural localization of low-frequency sound sources. Not only is absolute phase irrelevant in audition, but relative phase as well. For instance, if one hits the same pair of notes on a piano twice, the timing between the striking of the two keys will doubtless vary by at least a fraction of a millisecond from the one time to the next, enough so that the relative phases of the two fundamental frequencies will not be exactly the same in the two cases. But such slight differences go totally unnoticed. (A large time difference between two notes would of course be detected, but that involves quite a different process.) The auditory system, then, is almost totally dependent on decoding the temporal frequency spectrum to distinguish among and recognize different auditory patterns. Is the same true for the way in which the visual system deals with spatial patterns?

It is obvious that we are sensitive to phase to some degree in vision, contrary to the situation in audition. The dark bars of a grating are clearly different from the light bars, and we can readily say which is which (at least, for a low spatial frequency). To accomplish this requires knowledge of phase. Also, an $f + 3f$ combination in sine phase is clearly discriminable from the same combination in cosine phase. To say that we have some degree of sensitivity to both absolute and relative phase is only stating the obvious. What is not immediately apparent, however, is what elements of the visual system are phase sensitive and in what visual tasks phase plays an important role.

There have been various psychophysical demonstrations of sensitivity to pattern phase. For example, consider two rectangular wave gratings whose duty cycles sum to 1 (if the ratio of white to black in one is 1:3, say—a duty cycle of 0.25—the other will then have a ratio of 3:1, a duty cycle of 0.75). The luminance profiles of these two patterns will be mirror images of each other. The Fourier spectra of such patterns are identical in terms of the frequencies and amplitudes of their nonzero frequency components, differing only in their phase terms (they differ, however, in their DC levels). If a subject adapts to one of the two gratings, say one with wide white bars and narrow black bars, then looks at a square wave grating of the same fundamental frequency, the black and white bars of the square wave will no longer appear equal in width, but rather will be shifted in apparent width in opposite directions (K.K. De Valois, 1973, 1977a). The white bars of the test grating will appear to have shifted in width away from the white bars of the adaptation grating; the black bars of the test grating will appear to have shifted in width away from the black bars of the adaptation grating, as well. Thus, after adaptation to the grating just described (wide white bars, narrow black bars), the square-wave test grating appears to have narrow white bars and wide black bars (see Figure 8.1).

Inspection of Figure 8.2 will allow you to demonstrate this effect to yourself. After scanning the fixation bar between the two mirror image gratings on the left for about 60 s, the two square wave gratings on the right will appear quite different from each other, although they are physically identical. These results might be attributed to adaptation of a phase-sensitive system or, alternatively, to adaptation of separate black-bar and white-bar detectors. A subsequent study by Cavanagh, Brussell, and Stober (1981), however, indicates that adaptation of independent populations of black- and white-bar detectors cannot account for

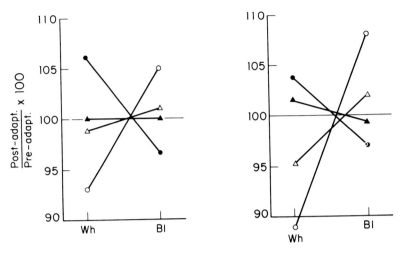

FIG. 8.1 Phase-selective effects following rectangular wave adaptation. Subjects adapted to vertical rectangular-wave gratings with duty cycles of 0.69 or 0.21, then set a test grating to an apparent duty cycle of 0.5 (square wave). The ratios of post- to preadaptation width settings for both black and white bars, and for both vertical and horizontal gratings are shown for each of two subjects. Circles: vertical test gratings. Triangles: horizontal test gratings. Open symbols: narrow-white, wide-black adaptation gratings. Filled symbols: narrow-black, wide-white adaptation (from K.K. De Valois, 1977a, *Vision Res., 17,* 209–215. Copyright 1977, Pergamon Journals, Inc. Reprinted with permission).

this effect. They had subjects alternate adaptation to a similar rectangular wave with adaptation to a sinusoidal grating of $2f$. The "bars" of the $2f$ grating were equal in width to the narrow bars of the rectangular wave pattern. One would thus predict that the alternating adaptation should reinforce the adaptational change on the narrow bars but counteract the adaptation on the broad bars, thus increasing the size of the effect—if bar width were the determining variable. This procedure, however, virtually eliminated the entire effect—as might be expected if the effect were not due to selective bar width adaptation, but instead to channels tuned to the relative phases of the two harmonics. Whatever elements subserve this effect are obviously also involved in the perception, as well as the detection, of the patterns.

Several other experiments have also demonstrated differential adaptation with patterns that differ only in the relative phase of their components. Tolhurst (1972a) had subjects adapt to either a left-facing or a right-facing Craik-Cornsweet edge. He found adaptation to one polarity reduced sensitivity (i.e., increased the threshold contrast) to the same pattern more than to the pattern of the opposite polarity. Stromeyer et al. (1973) demonstrated phase specificity in a McCollough aftereffect type of experiment. They had subjects adapt to alternating left- and right-facing sawtooth gratings in which one grating was illuminated with red light, the other with green light. After prolonged adaptation, a

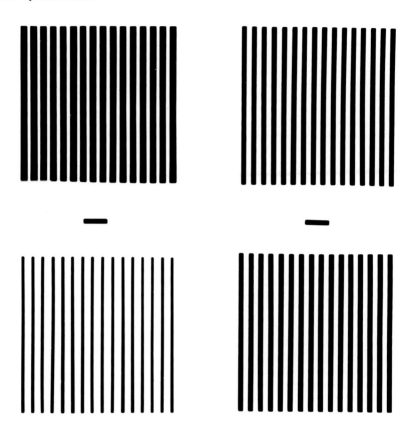

FIG. 8.2   Demonstration of phase-selective adaptation. Note first that the two gratings on the right are identical, then scan the fixation bar between the two gratings on the left for about a minute. Quickly shift your gaze to the right fixation bar. Do the two test gratings still appear identical?

sawtooth grating illuminated with white light appeared tinged with a color roughly complementary to that with which it was illuminated during adaptation.

Both of the experiments just described used patterns containing only one polarity of edge, either left-facing or right-facing. Perhaps for this reason both were interpreted as reflecting the responses of cells with odd-symmetric RFs (see Chapter 4). These are sometimes assumed to be identical with the "broad-band edge detectors" discussed by Shapley and Tolhurst (1973), who assessed the detectability of a luminance edge in the presence of an additional bright or dark line in various nearby positions. They found that a small bright line was more detectable just to the bright side of the edge than just to the dark side. A small black line was more detectable just to the dark side. The resulting sensitivity profile looked very like the RF profile of Hubel and Wiesel's asymmetric simple cells, which also are often considered to be edge detectors. On the basis of the Shapley and Tolhurst experiment and a similar one by Kulikowski and King-

Smith (1973), it was deduced that there were edge detector mechanisms in the human visual system and that these were rather broad band (as opposed to the fairly narrow-band spatial frequency channels discussed in Chapter 6). These experiments, when taken together with the Tolhurst and the Stromeyer et al. experiments described before, have led some to argue that sensitivity to relative phase in the human visual system is mediated by broad-band detectors with odd-symmetric RF profiles (Braddick, Campbell, & Atkinson, 1978).

There are problems with this notion. One concerns the simple interpretation of the Shapley and Tolhurst and the Kulikowski and King-Smith experiments. If sensitivity changes around an edge did in fact directly reflect the RF profiles of single cortical cells, those cells would have rather broad spatial frequency tuning. However, as Graham (1977) has demonstrated, if one considers probability summation among the outputs of different cells whose RFs are close or overlapping, results such as those of Shapley and Tolhurst can be produced by summation among narrow-band units. It is not necessary to postulate broadly tuned "edge detectors" to account for the experimental findings.

Another difficulty with the theory that postulated that broad-band edge detectors constitute the mechanism subserving phase detection is the rectangular wave adaptation experiment described earlier (K.K. De Valois, 1973, 1977a). Both Shapley and Tolhurst and Stromeyer et al. used patterns with either left- or right-facing edges, but not both. In the rectangular-wave adaptation experiment, however, the patterns used contained equal numbers of left- and right-facing edges. With the scanning technique used to reduce retinal afterimage formation, cells with odd-symmetric RFs facing both left and right should have been approximately equally adapted. Thus, there should be no differential adaptation effects if these cells alone are responsible for phase-specific adaptation.

A variety of other experiments have also demonstrated the importance of phase in vision. Legge (1976) compared the reduction in contrast sensitivity produced by adaptation to a grating to that produced by adaptation to a spatial impulse, i.e., a very narrow, bright bar. Although the spatial impulse and the grating were equated for total power present in a particular frequency band, the impulse was found to produce a smaller adaptation effect than would be predicted on the basis of its power spectrum. Legge argued that phase-independent spatial frequency channels could not account for this difference. If one were cognizant of the fixed relative phase of the frequency components of the spatial impulse and assumed phase-selective spatial frequency channels, however, the difference could be explained. (An alternative explanation for these results, however, could be inhibitory interactions among different spatial frequency channels, as discussed in Chapter 11. An impulse has a much broader spatial frequency spectrum than an extended grating and would thus be expected to excite many different channels. If these channels are mutually inhibitory, a broad-band stimulus should produce less excitation, and consequently less adaptation, in a given channel than would a narrow-band stimulus with the same total power in that frequency band.)

Burr (1980) has examined the ability to discriminate the relative phases of the two components of an $f + 3f$ pattern. He found a relative phase threshold of about 30°, independent of the absolute spatial frequency over a large range. Since the positional thresholds over this spatial frequency range go from 0.3 to 5′ arc while the relative phase thresholds remain constant, these results strongly suggest that phase rather than positional mechanisms are operating in this task.

Lawden (1983) has shown that relative phase relations can only be discriminated between gratings of nearby frequencies, those within about a 2-octave range, e.g., the phase of a $3f$ grating, relative to a grating of f, is readily discriminable, but that of f and $5f$ are not. He proposes that there may be broadband as well as narrowly tuned units responsive to each spatial frequency range, with phase being processed by broad-band cells tuned to a given frequency interacting with more narrowly tuned units tuned to somewhat higher frequencies. Thus broad-band units tuned to some frequency f would interact with narrowband units tuned to $3f$ to specify the phase relations between f and $3f$. Elsewhere, a group of cells with smaller RFs tuned to various spatial frequencies within the overlapping range of $3f$ to $9f$ would carry out a similar analysis over this higher spatial frequency range (the $3f$ cells in this group being, of course, more broadly tuned than those $3f$ cells which interacted with f). There would, in this system, be no way of comparing the relative phase of f and $9f$, since different groups of cells would be involved in the two cases. Lawden suggests that if the broadly tuned units were the most sensitive, one's inability to detect the relative phase of f and $3f$ at threshold (Nachmias & Weber, 1975) would be accounted for. One attraction of this proposal is that it would account for the presence of broadly as well as narrowly tuned cells at each spatial frequency range (R.L. De Valois, Albrecht, & Thorell, 1982).

In this discussion of phase we have been considering only monocular stimuli. However, additional evidence for phase sensitivity in the visual system comes from studies of binocular patterns. Bacon (1976), for instance, has shown that the interaction between gratings presented to the two eyes depends on their relative interocular phase. We will discuss additional experiments studying interocular phase differences in Chapter 10.

In the experimental situations discussed above phase was found to be an important variable. There are tasks, however, for which the relative phase of two gratings appears to be visually irrelevant. One is in the threshold detection of certain compound gratings. A grating composed of two spatial frequencies (say f and $3f$) will appear very different as a function of the relative phase of the two components if its contrast is well above threshold (although there is a contrast interval in which it is detectable but its phase is indiscriminable; Nachmias & Weber, 1975). Graham and Nachmias (1971) measured detection of compound gratings composed of two spatial frequencies, f and $3f$. If the amplitudes of the two components are kept equal, the total pattern contrast will depend on the relative phase at which the components are added. If the phase is such that peaks (and troughs) of the two gratings are aligned, the pattern contrast will be higher than if the peaks of one component are always aligned with the troughs of the other. Graham and Nachmias found that relative phase (and thus overall pattern contrast) did not affect the detectability of the two compound gratings at all: the peaks-add and peaks-subtract patterns were equally detectable.

SENSITIVITY TO ABSOLUTE PHASE OR POSITION

We have couched the discussion thus far in terms of phase and spatial frequency, but if it is to be relevant to the phenomena of spatial vision as a whole, then we must consider data from other types of experiments as well. One straightforward question to pose at this point is: How good are we at detecting the absolute position of a visual stimulus with no additional cues? It is a fairly difficult question to tackle experimentally. To devise a situation that has no additional information (other than absolute phase) but in which one can still ask the subject for a meaningful response is not simple.

One instructive, though not very quantitative, way to do this is to place a subject in a room that is totally dark except for a single point source of light. The subject, who can see nothing but that one point source, is asked to describe its position in space repeatedly. After some time, the point source will appear to begin to move (even though its veridical position never changes). This is known as the autokinetic phenomenon. The light may appear to undergo enormous movements, changing its apparent position in space by many degrees (Koffka, 1935). A point that is straight ahead of the subject, for example, may appear to be floating above his head or moving to the left or the right.

Some of the errors in localization in the autokinetic movement situation are attributable to eye movements. Eye position may change drastically in this situation, and our knowledge of the direction in which our eyes are pointing (in the absence of visual feedback) is by no means perfect. But drift in eye position alone may not be sufficient to account for the tremendous fluctuations in apparent position (Guilford & Dallenbach, 1928). This extreme situation shows that we are very deficient in our ability to localize objects absolutely in the absence of any framework or additional cues, despite the very precise retinotopic mapping of the visual field onto different cortical regions (see Chapter 4 and below).

Another example of our poor ability to judge absolute position comes from studies of a somewhat more complex stimulus arrangement, a dot within the framework of a box (Duncker, 1929). One can with extreme sensitivity detect whether or not a spot within a stationary frame is moving, unlike the situation in which autokinetic movement occurs. If the spot is made to oscillate over a small distance, it is seen to move back and forth within the frame. However, if the spot is kept stationary and the frame is moved back and forth laterally, the percept is exactly the same. That is, the frame again appears stationary and the spot appears to be moving back and forth within it (Duncker, 1929). One is thus incapable of distinguishing a movement of the frame alone from an opposite movement of the spot alone. It is, then, *relative*, not absolute, position or movement which is detected in this situation. Our sensitivity to absolute position must be feeble indeed since it can be so completely overridden.

It is somewhat paradoxical that while in some situations we are extremely poor at tasks involving spatial localization, in others we are phenomenally good. As Westheimer (1979) has pointed out, while vernier and stereoacuity measures are referred to as acuity tests, they actually depend upon spatial localization, not resolution (see Chapter 5). In these hyperacuity tasks, the fineness of our spatial discriminations is greater by an order of magnitude than our true acuity (i.e., resolution ability). The common factor in the various hyperacuity tasks is that they are all, in some manner, tests of our ability to localize a stimulus either relative to another stimulus or to its own position at a different time. For example, if a subject is shown a bright vertical line which then jumps a small distance to the left or the right, she can detect the direction in which it moved for astoundingly small displacements, changes as small as 3″ arc (Westheimer & McKee, 1978).

RELATIVE CONTRIBUTIONS TO LOCALIZATION OF PHASE AND POSITION

As was pointed out at the beginning of this chapter, a set of local spatial frequency filters in the cortex would provide two potential mechanisms for localization: encoding of spatial phase within a cortical region, and identification of which cortical region is activated. We know little about the relative contributions of these two potential mechanisms. They are, in fact, difficult to distinguish from each other experimentally. If, however, striate cortex cells are not functioning as local spatial frequency filters at all, but rather respond differentially to patterns on the basis of the position of some local feature such as a bright bar, an edge, or a zero-crossing, some interesting predictions can be made about our sensitivity to displacements of grating patterns.

For a single sine wave grating, a shift in position of a certain number of minutes of arc is the same as a phase shift of a certain number of degrees. Suppose a 1-c/deg vertical grating is shifted to the right by 15′ arc. Its absolute phase (relative to an arbitrary point) will have shifted 90°. Does a subject detect the shift because the position of a bright bar, say, has changed or because the phase has changed? Since the two are experimentally confounded, the question cannot be easily answered. Now, however, consider the same task with two grating patterns of different spatial frequencies. A particular amount of movement in minutes of arc will represent quite different phase shifts for the two frequencies. Correspondingly, the same phase shift for each will represent quite different positional changes. For example, consider two gratings of 1 and 10 c/deg, respectively. A 3′ arc positional shift would be an 18° phase shift of the 1-c/deg pattern, but a 180° phase shift of the 10-c/deg grating. By measuring sensitivity to displacements of gratings of different spatial frequencies, then, one should be able to tell whether the visual system is sensitive to phase shifts of spatial frequency components, or to positional displacements of local features.

Consider, for example, an extremely simple task of phase detection. A subject observes a sinusoidal luminance grating and is asked to detect a change in its position. The grating may either oscillate back and forth at some constant rate (e.g., 2 Hz), or it may be steady in one position then undergo a sudden jump to one side or the other. The latter is basically the same experiment as the West-heimer & McKee (1978) hyperacuity experiment described above. In this study, Westheimer (1978) used gratings of spatial frequencies ranging from 3 to 25 c/ deg, and found that the threshold displacement in seconds of arc was approxi-mately equal for all spatial frequencies. The displacement in degrees phase angle, therefore, rose as a function of spatial frequency. Westheimer interprets these results as indicating that not phase but spatial displacement of the bars is the relevant variable in our detection of changes in position. However, it is impor-tant to note that he used only relatively high spatial frequencies, those above 3 c/deg.

We (R.L. De Valois 1982; R.L. De Valois & K.K. De Valois, 1986), in similar experiments, used lower spatial frequencies and obtained quite different results. The subjects were shown a grating oscillating back and forth and their task was to adjust the amplitude of the oscillation to threshold. The results of this exper-iment, like those of Westheimer (1978), can be plotted in terms of either thresh-old spatial displacement in minutes of arc, or threshold phase angle. Above a spatial frequency of about 2 c/deg, our results are very similar to those of Westh-eimer. The threshold spatial displacement is roughly constant while threshold phase angle increases with spatial frequency. For lower spatial frequencies, how-ever, the relationship is reversed. Threshold phase angle remains constant while minimum spatial displacement decreases as spatial frequency increases (see Fig-ure 8.3). It appears, then, that at low spatial frequencies phase is the critical var-iable, whereas at high spatial frequencies position is more important (see also Figures 8.6 and 7).

The results, however, are somewhat more interesting, and in some sense sim-pler than that. All of the data, at all spatial frequencies, can in fact be well fitted by a single equation, the linear sum of a phase term and a positional term. For instance, threshold for a given subject might require a 5° phase shift plus a posi-tional shift of 20″ arc. It can be seen that at low spatial frequencies the positional term will be very small compared with the phase term, so the threshold is largely dependent on phase. At high spatial frequencies, the phase term becomes very small, so position is the main determinant of threshold. Consider the example given above of the threshold for a given subject being a 5° phase shift plus a 20″ positional shift. For a 1-c/deg grating, a 5° phase shift is 50″ arc positional change. The threshold would thus be 50″ + 20″ = 70″ arc, most of it due to the phase term. At 10 c/deg, however, a 5° phase shift is only 5″ arc, which plus the 20″ positional term would give a threshold of 25″ arc, most of it due to the positional term. One interpretation of such a result is that there may be two

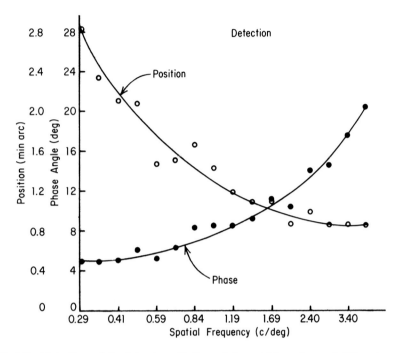

FIG. 8.3 Detection of the lateral oscillation of sinusoidal gratings of different spatial frequencies. The same data are plotted twice, once as the threshold positional change (in minutes of arc) and once as the threshold phase change (in degrees phase). Note that for spatial frequencies below about 2 c/deg the phase term is quite small and varies very little. For higher frequencies the positional term is almost constant, while the phase term increases rapidly.

successive processing stages, at one of which (the striate cortex?) the cells are phase sensitive, and at the next (some poststriate site?) position sensitive. If the units at each of these levels have a finite threshold, one would obtain our result, namely that to be detected a displacement must exceed a certain phase angle (to get past the striate stage), plus a certain positional shift (to get past the next stage).

PHYSIOLOGY OF PHASE AND POSITION SENSITIVITY

In the earlier chapters on retinal and cortical physiology, we discussed many of the characteristics of cells that are relevant to the question of how spatial location is neurally encoded. Here we will bring together and summarize these basic facts. It is clear that two separate processes are involved in spatial localization at the level of the striate cortex: the retinotopic mapping, which results in different cortical regions being stimulated, depending on the location of the stimulus in visual space; and the capacity of (some) cells in each cortical area to localize patterns within the restricted visual region from which they receive input. That is to say, striate cortex cells differ in their RF locations, and some can also differentially localize patterns *within* their RFs. These two mechanisms will be discussed in turn. Whether, as we suggested above, there is some later level at which phase information is recoded in terms of position is as yet unknown.

Retinotopic Mapping

It has long been realized that information from different regions of the retina is projected in a systematic way onto the striate cortex. The first evidence for a retinotopic projection came from observations of visual deficits following small cortical lesions. Destruction of restricted cortical areas was found to produce scotomas that were correspondingly restricted to particular parts of the visual field. More precise evidence for the nature of the retinotopic mapping on the cortex came from studies using evoked potential recording (Talbot & Marshall, 1941; Daniel & Whitteridge, 1961): the cortical point that gave maximum evoked potentials was found to vary systematically with stimulation in different parts of the monkey visual field. Still later studies, using the localization of the RFs of single cells or groups of cells in different cortical regions (Van Essen & Maunsell, 1980), confirmed and extended earlier results.

Recently, the 2-DG technique has been brought to bear on this problem (Tootell et al., 1982a). In Figure 4.1 we presented the cortical 2-DG uptake pattern produced by a stimulus pattern of rings and rays, each band being made up of small counterphase-flickering rectangles of various sizes. The cortical retinotopic map shown there, which confirms the earlier maps based on recording evidence, clearly demonstrates the overall pattern of cortical projection whereby stimuli in different parts of the visual field will activate different cortical regions. Insofar as the visual system maintains and utilizes information about which cortical region has been activated (and surely it must), this provides one basis for spatial localization. However, it is not clear at present how fine a basis for localization is provided by such mapping. That is to say, the spatial mapping from cortical module to cortical module across the cortex (from one of the dark patches to the next in Figure 4.1B) fairly unambiguously represents different locations in visual space. But is the same true for small displacements within a cortical module? A shift of, say, 100 μm from one cortical point to another will, we know, move from cells tuned to one orientation and spatial frequency to ones tuned to a different orientation and/or spatial frequency. As discussed in Chapter 4, if it also represents a change in spatial location, there would be a basic confounding of orientation and spatial frequency with location.

Phase-Sensitive and Phase-Insensitive Cells

Recording from cat ganglion cells, Kuffler (1953) first found evidence for two main cell types (see Chapter 3). The RFs of each consisted of separate excitatory and inhibitory areas (when measured with the luminance increments he used as stimuli); they differed in that one had an excitatory center and an inhibitory annular surround, whereas the other had an inhibitory center and excitatory surround. That these cells are sensitive to the spatial phase of a grating was first shown by Enroth-Cugell and Robson (1966), who named them X cells. Such cells give their maximum response to a grating (of the appropriate spatial frequency) in the phase in which a bright bar coincides with a region which is excitatory to increments. They show maximum inhibition to a grating shifted in phase 180° away from this (in which the black bar of the grating coincides with the excitatory area), and they respond not at all to the pattern at 90°, halfway between these points of maximum excitation and maximum inhibition. Thus Kuffler's two cell types differ in being 180° out of phase with respect to each other. If their RFs were precisely superimposed, the one cell type would fire maximally to a grating pattern of one phase; the other, to the same grating shifted 180° in phase.

In the same quantitative study of cat ganglion cells, Enroth-Cugell and Robson found evidence for another variety of cell, which they termed Y cells. These are largely insensitive to the spatial phase of the stimulus, firing to a grating pattern of the appropriate spatial frequency independent of the position of the grating with respect to the cell's RF.

While it is by no means certain (and is in fact rather unlikely) that cortical simple cells and complex cells are directly related to retinal X and Y cells, respectively (see Chapter 4), they are functionally similar in terms of their sensitivity (or lack of it) to spatial phase. A simple cell is extremely sensitive to the position of a grating pattern with respect to its RF. As was the case with a retinal X cell, a phase shift of 90° from the optimum position leads to no response, and a 180° phase shift, to maximum inhibition. On the other hand, complex cells are almost totally phase insensitive, often giving not only responses of the same polarity to gratings of various phase angles (as was the case for retinal Y cells), but of the same response amplitude as well to gratings in any phase with respect to the center of the RF (see Figure 4.6). When tested with flashed bars of light, a typical complex cell gives the same response to a white bar or a black bar in the same location in its RF.

In Hubel and Wiesel's original model, simple cells merely serve as inputs to produce complex cells; the latter form the sole output to later cortical regions. If that were the case, our visual systems would be totally lacking in information about spatial phase. As mentioned above and discussed further below, however, there is much psychophysical evidence to indicate that we are indeed sensitive to spatial phase, at least in the central visual field. For that and other reasons, we believe that simple cells constitute not just an intermediate step in forming complex cells (although they may well be that too), but also a separate system that must have an output from the striate. The presence of cells in later cortical areas that resemble simple cells more than complex cells provides physiological support for this. It seems to us much more likely that there are two parallel systems in the striate cortex, one—complex cells—with only two-dimensional spatial frequency information, and one—simple cells—with both two-dimensional spatial frequency information and phase information.

Odd- and Even-Symmetric Simple Cells

The retinal ganglion cells found by Kuffler (1953) have even-symmetric RFs. Cortical simple cells of the same two even-symmetric types are also found: ones with an excitatory center and two inhibitory flanks (to increments), or the reverse. These we can characterize as responding optimally to cosine gratings of 0 and 180°, respectively. In the cortex, however, as first noted by Hubel and Wiesel (1962), there are also two types of simple cells with odd-symmetric RFs. These would respond optimally to cosine gratings of 90 and 270°, respectively, if their RF centers were lined up precisely with those of the even-symmetric cells. One can also think of even-symmetric cells as responding optimally to a grating in cosine phase with respect to its RF center, and odd-symmetric cells as responding to the same pattern in sine phase. *If*, and it is an important if, these various cell types occur in a cortical region with precise alignment of their RFs, then they could by their relative activity rates encode the spatial phase as well as the spatial frequency content of a pattern in that location in the visual field (see discussion in Chapter 1). Pollen and Ronner (1981) have presented some evidence from recordings in cat striate cortex that such is the case. In 14 instances they recorded simultaneously with the same electrode from two simple cells and found one member of the pair to be even-symmetric and the other to be odd-symmetric. When the optimal phase of a grating was precisely determined for each member of the pair, they were found to be almost exactly 90° apart in each case, just as one would predict if they were encoding the sine and cosine components. Further confirmation of these important results with larger samples of cells would be desirable.

Phase Shift Versus Positional Change for Cells

One factor that led us to examine psychophysically the relative sensitivity of observers to phase versus positional shifts in a pattern was a consideration of the physiological data from cortical cells. Among the striking characteristics of striate cells to which we have repeatedly referred are their fairly narrow spatial frequency tuning, and the presence of cells within a given region tuned to a considerable range of spatial frequencies. Now consider how a group of such cells would respond to a flashed or counterphase-flickered grating in different locations with respect to their RFs (different phases). For a simple cell, as discussed above, the response would be maximal at one phase; 90° away (the null position) there would be no response; 180° away there would be maximal inhibition, etc. This is true for a cell tuned to a very low spatial frequency and for a neighboring one tuned to a much higher spatial frequency range (see Figure 8.4A). But the 90° phase shift that takes each of these cells from the maximum response rate down to no response is a very different *positional* shift (see Figure 8.4B). Striate simple cells tuned to different spatial frequency ranges thus have a certain constant phase sensitivity, but very different positional sensitivities. One would predict from the responses of units at this level alone, then, that a subject should require a much larger positional change of a low spatial frequency grating than of a high-frequency one for detection, but that there would be a constant phase threshold. As we discussed earlier, however, the psychophysical data indicate that this is only partially true, the results suggesting successive phase-sensitive and positional-sensitive stages. These physiological and psychophysical findings are not really in conflict, since the physiological data indicate that the phase-sensitive stage may be the striate cortex.

Variations in Cell Types With Eccentricity and Spatial Frequency

We suggested above that simple and complex cells form two parallel systems by which visual information is analyzed. It would be of interest to know how the proportions of these two cell varieties vary with different visual parameters. There appear to be data only with reference to two variables of interest here: spatial frequency and visual field eccentricity. Data on the relative proportions of simple and complex cells are very difficult to evaluate for technical reasons. In a region in which there are cells of different sizes and types, the precise single-cell recording conditions, particularly electrode tip size, critically determine which cells are most likely to be sampled. With large microelectrodes, for instance, it is very unlikely that extremely small cells will be isolated. Simple and complex cells may well have different morphologies and different average dimensions (J.P. Kelly & Van Essen, 1974). Since recording conditions, including electrode types and sizes, are not standardized across laboratories, one cannot place great weight on the varying percentages of different cell types reported by different investigators. Comparisons of recordings made by a single investigator are, of course, less subject to these problems. These caveats should be borne in mind when considering the evidence discussed below.

Variation With Eccentricity
In cat, the relative proportion of simple and complex cells is a function of eccentricity. J.B. Wilson and Sherman (1976), recording from cells at several cortical loci corresponding to various retinal eccentricities, found a consistent increase in the proportion of complex cells with increasing eccentricity. In the cortex related to central retina, about 30% of the cells in their sample were complex (considering only simple and complex cells); beyond about 15° peripheral, the

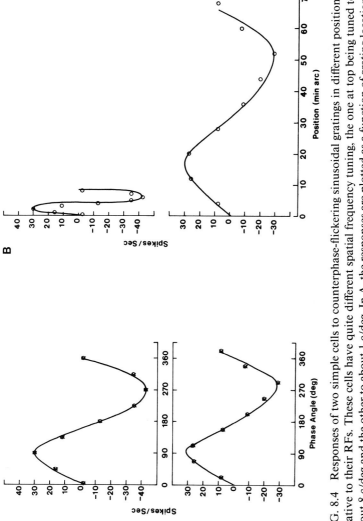

FIG. 8.4 Responses of two simple cells to counterphase-flickering sinusoidal gratings in different positions relative to their RFs. These cells have quite different spatial frequency tuning, the one at top being tuned to about 8 c/deg and the other to about 1 c/deg. In A, the responses are plotted as a function of grating location, expressed in degrees phase angle relative to a standard position. In B, the same data are plotted as a function of grating location, expressed in minutes of arc. Note that both cells show similar response selectivity when phase angle is the measure chosen. When positional shift is plotted, however, the higher spatial frequency cell on top is obviously sensitive to a much smaller positional change.

255

percentage of complex cells was found to be 50 to 60%. However, these results have been questioned by Berman and Payne (1982).

The proportion of simple and complex cells at different eccentricities has not been specifically examined in monkey over a wide range of eccentricities. We (R.L. De Valois, Albrecht, & Thorell, 1982) have found slightly more (42%) complex cells at 5° peripheral than in the foveal area (37%), but such a small difference is probably not significant. Investigators who have recorded from central cortex in monkey (Dow, 1974; Poggio, Baker, Mansfield, Sillito, & Grigg, 1975) have found a smaller percentage of complex cells than have others who recorded from more peripheral sites (Hubel & Wiesel, 1968). However, those findings are subject to the cross-experimenter problems discussed above.

Variation With Spatial Frequency

In our recordings from monkey striate cortex (R.L. De Valois, Albrecht, & Thorell, 1982), we have examined the distribution of the peak spatial tuning of simple and complex cells. The distributions of peak frequencies were largely overlapping, but complex cells tended to be tuned to somewhat higher spatial frequencies than were simple cells (see Figure 4.17). The same was found in another study in our laboratory, based on a different sample of cells (Thorell, 1981; Thorell et al., 1984). It is particularly notable that a considerable majority of those cells tuned to the very highest spatial frequencies (above, say, 8 c/deg) turned out to be complex cells.

One objection that might be raised is that the presence of eye movements would lead to an underestimation of the number of simple cells tuned to high frequencies. Despite the use of neuromuscular paralytics, residual eye movements do occur. If one averages the response of a simple cell over 10 or 20 s, significant eye movement could have occurred during the averaging period. If the stimulus used is a drifting grating, the eye movements would cause a shift in the apparent phase tuning of the cell during the stimulus presentation. For a high frequency grating, the apparent phase shifts caused by eye movements could be sufficient to mask the modulation of the response and make the cell appear to be phase insensitive (and therefore classified as a complex cell). Thus, one could argue that such experiments would almost inevitably underestimate the number of simple cells tuned to high spatial frequencies.

The counterargument can be made, however, that in the course of recording one can easily distinguish the sound of the modulated discharge a simple cell gives to a drifting grating from the unmodulated response of a complex cell. We were specifically attentive to the possibility that the responses of simple cells tuned to high frequencies might be shifting in phase (due to eye movement) during a stimulus presentation, making them appear to be complex cells. We were aware of no such cases.

One can conceive of reasons for the visual system's failing to maintain phase information at high frequencies. One is that small eye movements and vibrations would make it difficult to get precise phase information from high spatial frequencies. Another is the differing ways in which cells tuned to various spatial frequencies can localize patterns. A cell tuned to a very low spatial frequency has a very large RF. For instance, a cell tuned to 0.5 c/deg would have an RF of at least 3° diameter. A cell (particularly a complex cell, with no phase information) with a RF this size could give only very imprecise information about the position of a stimulus in the visual field. On the other hand, a cell with a comparable spatial frequency bandwidth but tuned to, say, 10 c/deg might have a total RF diameter of 0.2° or less. Even without phase information, such a high-frequency cell, by just firing or not firing, would convey fairly precise location information. Thus, one of the presumed functions of phase-sensitive mechanisms, absolute localization, is accomplished quite well by cells tuned to high frequencies without the need for their maintaining phase information.

Sensitivity to Relative Phase

The studies discussed above were concerned with the phase sensitivity of cells in their responses to a single grating. It is also of interest to examine how cells respond to the relative phase of the components of complex patterns. K.K. De Valois and Tootell (1983) quantitatively examined the responses of cat striate cortical cells to complex gratings composed of two harmonically related spatial frequencies: the cell's optimum frequency, and a second of either 1/4, 1/3, 1/2, 2, 3, or 4 times this frequency. This study was principally concerned with inhibitory interactions and will be discussed in more detail in Chapter 11. Its relevance here is that it involved examining the responses to two frequencies presented simultaneously, where one of the experimental variables was the relative phase of the two gratings.

For most of the complex cells studied, the addition of a second frequency to the cell's best frequency was found to have no effect on the response to f. Even for those complex cells showing two-frequency interactions, the interaction (whether facilitatory or inhibitory) was never dependent on the relative phase of the two components.

In the case of simple cells the situation was quite different. Nearly all simple cells showed significant two-frequency interactions. In slightly more than half, the response to f was inhibited in a non-phase-specific manner by one or more additional frequencies. This is particularly interesting in that it is a response which is independent of relative phase in a cell type whose responses are highly dependent upon absolute phase. The second type of two-frequency interaction found in simple cells was never seen in complex cells: a highly phase-dependent interaction of the two frequencies in a compound grating (see Figure 11.6). This type of cell responds not only to the spatial frequencies present in the pattern, but to a more complex attribute—the relative phase of two different frequencies. It is obvious from our ability to discriminate relative phase that it must somehow be encoded in the visual system. These cells have to some degree the requisite characteristics. It is interesting to note that the phase-specific interactions were almost always between f and either $2f$ or $3f$. It was quite rare to find phase-specific interactions between f and $4f$, and they occurred more often between f and $2f$ than between f and $3f$. If this accurately reflects the overall distribution of cell types, one might guess that our sensitivity to relative phase would be high for nearby frequencies but low for combinations of widely spaced frequencies. Stromeyer et al., (1973) reported this to be the case. They found adaptation-produced phase effects for combinations of frequencies as closely spaced as f and $3f$, but failed to find such effects for more widely spaced combinations.

PSYCHOPHYSICAL VARIABLES AFFECTING PHASE DETECTION

As we have pointed out above, it has been established that there are circumstances in which the visual system is sensitive to spatial phase. However, such phase sensitivity is not equal under all conditions. Indeed, there appear to be circumstances under which phase sensitivity is totally absent. It is of interest, then, to ask how perceptual sensitivity to spatial phase varies with different visual parameters, although the topic has received very little attention in the literature and the evidence is thus sparse. This question is of additional interest because of the physiological existence of some phase-sensitive striate cells (simple cells), and others (complex cells) which are not. It would be of interest to see whether variations in phase sensitivity reflect, as we would predict, variations in the characteristics and distributions of simple and complex cells.

Variation in Phase Sensitivity With Spatial Frequency

There is experimental evidence to indicate that our sensitivity to phase falls with increasing spatial frequency. Holt and Ross (1980) showed that one's ability to discriminate $f + 3f$ in square-wave versus triangular-wave phase is lost when $3f$ is above about 15 c/deg, even though the $3f$ component alone is well above threshold. This effect can perhaps be seen by viewing Figure 6.3 from a distance. Another demonstration of the lack of phase sensitivity at high spatial frequencies can be seen in Figure 8.5. Here are shown gratings of three different spatial frequencies, in which each is shifted 28° in phase five successive times. The phase shifts are obvious in the case of the low and middle spatial frequency patterns, but not at all so in the case of the high-frequency pattern at bottom. If each pattern is shifted by a constant *position*, however, the shifts become increasingly clear with increasing spatial frequency (see Figure 8.6).

Specific psychophysical evidence for variations in phase sensitivity with spatial frequency has already been presented in Figure 8.3 above. In that experiment, it will be remembered, we directly measured the observer's sensitivity to a phase shift in a grating as a function of the spatial frequency of the grating. The results indicate that at low spatial frequencies, a very small phase shift can be detected; at spatial frequencies above about 1 c/deg, the threshold starts to

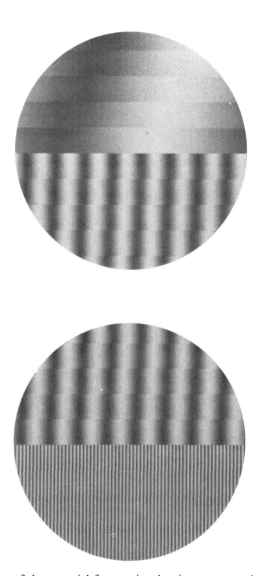

FIG. 8.5 Gratings of three spatial frequencies showing constant phase shifts. In each hemicircle there are five strips of grating. Each strip is shifted in phase by 28° from its neighbors. In the lower circle note that the shift is much less obvious for the highest spatial frequency grating (bottom half). Depending on the viewing distance, one may not even be able to detect the phase shifts in this high-frequency pattern. In the upper circle, the middle spatial frequency grating has somewhat less apparent shifts than does the lowest frequency one. (This is particularly clear if you slightly blur your eyes to eliminate the sharp transitions between the steps.)

FIG. 8.6   Gratings of three spatial frequencies with constant positional displacements. This differs from the preceding figure only in that each grating strip is displaced from its neighbors by the same positional shift, not the same phase shift. Note that the shifts are now increasingly obvious for the higher frequencies.

rise; and above about 2 c/deg the rise in threshold becomes quite steep. Finally, beyond about 15 c/deg the threshold reaches infinity (at least for moderately low contrast gratings): one can no longer detect movement of the pattern at all. This is also in accord with a number of psychophysical studies that have found quite different contrast sensitivity functions for stationary versus moving gratings. At low spatial frequencies movement considerably enhances detection of a grating. High spatial frequencies are equally detectable, however, whether or not a grating is moving, up to a moderate drift rate. In fact, a stationary and an oscillating grating cannot be distinguished from each other (Kulikowski, 1971). Put another way, if for such a high spatial frequency grating the white areas were suddenly to change to black and vice versa, one could not tell that anything had happened.

Now refer back to our earlier suggestion that almost all the units tuned to the highest spatial frequencies are complex cells. If information about very high spatial frequency patterns is carried only (or mainly) by complex cells, then we should be able to perceive the patterns quite readily (and discriminate their spatial frequency), but be unable to make any discriminations that depend on phase. This is exactly the situation we find psychophysically.

The suggestion that phase information is carried predominantly by cells tuned to low spatial frequencies also accords with Westheimer's (1979) observations discussed earlier. Sensitivity to small lateral displacements of a line was not affected by the imposition of as much as 1 diopter of spectacle blur, which in effect eliminates the high spatial frequency components of the pattern. In this case, at least, extremely accurate information about localization appears to be carried by low- and mid-spatial frequency channels.

Variations in Phase Sensitivity With Eccentricity

Sensitivity to spatial phase not only varies with spatial frequency but seems to vary with retinal eccentricity as well. Nachmias and Weber (1975) measured the detectability and the discriminability of patterns composed of $f + 3f$ in either sine or cosine phase. They report the existence of a contrast interval in which the compound grating can clearly be distinguished from a single grating—f and $3f$ are both perceived—but the relative phase of the two components cannot be discriminated. The compound grating appears identical, regardless of whether f and $3f$ are in sine or cosine phase.

Suppose that detection at threshold is based on the pooled responses of the most sensitive cells. With foveal stimulation this would presumably be some mixture of both simple and complex cells. Since all cells would carry frequency information but only a subset (simple cells) would carry phase information, there would be a relatively smaller signal correlated with pattern phase. Therefore one might reasonably expect to detect an f + 3f pattern (based on both simple and complex cell responses) at contrasts lower than those necessary to detect relative phase of the components (based only on simple cell responses). Since (in cat, at least) the simple/complex cell ratio may decrease with increasing eccentricity (J.B. Wilson & Sherman, 1976), this contrast interval should widen with increasing eccentricity.

Psychophysical data such as those we have been discussing are sometimes taken to be evidence of a quite different physiological model. It has been suggested that non-phase-specific frequency information is transmitted by narrow bandwidth channels but phase-specific information by broad-band detectors (cf. Braddick et al., 1978). Earlier in this chapter we discussed some problems with this theory. In addition, it is at variance with the direct physiological evidence of cortical cell characteristics (assuming, of course, that these cells have something to do with these kinds of visual behavior). It assumes that cells which are specific for stimulus phase are, in general, broadly tuned for spatial frequency, while those which are insensitive to phase are narrowly tuned for spatial frequency. In striate cortex of monkey and cat, this is clearly incorrect. There are unbroken, overlapping continua of tuning bandwidths for both simple and complex cells, but to the extent that they differ, phase-sensitive simple cells are more, not less, narrowly tuned for spatial frequency than phase-insensitive complex cells. There is no direct physiological evidence for a separate class of broadly tuned, phase specific cells.

Sensitivity to Color Phase

In our discussion of phase we have so far restricted ourselves to luminance-varying stimuli, but the topic is of equal importance with respect to color. A complete treatment of spatial vision must consider how the visual system analyzes spatial variations along each color axis—black-white, red-green, and yellow-blue. When one observes a red-green grating, it is phase sensitivity which allows one to identify which bars are red and which are green. At first glance, that the red and green bars in a red-green grating can be discriminated seems to be a trivial statement. If the grating can be seen at all, surely it must be because the red and green can be discriminated and identified. But that is not the case, as we discussed in Chapter 7. It is perfectly possible to perceive a pattern based on pure color differences without being able to tell which part of the pattern is which color, or perhaps even to identify the colors involved. Just this in fact happens for high spatial frequency pure color patterns. This may be compared to the situation we have discussed with respect to our perception of high spatial frequency luminance patterns.

We are able to perceive high spatial frequency isoluminant color patterns and to identify some of their spatial characteristics (e.g., orientation, spatial frequency). However, in the absence of phase information, we are unable to tell whether the pattern is formed by luminance variations or by color variations. The only information we can derive about color is the overall mixture color of the pattern, which would be carried by simple cells tuned to low frequencies. These peculiar perceptual appearances of high spatial frequency patterns could be understood, then, if the high spatial frequency color (and luminance) information were being carried by complex cells, but not by simple cells. This suggestion is directly consonant with our physiological evidence, as discussed earlier.

9

Two-Dimensional Patterns

Most of the psychophysical experiments examining evidence for multiple spatial frequency channels and the physiological experiments examining the tuning characteristics of cells have used one-dimensionally varying stimuli: gratings or bars sufficiently long as to be effectively varying only in the orthogonal direction. To use such simplified stimuli is of course a perfectly valid scientific approach and eminently sensible from a tactical point of view. But one should not lose sight of the fact that the retinal image is two-dimensional and that the visual nervous system must be performing a two-dimensional analysis.

It has long been known that the number of fibers in the optic nerve constitutes a significant proportion (perhaps 50%) of the total sensory input to the central nervous system in humans. A comparison to the auditory system, which in primates is the other main sense modality, is of particular interest. Each optic nerve has about 1,000,000 fibers, compared to about 30,000 fibers in each auditory nerve. A major reason for the much larger visual input is doubtless that while the auditory stimulus consists of only one-dimensional variations in sound pressure level, the visual system has to deal with variations in light across two-dimensional space.

One of the main purposes of this book is to present and evaluate the evidence that the visual system is performing a local spatial frequency filtering of the visual input as an early stage in its analysis. A two-dimensional spatial frequency specification of a pattern would consist of a combined specification of its spatial frequency and orientation content—that is, of the amplitude and phase at each spatial frequency at each orientation. The additional demands, above those required for one-dimensional filtering, would be for (1) multiple orientation channels, (2) an association between orientation and spatial frequency channels such that channels existed for each spatial frequency range at each orientation, and (3) some degree of independence between the orientation and the spatial frequency tuning of units, such that the orientation tuning does not change with spatial frequency and vice versa. In Chapter 6 we have already considered the evidence for one-dimensional spatial frequency channels. Here we will first consider the psychophysical, physiological, and anatomical evidence for orientation channels and their arrangement, and then evidence with respect to the relation between orientation and spatial frequency selectivity.

ORIENTATION CHANNELS

It is obvious that we can detect the orientation of patterns. The question we are raising here is whether this processing of orientation information takes place in a single channel subserved by radially symmetric RFs (presumably in the pure space domain), or in multiple orientation channels. We shall consider first the psychophysical and then the physiological and anatomical evidence for orientation channels, although the study of orientation selectivity forms an unusual case in which physiological evidence for the existence of a process preceded the psychophysical evidence for the process.

Psychophysics

One of the first clear psychophysical demonstrations of separate orientation channels was a masking experiment in which Campbell and Kulikowski (1966) measured the extent to which the simultaneous presence of a pattern of one orientation raised the threshold for the detection of the same pattern at another orientation. They found that a masking pattern sufficiently different in orientation from the test pattern did not interfere with its detection, although patterns of nearby orientations did. This result is difficult to reconcile with a model of a single channel processing information about all orientations and instead suggests separate channels for patterns of different orientations. The orientation bandwidth (the total number of degrees between the points at which the masking effect falls to half amplitude on each side of the peak) was found to be 24 and 30° for vertical/horizontal and oblique patterns, respectively.

There is also evidence for multiple orientation channels from adaptation experiments. One of the classic pieces of evidence for separate spatial frequency channels was the adaptation experiment of Blakemore and Campbell (1969), discussed in Chapter 6, in which they showed that adapting to a grating pattern of a certain spatial frequency led to a loss in contrast sensitivity restricted to a little more than an octave band about the adaptation frequency. That same series of experiments produced evidence for separate orientation channels as well: a subject who adapted to a grating of a particular spatial frequency and a particular orientation showed no loss in contrast sensitivity when tested with patterns of the same spatial frequency but of an orthogonal orientation. Gilinsky (1968) had earlier reported similar orientation specificity in an adaptation paradigm, though without examining the spatial frequency selectivity of the effect. These adaptation experiments make it apparent that patterns of all orientations are not being processed by a single mechanism, but that there are separate, at least partially independent, mechanisms at different orientations.

The Blakemore and Campbell experiment showed that patterns 90° apart in orientation act independently. By testing with a variety of different adaptation orientations, Blakemore and Nachmias (1971) and Movshon and Blakemore (1973) obtained measures of the bandwidth of this adaptation: about 15°, independent of the spatial frequency involved. The technique they used to measure the adaptation effect was that of equivalent contrast. It is not clear why the bandwidth measured in these experiments is so much smaller than in the masking experiments (15 versus 24–30°). However, it will be remembered (see Chapter 6) that this measurement technique, used in spatial frequency adaptation experiments (Blakemore et al., 1973), also gave lower spatial bandwidth estimates than other adaptation experiments, suggesting it may be the measuring procedure rather than masking versus adaptation that accounts for the discrepancy.

A third psychophysical technique, subthreshold summation, has also been used to test for separate orientation channels and estimate their bandwidths (Kulikowski, Abadi, & King-Smith, 1973). As was also the case with the use of this technique to test spatial frequency channels, the bandwidths found were extremely small, about 6°. As we discuss below, such narrow bandwidths are not in accord with the tuning properties of striate units, although the broader bandwidths measured with masking and adaptation experiments can readily be reconciled with cortical physiology.

Physiological and Anatomical Evidence

In many respects the most striking finding by Hubel and Wiesel in their first recordings from cat striate cortex (Hubel & Wiesel, 1959, 1962) was the presence of orientation selectivity in cortical units. For one thing, it was a quite unexpected cortical property, not having been previously predicted, as has usually been the case, from psychophysical or perceptual considerations. For another, even more than the discovery by Kuffler (1953) and Barlow (1953) of antagonistic center-surround retinal RFs, it made it clear that the visual cells were doing something more interesting than just relaying information about local light intensity from receptors to cortex.

The early reports that cortical cells had orientation selectivity have been amply supported by many electrophysiological and anatomical studies of both cat and monkey striate cortex, as discussed in more detail in Chapter 4. With respect to the anatomical arrangement, 2-DG autoradiographic studies of both cat and monkey cortex have revealed that only certain subpopulations of striate cells, arranged in columnar strips, are activated by patterns of just one orientation (Hubel et al., 1978; Tootell et al., 1981).

A number of recent studies have provided quantitative data on the orientation bandwidths of cells in both cat (Henry, Bishop, & Dreher, 1974; D. Rose & Blakemore, 1974; Watkins & Berkley, 1974) and monkey (Schiller et al., 1976b; R.L. De Valois, Yund, & Hepler, 1982). These findings can be summarized as follows: (1) A small percentage of striate cells (mainly in layer 4) have little more orientation tuning than do LGN cells, but the vast majority are orientation selective to various degrees. (2) The orientation tuning on the average is symmetric about a certain preferred orientation. (3) The preferred orientations seem to vary continuously around the clock, the cells with different preferences being systematically arranged with respect to each other in neighboring cortical regions, all the cells within a column through the 6 cortical layers having roughly the same orientation preference. (4) The bandwidths of cortical cells, even considering only those with clear orientation tuning, vary enormously from cell to cell, the range of bandwidths being from about 6 or 8 to 90° or more (to 360° if nonoriented cells are included, of course). (5) Both simple and complex cells have orientation tuning and have very similar bandwidths, although those of simple cells are slightly narrower on the average. (6) Cat cells are slightly more narrowly tuned for orientation than those in monkey, on the average. The respective median bandwidths for cat and monkey striate cells are about 35 and 42°, respectively (R.L. De Valois, Yund, & Hepler, 1982).

It can thus be seen that the psychophysical, physiological, and anatomical experiments agree completely in showing separate orientation channels tuned to every orientation around the clock. With respect to orientation bandwidths, however, the situation is more complex, both because of varying psychophysical estimates from different types of experiments, and because of the very great scatter of bandwidths seen physiologically among striate cells. The narrowest estimates of orientation bandwidths—about 6°, from subthreshold summation experiments—appear to be out of the range of cells seen in either cat or monkey striate, or at least are at the extreme limit of the most narrowly tuned cells. The estimates based on masking and adaptation experiments, however, are well within the range seen physiologically, corresponding to the more narrowly tuned cells.

We should note that neither the psychophysical *nor* the physiological data alone are sufficient to determine the perceptual channel bandwidths. The physiological data show the total range of selectivities of cortical cells, but do not by themselves indicate which cells may actually be involved in a given perceptual task. Some cells recorded from may be at intermediate levels in the production of orientation selectivity; others may be involved in circuits unrelated to orientation perception, e.g., eye movement control, or feedback to LGN or colliculus. On the other hand, psychophysical results can often be difficult to interpret or can be interpreted in multiple ways (e.g., probability summation may greatly modify estimates of bandwidths from subthreshold summation experiments; Graham, 1980). Thus a joint examination of physiological and psychophysical data, here as in other aspects of vision, is especially instructive. With respect to orientation selectivity, such a comparison suggests that the orientation channel bandwidths are 15 to 30°, as found by masking and adaptation experiments, and that this corresponds to the most selective third of the total cortical cell population, as measured in monkey (R.L. De Valois, Yund, & Hepler, 1982); see Figure 9.1.

Combined Orientation and Spatial Selectivity

We have already summarized in Chapter 6 and earlier in this chapter the considerable psychophysical and physiological evidence for separate spatial fre-

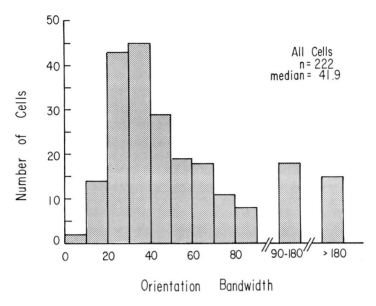

FIG. 9.1 Distribution of orientation bandwidths of a large (n = 222) population of macaque striate cortex cells. Orientation bandwidth is expressed in degrees. All cells were in the central projection area (from R.L. De Valois, Yund, & Hepler, 1982, *Vision Res., 22,* 531-544. Copyright 1982, Pergamon Journals, Inc. Reprinted with permission).

quency channels and for orientation channels. In principle, these orientation and spatial frequency channels could be unrelated to each other. That is, there could be some cells selective for spatial frequency but not for orientation and others with orientation but not spatial frequency tuning. For the visual system to perform a two-dimensional spatial frequency filtering would, however, require an association between spatial frequency and orientation channels such that there would be separate channels for each spatial frequency at each orientation. We need thus to consider briefly the psychophysical, physiological, and anatomical evidence for a relationship between these two parameters.

Psychophysical Evidence

The Blakemore and Campbell (1969) experiment that provided some of the first clear evidence for separate spatial frequency channels also showed that spatial frequency and orientation channels were interrelated. They found that adapting to a grating of a particular spatial frequency and a particular orientation (and thus at a particular two-dimensional spatial frequency locus) produced a loss in sensitivity only in the region of the adaptation frequency and orientation. It was left to other experiments to define precisely the orientation component of the selectivity, but nonetheless this experiment makes it clear that units with combined spatial frequency and orientation selectivity exist and are involved in the detection of grating patterns.

Physiological Evidence

Every investigator who has measured both spatial frequency and orientation tuning of striate cells has found that most cells are selective along both dimensions, thus showing that each responds to only a limited two-dimensional spatial frequency region. Of particular interest are those studies (Schiller et al., 1976b, 1976c; R.L. De Valois, Yund, & Hepler, 1982; R.L. De Valois, Albrecht, & Thorell, 1982; Webster & R.L. De Valois, 1985) which have quantitatively measured both orientation and spatial frequency tuning (or two-dimensional spatial frequency tuning) on a population of cells. Among monkey striate cells, both within the foveal projection and in a parafoveal site, the orientation and spatial frequency bandwidths of cells were found to be positively correlated (R.L. De Valois, Albrecht, & Thorell, 1982). It was in fact the largest correlation among the many examined between the various characteristics of the cells. Those cells which have narrow orientation tuning strongly tend to show narrow spatial frequency tuning as well, and nonoriented cells tend to have broad, often almost low-pass spatial frequency tuning.

A convenient way of representing two-dimensional spatial frequency is in a polar plot (see Figure 9.2), in which the orientation is given by the direction from the center, and the spatial frequency by the distance out from the center. Such

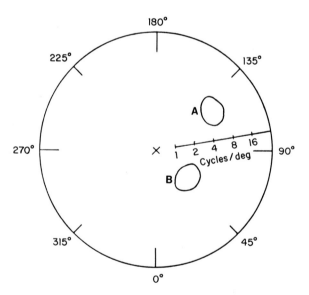

FIG. 9.2   Polar plot of the two-dimensional spatial frequency tuning of two macaque striate cortex cells. Spatial frequency corresponds to the distance out from the center; orientation is represented by the angle.

a plot, with a linear spatial frequency axis, would correspond to an optical two-dimensional Fourier power spectrum (see Chapter 1). On such a plot, a cell that responds (at half amplitude or more) only to patterns of orientations of, say, 110 to 140° and to spatial frequencies between 4 and 8 c/deg would have what we might term a two-dimensional response area as shown by cell A in Figure 9.2. On the other hand, cell B shown in that figure responds to a different orientation and to lower spatial frequencies and thus has a different two-dimensional response area. In Figure 9.3 are shown 9 grating patterns at the various combinations of three spatial frequencies and three orientations. Cell A in Figure 9.2 would respond optimally to the middle pattern in this array (assuming, of course, the appropriate distance). It would give little response to any of the other 8 gratings, all of which lie outside its half-amplitude bandwidth, with the "wrong" spatial frequency and/or orientation. Cell B in that figure would respond to none of these patterns.

FIG. 9.3   Nine grating patches chosen to illustrate the selectivity of striate cells. The spatial frequencies and orientations of these stimuli are such so that only the center one would produce a significant excitatory response from cell A of the previous figure. Each of the other patterns would lie outside the cell's passband in either spatial frequency, orientation, or both. Cell B would respond to none of these patterns.

The two-dimensional response areas diagrammed in Figure 9.2 can be thought of as the cells' receptive fields in the spatial frequency domain. For the visual system to be doing a local two-dimensional spatial frequency filtering, it must contain cells within each cortical region with all combinations of spatial frequency and orientation preferences. This can be restated diagrammatically as a requirement for such a polar plot to be completely paved with the spatial frequency RFs of cells.

In Figure 9.4A are shown the actual two-dimensional response areas of all of the narrowly tuned cells (including the two shown earlier) recorded from in a series of probes through a patch of near-foveal striate cortex in one monkey (R.L. De Valois, Albrecht, & Thorell, 1982). All of these cells had spatially overlapping RFs: they were processing information from a single region of visual space. But, as can be seen, each cell responded to a different portion of two-dimensional spatial frequency space, with the combination of orientation and spatial frequency tuning varying from cell to cell.

In both our physiological and our psychophysical discussions of spatial frequency tuning we have plotted data on a log spatial frequency scale and given the bandwidths in octaves. This is also true in Figures 9.2 and 9.4 here. It is convenient to use such a log frequency scale because then psychophysical channels and cells' tuning curves have approximately equal bandwidths regardless of spatial frequency peak (although somewhat narrower at high frequencies). Octave bandwidths are also much the same in cat and monkey striate, despite the much higher spatial frequency peaks of monkey cells on the average. The total range and shape of the behavioral contrast sensitivity functions of various animals are also quite similar, on a log scale, despite the virtually nonoverlapping ranges of spatial frequencies responded to by such animals as cats (Blake, Cool, & Crawford, 1974) and falcons (Fox, Lehmkuhle, & Westerdorf, 1976); see Figure 5.2. The constant octave bandwidths of cells regardless of peak spatial frequency tuning would be expected if the cells' RFs were of the same shape regardless of overall dimensions. Thus a cell with a central excitatory region and two antagonistic flanks would have a bandwidth of perhaps 1.8 octaves regardless of whether the three areas were very wide or quite narrow. A cell with additional sidebands would be more narrowly tuned in each case. It is instructive, nonetheless, to look at the cells' tuning on a linear spatial frequency scale. The data in Figure 9.4A so replotted are shown in Figure 9.4B. As can be clearly seen, the two-dimensional spatial frequency response areas of cells tuned to low spatial frequencies are now seen to be much smaller than those tuned to high frequencies. If the Fourier spectrum is represented on a linear scale (as is usually the case), the visual system is obviously much more selective at low spatial frequencies than at high. From the point of view of the linear spatial spectrum of objects, therefore, it is clear that the visual system is much better equipped to analyze low than high spatial frequency information.

The 20 cells shown in Figure 9.4 are the most narrowly tuned third of the cells recorded from in that patch of cortex. A total CM, containing all the cells dealing with a given region in space, consists of perhaps 150,000 cells (in monkey). In

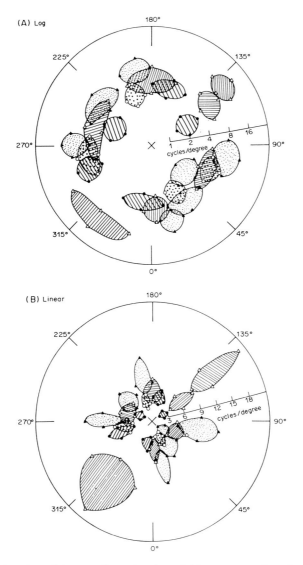

FIG. 9.4   Polar plots of the two-dimensional spatial frequency tuning of a sample of narrowly tuned cells recorded in one small foveal projection area in one macaque. Included
in this are the two cells illustrated in Figure 9.2. In A, spatial frequency is plotted on a
logarithmic axis; in B, on a linear axis. In such a plot cells that are not directionally selective will be represented by two patches (on opposite sides of center). Directionally selective cells will have only a single representation (from R.L. De Valois, Albrecht, & Thorell,
1982, *Vision Res., 22,* 545–559. Copyright 1982, Pergamon Journals, Inc. Reprinted with
permission).

that experiment, then, we probably recorded from less than 0.01% of all the cells in the CM. If all of the narrowly tuned cells in the whole CM had been recorded from and plotted in Figure 9.4, there would be more than 2,000 times as many of these two-dimensional response patches, with one cell or another then totally covering all of the two-dimensional frequency space. There would in fact be a great deal of overlap and duplication among the two-dimensional spatial frequency response areas of the various cells. The physiological evidence is thus consistent with the existence of a system that might serve to perform a two-dimensional spatial frequency filtering of the information in different parts of the visual world. Whether the visual system is in fact sufficiently linear and devoid of other complications to be accurately so described will be discussed below.

Anatomical Evidence
It is always useful in science to see whether the same answer results when a question is posed in as many different ways and with as many different techniques as possible. One's confidence in the answer increases greatly if very disparate approaches all lead to the same conclusion. It is thus of interest to look at the anatomical evidence for a possible two-dimensional spatial frequency filtering system in the cortex. The question of the overall cortical architecture possibly underlying two-dimensional spatial frequency analysis can also be best asked through anatomical techniques.

As we stated above, a two-dimensional spatial frequency filtering would require not only cells at least moderately selective for spatial frequency and for orientation, but an association between them such that cells tuned to each spatial frequency should be found among those tuned to each orientation. Furthermore, one would expect an orderly arrangement of cells tuned to different two-dimensional spatial frequency regions. This is hardly a logical necessity, but would be likely, given the advantages of such systematic arrangements for the construction of tuning functions by local interactions, for economy of genetic specification of connections, and perhaps for ease of extraction of the information by later regions.

As discussed in Chapter 4, Hubel and Wiesel have provided both physiological and anatomical evidence for a systematic arrangement of cells in striate cortex dealing with different orientations. The clearest demonstration of this comes from a study using the 2-DG technique (Hubel et al., 1978). A pattern of a single orientation was presented while radioactive 2-DG was being injected, then the brain was prepared for autoradiography. In cross sections of the cortex columns could be seen going through all the 6 cortical layers (except 4c), consisting of those cells in each neighboring CM tuned to the orientation presented. In tangential sections of the brain, the cells tuned to a given orientation were seen to cross the cortex in strips or slabs, rather like zebra stripes.

In the 2-DG study of orientation organization, Hubel et al. (1978) used a pattern containing many spatial frequencies, i.e., bars, which have a broad frequency spectrum. If they had not, they would have seen a combination of the spatial frequency and the orientation organization, instead of just the latter, for (see Chapters 4 and 6) there is also a systematic anatomical arrangement of cells in cat and monkey striate cortex according to their spatial frequency tuning. What of the relations between the anatomical organizations underlying orientation and spatial frequency? A two-dimensional spatial frequency filtering system demands a crossed relationship between the orientation and the spatial frequency slabs so that all combinations of spatial frequency and orientation would occur within each CM. There are two bits of anatomical evidence that such in fact is the case. The one constancy seen in the orientation slabs from cat to cat is that they appear always to meet the vertical meridian at right angles. The spatial frequency slabs, on the other hand, approach the vertical meridian at a nonperpendicular angle, perhaps radiating out from the area centralis (Silverman, 1984; Silverman, Tootell & R.L. De Valois, in preparation). Because of the irregular directions taken by the slabs elsewhere in the cortex, it is not possible, in comparisons across animals, to see what the relationships are in other cortical regions. But it is apparent from another experiment that the orientation and spatial frequency slabs do indeed intersect throughout the cortex. In a 2-DG experiment with either one orientation at all frequencies, or one spatial frequency at all orientations, one sees long cortical slabs. However, with one orientation and one spatial frequency, a dot-like pattern of 2-DG uptake appears, a leopard rather than a zebra pattern (Tootell et al., 1981). The dots clearly are the intersections of the orientation and the spatial frequency slabs.

Thus the anatomical evidence supports the physiological data in indicating a systematic cross relationship between the cortical spatial frequency and orientation organizations such that, within each CM, there are cells tuned to each orientation and spatial frequency combination. This, as we have seen, is what is required for a two-dimensional spatial frequency organization.

Constancy of Spatial Frequency and Orientation Tuning

The physiological studies of spatial frequency tuning of cortical cells have almost always used patterns of optimal orientation; tests of orientation tuning have likewise used gratings of optimal spatial frequency (or bars of optimal width). What would happen if nonoptimal patterns were used? What would the spatial frequency tuning of a cell be to off-orientation gratings? For a cell to encode faithfully the two-dimensional spatial frequency content of a pattern, it should respond only to a certain spatial frequency range, regardless of its orientation, and to a certain orientation range regardless of spatial frequency. Daugman (1980) has pointed out that a cell with a classic RF as described by Hubel and Wiesel (1962) would not have this property at all. Rather, its spatial frequency tuning would vary greatly depending on the orientation of the pattern, shifting to low spatial frequencies for very off-orientations. On the other hand, certain other suggested RF shapes, e.g., two-dimensional Gabor shape (Daugman, 1980) (a sinusoidal grating tapered in both directions by a gaussian), would show more independence of orientation and spatial frequency. Examining the responses of striate cells to various spatial frequency and orientation combinations, we have shown that cells respond only to patterns within a compact, delimited, two-dimensional spatial frequency (spatial frequency by orientation) region (Webster & R.L. De Valois, 1985). There is typically some change in spatial frequency tuning at off-orientations, but much less than would be predicted if the cells had the RF structure classically attributed to them by the Hubel and Wiesel model.

EVIDENCE FOR TWO-DIMENSIONAL SPATIAL FREQUENCY PROCESSING

We have summarized in the sections above the considerable anatomical, physiological, and psychophysical evidence that (1) there are both multiple spatial frequency channels and multiple orientation channels, based on deductions from psychophysical experiments; (2) in each section of the striate cortex there are cells with band-pass tuning for both orientation and spatial frequency, that is, for two-dimensional spatial frequency (3) the ensemble of cells within a region has two-dimensional spatial frequency selectivities scattered over the whole range of two-dimensional spatial frequencies to which the visual system is sensitive in that area, as a result of a systematic relationship between the columnar organizations for orientation and spatial frequency; and (4) the orientation tuning does not change significantly with spatial frequency or vice versa in most cells. Thus the basic organization appears to exist for the system to do a localized two-dimensional spatial frequency filtering of the visual information. The question we now raise is whether in fact it so operates in response to complex, two-dimensionally varying stimulus patterns. It is important to note that the tests used to establish the orientation and the spatial frequency tuning of the cells and of the psychophysical channels were simple one-dimensionally varying patterns. One cannot automatically assume from this that the visual system would function as predicted in response to other, more complex stimuli. For example, when striate cells are tested only with simple bars and edges of various orientations, it is easy to conclude that the critical factors are bar width and edge orientation; as we shall see below, that can be shown not to be the case when more complex patterns are used. Also, if there are interactions between various striate units, e.g., between those responsive to different orientations or different spatial frequencies, a cell's responses to complex patterns might be quite different from what one would predict from its responses to single gratings alone. It is thus very important to examine directly how striate cells and the system as a whole respond to more complex (and realistic) two-dimensional patterns.

Psychophysics

D.H. Kelly (Kelly & Magnuski, 1975; Kelly, 1976) was the first to compare detection of one- and two-dimensional patterns in psychophysical experiments. He examined the threshold for detection of sine wave gratings, compared with each of several two-dimensional patterns: certain radially symmetric patterns, and checkerboards. For these patterns, the predictions of detectability are quite different depending on whether detection is based on the amplitude of the two-dimensional spatial frequency components or on the spatial contrast of the patterns. He found, in every case studied, that the results were predictable from the two-dimensional Fourier spectrum of the stimulus pattern but not from the pattern contrast or the one-dimensional Fourier components.

Consider, for instance, the detection of a checkerboard pattern and of a square wave grating (Kelly, 1976). In Figure 1.6 both of these patterns are shown along with a representation of their Fourier power spectra. It is not relevant to this particular experiment (although it is for others discussed below), but one should note that the checkerboard pattern with the same edge orientation as the grating has its fundamental Fourier components shifted 45° to either side of the orientation of the grating's components. Furthermore, as is relevant for Kelly's experiment, the amplitude of each of the checkerboard fundamentals is smaller than that of the grating by $2/\pi$. The checkerboard and grating patterns, on the other hand, have identical pattern contrasts (same peak, trough, and mean luminance), so if it is *contrast* that is relevant for detection these patterns should be equally detectable. If, on the contrary, it is the *amplitude of the two-dimensional Fourier components* that is relevant, as it should be if the system were acting as a two-dimensional spatial frequency filter, then the grating ought to be more detectable by a factor of $\pi/2$. Kelly found that the relative detectability of these patterns corresponded to that predicted by the two-dimensional spectrum, but not at all that predicted from the spatial contrast.

In tests using two circularly symmetric patterns, produced by a Bessel function and by a circular cosine function, Kelly and Magnuski (1975) carried out a similar test of whether the contrast of a pattern or the amplitudes of its two-dimensional Fourier components better predict its detection. The contrasts of both of these patterns are independent of spatial frequency, so the contrast sensitivity function should resemble that for sine wave gratings if contrast were the relevant parameter. On the other hand, the amplitudes of the two-dimensional Fourier fundamentals of these patterns vary with spatial frequency, and in different ways for each pattern. Kelly and Magnuski showed that the detectability of these circular patterns was predictable from their two-dimensional Fourier fundamental amplitudes but not at all from the contrasts of the patterns.

In other studies of the detectability of two-dimensionally varying patterns, Mitchell (1976) found that the detection of spatially filtered two-dimensional patterns could be well predicted from their spatial frequency content. The same was found by Carlson, Cohen, and Gorog (1977) for patterns at a variety of spatial frequencies and luminance levels.

The checkerboard pattern described by Kelly was used in a quite different psychophysical test of how the visual system responds to two-dimensional stimuli, by Green, Corwin, and Zemon (1976) and by May and Matheson (1976). They utilized the McCollough aftereffect. It had been shown (McCollough, 1965) that prolonged inspection of a combined luminance and color pattern made up of vertical red-black bars and horizontal green-black bars produces an aftereffect on a subsequently viewed black-white striped pattern that depends on the orientation of the stripes: vertical white stripes now appeared greenish and horizontal ones reddish. This McCollough aftereffect has thus been described as dependent on color and edge orientation. But suppose it is not edge orientation but rather the orientation of the two-dimensional Fourier fundamentals which is the critical spatial determinant. In the original McCollough pattern these alternatives cannot be distinguished because they coincide, but in a checkerboard the Fourier fundamentals are at 45° with respect to the edge orientations. If one adapts with the two orthogonal colored gratings described above and then tests with a black-white checkerboard, the question is whether it is the orientation of the checkerboard edges which determines the colors seen, as it would be if the underlying cells were edge orientation specific, or if it is the orientation of the two-dimensional Fourier fundamentals, as it would be if cells were acting as spatial frequency filters.

Both May and Matheson and Green et al. found that the McCollough effect is contingent *not* on edge orientation, but on the orientation of the two-dimensional spatial frequency fundamentals (the higher harmonics are presumably too weak to make much of a contribution). In addition, Green et al. showed that the aftereffect was maximal not when the bar width of the adaptation pattern coincided with that of the test pattern, as had previously been thought, but when their two-dimensional spatial frequencies coincided (the spatial frequency of the checkerboard fundamental is $\sqrt{2}$ times that of the corresponding grating).

Another way of testing the extent to which the visual system behaves as a set of two-dimensional spatial frequency filters is to see whether complex two-dimensional patterns interact with simple sinusoidal gratings in a manner which is predictable from their two-dimensional Fourier spectra. K.K. De Valois and Switkes (1980) examined the effects of adapting to a pattern composed of randomly positioned pairs of dots, all pairs having the same interdot separation. The power spectrum of such a pattern is almost flat (i.e., very slowly changing) along one axis, but along the orthogonal axis there is a periodic fluctuation in power with spatial frequency. In Figure 9.5 are shown two such random dot pair patterns, for two different interdot spacings, along with their Fourier power spectra. It can be seen that the spacing of the oscillations in the power spectra is a function of the dot separation.

Adapting to such a pattern was found to produce a loss in contrast sensitivity for sinusoidal gratings that would be represented along the oscillatory axis. The spatial frequencies that are first affected can be precisely predicted by considering the dot pattern spectrum. At an orthogonal orientation, however, there is little loss in contrast sensitivity despite the presence of significant power in the

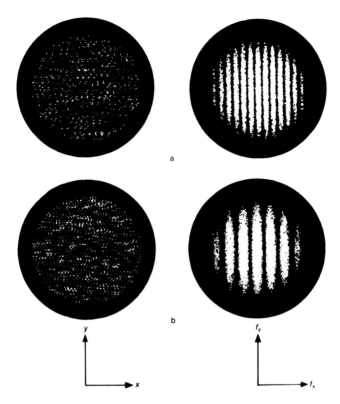

FIG. 9.5 Two-dimensional Fourier power spectra of two patterns of randomly positioned dot pairs. In each case the pattern (on the left) is composed of 500 pairs of dots laterally separated by a specific amount. The two dot patterns differ in the magnitude of the lateral translation. The corresponding power spectra are shown to the right. Note that there is oscillation in the power spectra due to the dot pairing (from K.K. De Valois & Switkes, 1980. Reprinted with permission).

spectrum. The most likely explanation of the absence of adaptation in this case is mutual inhibitory interactions, as discussed in Chapter 11. Thus, by considering the visual system to contain multiple two-dimensional spatial frequency filters one can predict the interactions between some, but not all, very dissimilar visual patterns.

Additional evidence that the visual system in fact can be treated as containing at some (striate) level a set of local two-dimensional spatial frequency filters comes from masking experiments. Weisstein (Weisstein, Harris, Berbaum, Tangney, & Williams, 1977; Weisstein & Harris, 1980), has studied backwards masking in a number of situations in which the test and masking stimuli were quite different in the space domain but had certain resemblances in the two-dimensional Fourier frequency domain. For instance, in one experiment (Weisstein et al., 1977) the masking stimulus was a spot of light, and the test stimulus was a bullseye target which overlapped hardly at all in space with the masking spot. One would thus not expect any masking either on the basis of spatial over-lap of the two, or on the basis of naturalistic resemblance between the two pat-terns. However, the two-dimensional Fourier spectra of the spot and bullseye have certain communalities that might lead one to expect on those grounds that the spot would mask the bullseye, as indeed it was found to do. However, in other situations the masking predicted from the two-dimensional Fourier spec-tra was not found to occur.

There are two problems in interpreting these particular masking experiments of Weisstein. One is that Fourier spectra of test and mask were only partially alike, so the degree of masking expected cannot easily be determined. More crit-ical, however, is the fact that these experiments implicitly assume a global Fou-rier analysis by the visual system, something which we have throughout this book argued is not in accord with the underlying striate physiology. In the case of stimuli such as the checkerboard and the random dot patterns discussed ear-lier, the patterns are highly repetitive so the *local* Fourier spectra (which is what we believe to be critically involved) are much the same as the global Fourier spectra. Therefore the predictions based on the overall global spectra of the pat-terns can be expected to apply, except when the patterns are so magnified that the local regions covered by cortical cell RFs would not encompass a whole sub-portion of the repetitive pattern. However, in the case of the patterns used by Weisstein and colleagues the local Fourier spectra could be quite different from the global Fourier spectra upon which the predictions were based.

The results from another, very different, experimental paradigm bear on the issue of two-dimensional spatial processing. Julesz (1975) has studied the ability of subjects to distinguish among patterns by "instantaneous" perception—as opposed to careful scrutiny with focal attention. He found that when highly complex texture patterns differ in their second-order statistics, or two-dimen-sional power spectra, they can be instantly distinguished, but not if they have identical power spectra. (By varying the phase relations one can readily produce patterns which differ but have identical global power spectra.) It is not at all obvious, when one carefully inspects a group of such patterns, which ones would be distinguished at a glance and which not. Thus this finding of Julesz would appear to provide some support for a two-dimensional spatial frequency model. However, Julesz, Gilbert, and Victor (1978) found clear exceptions to this rule: patterns with identical power spectra which are instantly seen as very different. Although a more thorough analysis is clearly needed, it appears that the critical factor could again be the issue of local versus global spectra. The initial patterns Julesz studied appear quite repetitive and similar throughout so that the local spectra should be statistically similar to each other and to the global spectrum (which is what he measured). However, the patterns found by Julesz et al. (1978), which do not follow the rule, are clearly different in various local regions so that the various local spectra doubtless are very different from each other. It could well be, then, that Julesz's initial conjecture was correct, but only if one considers the local rather than the global spatial frequency spectra.

There are two further points with respect to these studies of Julesz and coworkers which are worth noting as an aside. One is that if very simple patterns, e.g., gratings of only 2 spatial frequencies, were to be used, the results would be different. One can, for instance, clearly detect the difference between $f + 3f$ with $3f$ in sine phase, and f and $3f$ with $3f$ in cosine phase. The other is that with extended, focal attention any of these patterns can be differentiated on the basis of fine details, such as the width of a line here as opposed to there, or the contrast at this point versus that point. Subjects have been shown to judge on the basis of local contrast in other situations as well, where careful scrutiny is allowed (e.g., Badcock, 1984a, 1984b). This suggests that at some later, presumably poststriate stage visual information from the central retina may be resynthesized into a spatial representation. This does not negate, however, the view we have been presenting that at the earlier striate level the information is coded in the local spatial frequency domain.

Physiology

Both for reasons of convenience and for lack of theoretical reasons for doing otherwise, most physiological studies of cortex have utilized only one-dimensionally-varying stimuli such as bars, edges, or gratings (the other dimension being essentially uniform over an extent which is long with respect to the cell's RF). We have, however, examined cells in both cat and monkey striate cortex with a number of simple two-dimensional patterns (K.K. De Valois, R.L. De Valois, & Yund, 1979) The patterns used were chosen in particular to differentiate between bar-and-edge and spatial frequency models of cortical function, and to examine the extent of linearity of striate cortex function.

As mentioned above, checkerboard patterns have certain interesting features that make them particularly well suited to examine not only how well cortical cells can be described as two-dimensional spatial filters, but also to differentiate between that suggestion and the prominent alternative that they are bar-and-edge detectors. In the case of gratings and bars, the orientations of edges are the same as the orientations of the Fourier fundamentals and higher harmonics, as well. There is also a correspondence between bar widths and spatial frequency half cycles (of the fundamental frequency) for such patterns. Therefore, with such bar or grating patterns, it is hard to determine whether the cells are better described as responding to edges and bar widths or to the Fourier components. With checkerboard patterns, these various alternatives can be clearly separated.

In Figure 1.6 were shown a square wave grating and a checkerboard with check widths equal to the grating bar width. Also shown were representations of the Fourier power spectra of these two patterns. Although the grating and checkerboard have the same edge orientation (the checkerboard has additional edges 90° away, of course), their Fourier fundamentals are 45° apart. And although the grating and checkerboard have the same bar/check width, the spatial frequencies of their fundamentals differ, the checkerboard frequency being $\sqrt{2}$ times higher. Finally, the two patterns have exactly the same contrast, however contrast be

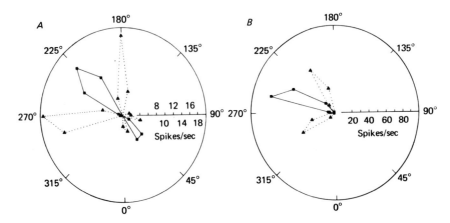

FIG. 9.6   Orientation tuning of two cortical cells to grating and checkerboard patterns. (A) shows responses of a cat simple cell, and (B) of a directionally selective monkey complex cell. Solid lines show the responses to gratings; dotted lines show the responses to checkerboards, with the "orientation" referred to being those of the patterns' edges. Note that each cell responds best to checkerboards shifted in orientation by 45° relative to the best grating pattern orientation, as would be predicted from their respective Fourier spectra (from K.K. De Valois et al., 1979. Reprinted with permission).

defined, since they have the same peak, trough, and mean luminance. But the Fourier fundamental amplitude of the grating is $\pi/2$ higher than that of the checkerboard. These properties of gratings and checkerboards have been used to test alternate bar and edge versus two-dimensional spatial frequency models psychophysically, as discussed above. They have also been used to test cortical cells directly to address the same questions (K.K. De Valois et al., 1979). Furthermore, additional manipulations of these patterns can provide additional tests: by varying the length and width of the checks independently, rectangular checkerboards can be made. These obviously have the same edge orientations as square checkerboards, but the Fourier fundamentals (and other components) have quite different orientations. The spatial frequencies of the rectangular checkerboard fundamentals are also different by precisely specifiable amounts from those of square checkerboards. Thus using gratings and these various checkerboards there are available a multitude of tests of the extent to which cortical cells' responses are in fact, as so often stated, determined by edge orientation and bar width or whether, on the contrary, they respond as would be predicted by the two-dimensional spatial frequency components.

The procedure for these experiments was to determine successively for each cortical cell studied the optimal orientation and spatial frequency (or bar width) for a grating, and then to do the same for one or more types of checkerboard. In experiments described later in which we examined the responses to the third and other higher harmonic components, gratings or checkerboards of three times the best width (one third the optimal spatial frequency) were also examined. The third harmonics of such patterns should then be at the cell's peak sensitivity.

The result of measuring the orientation tuning of cells was quite unequivocal: knowing the orientation tuning of a cell to a grating, one can predict its orientation tuning to the various checkerboards from the orientations of the fundamental components of the patterns, but *not at all* from the orientations of their edges. For instance, in Figure 9.6A is plotted in solid lines the orientation tuning of a simple cell to a grating pattern. It can be seen that it responded optimally to a grating of 225°. The cell showed no response at all, however, to a 1/1 checkerboard with edges at that orientation (dotted lines). Rather, the cell responded to a checkerboard oriented with its edges 45° to either side of the grating orientation, just as would be predicted from the two-dimensional spectra of the patterns. The same result can be seen for a monkey complex cell shown in Figure 9.6B.

Tests with checkerboards of various length/width ratios make this point even clearer. Such checkerboards obviously all have edges of exactly the same orientations. If it is edge orientation to which cells are tuned, then they should respond to these patterns in exactly the same orientations. If, however, it is not edge orientation, but the orientations of the two-dimensional spatial frequency components that are critical, then quite different orientation tuning would be expected to these various checkerboard patterns. As can be seen in Figure 9.7A, gratings and checkerboards of various length/width ratios give quite different orientation tuning where the "orientation of the pattern" is taken as the orientation of its edges. If, however (Figure 9.7B), one plots the same data with respect to the two-dimensional Fourier fundamental orientations, it can be seen that the cell's orientation tuning is the same for all these patterns. The orientation tuning of the cell to various patterns thus *cannot* be predicted from the edge

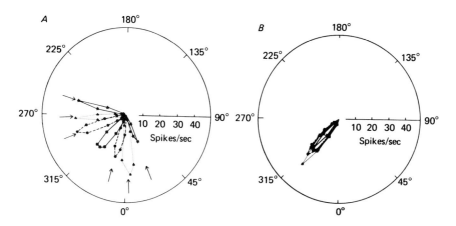

FIG. 9.7 Orientation tuning of a cat simple cell to a grating (squares and solid lines) and to checkerboards of various length/width ratios. In A the responses are plotted as a function of the edge orientation; in B as a function of the orientation of the Fourier fundamental of each pattern. It can be seen that the Fourier fundamental but not the edge orientation specifies the cell's orientation tuning (from K.K. De Valois et al., 1979. Reprinted with permission).

orientations at all, but can be precisely predicted if one considers the orientation of the two-dimensional spectra of each pattern. These tests were carried out on a sample of 41 cat and monkey simple and complex cells. Not one cell showed the orientation tuning one would predict from edges; every one responded as predicted from the orientation of the Fourier fundamentals.

Recording the responses of cortical cells to gratings and checkerboards allows one also to examine the predictions from alternate models with respect to the size tuning of the cells. Turning a grating into a 1/1 checkerboard does not change the bar widths or edge-to-edge distances. If these are the crucial spatial dimensions, then, cells should respond optimally to gratings and checkerboards of the same bar/check widths. On the other hand, if it is not bar width or edge-to-edge distance but spatial frequency which is the crucial spatial variable, one would have quite different predictions, since the checkerboard fundamental has a spatial frequency $\sqrt{2}$ times that of the grating with the same edge spacing. In Figure 9.8 is shown the spatial tuning of a cortical cell to gratings and various checkerboards. It can be seen that this cell shows quite different tuning to the grating and these various checkerboards when the data are plotted as a function of bar width (Figure 9.8A), but quite similar tuning when they are plotted as a function of the spatial frequency of the Fourier fundamentals (Figure 9.8B). It is thus clear that it is the spatial frequency of the Fourier components, not bar/check width, to which cells are tuned.

A third aspect of gratings and checkerboards that allows one to sharply distin-

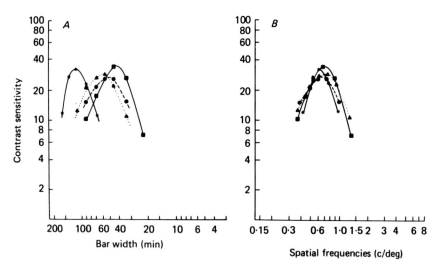

FIG. 9.8   Spatial tuning of a cat simple cell to gratings (squares, solid lines) and to checkerboards of various length/width ratios. In A the contrast sensitivity is plotted as a function of bar width (i.e., edge-to-edge separation of the checks); in B as a function of the spatial frequency of the pattern's Fourier fundamentals. The tuning functions are very similar in B, very different in A (from K.K. De Valois et al., 1979. Reprinted with permission).

guish between these two models of cortical function is with respect to the intensitive dimension. It has long been thought that pattern *contrast* is the crucial intensitive dimension: the retinal network has often been characterized as converting the visual system from an absolute luminance detecting system to one concerned with contrast (see Chapter 3). If contrast is, in fact, the crucial variable, then cells should be equally sensitive and responsive to the gratings as to the checkerboards used (K.K. De Valois et al., 1979) since they have identical peaks, troughs, and mean luminances and thus identical contrasts. On the other hand, if the system is in fact doing something like a local two-dimensional spatial frequency analysis, it would be the amplitude of the two-dimensional Fourier components, not contrast, that is relevant. The fundamentals of a checkerboard have an amplitude of only $2/\pi$ times that of a grating of the same contrast; cells should thus be less responsive to checkerboards. They in fact are. Not one cell studied was as sensitive or as responsive to a checkerboard as to a grating of the same contrast, and the difference in sensitivity was close to that (actually slightly more than that; see Chapter 11) predicted from the two-dimensional Fourier amplitudes.

One can examine further the extent to which striate cells follow linear predictions, and thus act as spatial frequency filters, by studying the effects of selectively attenuating various frequency components in checkerboard patterns. In the pattern shown in Figure 9.9A, the fundamentals of the checkerboard have been attenuated, with the higher harmonics (and thus the edges) unchanged; in Figure 9.9B the fundamentals are totally absent. (Note that these two patterns can be discriminated visually by viewing them from a distance. When the higher harmonics are all outside your visual system's sensitivity range, the missing-fundamental but not the diminished-fundamental pattern will disappear.)

In a study of cat striate cortex cells, Grosof, Skottun and R.L. De Valois (1985) found that cells tuned to the spatial frequency and orientations of the

A   B

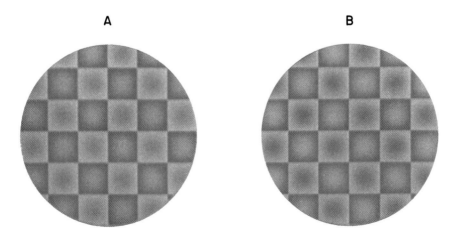

FIG. 9.9   Checkerboard patterns with the fundamentals attenuated (A) and absent (B).

checkerboard fundamentals gave considerable, but attenuated, responses to the diminished-fundamental pattern but responded not at all to the missing-fundamental pattern, as would be expected from a linear spatial frequency filter model. It is not at all obvious how striate cells might respond to these patterns from a consideration of anything but their spatial frequency content; conclusions drawn from a consideration of the edges would again be in error.

In the checkerboard experiments discussed above, gratings and checkerboards of optimal size for the cell being studied were used. These would be expected to be (and the evidence indicates that they are) of such a size that the fundamentals of the patterns are in the optimal spatial frequency range for the cell. It is also enlightening, however, to examine the responses of cells to patterns of such dimensions that not the fundamentals but the higher harmonics are within the cell's passband. This is of particular interest in comparing spatial filtering models with those which describe cells as bar and/or edge detectors. The latter description has no place in it for harmonic components. Thus if responses are found that are clearly associated with higher harmonic components, this would be a powerful argument against bar and edge detectors and in favor of spatial frequency filtering.

A checkerboard pattern has certain additional advantages for examining whether cells act as two-dimensional spatial frequency filters: one can take advantage of the fact that the different harmonic components are at different orientations. In the case of a square wave grating, the fundamental and all the higher harmonics are at the same orientation; in a checkerboard this is not the case. For a 1/1 checkerboard, the fundamentals are at 45° with respect to the edge orientation, but the third harmonics are 18 and 72° away. A cell should thus show the same orientation tuning to a square wave grating whether it is of optimum width (when the cell is presumably responding to the fundamental) or to one of 3 times optimum size (when it should respond to the third harmonic). In the case of a checkerboard, however, the orientation tuning should be predictably different for an optimum-size checkerboard and one 3 times that size. It can be seen in Figure 9.10 that that is precisely what is found. The complex cell pictured was tuned to 45° for a grating of either optimum or three times optimum size. To a checkerboard, however, the peak responses are 45° to either side of the grating orientation for the optimum-size checkerboard, as predicted from the orientation of the fundamental, but only about 15° to each side for the larger pattern in which the cell should be responding to the third (18° away) and fifth (11° away) harmonics.

All the results presented so far have been from studies of the responses of cells to luminance-varying patterns. However, pattern information can be carried by color variations as well (see Chapter 7). D.H. Kelly (1976) used red-green color-varying patterns in examining whether or not the sensitivity of human observers to checkerboards followed the two-dimensional Fourier predictions (it did). We have also examined a few monkey striate cells with pure color checkerboard patterns. The same results were obtained with these as with pure-luminance varying patterns: the orientation and spatial frequency tuning of the cells was

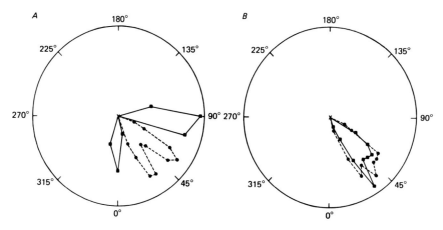

FIG. 9.10 Responses of a complex cell to grating and checkerboards of optimum dimensions, and 3 times optimum. In the former case, the pattern fundamentals (solid lines) fell within the cell's passband; in the latter case, the third harmonic (dashed lines) should have been within its passband. For a square wave grating (B), f and $3f$ have the same orientation, and the cell shows the same orientation tuning to the two patterns of different size. For a checkerboard (A), f is oriented 45° to either side of the grating orientation, and $3f$ 18° to either side. As can be seen, the cell shows the predicted difference in orientation tuning to these two checkerboard patterns (from K.K. De Valois et al., 1979. Reprinted with permission).

precisely predictable from the two-dimensional Fourier components, but not from the edges.

These responses of cells to the higher harmonics of checkerboard and grating patterns provide evidence that the cells dissect complex patterns into their harmonic components. Although it is not possible to record simultaneously from a particular selection of cells in an area, we know from successive recordings that a vertical sine wave grating of 1 c/deg will be responded to only by cells tuned to approximately 1 c/deg and with an orientation tuning of about 90°. A square wave grating of the same frequency (and the same bar widths) will be responded to by these same cells, plus additional cells tuned to about 3 c/deg, 5 c/deg, and probably to still higher spatial frequencies, all with 90° orientation tuning. A checkerboard made from this 1-c/deg vertical grating (multiplied by a horizontal grating of the same frequency) will produce no response by these cells tuned to 1 or 3 c/deg with 90° orientation tuning. Instead, it will activate cells tuned to 45° and 1.4 c/deg and other cells tuned to 135° and 1.4 c/deg, plus still other cells tuned to about 72° and 3.2 c/deg and still others to 108° and 3.2 c/deg, etc. In other words, consider that in the ensemble of cells in a given striate region are ones tuned to each two-dimensional spatial frequency range, as illustrated for an actual sample of such cells shown in Figure 9.4 above. A complex pattern will activate that particular subset of these cells whose two-dimensional Fourier response areas correspond to various parts of the two-dimensional spectrum of the pattern. One must keep in mind throughout, of course, the rather crude orientation and spatial frequency tuning of the cells. Any given cell may thus fail to differentiate among nearby parts of the spectrum of a very complex pattern. Since the response areas of the cells in an ensemble overlap to a considerable extent, however, the group of cells as a whole would have considerably greater resolution than any one cell would show.

Few two-dimensional patterns more complex than simple plaids and checkerboards have been explored in physiological experiments at the level of the striate cortex (those studying later areas have examined responses to much more complex figures—such as faces—but that is beyond the range of studies we are considering in this book). One exception is a pattern of random dots or textures. An array of random dots is in some sense the most complex pattern of all, and is the antithesis of a grating in that it contains power at all spatial frequencies and orientations. It has been reported (Hammond & MacKay, 1975) that complex, but not simple, cells respond to such random dot or highly textured patterns. A linear model would of course predict that all cells should respond to such patterns. These results have been partially confirmed by Maffei et al. (1979), who found that most but by no means all, simple cells were indeed unresponsive to such patterns. They interpreted their results as being due to inhibitory interactions among the many spatial frequency components and, in particular, the orientation components in such patterns. Maffei et al. go on to suggest that simple cells may therefore be a subsystem concerned with just detecting one-dimensional contours in patterns.

These conclusions that all (Hammond & MacKay, 1975) or most (Maffei et al., 1979) simple cells are unresponsive to highly textured patterns would have important consequences for models of visual function. However, Skottun, Grosof & R.L. De Valois (1985) have failed to replicate the original findings: almost all simple and complex cells were found to respond to random dots, although less well than to gratings. Simple cells are much less responsive than complex cells to these patterns, so a cursory analysis might lead one one to conclude that they do not respond to random dots, but in fact simple cells are about equally unresponsive as complex cells are to gratings as well. Thus the presence of inhibitory interactions between components at different orientations (Nelson & Frost, 1978) and at different spatial frequencies (K.K. De Valois & Tootell, 1983) makes striate cortex cells less responsive to highly textured patterns than they should be from purely linear considerations (and thus giving these patterns less adaptive power than gratings in psychophysical experiments [K.K. De Valois & Switkes, 1980], as discussed above). There do not, however, appear to be good grounds for concluding that simple cells respond only to one-dimensional contours.

Local and Global Spectra

Finally, we must emphasize again that all the psychophysical, physiological, and anatomical evidence indicates that the visual system at the striate cortex level is involved in only a local *patchwise* analysis of the visual scene. Anatomically, the cortex is broken up into perhaps 2,000 modules, each related to a given subregion of the visual world (see Chapter 4); physiologically, striate cells are found to have spatially limited RFs; and psychophysically much evidence supports the hypothesis that the system does a local frequency analysis as opposed to a global Fourier analysis. This being the case, in understanding the responses to patterns we need to consider the *localized* spectra rather than overall global spectra.

All of the gratings and checkerboard patterns (and even to a lesser extent the random dot patterns) we have been considering in the physiological and psychophysical studies discussed above are highly repetitive patterns in which any given patch (provided it is not too small, as discussed below) is representative of the whole. So although we have for convenience been presenting the global spectra of the patterns, it is really the local spectra that are relevant. We are justified in having just presented and discussed the global spectra of these particular patterns because in a repetitive pattern the spectrum of a patch would be similar to that of the whole pattern, except somewhat broadened. The same would obviously not be true of many nonrepetitive real-life scenes; in these cases the relevant data would be not the total two-dimensional Fourier spectrum but that of the individual patches.

Even in the case of repetitive grating and checkerboard patterns, however, the Fourier spectrum of the whole pattern is only representative of the local spectrum when the pattern is relatively repetitive within the extent of the RF concerned. In the extreme case, for instance, if a checkerboard were blown up so that a single check covered the whole RF of a cell, the pattern would in effect be not a checkerboard as far as the cell was concerned, but a uniform field (to which the cell would probably not respond). In the intermediate case, where just a part of a square wave grating or checkerboard was within a cell's RF, the relevant spectrum of the pattern would be that of an edge: a very broad spectrum with a single orientation. But only in the case of very large patterns with sharp edges stimulating units tuned to high spatial frequencies would that be the case. The majority of visual stimuli would probably have more than one edge within the RF of a cell. But it is important to realize that whether this is so or not, the cells' responses are still a function of the local Fourier spectrum.

Spatial Filtering and Receptive Fields

Some (see Ochs, 1979; MacKay, 1981) have suggested that there is a contradiction between cells' having certain RF properties and their acting as spatial frequency filters. However, we see no contradiction between a cell's having a certain RF structure in the space domain and having certain spatial frequency filtering characteristics in the frequency domain. Quite the contrary: insofar as the system acts as a linear filter, a certain two-dimensional spatial frequency selectivity not only is compatible with but *demands* a certain RF structure. The interconvertibility of the space and frequency domains in Fourier analysis is not only a well known mathematical property (see Chapter 1), but has been specifically pointed out in reference to cortical cell RFs (see Robson, 1975a, 1980; K.K. De Valois et al., 1979). That one can to a first approximation account for cortical cells' responses to patterns, e.g., checkerboards, on the basis of linear summation within classical simple cell RFs as mapped by Hubel and Wiesel (1962), for instance, in no way contradicts the position that the cells are performing a two-dimensional spatial frequency filtering of the stimulus.

Hubel and Wiesel (1962) first described the RFs of cortical simple cells and also stated that they responded optimally to edges and bars of certain widths and orientations. The latter statement has since been elaborated by others into models of visual processing by bar and edge detectors (e.g., Neisser, 1967; Lindsay & Norman, 1972). As a result, cortical cells have long been thought of as bar detectors. As we have discussed at length, however, cortical cells are *not* bar and edge detectors. There is in fact a basic contradiction between describing cells as bar and edge detectors and as showing linear summation within their RFs (K.K. De Valois et al., 1979).

It sometimes appears that the resistance to accepting the evidence that cortical cells are responding to the two-dimensional Fourier components of stimuli goes beyond the notion of bar and edge detectors to a general unease about positing that a complex mathematical operation similar to Fourier analysis might take place in a physiological structure like cortical cells. It is almost as if this evoked for some a specter of a little man sitting in a corner of the cell huddled over a calculator. Nothing of the sort is of course implied: the cells carry out their processing by summation and inhibition and other physiological interactions within their RFs. There is no more contradiction between a functional description of an ensemble of cortical cells as performing a spatial frequency analysis and their having RFs with certain physiological properties than there is between a functional description of some electronic component as being a multiplier and its being made up of transistors and resistors wired in a certain fashion. The one level functionally describes the process, the other states the mechanism. To give another example, the hydrodynamic properties of the cochlea provide the *mechanism* by which the auditory system performs a crude one-dimensional temporal Fourier analysis. Fairly linear summation within each cell in an array of striate cells with elongated RFs with oscillating sensitivity profiles of differing periods is the *mechanism* by which the visual system performs a crude, localized, two-dimensional spatial frequency analysis.

Finally, some have attempted to give continued life to the notion that cortical cells are bar and edge detectors by changing the meanings of the terms. It is a firm dictum of those who teach scientific methodology that the best theories are those which are stated in such a form as to be clearly testable and therefore subject to being proven false. Those acquainted with the reality as against the theory of science know this to be questionable advice: Freud will be with us long after others, whose testable theories of behavior have been examined and proven wrong, are forgotten. Vague theories stated in terms that have an ability to change meaning as required have great resilience. So it appears to be with

Spatial receptive field   Fourier response area

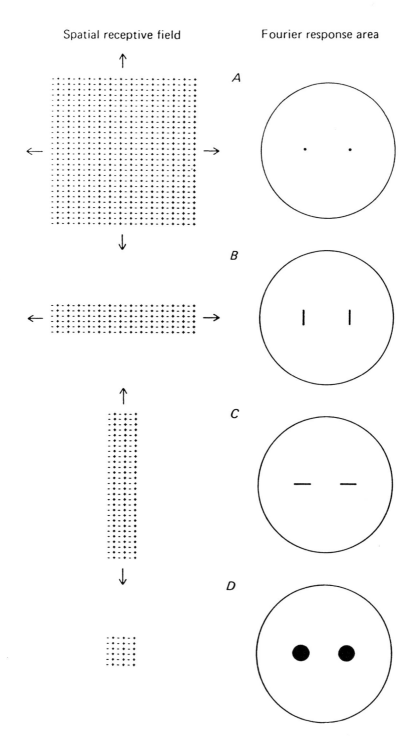

FIG. 9.11 Models showing the relationship between spatial RFs and Fourier response area. See text for discussion (from K.K. De Valois et al., 1979. Reprinted with permission).

notions of bar and edge detectors. "Bars" have started to assume peculiar shapes and on occasion to become blurred and sinusoidal, and "detectors" sometimes give graded responses. It is not clear, however, what benefit is to be gained from redefining bars as periodic structures and detectors as filters other than saving face for those with too great an investment in bar and edge detectors.

RF Model for Spatial Frequency Selectivity

We have been stating that there is no contradiction between cells' having certain RF shapes (rather like those described by Hubel & Wiesel, 1962) and their acting as local two-dimensional spatial frequency filters. Let us now consider this a little further. One could build an optical filter selective to just a certain two-dimensional spatial frequency location by having an array of elements that respond to light with varying positive $(+)$ or negative $(-)$ outputs and that are summed linearly, arranged in strips with a sinusoidal cross-section of sensitivity (see Figure 9.11). If the array were of infinite length and width (Figure 9.11A), it would respond to only one two-dimensional spatial frequency—only one spatial frequency and one orientation. One can think of an array as being the RF of a hypothetical cell. Such a cell would thus be an ideal, global two-dimensional Fourier filter. An ensemble of such cells in which the individual units had varying orientations and periods to their arrays would together carry out a global two-dimensional Fourier analysis.

If the spatial filter discussed above were modified to shorten its length (Figure 9.11B), its orientation tuning would be broadened somewhat, but it would still respond to only one spatial frequency at any orientation. Curtailing the width of the array but not its length (Figure 9.11C) would somewhat broaden the spatial frequency tuning but the cell would respond to only one orientation. If both the width and length of this hypothetical RF were limited (Figure 9.11D), a cell would be produced that responded to a range of orientations and a range of spatial frequencies. Such an RF, which strongly resembles the RFs of narrowly tuned cortical cells, would give some but far from perfect selectivity along both dimensions. From the responses of cells to patterns of various spatial frequencies and orientations one can determine the two-dimensional spatial frequency response area of the cell. From this, one can compute, by the inverse Fourier transform, the RF structure in the space domain within which linear summation would lead to the measured two-dimensional frequency selectivity. Figure 4.18 shows these for a typical striate cortex cell.

A cell such as that shown in Figure 4.18, then, would respond to a limited two-dimensional spatial frequency range. It would be acting only as a *local* spatial frequency filter, since its RF would encompass only a small portion of the total visual world. Striate cortex cells, then, have a spatial component in that they respond only to stimuli within a certain spatial region, and a frequency component in that they respond to the two-dimensional spatial frequency characteristics of the patterns within this spatial region.

10

Three-Dimensional Patterns

We live in a three-dimensional world, and our ability to perceive the third dimension is crucial. Yet the image of that three-dimensional world is mapped onto our two-dimensional retinae. One of the oldest and most enduring questions of spatial vision is how we analyze those two-dimensional images to derive information about variations in depth from which we construct a three-dimensional percept.

We often consider visual sensitivity to depth as being important primarily because it allows us to estimate the distance of objects from us. Certainly that is a necessary ability, particularly in the case of predators, which must accurately judge the position of potential prey. Imagine the disastrous consequences for an eagle, for example, if it overestimated the distance to a field mouse that it was diving down to catch. Or consider the problem of a cat that underestimates the distance to a bird at which it pounces—few birds wait around for a second compensatory jump. Although few of us depend on our skill at hunting for our food supply, we too require fairly veridical distance perception. Drivers who habitually overestimated the distance of the car ahead would not survive long, and even such simple tasks as walking up and down steps can be treacherously difficult without good depth perception.

Estimation of the distance of objects is crucial, but depth perception subserves certain other very important tasks, as well. Judgments of the relative depths of different parts of an object can aid greatly in determining the shape of the object. For example, in order to discriminate between a disk in the frontoparallel plane and a sphere, one must be able to determine whether the different parts of the object are at the same or different depths. Another, and perhaps even more important, function of depth perception is figure-ground segregation. Studies of figure-ground discrimination often use only two-dimensional stimuli, but this creates an artificially difficult task. Many visual objects differ from their backgrounds in depth, as well as in other characteristics. In such a case, the segregation of the visual image into different depth planes would also automatically accomplish the segregation of figure and ground.

There are many visual cues to depth or three-dimensional shape that can be obtained from the monocular visual image. The efficiency of monocular cues is attested to by the very good depth discrimination that can be achieved with only one eye. Indeed, we probably depend mainly on monocular cues for our estimates of object depth. Among the many monocular cues that are discussed in most accounts of depth perception are motion parallax, perspective, interposition, texture, aerial perspective, blurring and color changes with distance, and changing size. There is, in addition, instructive information to be obtained by comparison of the outputs of the two eyes, with their slightly different views of a three-dimensional world. We will discuss some, but not all, of these traditional monocular and binocular cues to depth here, with a selective emphasis upon how the types of information processing we know to take place in the striate cortex might play a role in this process.

MONOCULAR INFORMATION

Although some monocular decoding of depth requires complex analyses of object characteristics, the critical information in many cases is the local spatial frequency, orientation, and direction of movement of the pattern. As we have seen, these are the three main kinds of information that striate cells are extracting, in different parallel channels. We will discuss in turn below how these three kinds of information are used for obtaining estimates of depth.

Blur

Light Vergence
The one set of unambiguous, absolute monocular cues to depth (if, unfortunately, one difficult for the visual system to use) is the differing vergences of the light rays from objects at different distances. The nearer an object (e.g., a point source) is to an image-forming lens, the farther away will the image be brought to a focus. As the distance the object is from the lens increases, the rays that emanate from that object to strike the lens will become increasingly more parallel. Less dioptric power will be required to bring them into focus at a given point, or, alternatively, for a fixed lens, the image will be formed at closer and closer distances. If the eye had an optical system of fixed power, then, the image of an object would be formed farther forward (i.e., more anterior) in the eye as the object approaches. If it were possible to locate the focal point, then, one could in principle know the absolute distance of the object from the eye (although beyond about 3 m the rays become effectively parallel, making it most unlikely that information about depths greater than that could be utilized).

This vergence cue is sometimes referred to as monocular parallax, sometimes as the stimulus for accommodation, for the visual system of course does not have a fixed optical power, but a variable one. As an object gets closer, it requires increasing amounts of accommodation (increasing the power of the lens) to keep the image in focus on the retina. Monitoring the amount of accommodation required to bring an image to a sharp focus at a fixed point would thus be a way by which the visual system could utilize this cue to determine absolute depth (although there is little evidence that we actually do this).

A related situation is that in which the eye is focused on some one object among a group of objects at various depths. Depending on the depth of focus of the eye (as determined by pupil size), only objects within a certain range of depths around the fixation plane would be seen in sharp focus. Regardless of whether one had absolute depth information from knowledge of the precise accommodative state of the eye, the extent to which various objects were in or out of focus would give information about their distances from the fixation plane.

In both of these situations, the basic information that needs to be obtained from the retinal image is the extent to which objects are *blurred* by being out of focus. As discussed in Chapter 2 (see Figure 2.9), the effect of blur is selectively to attenuate high spatial frequencies, the range of high frequencies attenuated being systematically related to the degree of blur.

How might the visual system determine how blurred various parts of a visual scene are, and thus perhaps how distant? A simple, straightforward way would be to filter the image using multiple local spatial frequency channels and examine the relative amount of power at high frequencies present in various subregions. The images of most objects contain a broad range of spatial frequencies. A blurred pattern, then, could readily be identified as one missing high spatial frequencies, and the extent of the blur (and thus relative distance) could be assessed by a system with multiple spatial frequency channels in each region of the visual field. Alternative mechanisms that have been suggested for pattern analysis would have trouble obtaining this kind of information. For instance, blurring a pattern does not change the location of edges or zero crossings, or the width of bars, so a system analyzing for such would not have any ready way to assess this depth cue. Nor would a global spatial frequency analysis give the organism ready access to information about the extent to which objects in local regions are blurred by being distant or very close.

Atmospheric Blur

We pointed out in Chapter 2 that most optical imperfections of the eye and its media result in blur of the retinal image. The same applies to "imperfections" in the atmosphere. Particles in the air—mist, fog, or smog—scatter the light and blur the image presented to the eye. Such would also be true for temperature variations along the optical path between an object and the eye. Obviously, the more distant the object, other factors being constant, the more blurred its image will be.

Such atmospheric blur can clearly not serve as an absolute cue to distance, since the clarity of the atmosphere is quite variable. Early travelers across the Western Plains were misled by the (then) crystal-clear air into believing the

Rocky Mountains were only a few hours walk away when they were really some 100 km distant. On the other hand, viewed through a heavy fog or a cloud, objects only a few meters away may be blurred to invisibility. Nonetheless, at any given moment, the amount by which the images of various objects are blurred is an indication of the objects' depths. Blur is important because it is one of the few cues to the depth of very distant objects.

Again, the relevant information for the utilization of this cue to depth is the power in different spatial frequency bands in various local regions. The images of distant scenes will have little energy at very high spatial frequencies.

Spatial Frequency Gradients

Single Objects

A very important cue to depth is the variation in size of the retinal image of an object when it is at different distances from the eye. When a person is close by, his image subtends the whole retina and more; the image of a person 100 m distant would only cover about 1° visual angle. Retinal image size thus gives very powerful information about depth, and it is informative (as blur of objects off the fixation plane is not) at great distances. Obviously, knowing just the retinal image size, without knowledge of the physical dimensions of the object, would lead to ambiguity: size and distance are reciprocally related in determining retinal image dimensions, and neither can be specified without knowing the other (unless, of course, one knows the power of the optical system). But since most familiar objects have been seen from close enough to touch, we usually have the information required for judgments of absolute distance.

Any mechanism by which the size of objects is extracted by the visual system could clearly serve to obtain this cue to distance. Although there would be no special advantage here to spatial frequency filtering, the spatial frequency band in which the spectrum of an object's image peaked would clearly be a convenient source of distance information. Many striate cells, while tuned to different spatial frequency ranges, have roughly equal bandwidths on an octave, or logarithmic, scale (R.L. De Valois, Albrecht, & Thorell, 1982). As an object recedes in distance, the spectrum of its image shifts to higher and higher spatial frequencies, and their bandwidths increase on a linear scale. On a log frequency scale, however, the bandwidths would remain the same, so the only effect of a change in distance would be a shift to a different population of cortical cells.

Texture Gradients

Texture gradients are certainly among the most important cues to depth and three-dimensional shape in an extended scene, as Gibson (1950) has very forcefully argued. In any visual scene, the retinal images of objects that are farther from the viewer will be smaller and closer together, on the average, than those of nearer objects. In a field composed of uniform objects uniformly arranged, there would be a perfect inverse correlation between distance, on the one hand, and retinal image size, on the other, and object image density would increase

with distance. In the real world, of course, very few extended fields are composed of identical objects, but many visual scenes contain numerous small
objects of roughly the same size, for example, a sandy beach, a field of grass or
grain, leaf patterns (see Figure 10.1). Such patterns we can designate as having
a textured appearance. The texture gradients (variations in size and density) set
up when such a pattern varies in distance produce highly reliable cues to depth
and three-dimensional shape.

As a particular scene recedes from the viewer and average object image size
and density change, the spatial frequency spectrum of the scene also changes in
a regular way. Spatial frequency ratios remain constant, but the average spatial
frequency increases. In fact, some measure merely of the spatial frequency band
represented would be sufficient to provide the texture cue to depth and would
do so very economically. An overall representation of the power spectrum,
ignoring phase, in each patch of space would be sufficient. The sophisticated
discriminations among different textures of identical global power spectra,
which have been extensively investigated by Julesz and others (Julesz & Schumer, 1981), are not required in order to use texture as a cue to depth.

Cortical complex cells give just such a straightforward measure as would be
required for the visual system to economically encode texture information. They
do not encode phase, either absolute or relative, and do not, therefore, require
precise alignments of or interaction between two or more RFs. There is evidence
that we ignore phase in discriminating among different textures, at least in some
situations (Caelli & Julesz, 1979; Julesz, 1980a), as one would expect if it were
based on complex cell activity.

Complex cells not only are responsive to textured surfaces, but their responses
are quite sufficient to encode texture as a cue to depth. Consider some alternatives. It would obviously be extremely difficult and costly in terms of the number
of neurons required for the visual system to encode the locations, directions, and
orientations of all the millions of edges or zero crossings in the image of a sandy
beach, grassy field, or almost any other highly textured real-life scene. Suggestions of such should engender considerable skepticism. A global spatial frequency analysis would also not give ready access to local variations in spatial
frequency across a scene. A local spatial frequency analysis by simple cells, keeping phase information, would probably be more economical than locating all the
edges, due to the high degree of periodicity in textured scenes (see Chapter 12),
but would still contain superfluous phase information. But by encoding in the
responses of complex cells the average spatial frequency independent of phase
in each small retinal area, the visual system can economically extract and transmit much of the relevant information for perceiving depth and tilt.

Orientation

The early Renaissance painters were the first to discover many of the monocular
cues to depth; these they utilized to give a striking three-dimensional quality to
their paintings and carried to playful extremes in their *trompe l'oeil* paintings.

FIG. 10.1 Examples of textures in natural scenes.

Among the most important of their findings were the principles of perspective, of the way in which parallel lines appear to converge to a point in the distance, with the images of objects becoming increasingly smaller with increasing depth. This latter aspect of perspective we have already discussed, in terms of spatial frequency gradients, but the orientation information itself is also doubtless of importance.

A street or railroad track going across the visual field from left to right at a constant distance will be projected onto the retina with roughly parallel lines. If such a pattern is receding from one in depth, however, the lines will converge with distance. Since orientation is one of the principal stimulus dimensions being analyzed at the striate cortex, it is not surprising that we are extremely sensitive to the relative orientation of two lines, and even to absolute orientation around both the vertical and the horizontal planes. The slight deviation from parallelism of lines in a perspective drawing can by itself produce a powerful impression of depth, see Figure 4.18 for example.

It might be argued that while the spatial frequency gradients of perspective apply to natural as well as manmade scenes, the noncarpentered environment contains few parallel lines from which the pure orientation component of perspective could be extracted for depth information. However, rivers as well as roads have roughly parallel sides that converge into the distance: the Mississippi does not suddenly turn into a creek. Examination of the natural environment reveals that it in fact contains strongly oriented patterns (Switkes, Mayer, & Sloan, 1978), many of which are parallel, e.g., plants that grow vertically. One can have depth in the vertical as well as the horizontal plane, and the convergence of tree trunks, for instance, as you look up in a forest is a powerful stimulus to height (depth).

Orientation variations, like spatial frequency gradients, are not absolute indices of depth or distance, in the sense that they depend on assumptions about the nature of the environment. If railroad lines or rivers were wedge-shaped rather than parallel, and people came in a variety of sizes ranging down to 2 cm tall, we could be mistaken in using either deviations from parallel orientation or spatial frequency gradients as measures of depth. It is apparent that in this, as in many other aspects of vision, our ability to develop a coherent percept of the visual world depends not just on analysis of sensory input, but also on hypotheses about the nature of the world.

Motion Parallax

If you move your head while fixating a point, the image of the fixated point will of course maintain a constant retinal location, as eye movements compensate for the head movements. However, the images of objects closer than the fixated point will move opposite to the direction of the head movement, while those of more distant objects will move in the same direction. Such motion parallax has long been recognized as an important cue to depth (e.g., Gibson, 1950). For a convincing demonstration of the use of monocular motion parallax one need only walk into a monkey colony and watch the inhabitants. Many monkeys, at the sight of a stranger in the colony, immediately begin a rapid, side-to-side head motion, looking at the same scene from two slightly different perspectives. This movement parallax gives the monkey a very powerful cue to the relative distance of various objects in the scene. Since most monkeys have a considerably smaller interocular separation than humans, they have less binocular disparity and thus somewhat poorer stereopsis (Bough, 1970; Sarmiento, 1975). Monocular motion parallax may therefore be an even more important depth cue for monkeys and other animals with small heads than for humans.

One can consider a typical motion parallax situation to contain two separate types of information. One (the speed and direction of movement of objects) provides information about their distance from the fixation plane. We know (see Chapter 4) that there are many striate cortex units selectively sensitive to movement and differentially sensitive to movement in various directions. At this level, then, the visual system has considerable information from which to specify the direction of movement of various parts of the visual scene, and thus their relative depths. Such movement information would be available, of course, not just from oscillatory head movements, but from any movement of the body through space, as when one walks through a three-dimensional scene.

The second source of information in the motion parallax situation discussed above is the provision, at the end points of the movement, of two different views of the three-dimensional world. Stereopsis is based on the fact that the horizontally displaced eyes at each instant get slightly different views of the world, the positional differences being directly related to the depths of objects. Correspondingly, by moving the head laterally, one produces at two successive instants two retinal images which differ from each other to an extent dependent on the depth of various objects. It would be interesting to see to what extent the same paradigms that have proven fruitful in the study of stereopsis would, translated from simultaneous binocular to successive monocular presentation, be useful in studying depth perception by monocular movement parallax.

One psychophysical experiment has compared monocular motion parallax and (binocular) stereopsis (Rogers & Graham, 1982). It is interesting that the same (very low) spatial frequency range was found to be involved with both motion parallax and stereopsis. They found highest sensitivity to depth to be with gratings of about 0.4 c/deg, with lower sensitivity to both higher and lower spatial frequencies, whether stereopsis or motion parallax cues were involved.

BINOCULAR INFORMATION

Although considerable information from which to construct a three-dimensional world comes from the sorts of analyses of monocular information we have been discussing above, much additional useful information about depth can be obtained by virtue of our having two eyes displaced laterally by some distance from each other. This is particularly useful for determining the depths and three-dimensional shapes of nearby objects.

The primitive vertebrate pattern is to have two eyes on the sides of the head. Such an arrangement allows a panoramic view of much of the visual world, but the eyes have little binocular overlap. In some higher vertebrates, particularly carnivores and primates, the eyes have migrated to the front of the head. This produces a considerable shrinkage of the total field of view—we can obviously no longer see behind us and only partially to the side. The compensatory gain is that of binocular overlap between the visual fields of the two eyes, with the resulting possibility of gaining additional depth information by comparing the outputs of the two eyes.

When we fixate a point, the eyes turn to bring the image of that point to a focus on the center of each fovea. The amount of convergence of the eyes required to fixate a point depends on its depth. This binocular parallax or convergence cue potentially provides absolute depth information, although it clearly would operate only for objects quite close to the body. There is some evidence (Foley, 1978) that the convergence information is in fact used, but it does not appear to be a major factor in binocular depth perception.

Disparities in Binocular Images

The physicist Wheatstone (1838) was the first to realize that two eyes displaced slightly laterally with respect to each other would receive significantly different retinal images of a three-dimensional scene, and that these disparate views were actually utilized in depth perception (termed stereopsis); see Figure 10.2. Wheatstone went on to work out the whole geometry of the situation and invent the stereoscope, an instrument that presents the eyes with two slightly different drawings or photographs which, when fused, are perceived in depth.

There are two separate aspects to the problem of how the visual system combines the outputs of the two eyes. One is that of single versus double vision; the other, that of gaining depth information from a comparison of the two retinal outputs. Each eye sends to the cortex information about the whole forward visual field. In a three-dimensional environment we often see both of these images and perceive much of the world as double. However, objects very near the horopter (a roughly hemispherical surface going through the fixation point at which the images fall on corresponding points in the two eyes) are seen as single, the two retinal images being combined into one unified percept. The depth range of single vision, known as Panum's fusional area, is classically considered to be quite narrow (about 5' arc) in the foveal region (although see discussion below) and to expand to either side of the horopter with increasing retinal eccentricity. Objects outside this region, either nearer or farther, are seen as double.

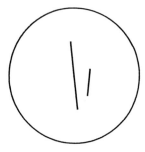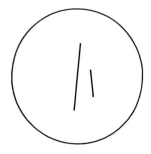

FIG. 10.2   Stereoscopic pattern. Attempt to fuse the images of these two patterns by converging your eyes such that the two outer circles are aligned. If this is accomplished, the two lines will appear to go through the paper in different directions. (If you find it difficult to fuse the images freely, try fixating on your finger held between your eyes and the page. After fusion, the two monocular images can be blocked out by holding your two hands at the appropriate separation.)

Stereopsis, gaining information about depth from the binocular input, is a related but somewhat different problem from that of single vision. The depth range over which stereopsis operates is much broader than Panum's fusional area: both single and double images can contribute to stereopsis (Westheimer & Tanzman, 1956). Also, binocular objects that differ from each other in color or shape, so much so that they cannot be fused, can nonetheless be combined to produce a percept of depth (Mitchell, 1969).

Wheatstone demonstrated that there would be point-by-point differences, or disparities, between the two retinal images of a three-dimensional scene. Clearly, then, if one somehow made a point-by-point comparison of the two images, the relevant stereoscopic information could be extracted. However, it does not follow that the visual system so operates. It is possible that, for reasons of efficiency in extracting stereoscopic output, or because the retinal information for some extraneous reason is not coded in a point-by-point spatial representation, other types of binocular comparisons might be made instead, e.g., spatial frequency, or phase, or orientation differences between the eyes. We thus need to examine the question of how the visual system actually operates in dealing with differences between the images in the two eyes.

Positional Disparity

The two retinae can be considered to have corresponding points to which the images of objects in different locations along the horopter would all be projected. Thus the center of the fovea in one eye corresponds to the foveal center in the other; 1° to the temporal side of the fovea in one eye corresponds to 1° nasal to the fovea in the other, etc. If two points are at different depths, however, their images will not both project to corresponding retinal points. If one point in space is binocularly fixated, its image will of course be at the center of the fovea in both eyes. However, light from some more distant point will fall on noncorresponding retinal points: for instance, 10' to the temporal side of the fovea in the left eye and 30' to the nasal side in the right. There would thus be a 20' *positional disparity* between the retinal points stimulated by this more distant object. The more distant the object from the fixation plane, the greater the positional disparity. Objects in front of the fixation plane will have a disparity in one direction (crossed); those behind will have a disparity in the other (uncrossed) direction. As Wheatstone made clear, an analysis of these point-by-point positional disparities between the two retinal images could give one precise depth information. Of course, such depth information would not be absolute, but only relative to the fixation plane. It is also apparent that useful stereoscopic information would demand exquisite sensitivity, since our eyes (to say nothing of those of cats and monkeys, on which most of the physiological studies have been carried out) are quite close together. Only tiny disparities are therefore present for different portions of a three-dimensional object or for objects that are nearby in depth. One can in fact detect stereoscopic differences of a few *seconds* of arc, in the hyperacuity range (Westheimer, 1981).

The initial reports of the locations in each eye of the RFs of binocular striate cells (Hubel & Wiesel, 1959, 1962) stated that they lay on corresponding retinal points. That is, if the RF for a binocular cell activated through the left eye was 3° away from the fovea, its RF in the right eye would also be 3° away. If such were the case, all binocular striate cells would be optimally stimulated by objects lying along the horopter, and there would appear to be no stereoscopic analysis taking place at this level (nor could it occur at any subsequent level receiving from such binocular cells, since once the inputs had been combined from corresponding points in the two eyes there is no obvious way in which positional disparity information could be retrieved). Subsequent studies of striate cells (Barlow et al., 1967; Nikara, Bishop, & Pettigrew, 1968) came to quite different conclusions. They reported that striate cells within a cortical region differed in the positional disparities of the RFs in the two eyes, so that one cell would respond to light from corresponding retinal points while others nearby were picking up from disparate locations in the two eyes. The various cells within a region, then, would together respond to patterns on the horopter, and at various crossed and uncrossed disparities.

Experimental problems make the issue of whether striate cells have various positional disparities in their binocular RFs a difficult one to settle. It is technically very difficult to determine the precise location of the RF of a binocular cell in each eye (particularly in a cat, which has no fovea, but only a vaguely defined area centralis), and very difficult to completely eliminate eye movements in the course of a recording experiment. If the eyes move relative to each other between the mapping of RFs in two successive cells, it would appear that these had different disparities even if they were in fact the same. Such errors can be large relative to the very small disparities likely to be found, given the fineness of stereoacuity.

The discrepancies between the reports, on the one hand, of no striate stereo-scopic analysis (Hubel & Wiesel, 1962, 1970) and, on the other hand, of a graded series of cells tuned to various disparities (Barlow et al., 1967; Nikara et al., 1968) seem to have been largely resolved by studies using more precise measures of eye position. Poggio and Fischer (1977) recorded from awake monkeys that had been trained to fixate a spot at a particular depth. The responses of cells to patterns presented at various depths with respect to this fixation point could then be recorded. Von der Heydt, Adorjani, Hänny, and Baumgartner (1978) recorded the binocular RFs of cells in cat while periodically photographing the fundus of the eye. They used the pattern of blood vessels to precisely assess, and compensate for, any drift in eye position.

Both groups reported many disparity-specific units in striate cortex, cells that fire to a pattern at only a narrow range of depths. Most of these appeared to be tuned to the horopter or very slightly to either side (that is, to zero or near-zero disparity). In addition, disparity-selective units with broader disparity tuning were reported. Some would fire to a pattern anywhere behind the fixation plane (any uncrossed disparity) and inhibit to those in front; other fired to patterns in front of the fixation plane (any crossed disparity) and were inhibited by those behind. Similar units were also reported to be present in V2 (Poggio & Fischer, 1977). Still undetermined is the question of whether the narrowly depth-tuned cells all have RFs precisely on the horopter, or whether they systematically vary in their depth tuning over a narrow range to either side. Such striate and pre-striate cells could clearly provide a physiological basis for local stereoscopic depth analysis.

Phase Disparity of Frequency Components

From the time of Wheatstone, the patterns used in stereoscopic studies, both psychophysical and physiological, have consisted of lines or edges or, more recently (Julesz, 1971), random dots. The disparities were then measured in terms of the differences in location (positional differences) between the images of points in the two eyes.

We have in this book summarized considerable evidence that, early in the visual path, patterns are analyzed into their local spatial frequency components. This suggests that the *phase* of the sine wave components rather than the *position* of such naturalistic features as edges may be the more relevant variable in stereopsis, at least at the striate level. A change in position of a given sine wave is equivalent to a change in phase. Thus, for a 1-c/deg grating, a positional dis-placement of 1′ is the same as a phase change of 6°. However, for a 10-c/deg grating, the same 1′ positional shift would be not a 6 but a 60° phase shift. So when one is considering patterns other than a simple grating of one frequency, phase and position are not equivalent.

For lateral, monocular displacements of patterns on the retina, it is clear that striate simple cells have in common a certain *phase* sensitivity, not a certain positional sensitivity, as discussed in Chapter 8. Thus if one determines the optimum location of a grating to stimulate any simple cell, then moves it 90° in phase, the response goes to zero; a 180° phase shift moves the pattern to a location that produces maximum inhibition. This is true for a cell tuned to a high spatial frequency, as well as one tuned to a low frequency (see Figure 8.4), but the positional displacements for these two cells will be quite different. Thus each of the cells shown there gives about the same change in firing to a 20° phase change; but this is a 0.4′ positional change for the one cell and a 3.6′ positional change for the other.

It is clear for changes in lateral position, then, that striate simple cells can detect a certain phase change: it is phase, not position, that is the critical variable. The same is very likely true for stereoscopic stimulation of binocular cells as well, although that does not appear to have been specifically investigated. If so, cells tuned to high and low spatial frequencies would be about equally responsive to binocular phase changes, which would mean that cells tuned to high spatial frequencies would detect very small depth changes, and those tuned to low spatial frequencies, only larger changes in depth. Also, high spatial frequency cells should only be able to signal depth changes, or subsume single vision, over a narrow range, whereas cells tuned to low spatial frequencies should be able to operate over much larger ranges of depths. The narrowly-tuned depth cells of Poggio and Fischer (1977) might thus just be cells tuned to high spatial frequencies, and the coarsely-tuned depth units those sensitive to low frequencies, rather than these two classes of cells constituting separate depth systems.

The fact that Panum's fusional area, as classically measured, is narrow in the fovea and widens with eccentricity is predictable if the phase difference, not positional disparity, is the critical determinant of single vision. The average spatial frequency tuning of units and the highest peak spatial frequencies shift to lower spatial frequencies with retinal eccentricity, so one might well expect the fusional range to increase correspondingly. Such an analysis also suggests that Panum's area, as classically defined in terms of a certain range of positional disparities over which single vision occurs, would not be a constant at a given eccentricity. Rather it should, and does, depend on the spatial frequency content of the stimulus. One can readily demonstrate that with a foveally presented binocular stimulus of low spatial frequency, there is single vision for very large disparities, far beyond the 5′ classically measured (Schor & Tyler, 1981). An extended grating of a high spatial frequency, on the other hand, can only be seen in depth over a narrow range (one should note that a 360° phase shift of an extended grating is equivalent to no change at all, so a high-frequency grating can in principle be displaced only over a narrower range than a low-frequency pattern). Kulikowski (1978) showed that blurring a target (thus reducing its high spatial frequency content) increases Panum's fusional area. Schor, Wood, and Ogawa (1984), using targets with difference-of-gaussians (DOG) profiles, have reported variations in the maximum extent of Panum's area at the fovea ranging from 5 to 400′, with larger areas for low spatial frequency targets. The fusion ranges for the largest (i.e., lowest spatial frequency) targets were limited by a constant phase disparity equal to a quarter of a cycle (90°). Panum's area, then, needs to be redefined in terms of phase. We have single vision over a certain range of phase disparities between the eyes (approximately 90°), not over a certain fixed distance.

Other psychophysical studies also suggest that it is the amount of phase disparity between the separate spatial frequency components in a pattern, rather than the size of the positional disparities between points or contours, which is critical for binocular single vision. Levinson and Blake (1979) showed that fusion is not possible unless the spatial frequency content of the patterns is similar in the two eyes. Patterns with similar contours in both eyes but in which the interocular spatial frequency contents differ cannot be fused. For instance, a grating pattern of frequency f cannot be binocularly fused with a missing-fundamental pattern $(3f + 5f + 7f\ldots)$, even though these two patterns have identical periods, because they have their power in non-overlapping spatial frequency bands. On the other hand, a square-wave grating $(f + 3f + 5f\ldots)$ *can* be fused with a pattern of $3f$. In this case, the contours and periods of the patterns do not correspond, but the underlying spatial frequencies do overlap (Levinson & Blake, 1979). It has also been shown (Mayhew & Frisby, 1976) that a random dot stereogram which is spatially filtered so that the left- and right-eye portions do not overlap in spatial frequency content cannot be fused.

A complication arises when a complex object, made up of multiple spatial frequencies but perceptually single, is viewed at some distance from the fixation plane. If the low frequencies were seen as single but the high frequencies as double, the object should perceptually disintegrate. This does not happen, at least in real-life objects. It appears that when multiple spatial frequencies are present the higher spatial frequency components (if they can be detected, with central vision) somehow limit the range of single vision for the whole pattern. Kulikowski (1978), for instance, showed that a sine wave grating, out of phase in the two eyes, can be fused and then appears to be at a considerable depth with respect to a background frame, whereas a square wave grating of the same frequency, 180° out of phase, cannot be fused. A possible explanation for this appears to be that the higher harmonics in the square wave cannot be seen as single at the great depth that would correspond to the disparities in the fundamental, and that they prevent the whole pattern from being seen as single.

The question of whether phase or positional disparities are critical can also be raised for the perception of depth in stereopsis. Observations similar to those which showed single vision operating over different ranges, depending on the spatial frequency of the stimulus (Schor et al., 1984), also indicate that the stereoscopic depth range varies correspondingly (Felton, Richards, & Smith, 1972; Richards & Kaye, 1974; R.L. De Valois, 1982; Schor & Wood, 1983). Marr and Poggio's revised computational model of stereopsis (1979) takes this variation into account. Very fine disparities of low spatial frequency targets do not produce a percept of depth, nor do very large disparities of high spatial frequency patterns.

One aspect of this question is whether, in depth changes, one is sensitive to a constant positional change in the pattern, independent of its spatial frequency, or to a constant phase shift. As discussed in Chapter 8, we have examined this question (R.L. De Valois, 1982; R.L. De Valois & K.K. De Valois, 1986) and find that the sensitivity at different spatial frequencies can be modeled by a linear combination of a phase term and a positional term. At low spatial frequencies the positional term is negligible and one has almost constant phase sensitivity; at higher spatial frequencies the contribution of the phase term is very small and positional sensitivity is almost constant. This sort of a linear summation of a phase term and a positional term might be expected if there were two successive stages in the processing of stereo information, one (perhaps the striate cortex) being phase sensitive, and the other (perhaps later prestriate levels) being positional sensitive. The results of Schor and Wood (1983), using DOG patterns which are delimited in space as well as in spatial frequency, are consistent with such a model.

Orientation Disparity

If you fixate a vertical line, it will be imaged at the same orientation in each eye. If, however, it is tilted in the front-back plane (rotated around a horizontal axis lying in the frontoparallel plane), the images of the line in the two eyes will be at different orientations. The extent of the orientation difference between the eyes, the orientation disparity, will increase with the tilt, reaching 180° difference for an object pointing directly towards the nose. (If you look at a pen pointing directly out from the bridge of the nose and close each eye in turn, you can see that the tip of the pen points to the left in the left eye and to the right in the right.) An example of a smaller orientation disparity can be seen in Figure 10.2.

In most situations in which there is an orientation disparity, the depth seen can in principle be accounted for on the basis of the point-by-point position disparities involved (or, as we have been pointing out above, from the phase disparities). If, in Figure 10.2, the circle is fused (and thus seen in the fixation plane), a point at the center of each line will also have zero disparity and thus will be seen in the fixation plane as well; points further and further above the center of the line will have increasing amounts of crossed positional disparities and should thus be seen increasingly closer. However, saying that such patterns can be analyzed in terms of point-by-point positional disparities is not the same as saying that that is how the visual system actually proceeds to analyze them.

It has been clear since the first reports of Hubel and Wiesel (1959, 1962) that most striate cells respond best not to spots of light but rather to elongated patterns of a particular orientation, the orientation preference varying from cell to cell. Lines such as those in Figure 10.2 would thus be excellent stimuli for a striate cell. The possibility therefore arises, as first suggested by Blakemore, Fiorentini, and Maffei (1972), that the visual system might analyze tilt around the horizontal axis not by point-by-point positional disparity computations, but by a comparison of orientation differences between the images in the two eyes, by direct use of the orientation disparity. Such an analysis would clearly be highly economical. A single unit responsive to a certain orientation disparity could detect the tilt of each line in Figure 10.2; it would require dozens of units computing the disparities at each pair of positions down the lines to calculate the same answer. That the visual system may utilize orientation disparities directly is thus in accord with our general knowledge of striate cortical function, and could also be much simpler.

Although cortical cells have an orientation selectivity, the optimum orientation is in general the same in each eye for a binocular cell. Such a cell would thus respond optimally to a line or grating in the frontoparallel plane. To take advantage of the simplicity of computing tilt by analyzing orientation disparity would require a system of cortical cells with differing orientation selectivities in the inputs from the two eyes, e.g., 5° clockwise to vertical in the left eye and 5° counterclockwise to vertical in the right.

What psychophysical and physiological evidence is there for such a system of directly extracting information about orientation disparities? In examining various tilted patterns, we (K.K. De Valois, von der Heydt, Adorjani, & R.L. De Valois, 1975; von der Heydt, 1979) found evidence for a very profound adaptation tilt aftereffect. If one inspects a pattern such as a triangle with the top tilted back for 3 or 4 min (with lateral movement to prevent receptor-specific adaptation), it will gradually lose its apparent backward tilt, and vertical patterns subsequently presented will appear to be tilted forward. To make another pattern now appear vertical, it must be tilted far back. You can perhaps see this aftereffect for yourself in inspecting Figure 10.3. In the extreme case, with pro-

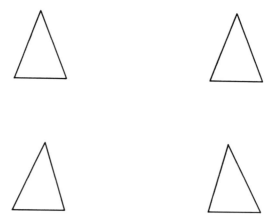

FIG. 10.3 Three-dimensional tilt aftereffect. First fuse these two sets of triangles. Notice that the top fused triangle appears to be oriented vertically (the book must be held vertically). Now inspect the lower fused triangle for about 3 min (allow your eyes to move around the pattern enough to prevent retinal afterimages). After adapting, look immediately at the top fused triangle again, to see whether it now appears tilted in depth.

longed exposure and a very sensitive subject, adaptation to a backward tilt will make it impossible for a few seconds to see any pattern as tilted back at all. Similar aftereffects are found with adaptation to a forward tilt. Such a tilt aftereffect by itself could be produced from adaptation either of a point-by-point positional disparity system or of an orientation disparity system. However, other aspects of the aftereffect cannot be readily explained by positional disparity alone. One is that such adaptation generalizes to tilted patterns at other distances relative to the fixation point as well, as one would expect from orientation but not from point-by-point position disparity adaptation. Furthermore, if a tilted pattern is moved vertically during adaptation, every point along a central vertical strip would have been exposed to the same range of depths. The positional disparity adaptation within this region should thus be uniform; one would expect no tilt aftereffect. However, such a vertically moving pattern would produce constant, selective stimulation of units tuned to a certain orientation disparity. From this one would predict a tilt aftereffect in this situation as well, and such an aftereffect was found.

Even more convincing evidence against tilt's being detected solely from point-by-point positional disparities comes from an experiment by von der Heydt, Hänny, and Dursteller (1981), in which they produced a binocular pattern of dynamic tilted random lines. Since the lines in the two eyes were randomly related to each other, the positional disparities were random in direction and amount. However, the lines were of different orientations in the two eyes and thus had a consistent orientation disparity. Such a pattern is clearly perceived as tilted.

The physiological evidence for orientation disparity units in cortex is more ambiguous. Blakemore et al. (1972) reported finding units with somewhat different orientation tuning for patterns in the two eyes, just as would be required to encode orientation disparities. However, cells show considerable variability in response, and orientation tuning is difficult to specify precisely. The different orientation tuning in the two eyes might thus just be due to random errors of measurement, as Bishop (1978) has claimed. However, Hänny, von der Heydt, and Poggio (1980) have found a subpopulation of disparity-specific prestriate cortical cells that respond specifically to dynamic random tilted lines. There is thus evidence from both psychophysics and physiology for the notion that slant around the horizontal axis is processed not solely by positional or phase disparity detection, but at least partly from the orientation disparities involved.

Spatial Frequency Disparity

If one binocularly inspects a grating patch which is in the frontoparallel plane, its projections onto the two retinae will be of the same spatial frequency. If, however, the grating is rotated about the vertical axis so that, say, the left edge is closer to the eyes than the right edge, the image in the left eye will be of a higher spatial frequency than that in the right. It was first suggested by Blakemore (1970) that such interocular spatial frequency differences might be utilized as a depth cue. Such a cue could potentially be used to judge the slant of not only grating patterns, but of any pattern, since of course any pattern can be analyzed into spatial frequency components. It is to be noted that only spatial frequency differences related to vertical gratings would be relevant in this situation. It is also important not to confuse the spatial frequency difference between the two eyes, which is what we are concerned with here, with the phase difference between the same frequency in each eye, which was discussed earlier as a depth cue.

A pattern rotated about the vertical axis provides, of course, not only an interocular spatial frequency difference, but also point-by-point positional disparity differences between the eyes. A pure positional disparity system, therefore, would be sufficient to decode the tilt in depth. One can make the same argument here, however, as we did with respect to orientation disparity analysis, namely, that it would be much more economical for the visual system to deal with binocular spatial frequency differences instead of just positional disparities. A single cortical cell tuned to a binocular spatial frequency difference could accomplish the same task that would require many more positional disparity cells.

Since a large proportion of cells in V1 and V2 are spatial frequency selective and have binocular inputs, an attractive possibility to consider is that some of these units might be sensitive to binocular spatial frequency disparities. There is to date, unfortunately, no physiological evidence bearing directly on this issue. Several psychophysical experiments, however, support the existence of such a spatial frequency disparity system.

Blakemore (1970) provided evidence that a comparison between the spatial frequencies of the patterns in the two eyes, rather than a point-by-point or bar-by-bar positional comparison, may be involved, at least in certain situations. Grating patterns with less than 10% or so difference in frequency between the eyes can be fused and appear as a single surface slanted in depth by an amount proportional to the frequency difference (see Figure 10.4). If such a pattern is several cycles wide, it will have more bars in the pattern to the one eye than in that to the other. It is difficult to see how the visual system, by using point-to-point positional disparity, could compare, say, 7 bars in one eye with 8 in the other, as in Figure 10.4, to produce the percept of a single slanted grating (the positional disparity information would instead predict multiple slanted surfaces; see below).

When a real grating is seen at a slant, there is not only a spatial frequency difference between the two eyes, but a spatial frequency gradient in each monocular stimulus, the more distant part being at a higher frequency. H.R. Wilson (1976) found that greater slants are perceived when both monocular spatial frequency gradients and binocular spatial frequency disparities are present than with just the latter alone, as one might well expect. He argued against the existence of a spatial frequency disparity mechanism, since the overall global spectra of the patterns in the combined gradient plus disparity situation cover overlapping but somewhat different spatial frequency ranges. His arguments, however,

FIG. 10.4 Apparent depth produced by patterns differing in spatial frequency. When the patterns are fused, the two gratings of different spatial frequency (and thus different numbers of bars across the pattern) will appear as a single tilted grating.

only apply to a single, global spatial frequency disparity system, and do not argue against the operation of the patch-by-patch analyses suggested by cortical physiology.

A second, more compelling demonstration for the existence of a spatial frequency disparity system is that a pattern of two different frequencies can still be seen as slanted in depth when one of the gratings is moving and the other stationary (Blakemore, 1970). It does not appear to be possible to account for this on the basis of an analysis of point-by-point positional disparities. Tyler and Sutter (1979) extended this situation one step further by producing in the two eyes gratings of different spatial frequencies that were made to move rapidly in opposite directions. Here the positional disparity information would be chaotic, but the pattern is nonetheless seen as slanted. In fact, as discussed below, it is even more clearly slanted than in the static situation, in which positional disparity information is also available.

Tyler and Sutter offer a third powerful type of evidence for the visual system's use of spatial frequency disparity. They presented a dynamic display of filtered random noise patterns, with the line patterns in the two eyes being uncorrelated. Nonetheless, a slanted surface was seen when the spatial frequency band in one eye was shifted in average spatial frequency with respect to that in the other.

We have been writing as though the perception of slanted surfaces in these experimental conditions could be equivalently decoded by either positional disparity or by spatial frequency disparity (except, of course, in those situations designed to eliminate the former). In most naturalistic scenes that would be the case, but it is not really true with these highly periodic grating patterns. Consider a pattern of, say, 9 bars in the left eye and 11 in the right (see Figure 10.5). One would expect to see a single slanted surface from spatial frequency disparity because the right eye pattern is everywhere of a higher frequency than that in the left. However, if the positional disparity system were to associate each bar in one eye with the closest bar in the other, the depth being given by the amount

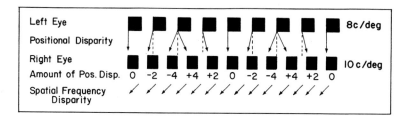

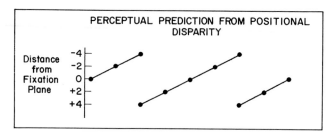

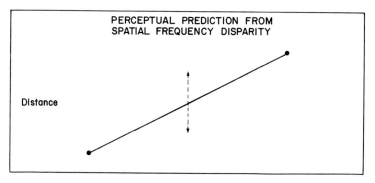

FIG. 10.5   Predictions of stereoscopic depth percepts from positional disparity and from spatial frequency disparity. See text for explanation.

and direction of the disparity involved, a quite different percept would result. Starting from the left, each successive bar would have a larger disparity, and a slanted surface would be seen. The third bar in the left eye would be equally close to two different bars in the right eye. One match-up would correspond to a still greater disparity in the same direction as the earlier ones; the other match-up to a large disparity in the opposite direction. Continuing along, one would again have a regular shift in disparity, and so on. The result, then, would be of three parallel slanted surfaces, like a partially opened vertical venetian blind. (This would also take care of the "extra" bars in the higher frequency pattern.) When one inspects a static stimulus like this, one does indeed on occasion see just such a venetian blind, in a state of rivalry with the percept of a single slanted surface, and the number of slats seen is predictable from these simple considerations of the positional disparities involved. However, as reported by Tyler

and Sutter, when the patterns are drifted rapidly to eliminate positional disparities, only a single, stable slanted surface is seen, the percept predicted from spatial frequency disparity alone. Furthermore, a single slanted surface is seen even
with a 100% frequency difference, far beyond the difference at which a stationary
display breaks up into slats.

It appears, then, that both positional and spatial frequency disparity analyses
are involved in the perception of slanted surfaces. In most naturalistic situations, both doubtless give the same answer and cooperate in producing the percept of depth and of three-dimensionality. When one inspects highly repetitive
simple grating patterns, however, the two separate mechanisms give partially
different answers and the percept alternates between the two rivalrous solutions.

One of the virtues of both an orientation disparity system and a spatial frequency disparity system is that they do not require specific positional or phase
information: the overall orientation and spatial frequency in a region (the two-
dimensional spatial frequency power spectrum) of one eye compared with that
in the other would be sufficient to encode tilt and slant. Therefore, the requisite
information should be obtainable from the output of a few complex cells that
integrate the responses of groups of simple cells.

Movement Disparity

When an object moves in depth, or when we ourselves move through a three-
dimensional environment, there will be differential movement of patterns in the
two retinal images. For instance, the image of an object directly approaching the
head will move in different directions in the two eyes, whereas an object going
from right to left at a constant distance will have images moving in the same
direction and at the same speed. For intermediate angles between these
extremes, the direction of movement will be the same but the speed of the image
movement will differ in the two eyes.

In the various situations described above involving movement in depth, the
stimuli over successive time intervals are the same as those we were considering
earlier in our discussions of orientation and spatial frequency disparity. For
instance, a line pointed at the bridge of the nose will have images with 180°
orientation disparity; a ball following the same course towards the head will at
successive time intervals follow down the same divergent paths in the two eyes.
As was true for those other situations, the patterns of movement in depth can
also be specified by successive position disparities between the eyes. The critical
question, however, is whether the visual system may not have specialized systems for analyzing such patterns. The answer again clearly seems to be yes.

Most striate cells respond to appropriate spatial patterns moved across their
receptive fields in any direction or to stationary patterns flickered on and off in
place. However, a sizable subpopulation of about 25% of cells respond well to a
pattern moved in one general direction, but are inhibited by the same pattern
moved in the opposite direction; a much higher percentage of cells in the post-

striate area MT are of this type (see Chapter 4). Such cells in general respond poorly to stationary flickering patterns. These cells can potentially not only respond to moving patterns, but signal the direction of movement. However, if the direction selectivity is the same in both eyes of a binocular movement-selective cell, it would respond optimally to movement in the frontoparallel plane, not in depth.

In recordings from poststriate cells, Pettigrew (1973) first found the presence of an occasional cell that responded to movement in one direction in one eye and the opposite direction in the other. Such cells were also noted by Zeki (1974), and studied in detail by Cynader and Regan (1978). In addition to finding such cells, some of which responded optimally to movement directly toward the head and others directly away, Cynader and Regan also noted other units that responded optimally to movement in oblique depth planes. The cells responsive to movement directly toward or away from the head were found to be quite narrowly tuned for direction; those responsive to more oblique planes were broader in their direction tuning.

Psychophysical evidence for specialized movement-in-depth systems based on movement disparity was provided by Regan and Beverly (1978). Adaptation to a pattern moving in depth along one plane was found to produce selective loss in sensitivity to movement in that general direction. Narrower tuning curves were found for movements that would come close to the head, in accord with the physiological evidence.

We would suggest, as we did for orientation and spatial frequency disparity, that a movement disparity system might well be much simpler and more economical than one extracting the same information from a point-by-point (and time-by-time) positional disparity analysis.

Local Versus Global Stereopsis

Julesz's (1971) introduction of random dot stereograms to vision made many contributions to the study of stereopsis and raised several important issues. See Figure 10.6 for an example of a random dot stereogram. One point emphasized by Julesz is that the fact that one can see a pattern in depth in a random dot stereogram, in which there are no monocular cues to the pattern, makes it apparent that stereopsis does not require a prior discrimination of form. This feature also makes such patterns extremely useful tools for studying stereopsis in animals and children; the shape of a pattern standing out in depth, or whether it is in front of or behind the background, cannot be discriminated in the absence of stereopsis; there is no way that it can be deduced from monocular cues alone. A response to the binocularly produced pattern, thus, implies functioning stereopsis.

The random dot stereograms of Julesz also seemed to provide powerful support for point-by-point positional disparity analysis in stereopsis, since they had in them no lines, only individual, randomly located dots. However, with the

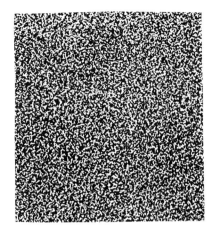 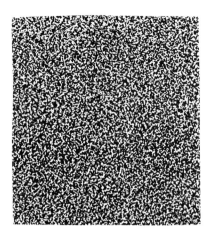

FIG. 10.6 Apparent depth produced by random dot pattern. The patterns for the two eyes are the same, except that two segments have been displaced (in opposite directions) in one eye relative to the other. When these patterns are fused, one should see a disk and a square in depth relative to the background, one in front and one behind.

application of linear systems analysis to vision (Campbell & Robson, 1968), we have come to realize that such random dot patterns contain a broad spatial frequency spectrum and that the detection of the stereo information may well be through separate spatial frequency channels. Indeed, Julesz showed that filtering high spatial frequencies from a random dot pattern does not much affect the perception of depth.

The presence of stereo patterns made up of thousands of identical dots also raised the issue of local versus global stereopsis. Most discussions of stereopsis and its physiological basis consider just the problems of local disparity processing—assessing the degree of disparity between comparable points in the patterns in the two eyes. However, with random dot stereograms, any one point in the pattern in one eye can equally well be associated with dozens of points in the other. Each of these comparisons would lead to a different depth estimate for that region in space. The question, therefore, is how the visual system comes up with a single global solution to this problem. Local point-by-point disparity analyses are not sufficient to explain the process. Julesz (1971) and Nelson (1975) developed models to account for global stereopsis, the latter's theory being based on a combination of facilitation among units tuned to the same disparity and inhibition among units tuned to different disparities.

The apparently massive problem of global stereopsis in random dot stereograms, however, comes from the implicit consideration of these patterns as consisting of individual dots which are being detected and responded to as such. The ambiguities then arise because of the great number of identical dots, any one of which can be correlated with any other in the other eye. However, if one considers such patterns instead in terms of their spatial frequency spectra, much of the ambiguity that leads to the problem of global stereopsis disappears (Marr & Poggio, 1979). There is little ambiguity in the low spatial frequency components of the two images. These could thus be used to perform the initial, rough alignment of the patterns. The components of successively higher spatial frequency would then provide more and more precise alignment of the patterns, considerably reducing the correspondence or global stereopsis problem. In normal visual conditions the problem of correspondence between the right and left eye images would be considerably smaller than is the case with random dot patterns. It should be noted that the fact that global stereopsis can occur without monocular contours does not mean that such monocular patterns might not play an important role when they are present.

Hypercyclopean Channel

It is likely that the disparity processing seen in area 17 is only a very early stage in stereopsis, with the processing of visual depth information continuing beyond area 17. For example, in their impressive series of studies of changing size and direction as cues to depth, Regan and Cynader (Cynader & Regan, 1978; Regan & Cynader, 1979) found cells in area 18 but not 17 that appeared to be specifically responsive to those cues. Julesz and Schumer (1981) discuss psychophysical evidence which suggests that depth information is processed in areas more central than striate cortex. Thus it is possible that up through area 17 much visual information is analyzed and encoded in terms of spatial frequencies, and that when this information is further processed to derive complex characteristics such as depth it is again transformed, this time in some more object-oriented fashion.

One curious fact immediately appears, however: there is a significant amount of evidence now that the visual system operates with spatial frequency channels beyond the point at which stereopsis occurs. These mechanisms, which Julesz and Schumer call "hypercyclopean channels," are of particular interest because they must arise beyond the point at which stereopsis occurs. They cannot simply be a later reflection of the monocularly measured spatial frequency channels we have discussed throughout this book, because the information upon which they operate is not available to the system until after binocular combination has taken place.

These hypercyclopean spatial frequency channels are similar to their monocular counterparts in showing orientation specificity as demonstrated by a tilt aftereffect. Adaptation to a single spatial frequency seen only in depth produces a shift in the apparent spatial frequency of a similar grating (Tyler, 1975), like that reported by Blakemore and Sutton (1969) for monocular gratings. Using both subthreshold summation and spatial frequency adaptation, Schumer and Ganz (1979) found that the hypercyclopean channels are band-pass, with bandwidths considerably broader (2–3 octaves) than those seen for the corresponding monocular channels. Tyler and Julesz (1978), using narrow-band masking noise, reported somewhat narrower bandwidths.

The point of particular interest concerning the existence of hypercyclopean spatial frequency channels is that the visual system apparently finds the analysis of the visual scene in terms of spatial frequency (or its linear transformation) to be so useful that it would repeat the process at a later stage. In order to accomplish stereopsis in terms of objects rather than spatial frequency components (which the visual system surely must do), a spatial frequency kind of representation of the visual image must be either abandoned or severely modified. Very powerful advantages must accrue to the system from this sort of quasilinear analysis, or the investment it requires would surely not be expended.

11

Nonlinearities

Throughout most of this book we have discussed the visual system in terms of spatial frequency analysis using a linear systems approach. This has a number of attractions, one being that the mathematics used in linear systems analysis is both well developed and straightforward. The advantages of being able to make quantitative predictions and thus devise rigorous tests of a theory are tremendous. A scientific theory which is so imprecise that it can accommodate any results is useless and cannot advance one's understanding. Only to the extent that a model is capable of being disproven can it be of value. Thus an approach which allows a precise, quantitative prediction for any given experiment is of great value.

But neither linear systems analysis nor any other mathematical approach, no matter how elegant and precise, can be of use unless the conditions necessary for its application are met. In the case of linear systems analysis the basic requirement is, of course, that the system under consideration be linear. With respect to the visual system such an assumption seems, at first blush, to be almost laughably inappropriate. The known nonlinearities of the visual system are so great that one is forced to wonder what prompted anyone even to consider applying a linear systems approach. There are three counterarguments to this objection.

T.N. Cornsweet (1970) has made one of these points quite clearly. Consider a slowly changing function without sharp inflection points, such as the visual system's response to changes in light level. The light increment necessary to produce a constant response (say a just noticeable difference, jnd) when the visual system is adapted to a low light level is much smaller than the increment necessary to produce the same response at a high adaptation level. In a linear system, a given input should always produce the same response, and to the extent that this fails to happen the system is nonlinear. But think of the overall intensity-response function of the visual system. Although the whole function is certainly quite nonlinear, any one small section of it deviates only slightly from linearity. So, as long as one deals only with points within a fairly restricted intensity range (as one does in most visual scenes), the system closely approximates linearity and can be successfully modeled as a linear system. Thus, the existence of the nonlinearities represented by very slowly changing functions does not necessarily preclude the applicability of linear systems analysis in restricted situations.

The second argument concerns the types of nonlinearities present. There can be nonlinearities in the input-output relationship which are superimposed on a basically linear input analysis. This point was made by Enroth-Cugell and Robson (1966) with respect to the behavior of retinal X cells. If one adopts a constant response criterion (e.g., 10 spikes in the case of a cell or detection in the case of psychophysics), then it is possible to measure the degree of linearity of input summation without regard to the possible output nonlinearities. This has proven to be a very useful technique for both physiology and psychophysics.

The third point is that linear systems analysis is useful even in the case of a nonlinear system, in that it allows one to identify the circumstances under which nonlinearities appear and the types of nonlinearities to be found. If the visual system behaves in a fairly linear manner under many conditions, that much can be simply understood. Special modifications or adjustments can then be introduced to handle the nonlinearities in the circumstances in which they are known to appear. Without the ability to make quantitative predictions based on a rigorous mathematical analysis, none of this would be possible.

For these three reasons, then, we believe it is reasonable to attempt to apply linear systems analysis to the visual system. Its utility has been strikingly demonstrated in the correct predictions made in many diverse experiments. In this chapter, however, we wish to describe a variety of situations in which linearity demonstrably does not hold. A study of the nonlinear responses of the visual system allows one to understand its operations more fully.

Threshold Nonlinearity

One type of nonlinearity which we wish to consider is that of a threshold. Signal detection theorists (e.g., Green & Swets, 1966) have cautioned repeatedly about the inadvisability of applying a strong threshold model to most psychophysical detection tasks. They have demonstrated that what appears to be a firm, objectively determined "threshold" can in fact be pushed around considerably by various procedures that cause a subject to change his criterion. Subjects can not only make a binary detection decision ("I see it," or "I do not see it"), but can describe a whole psychometric function by using a probability rating scale (ranging, for example, from "definitely present" through various degrees of uncertainty to "definitely not present"). Those cautions are well taken and should be kept in mind during any discussion of threshold-type mechanisms. Nevertheless, at some stage there must be threshold mechanisms operating. When a visual stimulus is the impetus for some particular behavioral response, a binary decision must be made as to whether or not the response should occur. Any time such a binary decision must be made, there is a threshold, although that threshold may relate more to judgmental processes than to strictly sensory processes. It may well be that that threshold is not rigid and unchanging; it may be capable of being moved up or down by various external factors. But wherever it sits at a given moment and whatever the factors that determine its position, it nonetheless functions as a real threshold. Stimuli below its level do not result in the given behavior; stimuli above its level do. To the extent that a given increment produces different results above and below threshold, the system is nonlinear. Any point at which a binary decision about the presence or absence of a stimulus must be made is a threshold point, and there will, at that point, be a nonlinear input-output relationship.

In this book we are almost totally restricting our consideration of physiological processes (and psychophysical processes associated with them) to those which occur at the level of the striate cortex or earlier, mainly for lack of strong evidence as to the nature of the processing in later visual areas. It seems unlikely that the threshold function associated with binary decisions would be operating at this level.

Phase Nonlinearity

A second type of nonlinearity which may be involved in visual function is what we may term phase nonlinearity. We have repeatedly discussed the evidence that some cells in the visual pathway (retinal and geniculate X cells and cortical simple cells) sum linearly within subregions of their RFs, whereas others (retinal and LGN Y cells and cortical complex cells) fail to show such linear summation. The nonlinear character of the summation within the RFs of complex cells is reflected in an insensitivity to absolute stimulus phase (although, note, not necessarily to relative phase, or to the change in phase associated with movement): the response of such a cell is the same regardless of the position of the stimulus on its RF.

Although phase insensitivity may be described as a nonlinearity of summation within the RF, it does not represent quite the same kind of phenomenon as the other nonlinearities we are discussing. It does not produce a transformation of information (such as adding power at frequencies not present in the stimulus), but rather just loses some of the information present, specifically, information about spatial phase. However, we have argued that simple and complex cells must form at least partially parallel paths, each with an output from the striate. So although the complex cells are lacking in phase information, under most circumstances simple cells responsive to the same stimuli will be carrying such phase information. Possible exceptions are at very high spatial frequencies and in the far periphery of the visual field (see Chapter 8). We shall discuss below the interesting manner in which phase-insensitive mechanisms can interact with cortical simple cells to produce nonlinear behavior in these otherwise rather linear cells.

Nonlinear Contrast-Response Functions

One type of nonlinearity which is very obvious in the responses of cortical cells is a response amplitude nonlinearity. For several years most studies applying linear systems analysis to the visual system dealt only with behavior near threshold (e.g., Campbell & Robson, 1968; Campbell, Carpenter, & Levinson, 1969) and demonstrated a remarkable degree of linearity. Significant nonlinearities were found, however, when people began considering not threshold detection but the appearance of suprathreshold stimuli. For increasing stimulus contrast of a single spatial frequency, Cannon (1979) has shown by magnitude estimation that apparent contrast increases as a linear function of physical contrast up to at least 60% contrast. However, if one compares the increase in apparent contrast as a function of physical contrast for different spatial frequencies, quite different slopes appear just above threshold. Apparent contrast increases more rapidly for both high and low spatial frequencies (once they exceed their higher thresholds) than it does for middle spatial frequencies. Thus, by some moderate physical contrast (ca. 10–20%), all spatial frequencies will be of roughly equal apparent contrast even though their contrast thresholds are vastly different (see Figure 5.11). This flattening out of the perceived contrast function across spatial frequencies at suprathreshold levels was reported by Georgeson and Sullivan (1975), who suggested that these frequency-dependent nonlinearities allow the visual system to compensate for its lower sensitivity to high and low spatial frequencies.

The contrast-response functions for individual cells in the visual pathway vary considerably from cell to cell. Figure 11.1 shows contrast-response functions from four striate cortical cells. Although the response of each cell increases linearly with contrast (or with log contrast) over a fairly extended range, the

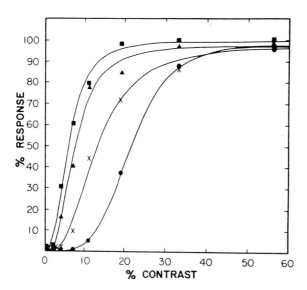

FIG. 11.1 Physiologically determined contrast response functions for the four striate cortex cells (from Albrecht & Hamilton, 1982. Reprinted with permission).

slopes of the functions and the contrast level at which they are linear differ somewhat from cell to cell.

Figure 11.1 also illustrates a type of response amplitude nonlinearity that typically occurs with large signals. The cells show a fairly linearly increasing response with increasing contrast up to some contrast level at which the response has reached its asymptote, and it remains at that level (or may even, in occasional cells, decrease slightly) as contrast continues to increase. Such response saturation occurs in most striate cortical cells, often at relatively low contrasts. One cell shown in Figure 11.1, for example, saturates at about 15% contrast whereas another not until about 40% contrast. The effects of response saturation at high contrasts would be lessened by the contrast gain control found by Ohzawa, Sclar, and Freeman (1982): in the presence of continued high-contrast patterns, many cells decrease their response and now show differential responses to patterns over this high-contrast range to which they previously gave a uniform (saturated) response. However, Albrecht et al. (1984) have shown that most cells show only a partial contrast gain control.

The overall effect of the amplitude nonlinearities of cortical cells is to decrease the effectiveness of high-contrast components of stimuli: response saturation is common, downturns are seen on occasion, but one almost never sees an upturn at high contrasts in a cell's contrast-response function. It is hard to predict the extent to which perceptual distortions would result from this because there is little evidence as to the contrasts of natural visual stimuli. It is a common criticism of threshold psychophysics to say that most natural stimuli are of very high contrast, far above threshold. However, such a glib dismissal of threshold psychophysics needs to be examined more closely. Many stimuli are undoubtedly of high contrast, but the critical issue, given the evidence for multiple channels, may be not the overall pattern contrasts but the amplitudes of the spatial frequency components of the patterns. In the case of many naturalistic stimuli of quite high pattern contrast but of broad spatial frequency spectra, it could well be that the power per octave, for instance, is actually quite low, within the linear range of the cells that would be responding to it.

Another factor to be taken into consideration in evaluating the significance of the nonlinearity of the saturating intensity-response functions of cortical cells is the likely presence of inhibitory interactions, as discussed in the next section. We only note here that when presented with complex, broad-spectrum patterns (as most natural stimuli are) rather than sine wave gratings, cortical cells might be subject to sufficient inhibition that they do not attain the high, saturating rates of firing seen in responses to simple high-contrast gratings.

Half-Wave Rectification

Another major nonlinearity which is particularly obvious in the responses of many cortical cells is that they show some degree of half-wave rectification. Since most cortical cells, especially simple cells, have very low maintained discharge rates, they cannot respond with symmetrical increases and decreases in firing from the maintained rate. Consider the difference between a retinal ganglion X cell and a cortical simple cell. Both respond to a drifting grating in a phase-locked manner, showing excitation only when the grating is in certain positions with respect to the cell's RF. However, since retinal ganglion cells typically have quite high maintained (spontaneous) rates, they show not only excitation to the stimulus in one phase but a fairly symmetrical amount of inhibition to the pattern shifted 180° in phase. There may be large modulated responses but little if any change in the overall mean firing rate to a drifting grating. Such ganglion cells thus show highly linear stimulus-response relationships. But cortical simple cells, which have similar phase specificity, typically have extremely low maintained rates and thus cannot show a decrease in response to a grating that is in the inhibitory phase. The result is similar to half-wave rectification in an electrical circuit. One effect of such rectification is to introduce frequencies into the response that are not present in the stimulus. It also produces an increase in the mean firing rate, since the excitatory response to the pattern in one phase is not canceled by a decrease in firing to another phase. Thus the passage of a grating across a simple cell's RF produces not only a modulated discharge but an increase in mean firing rate as well.

Half-wave rectification in the striate cortex is a significant nonlinearity. However, there are two mitigating circumstances to be considered. One is the presence of simple cells tuned 180° out of phase with respect to each other. Among simple cells with even-symmetric RFs, for instance, those with excitatory RF centers (to increments) and those with inhibitory centers are found equally often. Since each of these cells would respond fairly linearly to one half cycle of a grating (although not responding at all to the other half cycle), the *difference* between their responses would give a linear output to the whole pattern if they had the same RF center point.

The other point to be considered is the extent to which the level of the maintained discharge of cortical cells seen in physiological recording experiments realistically reflects the situation in an animal's ordinary life. It is clear, for instance, that barbiturates can have a strong suppressive effect on a cortical cell's maintained discharge rate. The same is probably true at least to some extent for most other anesthetics used in recording experiments. It is entirely possible that the maintained discharge rates of cortical cells in an unanesthetized and attentive animal might be considerably higher than those typically measured. Insofar as that is so, the magnitude of the half-wave rectification nonlinearities seen in most physiological experiments would be artifactually high.

Nonetheless, some half-wave rectification undoubtedly occurs at cortical levels and may explain some of the nonlinearities seen in psychophysical experiments. Henning, Hertz, and Broadbent (1975) examined a very interesting pattern made up of a combination of three harmonically related spatial frequencies, $4f + 5f + 6f$. Such a pattern produces "beats" at a frequency of f. That is, the overall contrast of the pattern waxes and wanes as the component frequencies come in and out of phase with respect to each other, with a spatial periodicity of f (see the pattern at the top of Figure 11.2). Perceptually, such a pattern

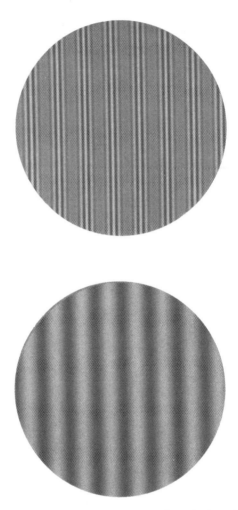

FIG. 11.2   An amplitude-modulated grating and a sinusoidal grating of the same periodicity. The upper pattern is produced by the addition of three gratings of 4*f*, 5*f* and 6*f*.
Its period is the same as that of the sinusoidal grating of frequency *f* below, but the compound grating contains no component at *f*.

appears somewhat similar to a grating of frequency *f*, shown at the bottom of
Figure 11.2, although there is no power at all in its spatial spectrum at that frequency. One might note that this pattern is similar in the spatial domain to the
"missing fundamental" pattern in the temporal domain, a pattern which has
been widely investigated in audition. Perceptually, a complex auditory waveform made up of higher harmonics of some fundamental frequency but with no
power at the fundamental itself nonetheless clearly has the pitch of the
fundamental.

The $4f + 5f + 6f$ pattern has certain resemblances to a grating of frequency f. To account for its appearance and for some masking results discussed below, Henning et al. suggested that channels tuned to low spatial frequencies might receive excitatory inputs from high-frequency channels which are modulated in contrast in this pattern. Such a schema, if true, would seem to negate the idea that the visual system analyzes patterns by means of separate spatial frequency selective channels at early neural levels. It is thus of interest to examine how cortical cells respond to such a "missing fundamental" pattern. Albrecht and R.L. De Valois (1981) recorded responses of cat and monkey striate cells to these patterns, both when $4f + 5f + 6f$ was centered on the passband of the cell, and when the "missing" f was so centered. In no case did we find a cell tuned to f that responded to the beat of $4f + 5f + 6f$ (see Figure 11.3A). The sort of major distortion of the separate channel system postulated by Henning et al. was thus not found at the striate level.

However, Albrecht and De Valois found that simple cells tuned to the region of 4 to $6f$ showed a periodic change in mean firing when the $4f + 5f + 6f$ pattern was drifted across their RFs (see Figure 11.3B). This change had a periodicity of $1/f$. In a region in which the pattern contrasts summed (so that there was a lot of power in the local spatial frequency spectrum), the cells fired. Where the pat-

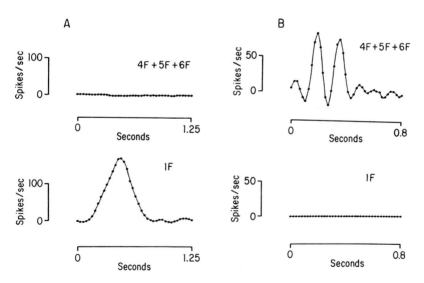

FIG. 11.3   Responses of two cortical simple cells to the patterns shown in Figure 11.2 drifted across their RFs. In A are shown the responses of a cell tuned to a frequency f. It gives a large response to f but does not respond to the $4f + 5f + 6f$ pattern that beats at f. In B are the responses of a cell tuned to $5f$. It responds to the contrast-varying beat pattern with a waveform mimicking its profile, but gives no response to the grating of f. Thus, the psychophysical masking interactions between these two patterns cannot be accounted for on the basis of cells at this level (from Albrecht & R.L. De Valois, 1981. Reprinted with permission).

tern contrasts canceled (with a consequent absence of power in the local frequency spectrum), the cells remained silent. If, then, it were possible to measure the mean response rate of all cells within each cortical locus across an extended region of the cortex in V1, a spatially periodic pattern should emerge. Although no cells tuned to f would be firing differentially, there would be a periodic variation in activity across the cortical surface. Ignoring the complications of differential cortical magnification, this variation would have a periodicity corresponding to $1/f$. Thus if a later cortical region were able to read out this pattern of response variation, it could generate the percept of a pattern which was periodic with a frequency of f.

Carlson, Anderson, and Moeller (1980) studied a quite different pattern, the perception of which might be accounted for in a similar fashion. They constructed a center-surround stimulus (like a Mexican hat) which had power over a limited band of high spatial frequencies. They then put together a string of such center-surround patches to form the shape of the Muller-Lyer illusion pattern (in which a line with outward-facing end lines appears longer than one with inward-facing, arrow-like end lines). Ginsburg (1971) had earlier suggested that the Muller-Lyer (as well as certain other spatial illusions) could be accounted for on the basis of our judging the length of lines from just low spatial frequency information, since in the low-frequency image the two lines in the Muller-Lyer pattern are of different lengths, as they appear perceptually. However, in the high-pass Carlson version of this illusion, each of the components contained only high spatial frequency components, the overall pattern being therefore devoid of low spatial frequencies. Yet, as Carlson et al. showed, not only is the overall pattern visible, but the illusion occurs also (albeit weakened).

Consider the representation of this pattern across the cortical surface. There will be a net increase in mean firing rate to each pattern element within the figure, and these responses will be distributed across the cortex in the overall shape of the Muller-Lyer figure. Again, later cortical areas, by putting together the output from different striate subregions, may build up the percept of an overall pattern of lines from these localized changes in mean firing rate.

In our discussion of these patterns, we have tried to make three points which we would like to make explicit and to reiterate for emphasis. One is that striate cortex cells show a half-wave rectification nonlinearity, and that this nonlinearity would produce a net increase in cortical activity under circumstances in which that would not be expected from purely linear considerations. The second point is that we need to be careful to avoid the trap of considering the striate cortex as performing a global spatial frequency analysis. Rather, as we have repeatedly emphasized, each striate region is only processing information from a limited region of visual space. There is no striate cortex cell which is "looking at" all of the $4f + 5f + 6f$ beat pattern across many degrees of the visual field, or at the large overall Muller-Lyer illusion pattern made up of center-surround elements. Rather, each cell in striate cortex is concerned only with small subregions within each of these patterns. This leads directly to the third point, which is that later cortical regions must put together information from various striate modules to form our percepts of large patterns. Both the spatial frequency characteristics within each module and the changes in mean firing rate produced by half-wave rectification presumably provide inputs to this later stage.

Spatial Frequency and Orientation Interactions

The final type of nonlinearity we would like to discuss is that of interactions between different spatial frequencies. In a truly linear system, the various spatial frequency channels would operate quite independently of each other. However, there is considerable evidence—psychophysical, physiological and anatomical—showing that there are significant inhibitory interactions among channels tuned to different spatial frequencies.

Psychophysical Evidence

The first suggestion of inhibitory spatial frequency interactions between channels came from an adaptation experiment by Tolhurst (1972b). He compared the loss in contrast sensitivity resulting from adaptation to a sinusoidal grating and to a square wave grating in which the two gratings were equated for the amplitudes of their fundamentals, f. If the channels responsive to different spatial frequencies were independent, the two conditions should have produced identical sensitivity losses at f. In fact, adaptation to the square wave grating was found to produce a smaller loss in contrast sensitivity than adaptation to the sine wave. Since the two gratings had been equated for power at f, their spectra differed only in that the square wave contained additional higher frequency components. The most straightforward interpretation of these results, as Tolhurst suggested, is that the channels responsive to f and to $3f$ (and/or $5f$) in the square wave are mutually inhibitory. The channel responsive to $3f$ would be stimulated in the square wave case and thus inhibit the channel responsive to f. As a result, the net excitation in the channel centered at f would be less than for the sine wave with equal power at f, and there would therefore be less adaptational loss in contrast sensitivity, exactly the result that Tolhurst reported.

Similar evidence for spatial frequency interactions was found by Stecher, Sigal, and Lange (1973), who showed that the addition of a second spatial frequency lessened the adaptational effect of an adapting grating. This was found to hold for nearby, nonharmonic spatial frequency combinations, suggesting that Tolhurst's findings did not reflect some peculiar characteristic of square wave gratings. These experiments may lead one to question how Campbell and Robson (1968) found the exact correspondence between contrast sensitivity and fundamental amplitude for sine and square wave gratings, as discussed in Chapter 6. They found that contrast sensitivity for a square wave is $4/\pi$ times greater than contrast sensitivity for a sine wave of the same spatial frequency, the factor of $4/\pi$ being the ratio of the amplitudes of the fundamentals of square and sine waves of identical pattern contrast. The difference may lie in the fact that Tolhurst used suprathreshold patterns while Campbell and Robson measured absolute detection. At threshold contrast (for all but very low spatial frequencies) only the square wave fundamental has sufficient power to be detected. The third harmonic is, of course, physically present, but since its amplitude is subthreshold it cannot exert any significant inhibitory influence. It is likely that two components interact only when each exceeds its own threshold. For this reason, many experiments have demonstrated apparent linearity and independence of channels at threshold, although the same patterns at suprathreshold contrasts show obvious frequency interactions. One must be cautious in drawing strong conclusions about the independence of channels based on experiments using only very low-contrast patterns.

K.K. De Valois (1977b) demonstrated interchannel inhibition in another adaptation paradigm. Adaptation to a high-contrast grating of a single spatial frequency produces a band-limited loss in contrast sensitivity centered on the adaptation frequency, as Blakemore and Campbell (1969) first reported. De Valois found, however, that careful measurements also reveal an increase in contrast sensitivity to spatial frequencies two or three octaves away from the adaptation frequency (see Figure 6.6). The simplest explanation of this finding is that spatial frequency channels normally inhibit one another. The adaptation of one channel would result in a temporary reduction in its activity, thus also reducing the amount of inhibition it exerts on other channels. The consequence of that release from inhibition would be an increase in the contrast sensitivity of the inhibited channels. The inhibition demonstrated in this experiment seems to occur approximately equally for both higher and lower spatial frequencies, but that found in physiological experiments is less symmetrical. Still other psychophysical evidence suggesting inhibitory interactions among spatial frequency channels comes from the study of adaptation to random dot patterns by K.K. De Valois and Switkes (1980), discussed in Chapter 9.

A perceptual illusion has also suggested inhibitory interactions among cells tuned to different spatial frequencies. Inhibitory interactions in the space domain have long been invoked to explain Mach bands (Ratliff, 1965). MacKay (1973) has described a spatial frequency analog of Mach bands. If two regions of different spatial frequency are connected with a sharp spatial frequency ramp (i.e., a frequency-modulated grating), a strip of the grating at the edge of the high spatial frequency portion appears to be of a higher spatial frequency than the rest of the physically equal part; a strip at the edge of the ramp on the low-frequency part appears to be of a lower spatial frequency than the rest of the low-frequency portion. By an argument analogous to that used to explain classical Mach bands, mutual inhibition among spatial frequency channels could explain these spatial frequency Mach bands.

There is also psychophysical evidence for inhibitory interactions between lines of different orientation. Blakemore, Carpenter, and Georgeson (1970) showed that the apparent orientation of a line was changed perceptually by the presence of another line of neighboring orientation. The effect was found to fall off systematically as the two lines diverged more and more from each other in orientation. A grating of a particular orientation also has its apparent orientation changed by a surrounding grating of slightly different orientation (Tolhurst & Thompson, 1975). It has also been shown (Thomas & Shimamura, 1975) that two lines of slightly different orientation are less detectable than ones more widely separated in orientation, as one would predict from mutual inhibition among neighboring orientation columns. Such mutually inhibitory interactions between patterns of nearby orientations have long been postulated to account for the visual distortions in the shape of certain patterns, as dramatized in the Hering, Poggendorf, and Zollner illusions.

Physiological Evidence

What has come to be known as the "classic receptive field" of a cell is that region from which responses can be evoked with direct stimulation. Stimulation of regions outside this area, in what we may term the far surround, while ineffective alone in driving a cell, can often nonetheless influence the responses to stimuli presented simultaneously within the classic RF. The most commonly observed interactions of this sort are inhibitory. Blakemore and Tobin (1972) examined the effect of varying the orientation of a grating presented in the far surround on the responses of striate cells to an optimal stimulus within the classic RF. They found large inhibitory effects which were orientation specific: the cell was maximally inhibited by a far-surround grating of the same orientation as the optimal (excitatory) grating presented to the classic RF. The inhibition was found to drop gradually as the orientation of the surround grating was changed, falling to zero for an orientation which was orthogonal to the central pattern. Similar orientation-specific inhibition has also been reported by Maffei and Fiorentini (1976), Nelson and Frost (1978), and Morrone, Burr, and Maffei (1982).

Such inhibitory-excitatory interaction in the orientation domain is in some ways analogous to the interactions in the space domain seen at the level of bipolar and ganglion cells (as discussed in Chapter 3), which produce a center-surround organization in space. An excitatory input to RF center with a certain fairly narrow orientation selectivity, and a weaker inhibitory input to far surround with a broader orientation tuning but same peak, would combine (albeit apparently nonlinearly) to make a cell fire to a full-field grating of optimal orientation but be inhibited by off-orientations. Such interactions should have the effect of narrowing a cell's orientation tuning.

There is also physiological evidence for spatial frequency interactions. K.K. De Valois and Tootell (1983) examined how striate cortex cells respond to patterns of two different spatial frequencies. The optimum grating stimulus (best spatial frequency, contrast, and orientation) was determined for each cell. Then the response of the cell was recorded to that stimulus both alone and in combination with gratings of other harmonically related frequencies ($\frac{1}{4}$, $\frac{1}{3}$, $\frac{1}{2}$, 2, 3, and $4f$, respectively) of equal contrast. Virtually all simple cells (97%) showed a reduced response to their optimal grating stimulus when it was presented in conjunction with one or more of the other gratings, most cells being maximally inhibited by the addition of either $2f$ or $3f$, with only a few cells showing significant inhibition to any lower spatial frequencies. Complex cells were less likely to show inhibitory interactions. Only 29% were inhibited by the addition of higher spatial frequencies, and 8% by lower frequencies.

The two-frequency inhibition found in cortical cells can be quite profound. In the case of simple cells it may be a function not only of relative frequency but also of the relative phase of the two gratings. Complex cells, on the other hand, were never found to exhibit phase-specific interactions. Figure 11.4A shows the responses of a typical simple cell, which is inhibited in a non-phase-specific manner. The experiment was run with the two gratings combined in relative phase angles of 0, 90, 180, and 270o. As can be seen, this cell was unaffected by the addition of frequencies lower than its best frequency but was profoundly inhibited by the addition of either a $2f$ or a $3f$ grating. In Figure 11.4B are the responses of the same cell to the $f + 2f$ combinations in eight different relative phases. There was no significant effect of the relative phase at which the second grating was added. The non-phase-specific inhibition of a simple cell response cannot reflect a simple linear summation within RF subregions. The most obvious basis for such phase-independent interactions would be if the simple cell were being inhibited by a (phase-independent) complex cell tuned to $2f$. The prevalence of such inhibition suggests the possibility of a major input from complex cells onto simple cells, an organization which is of course opposite to the classical model of simple cells feeding into complex cells.

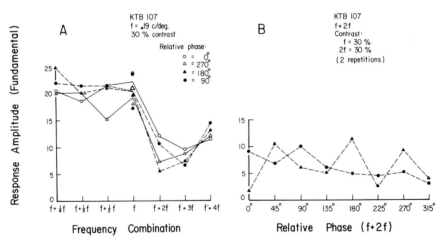

FIG. 11.4   Phase-independent interactions in a cat simple cell. The modulated response to f (the cell's preferred frequency) is shown for various combinations of two spatial frequencies. The response to f alone is shown for comparison. Response amplitude is plotted as a function of the frequency combination (A) on the left and as a function of the relative phase of the $f + 2f$ combination (B) on the right. Note that although the addition of $2f$ profoundly inhibits the response to f, the inhibition does not depend on the relative phases of the $f + 2f$ combination (from K.K. De Valois & Tootell, 1983. Reprinted with permission).

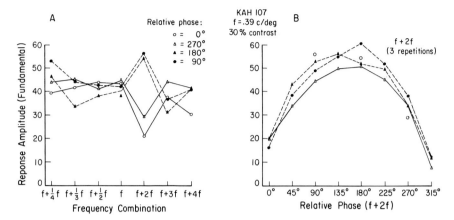

FIG. 11.5   Phase-dependent frequency interactions in a simple cell. In A are plotted the responses to the cell's best frequency, *f*, alone and in combination with 6 other harmonically related frequencies. Each combination was presented in four different relative phases. Note that the response to *f* + 2*f* is highly phase dependent. In B are the responses to the *f* + 2*f* combination in 8 different relative phases (from K.K. De Valois & Tootell, 1983. Reprinted with permission).

   The responses of a simple cell with phase-dependent interactions are shown in Figure 11.5. It can be seen there that for the lower frequencies and for 3*f* and 4*f*, very little interaction occurs, but when *f* is combined with 2*f*, the cell's response may be either increased or decreased, depending on the relative phase angle with which the two gratings are combined. It is possible that some such phase-specific interactions between gratings of two spatial frequencies reflect linear summation within the RF of a simple cell. To the extent that that is true, they are not of particular relevance to this discussion of nonlinearities. The other possibility is that phase-specific two-frequency interactions do not reflect linear summation within the RF subregions of a single cell, but rather interactions between two separate cells, each of which responds primarily to one component of the compound grating. If this is the case, the cell exerting the modulating influence must itself be a simple cell, since the modulated (interactive) response is phase specific. This would be an example of the nonindependence of two cells with different frequency tuning.
   It is interesting to speculate about the functions served by spatial frequency interactions. The most obvious result of mutual inhibition between cells tuned to different spatial frequencies is a narrowing of their spatial frequency response bandwidths. Although such inhibitory interactions would be a kind of nonlinearity, they would have the effect of increasing the selectivity of the individual cells and therefore of the system as a whole. In a system that starts out with very broadly tuned detectors, the lack of independence introduced by inhibitory interactions may be more than compensated for by the increased narrowing of channels that results.

While there is some reason for believing that frequency-specific inhibition is at least partly responsible for the narrowing of spatial frequency selectivity found in the cortex, the evidence is not compelling. The most obvious discrepancy is in the asymmetry of the inhibitory interactions. Although most LGN cells have relatively sharp high-frequency cuts in their spatial frequency tuning functions, the fall-off on the low-frequency end is typically quite gradual. The most striking difference seen in the spatial frequency tuning of cortical cells is that they have acquired sharp low-frequency cuts. One might expect, then, that if this narrowing of tuning functions were accomplished by inhibitory interactions among cells tuned to different spatial frequencies, any given cell would be much more likely to show inhibition from lower spatial frequencies, but the opposite was found. The evidence for the involvement of spatial frequency inhibition in the narrowing of tuning functions is not entirely negative, however. Simple cells are, on the average, somewhat more narrowly tuned than complex cells, and, as discussed above, simple cells are much more likely (97%) to show two-frequency inhibition than are complex cells (37%). Furthermore, those complex cells which do show two-frequency inhibition are, on the average, more narrowly tuned for spatial frequency than those which do not, although the differences are small (K.K. De Valois & Tootell, 1983).

If the narrowing of spatial frequency sensitivity is not the only *raison d'être* for inhibitory interactions, what other functions might they serve? Blakemore and Campbell (1969) have suggested that detectors tuned to specific ratios of spatial frequencies could subserve an object constancy function. Since many cortical cells seem to be particularly sensitive to a spatial frequency ratio of 1:2 or 1:3, it is tempting to suggest that this is the particular stimulus characteristic which they signal. However, that would be in error. It is not the ratio of the frequency components which determines when inhibition occurs, but rather the absolute spatial frequency content. Consider a cell that is excited by f and inhibited by an $f + 2f$ combination. If this cell is shown a grating of ⅔ f, it will give an excitatory response, since ⅔ f is still within its excitatory passband. If the inhibition were specific to the ratio of stimulus frequencies, the peak inhibition should now occur when the second grating had a frequency of ⅘ f, twice that of the lower, excitatory grating. In fact, however, the maximum inhibition will still occur when the second grating has a spatial frequency of $2f$ (K.K. De Valois & Tootell, 1983). The inhibition, which is often quite narrowly tuned, occurs to a particular spatial frequency band, not to a specific spatial frequency ratio.

The nonlinear, two-frequency interactions we have been discussing above may be the beginning of another, more complex type of analysis which we do not yet understand. It would appear that the next stage operates in an as yet unspecified manner upon the outputs of the quasilinear spatial frequency filters seen at the earlier level. The prevalence of phase-independent interactions, however, suggests that it is *not* just the geometric profile of the stimulus upon which the further analysis is carried out. Rather, the spatial frequency content of the stimulus is also important.

Anatomical Evidence

Anatomical studies (Tootell, Silverman, & R.L. De Valois, 1981) of the spatial frequency organization have also produced evidence for spatial frequency interactions. When a cat is presented with a single high spatial frequency grating while being injected with 2-DG, autoradiography of the striate cortex sections shows bands of cells, those tuned to this high spatial frequency (see Figure 4.22). Relevant to our discussion here is the fact that the regions *between* these high spatial frequency columns are lighter than other, unstimulated regions of striate cortex. This has been quantitatively established by densitometric measures, reading across the columns (see Figure 11.6). This indicates that these neighboring regions within each cortical module, presumably containing those cells tuned to lower spatial frequencies, are less active than if they had not been within the stimulated area at all. The conclusion we would draw, of course, is that these cells were being actively inhibited during the 2-DG administration by those cells in neighboring columns which were excited by the high spatial frequency stimulus pattern being presented. Evidence consistent with this interpretation is that such lightening between spatial frequency columns is seen more prominently in high spatial frequency cases than when the stimulus pattern was of a low spatial frequency. This would agree with the asymmetric inhibitory interactions seen between high and low spatial frequencies in other situations: high spatial frequencies inhibit low more than low inhibit high.

In summary, the visual system cannot in any sense be considered a truly linear device, but under restricted conditions (e.g., just-suprathreshold contrast), its behavior closely approximates that of a linear system. Furthermore, most of the

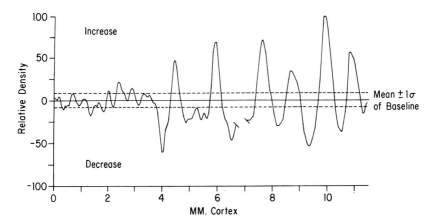

FIG. 11.6   Densitometric measurement across the 2-DG spatial frequency pattern shown in Figure 4.22. It can be seen that the density increases in those bands containing cells responsive to the high spatial frequency pattern shown, and *decreases* between the columns, relative to unstimulated cortex on the left (from Tootell et al., 1981, *Science, 214,* 813–815. Copyright 1981, AAAS. Reprinted with permission).

nonlinearities that have been found in the early stages of its operation apply only to the extent to which the absolute amplitude of the response is considered. Such gross nonlinearities as a cell's responding to stimuli quite different than one would predict have not been found. Thus even under suprathreshold conditions, qualitatively correct predictions can often be made. Furthermore, by treating the visual system as a quasilinear local spatial frequency analyzer, one can accurately predict its responses to a large variety of dissimilar stimuli, and the failures of prediction allow one to identify the types and perhaps the sources of the nonlinearity. It seems both reasonable and profitable, therefore, to think of the early stages of processing by the visual system as carrying out a flawed but nonetheless effective quasilinear spatial frequency filtering of the image on a patch-by-patch basis.

12

Why Localized Spatial Frequency Filtering?

One sometimes talks about the visual system's performing a spatial frequency analysis—indeed, we have repeatedly used the phrase ourselves in this book—but strictly speaking, spatial filtering is not an analysis at all. Insofar as spatial information is being linearly transformed from the space domain at the level of the receptors into a combined space-frequency domain at the cortex, no *analysis* is taking place at all. The information is merely being put into another (presumably more useful) form. In this sense, such a filtering model is a step back from a model of cortical feature detectors which, as very nonlinear elements signaling by their activity the presence of "their" feature in the visual scene (Barlow, 1972), would be acting to detect and identify naturalistic features of the environment. One might reasonably ask what purpose, if any, would be served by devoting the first stages of visual processing to such a quasilinear transformation. There are two aspects to this question. One is, why does the visual system do a spatial frequency filtering of the visual information? The other is, given that the information is spatial frequency filtered, why does the visual system do it in a local, patch-by-patch way rather than on an overall global basis? We have discussed various issues related to these questions and provided some possible answers throughout this book. It might be useful, however, to bring the various thoughts and speculations together and expand upon them here.

WHY SPATIAL FREQUENCY FILTERING?

Efficient Summary of Retinal Information

The synaptic interactions at various levels in the retina and central nervous system do not just relay the receptor output, but rather process the visual information. There is more to it than that, however. The overall arrangement of the visual pathway presents the visual system with an additional problem: the optic nerve constitutes a serious bottleneck in the visual path. There are some 126 million receptors and 500 to 1,000 million striate cortex cells, but only about 1

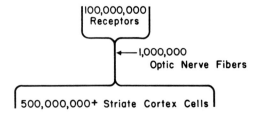

FIG. 12.1 Optic nerve as a bottleneck in the visual system. Information from the roughly 130 million retinal receptors must be greatly condensed in order to be transmitted by the 1 million or so optic nerve fibers. The number of available cells in visual cortex is larger by a factor of 500 to 1,000. The retina, therefore, must serve as an extremely efficient information-processing system, not just as a passive transmission device.

million optic nerve fibers and LGN cells connecting the eye with the cortex (see Figure 12.1). The receptor output must therefore be severely condensed and summarized. As a result of this bottleneck, the form in which the receptor information is encoded is not a matter of indifference. We suggest that visual information is more efficiently condensed, with less loss of crucial information, if it is transformed to the (localized) frequency domain than if left in the pure space domain. Below we shall discuss several bases for this suggestion.

Complete Representation of Visual Stimuli

An important requirement for the visual system of higher vertebrates is that visual information be represented in the cortex in a universal form. Some lower vertebrates have very limited life styles; it is possible that there are correspondingly limited numbers of visual objects which they can discriminate and recognize. A frog, for instance, might encode information about moving flies but not about stationary (dead) ones, or about many other objects. Higher vertebrates, however, are much more generalized animals, adapted to many habitats. They thus need to encode and potentially analyze a much wider range of visual stimuli, and with the evolution of the geniculostriate system have developed the capacity to do so.

It is well known (see Chapter 1) that any waveform can be Fourier analyzed into (or synthesized from) the sum of sine and cosine waves of specified frequency and amplitude. With the addition of an orientation component, the same is true for any two-dimensional waveform or pattern. (That of course is the basis for the wide application of frequency analysis in many fields.) The fact that *any* waveform can be analyzed in this manner means that the luminance profile of any retinal image could be analyzed (and thereby encoded) by units selectively responsive to different spatial frequency components at each orientation. Such an encoding could thus provide a complete representation of any visual stimulus.

The psychophysical and physiological evidence that we have been summarizing in this book, however, indicates that the visual system does not perform the global analysis implied by the discussion above. Rather, the receptive fields of units are spatially delimited and localized. Any spatial frequency analysis must therefore be a patch-by-patch one. However, it has been shown (see Chapter 1) that a piecewise analysis based on units with gaussian-shaped sensitivity profiles can also give a complete representation (Helstrom, 1966). Although the same may be true for other kinds of units into which visual information might be analyzed, it is by no means certain that it is for all the systems that have been suggested.

Separating Illuminant From Objects

In Chapter 5 we discussed the problem of how the visual system could separate out the relatively minor luminance variations due to the reflective characteristics of visual objects from the massive luminance contributions due to the illuminant. Attenuating very low spatial and temporal frequencies constitutes a large first step towards this goal. Most of the visually interesting luminance information in the visual field occurs in the middle spatial frequency range: there are few objects which extend uniformly across large parts of the visual world. Light from the illuminant, on the other hand, tends to be more uniform across the visual field (except for shadowing). The same is true in the temporal domain. The intensity of light from the sun varies only gradually through the day, whereas objects that move, or whose images move because of eye movements, produce temporal variations at much higher frequencies. Thus attenuation of zero or very low spatial and temporal frequencies, as produced by the center-surround antagonism in retinal RFs, tends to minimize contributions of the illuminant while maintaining information relevant to visual objects. Such discarding of largely irrelevant very low-frequency information results in a considerable economy in the retinal encoding of information.

The Peripheral Retina

Although there should be some degradation of resolution in the periphery because of the decreasing cone population, psychophysical measures indicate a more drastic loss. This is quite compatible with the distribution of ganglion cell axons, which shows a sharp fall-off with eccentricity (see Chapter 3). Thus the visual system extracts a maximum amount of information from the foveal image, but it must discard much information about the peripheral image. Doubtless the optic nerve could not transmit nor the cortex process all the information present in the receptor array. The visual system must process and encode the peripheral receptor output in such a way as to preserve the most important information, given that not all can be transmitted.

In a truly linear system, the space and frequency domains are completely equivalent in the sense that information can be transformed from one to the other without loss, and in general the same number of units would be required to specify information in either domain. Where all the information is not to be maintained, however, as in the retinal periphery, the issue of whether the information is encoded in the space or frequency domain is no longer a matter of indifference. A small number of units may very well be able to encode the visually most important information in the local frequency domain better than in the pure space domain.

Consider first a system that just reports the spatial locations of luminance changes. If all the luminance steps were to be monitored and relayed, the complete retinal (luminance) information would be transmitted. But what if only, say, one tenth enough neurons are present to accomplish this, as is the case in the retinal periphery? What then? Which borders or contours are to be reported and which ignored? The problem is that the visual field may contain a great many contours, some of which are important in characterizing the scene, and some largely irrelevant. Those that are irrelevant do not necessarily have the smallest luminance or color steps, or other characteristics that would allow them to be segregated out by simple stratagems. In a forest, for instance, there are contours at the edges of each tree trunk—but also many edges within the image of each trunk, discontinuities in the bark, or shadows in the field. In general, visual objects have both external contours, which define their overall shape, and many internal contours, which are of secondary perceptual importance or even quite irrelevant. An encoding based just on contour location would not be able to distinguish between these.

Consider, however, an encoding in terms of spatial frequency, even with channels having the very broad filtering characteristics of retinal ganglion cells. One could (and does) have a decreasing number of units tuned to high spatial frequencies with increasing eccentricity while maintaining low frequency units. Many high frequency units would be required to cover the same spatial region as could be covered by one unit tuned to a low spatial frequency (R.L. De Valois, Albrecht, & Thorell, 1982; Sakitt & Barlow, 1982). For instance, given a two-dimensional array, 4 units tuned to 16 c/deg would be needed to cover the same spatial range as could be covered by one unit tuned to 8 c/deg, given comparable bandwidths. Curtailing the high end of the spatial spectrum from 16 to 8 c/deg would thus drastically diminish the number of cells required while eliminating only a relatively small part of the spatial frequency spectrum. The critical point, however, is that the most vital visual information would be maintained since low spatial frequencies may transmit the essential "object" information. Elimination of cells tuned to high spatial frequencies would primarily lead to a loss of information about internal contours and fine details, which can be most readily sacrificed. A local spatial frequency encoding would thus provide the visual system with the possibility of transmitting sufficient information from the periphery, in the low spatial frequency image, to give a picture of the overall nature and arrangement of objects in the environment. From the fovea there would also be transmitted detailed high-frequency information. (Note that we refer to the moderate-to-low spatial frequency range here, not the *very* low spatial and temporal frequencies which serve primarily to carry the less interesting information about the illuminant.)

Visual Stimuli Are Periodic

If the visual world were spatially periodic, there would clearly be a major advantage to spatial frequency encoding and/or analysis, as opposed to encoding in terms of the spatial location of such features as edges or bars of different widths. A periodic distribution of light over a few cycles can be specified by a few numbers (its frequency, amplitude, and phase), whereas a specification in terms of the location and direction of each edge might require a dozen or more. Of course the relative advantage to a spatial frequency specification would depend on the extent of the periodicity, increasing with the number of cycles, but even a trivial periodicity of two cycles could be more economically specified by its frequency.

The argument here is akin to ones made by Attneave (1954), Barlow (1961), and others—namely, the need for reducing redundancy in the encoding of visual information. They emphasized that in order to deal with the vast amount of information in a visual scene, the visual system must somehow eliminate redundant information. In proposing mechanisms to accomplish this, they principally considered redundancies due to uniformity, such as the fact that the sky varies little over large visual expanses and so need not have its color and brightness specified at each point. Here we consider redundancies due to periodicity.

We have heard it argued that it makes sense for the auditory system to do a (temporal) frequency encoding because there are many naturally periodic auditory stimuli. Various objects have characteristic resonant properties, and when struck or otherwise set into motion will vibrate at a particular frequency. However, so the argument goes, visual stimuli are not naturally spatially periodic; since no physical processes produce spatial periodicities, a frequency encoding or analysis of visual stimuli would not be similarly advantageous. If the basic premise of this argument—that natural visual stimuli are not spatially periodic—were true, one strong argument for spatial frequency encoding certainly would be gone. It seems to us, however, that this is clearly not the case. A large proportion of visual stimuli are in fact spatially periodic, and one can readily identify a number of physical and biological principles that might account for such periodicities.

Perhaps one difficulty some have in recognizing the numerous visual periodicities is that they seek spatial periodicities of very large extent. Only rarely do spatial periodicities extend over many cycles, across a large part of the visual scene (e.g., ripples on a lake), but we are not mainly concerned with such highly repetitive stimuli. There is in fact no evidence for (and much against) the visual system's performing the extended, global frequency analysis that would be required to take advantage of such extended periodicities. Rather, as we have emphasized, the evidence indicates that each cell in the system (through the striate) has a spatially restricted RF. Therefore, the repetitive stimuli we must consider are those which extend 2 or 3 to at most half a dozen cycles. Such local spatial periodicities in the visual world are very common indeed.

Man-Made Periodicities

A large number of manmade objects are obviously spatially periodic. We are not primarily concerned with those in this argument, since our visual system obviously evolved long before the advent of human carpentry. Nonetheless, we might mention in passing such things as corrugated or shingled roofs, regularly repeated windows in houses, brick buildings, pillars, striped, check, or plaid clothing, etc. In fact, a very large proportion of man-made objects are highly periodic, and their visual images thus contain much redundant information.

Biological Periodicities

Those decreasing numbers of the human race who live among trees, grass, or sand probably encounter at least as many highly periodic spatial patterns as their city relatives. Most plants have highly repetitive structures. The leaves of bushes, ferns, and trees and the needles of evergreens tend to be numerous, to differ in size from plant to plant, and to be arranged in fairly regular patterns on a single plant. Most plants thus present quite periodic visual patterns, and the dominant spatial frequencies are a highly distinguishing characteristic (see Figure 12.2).

There are good biological reasons for plants to have repetitive structures. For example, if the leaves were too far apart the amount of photosynthesizing surface would be decreased; if too close together they would shade each other. Leaves and needles are therefore often arranged in a regular fashion along a branch. Further, the spacing of leaves tends to be proportional to their width. Thus thin pine needles are much closer together than large maple leaves, for instance. In a given country or jungle scene there may be literally thousands of leaves in view. To specify such a scene by the location and orientation and direction of each edge would require an immense number of cells. Because of the periodicities, however, the patterns can be summarized much more economically by their respective local spatial frequency spectra.

The biological constraints underlying the periodicity of leaf patterns apply to a lesser extent to the branches of trees as well, which therefore tend to be somewhat regularly spaced. The same is true for the spacing of individual trees in a forest. Again, simple biological factors that act to produce periodicities can be readily found. If a tree grows too close to another it will be shaded. If it grows too far away it will lack protection from wind and/or provide an opening in which another tree will grow. Therefore trees tend to assume somewhat regular patterns in a forest, the spacing of their trunks depending on the type of tree (and doubtless other factors). The same is also the case with grass. Again, such very redundant periodic patterns can be much more economically encoded in the frequency domain than in the pure space domain.

FIG. 12.2   Examples of naturally occurring periodic patterns in plants. The very regular spacing of leaves, as in these examples, is representative of many varieties of plants.

There are also spatial periodicities in the fine structures of animals. Among the countless examples that come readily to mind are the hairs on the body surface, birds' feathers, scales (see Figure 12.3), wrinkle patterns in the skin, the segments of segmented animals, legs of centipedes. We would submit that such periodic structures are the norm not the exception. Many biological constraints doubtless operate to produce them. One is related to a consideration we discussed with respect to visual spatial frequency encoding: it is genetically easier to specify a regular, repetitive pattern than a highly aperiodic one. For instance, it would require less genetic information to specify that 100 cells all be the same shape and size than that each be different from the others. A periodic pattern is easier for a plant or animal to encode genetically because of its redundancy; for the same reason, it is easier for the visual system to decode such a pattern in the spatial frequency domain.

There are also many highly periodic structures that gain their repetitive character from growth factors. For instance, snails and other animals make regular increments to their shells, which then acquire very periodic appearances. Many other animals, e.g., zebras, tigers, giraffes, have regular markings. This presumably serves to camouflage them in the surrounding vegetation. That their stripes

FIG. 12.3   Naturally occurring periodic patterns in animals. In addition to the numerous striped and spotted animals, there are many others which have very periodic structures of scales or skin, such as crocodiles, lizards, snakes and, as seen in this photograph, armadillos (armadillo kindly provided by E.R. Hafter).

do perform such a function can be considered as further evidence for the high degree of periodicity in the vegetative environment. Altogether, then, there are a number of factors that result in repetitive, periodic, biological structures. The visual images of these patterns can be more economically encoded and analyzed in the spatial frequency domain than in the space domain.

Nonbiological Structures

Visual periodicities are certainly not restricted to the images of biological structures, as common as those are. For instance, many rocks (or whole mountainsides) constitute highly periodic visual stimuli due to stratification from having been laid down in different geological periods. Perhaps the most common mineral periodicities, however, are produced by patches of rocks or regions containing gravel or sand. Such groupings often have elements of roughly the same size, which produce quite periodic patterns. Several factors may operate to produce such groupings of rocks by size. In a river, for instance, progressively smaller stones will be washed further and further downstream so that those that settle at any point may be of approximately constant size. On a beach, waves break rocks into sand, and probabilistic considerations result in particles of about the same size.

Finally, nonbiological spatial periodicities can be produced by the action of wind on water or sand. The results are such highly periodic spatial configurations as ripples on a lake, waves in the sea, and wave formations in blown sand dunes.

We have not attempted to give a comprehensive account of various spatial periodicities or of the physical and biological processes giving rise to them. Our intent is merely to emphasize the ubiquity of such repetitive patterns and the fact that there are many factors that produce periodicities. Indeed, we would suggest that spatially periodic patterns (of limited extent) among visual stimuli are the rule, not the rare exception. They may in fact be as common as temporally periodic auditory patterns. Where spatial periodicities occur, the redundant information can be more economically transmitted by a frequency encoding than by requiring specification of the location of each separate edge or zero-crossing or bar.

Texture

In the preceding sections we listed some of the many repetitive spatial patterns in the natural world. There is an important distinction to be made among such patterns, however, which we would now like to consider. For some stimuli one needs precise spatial frequency and phase information; there are others for which phase is largely or totally irrelevant, the average power in various frequency bands being sufficient. The importance of this distinction is that for the latter patterns, which we will hereafter group together and refer to as "texture," a great further advantage accrues to a frequency encoding, a great economy in the number of units required. It is not clear how phase is encoded by the visual system, but at least two units of different type would be required at each location (see Chapter 8). Eliminating phase information would at least halve the requisite number of cells. If in addition one needed to know only the dominant spatial frequency band in a patch of visual space instead of each of dozens of individual frequency components, a still greater additional economy would be forthcoming.

Consider the examples mentioned above of sand on a beach or the needles on a pine tree. In each case there may be literally millions of edges and contours in a section of the visual field. It would clearly be beyond the capacity of even the enormous primate visual system to encode and process all the vast information about the location, orientation, and direction of each of these millions of edges. But the visual system cannot afford to ignore such complex stimuli, both because of their prevalence and because they contain important visual information. Very precise information may be required about such patterns for useful depth discrimination, for instance. Such information could very well be obtained by a few phase-insensitive complex cells tuned to a few overlapping, rather broad spatial frequency bands at high frequencies. Such cells would only reflect something like the average power within their frequency passbands, but comparing the outputs of a few such cells (at each location) could provide just the information the visual system needs: the average spatial frequency in that region.

One can envision such a texture system functioning in a manner analogous to the way in which the visual system deals with color. Our visual system does not give us precise information about the wavelength distribution of light in a region—far from it. For example, some combination of monochromatic lights of, say, 540 and 640 nm will be indistinguishable from a monochromatic light of 580 nm; or, again, some mixture of 480 and 620 nm will be indistinguishable from some mixture of lights of all wavelengths, etc. There are in fact an infinite number of such chromatic metamers, different wavelength combinations all of which visually appear identical. However, by comparing the outputs of cones each containing one of three pigments with very broad overlapping absorption spectra, the system gains precise—very precise—information about the (weighted) *average* spectral input from a patch of space. This is a far simpler thing for the visual system to do than to determine the actual wavelength distribution, and it is quite sufficient to allow us to distinguish between almost any two colored objects in the real world.

So also, for many (but by no means all) visual purposes knowledge of just the average spatial frequency without phase in a patch of space is sufficient for pattern and depth discrimination. Insofar as this were so, it would constitute a vast simplification for the visual system. A consequence, however, is that one would expect to find many *spatial metamers,* different spatial configurations that look alike. There are such. Consider the examples we have been mentioning of needles on a pine tree and sand on a beach. As the spacings of pine needles are shuffled around by a passing breeze, the spatial frequency and phase distribution in a region are changed without changing the average frequency. The appearance before and after would probably not be discriminated. The *average* spatial frequency is critical to our recognition of the pattern as a pine branch and for depth estimates, but the particular combination of frequencies and phases in a given locus may be largely irrelevant. Or consider a beach on which each successive wave redistributes the sand particles, thus changing the precise spatial waveform but not the average spatial frequencies. We do not notice the difference, for although the average frequency is important for depth discrimination and for recognizing the pattern as being sand, the particular individual frequencies and phases are not important. The stereoscopic patterns shown in Figure 10.6, when viewed monocularly, are examples of such spatial metamers.

Let us return to the main point, which is that in many instances a specification of the overall mean spatial frequency of the pattern in a given locus (which can be done very simply with few units) gives the visual system important information that would be virtually impossible to encode in terms of individual spots or edges. We would emphasize that such a system could be exquisitely sensitive. It does not provide just a crude summary. However, it would be carrying very precise information only about the average spatial frequency of the pattern, just as our color vision is extremely sensitive but only to the average spectral input.

There are at least two types of situations in which such a "texture" system can play an important visual role. One is in the identification of objects. One needs only average frequency, or texture, information to distinguish a pine from an ash from a maple tree, or to tell sand from rocks from grass. There are, in other words, many visual objects for which complex internal contours are not critical identifying characteristics. The frequency-but-not-phase-specific complex cells give the visual system an extremely economical way of dealing with such patterns. Much of the information in such "texture" patterns is at high spatial frequencies, and we note again the finding (R.L. De Valois, Albrecht, & Thorell, 1982; Thorell, De Valois, & Albrecht, 1984) that the striate cells tuned to the highest spatial frequencies tend to be complex cells. However, we should not think of texture as exclusively involving high frequencies. One can readily think of other situations, particularly involving the peripheral retina, in which information about the average spatial frequency (but not all the individual frequency and phase components) would be useful in the low spatial frequency range, as well. For instance, in walking past a forest it is useful to know of the continued presence of tree trunks in the far periphery, but not necessarily to know their precise positions and individual spacing. The average (in this instance, comparatively low) spatial frequency without phase in this peripheral locus would give the requisite information.

Local frequency encoding of "texture" might also play an important simplifying role in monocular depth discrimination. Gibson (1950) has shown that spatiotemporal variations in texture contribute to the perception of the slant of surfaces, of the depth of various objects, and of the direction of movement (he concluded that these were *the* critical cues). For instance, on any complex, fairly uniform surface, such as a sandy area, gravel, or greensward, the density of the texture, or the average spatial frequency, shifts progressively with distance. This can be shown (Gibson, 1950) to provide a powerful monocular cue to depth. Gibson did not attempt to provide physiological explanations of perceptual phenomena, but we can readily see how a minimal number of complex cells tuned to different spatial frequency bands within each patch of cortex could provide this important depth information. To analyze such a pattern on the basis of the spatial locations of individual edges or other features would require massive numbers of cells.

Blur

As discussed in Chapter 2 and shown in Figure 2.9, defocus of the retinal image produces a systematic change in the stimulus spectrum: high spatial frequencies are progressively attenuated more than low (Westheimer, 1964). Spherical and chromatic aberrations of the eye have similar effects. Certain clinical conditions such as cataracts can similarly selectively attenuate high spatial frequencies. Finally, atmospheric blur, produced by particles in the air and thus accentuated with increasing distance from the object, also attenuates mainly high spatial frequencies.

Since blur produces systematic changes in the spatial frequency spectrum but not in bar width or edge location (although edge sharpness is reduced, of course), a spatial frequency encoding of the image could provide a number of advantages for the visual system. We shall enumerate and briefly discuss what we see as some of these advantages.

A major problem for the visual system is that of maintaining visual stimuli in focus through accommodative changes in the lens. The fact that as the spatial frequency increases, the loss of contrast with defocus does also, provides a possible mechanism for detecting the need for accommodative change and determining whether or not the change made is in the correct direction. The system may, for instance, try to maintain a maximum high/low spatial frequency ratio in the retinal image (Switkes, personal communication).

The visual system could also take advantage of the fact that the optical degradation of visual images is systematic in the frequency domain by selectively compensating for it (Georgeson & Sullivan, 1975). Insofar as the visual system analyzes a pattern by means of separate spatial frequency selective channels, it can easily determine the power in each frequency band in a visual region. If, in addition, the system "knows" its optical attenuation characteristic at each spatial frequency, it can potentially compensate for this neurally. For instance, if the eyes' optics degrade 12 c/deg fivefold and 8 c/deg twofold, the system could multiply whatever was detected in the 8-cycle band by 2, and in the 12-cycle band by 5, etc., to produce a much sharper percept than would apparently be permitted by the rather poor optics of the eye. This could be easily accomplished neurally. Suppose, for instance, some unit were summing the outputs from a variety of different spatial frequency channels to detect an edge at given locus. If the axons from the high spatial frequency units were to make synaptic contact on the cell body of this later cell, and units tuned to lower spatial frequencies synapsed progressively farther out along the dendrites, the high frequencies would be given greater effective weight and thus amplified. Note that a prerequisite for this is that the system initially filter the information into different spatial frequency bands. Georgeson and Sullivan have not only suggested this possible role for spatial frequency analysis, but have presented psychophysical data which suggest that the visual system may be doing something of the sort.

Finally, the blurring of patterns in the distance, one of the classic monocular cues to depth, would be easily and economically detected with a system containing multiple spatial frequency channels. Again, to do this with a system of edge detectors, for instance, would be more difficult.

Invariance of Low-Frequency Information

We have been discussing the consequences of the fact that optical blur mainly affects high spatial frequencies. The opposite side of this coin is that various factors which blur the optical image minimally affect low spatial frequencies. Low spatial frequency information thus potentially provides the visual system with constant features in a scene. A general problem for perception, of which this is only a small part, is that of constancy. How do we perceive objects as being the same from one situation to another, despite the presence of many changes in the retinal image? Among these changes are variations in the sharpness of the image. But insofar as the visual system analyzes a scene into separate spatial frequency channels, the low-frequency channels' outputs would remain relatively constant, thus providing a possible basis for some perceptual constancies.

Bridging Gaps

The receptor array throughout the retina is fairly regular. Outside the fovea, however, there are numerous blood vessels shading some of the receptors, producing, in effect, gaps and irregularities in the receptor array. A more severe problem which produces similar gaps in the field occurs with the death of cells through trauma or aging. There is also, of course, the presence of the optic disk, which bites a 5°-diameter piece out of the receptor array.

All of these factors should produce problems for any highly localized, point-by-point representation of the visual field, in which the location of luminance changes is encoded. Gaps and the shadows of blood vessels introduce false contours. A spatial frequency representation might allow the system to overcome many of these problems. By its very nature, a spatial frequency encoder samples across some (nonpunctate) extent of the retina; it is a spatially distributed rather than a strictly localized representation. A shadow of a blood vessel or a gap in the receptor array would have relatively little effect on the amplitude of some low frequency within the region. The local low spatial frequency representation within the peripheral retina, then, could allow the visual system to bridge gaps in the image array.

Simplicity of Genetic Specification

A major problem for the organism as a whole is that of wiring up a nervous system containing billions of cells with a very limited set of genetic instructions. All sorts of clever stratagems must be employed to accomplish this. One of these surely is to allow as much randomness as possible in wiring. It is much easier to specify that a neuron make random connections with the surrounding neurons than that it make certain highly specific contacts. (Consider, for example, the numbers of instructions required to wire up and program a computer to carry out even much simpler tasks.)

A random distribution of excitatory inputs, plus a larger but again random set of inhibitory inputs, would give a retinal ganglion cell a center-surround RF organization, such as Rodieck and Stone (1965) modeled as the difference of two gaussians. Such an RF acts as a broadly tuned bandpass spatial frequency filter, as we have pointed out (Chapter 3). A further subtraction of two of these can lead to the narrow bandpass tuning characteristics of narrowly tuned cortical cells. Cells with narrow spatial frequency tuning can thus be made with a minimum of specification.

To produce cells that are true bar detectors or ones that would only respond to an edge would require a more complex RF, one not made up of simple, gaussian distributions. So it may be that one pressure to develop a system of local spatial-frequency-tuned units came from the fact that this is a very simple network and thus one that the organism can build with its very limited number of wiring instructions.

Spatial Filtering Useful for Stereopsis

Julesz's (1971) study of random dot stereograms has clearly identified a serious problem faced by the visual system, that of accomplishing global stereopsis. Given the huge number of edges and contours in the visual image in each eye, how does the visual system determine which contour in one eye to associate with which in the other at each point in the visual field? Julesz (1971) and Nelson (1975) each developed models dependent on interactions among local stereopsis units to accomplish this. Marr and Poggio (1976) demonstrated that a mechanism similar to that proposed by Nelson could indeed be made to work in a computer simulation, but that it was very slow and cumbersome. In a later simulation, Marr and Poggio showed that the process of global stereopsis could be greatly facilitated if a stage of spatial frequency filtering preceded the level of binocular comparison. Matching the low-frequency patterns from each eye is fairly simple, and once accomplished it resolves much of the ambiguity in comparing the binocular information from other spatial frequency bands. Such a mechanism was found to be much more efficient than one operating purely in the space domain, comparing individual contours.

WHY LOCAL (RATHER THAN GLOBAL) SPATIAL FREQUENCY FILTERING?

Throughout this book, we have been presenting psychophysical, physiological, and anatomical evidence that the visual system up to and at the level of the striate cortex performs a local, patch-by-patch spatial frequency filtering of the visual information, rather than the global Fourier analysis proposed, for instance, by Kabrisky (1966). We would like here to consider some of the reasons why local rather than global processing might be advantageous.

Only Local Texture Information Useful

We suggested above that a spatial frequency analysis would be a particularly useful and economical way to extract information from complex textured surfaces. Such texture information could be used by the system both to identify objects and as a powerful cue to the depth and slant of the textured surface. Texture information, however, would only be useful on a local basis. A global analysis giving the average spatial frequency over a whole section of beach would not allow one to identify its slant, for instance, or to determine that regions higher and higher in the visual field are progressively farther and farther away. For that purpose, what is required is the average spatial frequency within each of a series of patches. Such an analysis would reveal a gradual shift to higher and higher frequencies (and therefore greater distances) the higher the location in the visual field. The same argument holds, of course, for the use of texture information to determine the slant of a surface.

Spatial Localization of Objects in the "Real" World

In a global, two-dimensional Fourier analysis, the frequencies and phases at any given orientation would be determined by the visual stimulation at every point across the visual field. A change anywhere in the field would therefore produce a change in the global frequency spectrum. For the most part, the visual world is made up of unchanging objects: trees, rocks, ground. It would be a vast simplification if the unchanging background could be visually decoded and stored just once, to allow the system to concentrate on just the small fraction of the world which is changing. Breaking up the visual representation into parts by doing a local patch-by-patch analysis would facilitate this sort of simplification of the visual problem.

Not only is the world made up objects, but those objects are for the most part spatially compact. That is to say, all of the parts that go together to make a functional object tend to be adjacent to each other. A rare exception to this would be a spider web, which is spatially dispersed, with other objects to be seen in the midst of it (through it). But since most objects are compact, they can most readily be dealt with on a local basis.

Three-Dimensional Transformations Solvable on a Local Basis

One of the considerable problems that the visual system must solve is how to maintain object constancy in the presence of three-dimensional transformations of objects. Almost any object presents very different two-dimensional retinal images as it is viewed from different locations in space. For instance, viewed from one angle, a table top is a rectangle; from other angles, its image would be projected onto the retina as one of a variety of trapezoids. From one angle the legs would come off at right angles with respect to the top; at other angles of regard they would come off at quite different angles. The question is, how do we perceive all of these very different retinal images as being that of the same table? It is beyond the scope of this book to discuss this complex and fascinating question at length; we raise the issue here only because of its relevance to the issue of local versus global analysis. The geometrical transformations which the two-dimensional image of an object undergoes as it rotates in three dimensions are predictable and solvable. There are many computer programs that allow one to manipulate an "object" that has been produced on a display monitor by rotating it in three dimensions. The visual system, operating similar algorithms in reverse, could potentially identify a set of two-dimensional retinal patterns as having been produced by particular three-dimensional positions of a specific object. However, such solutions depend upon breaking the field into spatially localized objects. The transformations in the total field produced by objects at various three-dimensional positions would be a quite different problem, possibly an insolvable one.

Illuminant Must be Locally Evaluated

We have discussed above and in Chapter 5 how attenuation of near-zero spatial frequencies can aid the visual system's segregation of variations due to visual objects from those due to the illuminant. The mean light level, in other words, is largely due to the time of day, not to the presence of any particular object in the field. It can thus be largely ignored. However, when one considers the prevalence of shadows in any visual environment other than desert or ocean, it is clear that the illuminant needs to be evaluated on a local basis. It is not the mean across the whole field, but the regional mean which needs to be subtracted out, since the level of illumination in and out of shadows may be quite different.

It is apparent that the visual system in fact compensates for the local, not the global, illumination level. A piece of white paper in deep shadow on a sunny day looks white, and a piece of coal in a sunny part of the same scene looks black. Photometric measurements would reveal more light reflected from the coal than from the paper. The color (and brightness) appearance thus cannot be attributed to the objects' luminances relative to the overall level. But it is obvious that the paper reflects much more and the coal much less than their immediate backgrounds. Thus it is clear that the contribution of the illuminant is being evaluated on a local, patch-by-patch basis.

Limits to Growth and Interaction

A rather mundane but nonetheless possibly crucial consideration is that a global analysis of the visual scene (whether a Fourier-type analysis or some other) would involve interactions among units in all parts of the striate cortex, those receiving input from all retinal regions. The sheer extent and complexity of the wiring required for such extensive interconnections might be beyond the capabilities of the nervous system. A local spatial frequency filtering, on the other hand, would require only spatially limited interconnections within the cortex. Although more widespread connections occur in later visual regions, it is clear that within the striate cortex most neuronal processes connect only with other neurons in a fairly localized region.

Visual World is Locally, but Not Globally, Periodic

We suggested above that one argument for encoding visual information in terms of spatial frequency is that the visual world is periodic and can thus be more efficiently encoded in the spatial frequency domain than in the pure space domain. However, insofar as visual patterns are only *locally* periodic, a local but not a global frequency analysis would take advantage of such redundant patterns. It may well be that spatial periodicities in fact rarely extend over more than a small fraction of the visual field. Thus spatially localized, patch-by-patch spatial frequency encoding would be most adaptive, more so than more global processing.

References

Abney, W. deW. (1913). *Researches in colour vision.* London: Longmans, Green.

Abney, W. deW., & Festing, E.R. (1886). Colour photometry. *Phil. Trans. R. Soc. Lond., 177,* 423–456.

Adler, F.H. (1965). *Physiology of the eye.* St. Louis: Mosby.

Albrecht, D.G. (1978). *Analysis of visual form.* Doctoral dissertation, University of California, Berkeley.

Albrecht, D.G., & De Valois, R.L. (1981). Striate cortex responses to periodic patterns with and without the fundamental harmonics. *J. Physiol. (Lond.), 319,* 497–514.

Albrecht, D.G., & Hamilton, D.B. (1982). Striate cortex of monkey and man: contrast response function. *J. Neurophysiol., 48,* 217–237.

Albrecht, D.G., De Valois, R.L., & Thorell, L.G. (1980). Visual cortical neurons: Are bars or gratings the optimal stimuli? *Science, 207,* 88–90.

Albrecht, D.G., Farrar, S.B., & Hamilton, D.B. (1984). Spatial contrast adaptation characteristics of neurones recorded in the cat's visual cortex. *J. Physiol. (Lond.), 347,* 713–739.

Albus, K. (1975). A quantitative study of the projection area of the central and paracentral visual field in area 17 of the cat. I. The precision of topography. *Exp. Brain Res., 24,* 159–179.

Allman, J.M., Baker, J.F., Newsome, W.T., & Petersen, S.E. (1981). Visual topography and function: Cortical visual areas in the owl monkey. In C.N. Woolsey (Ed.), *Cortical sensory organization: Vol. 2. Multiple visual areas* (pp. 171–185). Clifton, NJ: Humana Press.

Andrews, B.W., & Pollen, D.A. (1979). Relationship between spatial frequency selectivity and receptive field profile of simple cells. *J. Physiol. (Lond.), 287,* 163–176.

Applegate, R., & Bonds, A.B. (1981). Induced movement of receptor alignment toward new pupillary aperture. *Invest. Ophthalmol. Vis. Sci., 21,* 869–873.

Arend, L.E., & Skavenski, A.A. (1979). Free scanning of gratings produces patterned retinal exposure. *Vision Res., 19,* 1413–1419.

Attneave, F. (1954). Informational aspects of visual perception. *Psychol. Rev., 61,* 183–193.

Bacon, J.H. (1976). The interaction of dichoptically presented gratings. *Vision Res., 16,* 337–394.

Badcock, D.R. (1984a). Spatial phase or luminance profile discrimination? *Vision Res., 24,* 613–623.

Badcock, D.R. (1984b). How do we discriminate relative spatial phase? *Vision Res., 24,* 1847–1857.

Bailey, I.L., & Lovie, J.E. (1976). New design principles for visual acuity letter charts. *Am. J. Optom. Physiol. Opt., 53,* 741–745.

Barlow, H.B. (1953). Summation and inhibition in the frog's retina. *J. Physiol. (Lond.), 119,* 69–88.

Barlow, H.B. (1961). Three points about lateral inhibition. In W.A. Rosenblith (Ed.), *Sensory communication* (pp. 782–786). New York: Wiley.

Barlow, H.B. (1972). Single units and sensation: A neuron doctrine for perceptual psychology? *Perception, 1,* 371–394.

Barlow, H.B. (1979). Reconstructing the visual image in time and space. *Nature, 279,* 189–190.

Barlow, H.B. (1981). Critical limiting factors in the design of the eye and visual cortex. *Proc. Roy. Soc. (B), 212,* 1–34.

Barlow, H.B., Blakemore, C., & Pettigrew, J.D. (1967). The neural mechanism of binocular depth discrimination. *J. Physiol. (Lond.), 193,* 327–342.

Baylor, D.A., & Fuortes, M.G.F. (1970). Electrical responses of single cones in the retina of the turtle. *J. Physiol. (Lond.), 207,* 77–92.

Baylor, D.A., & Hodgkin, A.L. (1973). Detection and resolution of visual stimuli by turtle photoreceptors. *J. Physiol. (Lond.), 234,* 163–198.

Baylor, D.A., Fuortes, M.G.F., & O'Bryan, P.M. (1971). Receptive fields of cones in the retina of the turtle. *J. Physiol. (Lond.), 214,* 265–294.

Berman, N., & Payne, B.R. (1982). Variation in response properties of cortical neurons with locations in the visual field. *Invest. Ophthalmol. Vis. Sci. (Suppl.), 22,* 11.

Bishop, P.O. (1978). Orientation and position disparities in stereopsis. In S.J. Cool & E.L. Smith (Eds.), *Frontiers in visual science* (pp. 336–350). New York: Springer Verlag.

Blake, R., Cool, S.J., & Crawford, M.L.J. (1974). Visual resolution in the cat. *Vision Res., 14,* 1211–1217.

Blakemore, C. (1970). A new kind of stereoscopic vision. *Vision Res., 10,* 1181–1199.

Blakemore, C., & Campbell, F.W. (1969). On the existence of neurones in the human visual system selectively sensitive to the orientation and size of retinal images. *J. Physiol. (Lond.), 203,* 237–260.

Blakemore, C., & Nachmias, J. (1971). The orientation specificity of two visual after-effects. *J. Physiol. (Lond.), 213,* 157–174.

Blakemore, C., & Sutton, P. (1969). Size adaptation A new aftereffect. *Science, 166,* 245–247.

Blakemore, C., & Tobin, E.A. (1972). Lateral inhibition between orientation detectors in the cat's visual cortex. *Exp. Brain Res., 15,* 439–440.

Blakemore, C., Carpenter, R.H.S., & Georgeson, M.A. (1970). Lateral inhibition between orientation detectors in the human visual system. *Nature, 228,* 37–39.

Blakemore, C., Fiorentini, A., & Maffei, L. (1972). A second neural mechanism of binocular depth discrimination. *J. Physiol. (Lond.), 226,* 725–749.

Blakemore, C., Muncey, J.P.J., & Ridley, R.M. (1971). Perceptual fading of a stabilized cortical image. *Nature, 233,* 204–205.

Blakemore, C., Muncey, J.P.J., & Ridley, R.M. (1973). Stimulus specificity in the human visual system. *Vision Res., 13,* 1915–1931.

Blakemore, C., Nachmias, J., & Sutton, P. (1970). The perceived spatial frequency shift: Evidence for frequency-selective neurones in the human brain. *J. Physiol. (Lond.), 210,* 727–750.

Bonds, A.B. (1984). Spatial adaptation of the cortical visual evoked potential of the cat. *Invest. Ophthalmol. Vis. Sci., 25,* 640–646.

Bonds, A.B., & MacLeod, D.I.A. (1978). A displaced Stiles–Crawford effect associated with an eccentric pupil. *Invest. Ophthalmol. Vis. Sci., 17,* 754–761.

Borwein, B. (1981). The retinal receptor: A description. In J.M. Enoch & F.L. Tobey, Jr. (Eds.), *Vertebrate photoreceptor optics* (pp. 11–81). Berlin: Springer Verlag.

Borwein, B., Borwein, D., Medeiros, J., & McGowan, J. (1980). The ultrastructure of monkey foveal photoreceptors, with special reference to the structure, shape, size, and spacing of foveal cones. *Am. J. Anat., 159,* 125–146.

Bough, E.W. (1970). Stereoscopic vision in the macaque monkey: A behavioural demonstration. *Nature, 225,* 42–44.

Bowmaker, J.K., Dartnall, H.J.A., & Mollon, J.D. (1980). Microspectrophotometric demonstration of four classes of photoreceptors in an old world primate *Macaca fascicularis. J. Physiol. (Lond.), 298,* 131–143.

Boycott, B.B., & Dowling, J.E. (1969). Organization of the primate retina: Light microscopy. *Phil. Trans. R. Soc. Lond. (B), 255,* 109–184.

Boycott, B.B., & Kolb, H. (1973). The horizontal cells of the rhesus monkey retina. *J. Comp. Neurol., 148,* 115–140.

Boycott, B.B., & Wässle, H. (1974). The morphological types of ganglion cells of the domestic cat's retina. *J. Physiol. (Lond.), 240,* 397–419.

Boynton, R.M. (1979). *Human color vision.* New York: Holt, Rinehart & Winston.

Boynton, R.M., & Kaiser, P.K. (1968). Vision: The additivity law made to work for heterochromatic photometry with bipartite fields. *Science, 161,* 366–368.

Boynton, R.M., Hayhoe, M.M., & MacLeod, D.I.A. (1977). The gap effect: Chromatic and achromatic visual discrimination as affected by field separation. *Optica Acta, 24,* 159–177.

Bracewell, R.N. (1965). *The Fourier transform and its application*. New York: McGraw-Hill.

Braddick, O., Campbell, F.W., & Atkinson, J. (1978). Channels in vision: Basic aspects. In R. Held, H.W. Leibowitz, & H.-L. Teuber (Eds.), *Handbook of sensory physiology: Vol. 7* (pp. 3–38). Berlin: Springer Verlag.

Bradley, A., Switkes, E., & De Valois, K.K. (1985). Orientation and spatial frequency selectivity of adaptation to isoluminant color patterns. *Invest. Ophthalmol. Vis. Sci. (Suppl.), 26,* 182.

Brown, J.E., Major, D., & Dowling, J.E. (1966). Synapses of horizontal cells in rabbit and cat retinas. *Science, 153,* 1639–1641.

Brown, K.T., Watanabe, K., & Murakami, M. (1965). The early and late receptor potentials of monkey cones and rods. *Cold Spring Harbor Symp. Quant. Biol., 30,* 457–482.

Bullier, J., & Henry, G.H. (1979a). Ordinal position of neurons in cat striate cortex. *J. Neurophysiol., 42,* 1251–1263.

Bullier, J., & Henry, G.H. (1979b). Neural path taken by afferent streams in striate cortex of the cat. *J. Neurophysiol., 42,* 1264–1270.

Bullier, J., & Henry, G.H. (1979c). Laminar distribution of first–order neurons and afferent terminals in cat striate cortex. *J. Neurophysiol., 42,* 1271–1281.

Burr, D.C. (1980). Sensitivity to spatial phase. *Vision Res., 20,* 391–396.

Caelli, T.M., & Julesz, B. (1979). Psychophysical evidence for global feature processing in visual texture discrimination. *J. Opt. Soc. Am., 69,* 675–678.

Campbell, F.W., & Green, D.G. (1965). Optical and retinal factors affecting visual resolution. *J. Physiol. (Lond.), 181,* 576–593.

Campbell, F.W., & Gubisch, R.W. (1966). Optical quality of the human eye. *J. Physiol. (Lond.), 186,* 558–578.

Campbell, F.W., & Kulikowski, J.J. (1966). Orientation selectivity of the human visual system. *J. Physiol. (Lond.), 187,* 437–445.

Campbell, F.W., & Robson, J.G. (1968). Application of Fourier analysis to the visibility of gratings. *J. Physiol. (Lond.), 197,* 551–566.

Campbell, F.W., Carpenter, R.H.S., & Levinson, J.Z. (1969). Visibility of aperiodic patterns compared with that of sinusoidal gratings. *J. Physiol. (Lond.), 204,* 283–298.

Campbell, F.W., Cooper, G.F., & Enroth-Cugell, C. (1969). The spatial selectivity of the visual cells of the cat. *J. Physiol. (Lond.), 203,* 223–235.

Campbell, F.W., Kulikowski, J.J., & Levinson, J. (1966). The effect of orientation on the visual resolution of gratings. *J. Physiol. (Lond.), 187,* 427–436.

Cannon, M.W. (1979). Contrast sensation: A linear function of stimulus contrast. *Vision Res., 19,* 1045–1052.

Carlson, C.R., Anderson, C.H., & Moeller, J.R. (1980). Visual illusions without low spatial frequencies. *Invest. Ophthalmol. Vis. Sci. (Suppl.),* 165–166.

Carlson, C.R., Cohen, R.W., & Gorog, I. (1977). Visual processing of simple two–dimensional sine-wave gratings. *Vision Res., 17,* 351–358.

Carter, B.E., & Henning, G.B. (1971). Detection of gratings in narrow–band visual noise. *J. Physiol. (Lond.), 219,* 355–365.

Cavanagh, P. (1982). Functional size invariance is not provided by the cortical magnification factor. *Vision Res., 22,* 1409–1412.

Cavanagh, P., Brussell, E.M., & Stober, S.R. (1981). Evidence against independent processing of black and white pattern features. *Percept. Psychophys., 29,* 423–428.

Cleland, B., Dubin, M.W., & Levick, W.R. (1971). Sustained and transient neurones in the cat's retina and lateral geniculate nucleus. *J. Physiol. (Lond.), 217,* 473–496.

Cohen, A.I. (1970). Further studies on the question of the patency of saccules in outer segments of vertebrate receptors. *Vision Res., 10,* 445–453.

Cohen, A.I., Hall, J.A., & Ferrendelli, J.A. (1978). *J. Gen. Physiol., 71,* 595–612.

Colonnier, M. (1968). Synaptic patterns on different cell types in the different laminae of the cat visual cortex. An electron microscope study. *Brain Res., 9,* 268–287.

Connolly, M., & Van Essen, D. (1984). The representation of the visual field in parvocellular and magnocellular layers of the lateral geniculate nucleus in the macaque monkey. *J. Comp. Neurol., 226,* 544–564.

Cooper, G.F., & Robson, J.G. (1968). Successive transformations of spatial information in the visual system. *IEE Conf. publ., 47,* 134–143.

Copenhagen, D.R., & Owen, W.G. (1976). Coupling between rod photoreceptors in a vertebrate retina. *Nature, 260,* 57–59.

Cornsweet, T.N. (1970). *Visual perception.* New York: Academic Press.

Craik, K.J.W. (1940). The effect of adaptation on subjective brightness. *Proc. R. Soc. Lond. (B), 128,* 232–247.

Crawford, B.H. (1937). The luminous efficiency of light entering the eye pupil at different points and its relation to brightness threshold measurements. *Proc. R. Soc. Lond. (B), 124,* 81–96.

Creutzfeldt, O.D., Kuhnt, U., & Benevento, L.A. (1974). An intracellular analysis of cortical neurons to moving stimuli: Responses in a cooperative neuronal network. *Exp. Brain Res., 21,* 251–274.

Crick, F.H.C., Marr, D.C., & Poggio, T. (1981). An information-processing approach to understanding the visual cortex. In F.O. Schmitt, F.G. Worden, G. Adelman, & S.G. Dennis (Eds.), *The organization of the cerebral cortex* (pp. 505–533). Cambridge, MA: MIT Press.

Cynader, M., & Regan, D. (1978). Neurons in cat parastriate cortex sensitive to the direction of motion in three-dimensional space. *J. Physiol. (Lond.), 274,* 549–569.

Daitch, J.M., & Green, D.G. (1969). Contrast sensitivity of the human peripheral retina. *Vision Res., 9,* 947–952.

Daniel, P.M., & Whitteridge, D. (1961). The representation of the visual field on the cerebral cortex in monkeys. *J. Physiol. (Lond.), 159,* 203–221.

Daugman, J.G. (1980). Two-dimensional spectral analysis of cortical receptive field profiles. *Vision Res., 20,* 847–856.

Dealy, R.S., & Tolhurst, D.J. (1977). Is spatial frequency adaptation an aftereffect of prolonged inhibition? *J. Physiol. (Lond.), 241,* 261–270.

de Lange, H. (1952). Experiments on flicker and some calculations on an electrical analogue of the foveal systems. *Physica, 18,* 935–950.

de Monasterio, F.M., Gouras, P., & Tolhurst, D.J. (1975a). Trichromatic colour opponency in ganglion cells of the rhesus monkey retina. *J. Physiol. (Lond.), 251,* 197–216.

de Monasterio, F.M., Gouras, P., & Tolhurst, D.J. (1975b). Concealed colour opponency in ganglion cells of the rhesus monkey retina. *J. Physiol. (Lond.), 251,* 217–229.

de Monasterio, F.M., Schein, S.J., & McCrane, E.P. (1981). Staining of blue-sensitive cones of the macaque retina by a fluorescent dye. *Science, 213,* 1278–1281.

Derrington, A.M., & Lennie, P. (1984). Spatial and temporal contrast sensitivities of neurones in lateral geniculate nucleus of macaque. *J. Physiol. (Lond.), 357,* 219–240.

Derrington, A.M., Krauskopf, J., & Lennie, P. (1984). Chromatic mechanisms in lateral geniculate nucleus of macaque. *J. Physiol. (Lond.), 357,* 241–265.

De Valois, K.K. (1973). *Phase-and color-specific adaptation.* Doctoral dissertation, Indiana University, Bloomington, Indiana.

De Valois, K.K. (1977a) Independence of black and white: Phase-specific adaptation. *Vision Res., 17,* 209–215.

De Valois, K.K. (1977b). Spatial frequency adaptation can enhance contrast sensitivity. *Vision Res., 17,* 1057–1065.

De Valois, K.K. (1978). Interactions among spatial frequency channels. In S.J. Cool, & E.L. Smith (Eds.), *Frontiers in visual science* (pp. 277–285), New York: Springer Verlag.

De Valois, K.K., & Switkes, E. (1980). Spatial frequency specific interaction of dot patterns and gratings. *Proc. Natl. Acad. Sci. USA, 77,* 662–665.

De Valois, K.K., & Switkes, E. (1983). Simultaneous masking interactions between chromatic and luminance gratings. *J. Opt. Soc. Am., 73,* 11–18.

De Valois, K.K., & Tootell, R.B.H. (1983). Spatial-frequency-specific inhibition in cat striate cortex cells. *J. Physiol. (Lond.), 336,* 359–376.

De Valois, K.K., De Valois, R.L., & Yund, E.W. (1979). Responses of striate cortex cells to grating and checkerboard patterns. *J. Physiol. (Lond.), 291,* 483–505.

De Valois, K.K., von der Heydt, R., Adorjani, Cs., & De Valois, R.L. (1975). A tilt aftereffect in depth. *Assoc. Res. Vision Ophthalmol., 15,* 90.

De Valois, R.L. (1965). Analysis and coding of color vision in the primate visual system. *Cold Spring Harbor Symp. Quant. Biol., 30,* 567–579.

De Valois, R.L. (1972). Processing of intensity and wavelength information by the visual system. *Invest. Ophthalmol., 11,* 417–427.

De Valois, R.L. (1982). Early visual processing: feature detection or spatial filtering? In D.G. Albrecht (Ed.), *Recognition of pattern and form* (pp. 152–174). Berlin: Springer Verlag.

De Valois, R.L., & De Valois, K.K. (1975). Neural coding of color. In E.C. Carterette, & M.P. Friedman (Eds.), *Handbook of perception: Vol. 5,* (pp. 117–166). New York: Academic Press.

De Valois, R.L., & De Valois, K.K. (1986). Phase vs position. *Invest. Ophthalmol. Vis. Sci. (Suppl.), 27,* 342.

De Valois, R.L., & Jacobs, G.H. (1968). Primate color vision. *Science, 162,* 533–540.

De Valois, R.L., & Jacobs, G.H. (1984). Neural mechanisms of color vision. In J.M. Brookhart & V.B. Mountcastle (Eds.), *Handbook of physiology—The nervous system III* (pp. 425–456). Bethesda, MD: American Physiological Society.

De Valois, R.L., Abramov, I., & Jacobs, G.H. (1966). Analysis of response patterns of LGN cells. *J. Opt. Soc. Am., 56,* 966–977.

De Valois, R.L., Albrecht, D.G. & Thorell, L.G. (1977). Spatial tuning of LGN and cortical cells in the monkey visual system. In H. Spekreijse & H. van der Tweel (Eds.), *Spatial contrast* (pp. 60–63). Amsterdam: Elsevier.

De Valois, R.L., Albrecht, D.G., & Thorell, L.G. (1978). Cortical cells: bar and edge detectors, or spatial frequency filters? In S.J. Cool & E.L. Smith (Eds.), *Frontiers in visual science* (pp. 544–556). New York: Springer Verlag.

De Valois, R.L., Albrecht, D.G., & Thorell, L.G. (1982). Spatial frequency selectivity of cells in macaque visual cortex. *Vision Res., 22,* 545–559.

De Valois, R.L., Jacobs, G.H., & Abramov, I. (1964). Responses of single cells in visual system to shifts in the wavelength of light. *Science, 146,* 1184–1186.

De Valois, R.L., Jacobs, G.H., & Jones, A.E. (1962). Effects of increments and decrements of light on neural discharge rate. *Science, 136,* 986–988.

De Valois, R.L., Morgan, H., & Snodderly, D.M. (1974). Psychophysical studies of monkey vision III. Spatial luminance contrast sensitivity tests of macaque and human observers. *Vision Res., 14,* 75–81.

De Valois, R.L., Thorell, L.G., & Albrecht, D.G. (1985). Periodicity of striate-cortex-cell receptive fields. *J. Opt. Soc. Am. A, 2,* 1115–1123.

De Valois, R.L., Yund, E.W., & Hepler, N. (1982). The orientation and direction selectivity of cells in macaque visual cortex. *Vision Res., 22,* 531–544.

De Valois, R.L., De Valois, K.K., Ready, J., & von Blanckensee, H. (1975). Spatial frequency tuning of macaque striate cortex cells. *Assoc. Res., Vision Ophthalmol., 15,* 16.

De Valois, R.L., Morgan, H., Polson, M.C., Mead, W.R., & Hull, E.M. (1974). Psychophysical studies of monkey vision. I. Macaque luminosity and color vision tests. *Vision Res., 14,* 53–67.

De Valois, R.L., Smith, C.J., Karoly, A.J., & Kitai, S.T. (1958). Electrical responses of primate visual system, I. Different layers of macaque lateral geniculate nucleus. *J. Comp. Physiol. Psychol., 51,* 662–668.

De Valois, R.L., Smith, C.J., Kitai, S.T., & Karoly, A.J. (1958). Responses of single cells in different layers of the primate lateral geniculate nucleus to monochromatic light. *Science, 127,* 238–239.

De Valois, R.L., Snodderly, D.M., Yund, E.W., & Hepler, N. (1977). Responses of macaque lateral geniculate cells to luminance and color figures. *Sensory Processes, 1,* 244–259.

De Valois, R.L., Webster, M.A., De Valois, K.K., & Lingelbach, B. (1986). Temporal properties of brightness and color induction. *Vision Res., 26,* 887–897.

De Vries, H. (1943). The quantum character of light and its bearing upon the threshold of vision, the differential sensitivity and the acuity of the eye. *Physica, 10,* 553–564.

Ditchburn, R.W., & Ginsborg, B.L. (1952). Vision with a stabilized retinal image. *Nature, 170,* 36–37.

Dow, B.M. (1974). Functional classes of cells and their laminar distribution in monkey visual cortex. *J. Neurophysiol., 37,* 927–946.

Dow, B.M., Snyder, R.G., Vautin, R.G., & Bauer, R. (1981). Magnification factor and receptive field size in foveal striate cortex of the monkey. *Exp. Brain Res., 44,* 213–228.

Dowling, J.E. (1968). Synaptic organization of the frog retina: An electron microscopic analysis comparing the retinas of frogs and primates. *Proc. R. Soc. Lond. (B), 170,* 205–228.

Dowling, J.E., & Boycott, B.B. (1966). Organization of the primate retina: Electron microscopy. *Proc. R. Soc. Lond. (B), 166,* 80–111.

Dowling, J.E., & Ehinger, B. (1975). Synaptic organization of the amine-containing interplexiform cells of the goldfish and cebus monkey retinas. *Science, 188,* 270–273.

Dreher, B., Fukada, Y., and Rodieck, R.W. (1976). Identification, classification and anatomical segregation of cells with X-like and Y-like properties in the lateral geniculate nucleus of Old-World primates. *J. Physiol. (Lond.), 258,* 433–452.

Duncker, K. (1929). Über induzierte Bewegung. *Psychol. Forsch., 12,* 180–259.

Enoch, J. (1961). Nature of transmission of energy in retinal receptors. *J. Opt. Soc. Am., 51,* 1122–1126.

Enoch, J.M., & Birch, D.G. (1981). Inferred positive phototropic activity in human photoreceptors. *Phil. Trans. R. Soc. (B), 291,* 323–351.

Enroth–Cugell, C., & Robson, J.G. (1966). The contrast sensitivity of retinal ganglion cells of the cat. *J. Physiol. (Lond.), 187,* 517–552.

Fain, G.L., Gold, G.H., & Dowling, J.E. (1976). Receptor coupling in the toad retina. *Cold Spring Harbor Symp. Quant. Biol., 40,* 547–561.

Famighetti, E.V., Jr., & Kolb, H. (1976). Structural basis of ON- nand OFF-center responses in retinal ganglion cells. *Science, 194,* 193–195.

Famighetti, E.V., Jr., Kaneko, A., & Tachibana, M. (1977). Neuronal architecture of on and off pathways to ganglion cells in carp retina. *Science, 198,* 1267–1269.

Felton, T.B., Richards, W., & Smith, R.A. (1972). Disparity processing of spatial frequencies in man. *J. Physiol. (Lond.), 225,* 349–362.

Fischer, B. (1973). Overlap of receptive field centers and representation of the visual field in the cat's optic tract. *Vision Res., 13,* 2113–2120.

Fisher, S.K., & Boycott, B.B. (1974). Synaptic connexions made by horizontal cells within the outer plexiform layer of the retina of the cat and rabbit. *Proc. R. Soc. Lond. (B), 186,* 317–331.

Foley, J.M. (1978). Primary depth perception. In R. Held, H.W. Leibowitz, & H.-L. Teuber (Eds.), *Handbook of sensory physiology: Vol. 7* (pp. 181–214). Berlin: Springer Verlag.

Foley, J.M., & Legge, G.E. (1981). Contrast discrimination and near-threshold discrimination in human vision. *Vision Res., 21,* 1041–1053.

Foster, K.H., Gaska, J.P., & Pollen, D.A. (1983). Spatial and temporal frequency selectivity of V1 neurons in the macaque monkey. *Invest. Ophthalmol. Visual Sci. (Suppl.), 22,* 228.

Fox, R., Lehmkuhle, S.W., & Westerdorf, D.H. (1976). Falcon visual acuity. *Science, 192,* 263–265.

Fuortes, M.G.F., Schwartz, E.A., & Simon, E.J. (1973). Colour-dependence of cone responses in the turtle retina. *J. Physiol. (Lond.), 234,* 199–216.

Gabor, D. (1946). Theory of communication. *J. Inst. Elect. Eng. (London), 93,* 429–457.

Geisler, W.S. (1984). The physical limits of acuity and hyperacuity. *Invest. Ophthalmol. Vis. Sci. (Suppl.), 25,* 315.

Georgeson, M.A. (1976). Psychophysical hallucinations of orientation and spatial frequency. *Perception, 5,* 99–112.

Georgeson, M.A., & Sullivan, G.D. (1975). Contrast constancy: Deblurring in human vision by spatial frequency channels. *J. Physiol. (Lond.), 252,* 627–656.

Gibson, J.J. (1950). *The perception of the visual world.* London: Allen and Unwin.

Gilbert, C.D. (1977). Laminar differences in receptive field properties of cells in cat primary visual cortex. *J. Physiol. (Lond.), 268,* 391–424.

Gilbert, C.D., & Wiesel, T.N. (1979). Morphology and intracortical projections of functionally characterised neurones in the cat visual cortex. *Nature, 280,* 120–125.

Gilinsky, A.S. (1968). Orientation–specific effects of patterns of adapting light on visual acuity. *J. Opt. Soc. Am., 58,* 13–18.

Ginsburg, A.P. (1971). *Psychological correlates of a model of the human visual system.* M.A. thesis GE/EE/715-2, Wright-Patterson AFB, Ohio, Air Inst. Technol.

Glezer, V.D., & Cooperman, A.M. (1977). Local spectral analysis in the visual cortex. *Biol. Cybern.,* 28, 101–108.

Glezer, V.D., Ivanoff, V.A., & Tscherbach, T.A. (1973). Investigation of complex and hypercomplex receptive fields of visual cortex of the cat as spatial frequency filters. *Vision Res., 13,* 1875–1904.

Goodman, J.W. (1968). *Introduction to Fourier optics.* New York: McGraw-Hill.

Gouras, P. (1974). Opponent-color cells in different layers of foveal striate cortex. *J. Physiol. (Lond.), 238,* 583–602.

Gouras, P., & Zrenner, E. (1979). Enhancement of luminance flicker by color-opponent mechanisms. *Science, 205,* 587–589.

Graham, N. (1977). Visual detection of aperiodic spatial stimuli by probability summation among narrowband channels. *Vision Res., 17,* 637–652.

Graham, N. (1980). Spatial frequency channels in human vision: detecting edges without edge detectors. In C.S. Harris (Ed.), *Visual coding and adaptability* (pp. 215–262). Hillsdale, NJ: Lawrence Erlbaum Assoc.

Graham, N., & Nachmias, J. (1971). Detection of grating patterns containing two spatial frequencies: A comparison of single channel and multichannel models. *Vision Res., 11,* 251–259.

Graham, N., Robson, J.G., & Nachmias, J. (1978). Grating summation in fovea and periphery. *Vision Res., 18,* 815–825.

Granger, E.M. (1973). *Specification of color image quality.* Doctoral dissertation, University of Rochester, Rochester, New York.

Granger, E.M., & Heurtley, J.C. (1973). Visual chromaticity-modulation transfer function. *J. Opt. Soc. Am., 63,* 1173–1174.

Graybiel, A.M., & Berson, D.M. (1981). On the relation between transthalamic and transcortical pathways in the visual system. In F.O. Schmitt, F.G. Worden, G. Adelman, & S.G. Dennis (Eds.), *The organization of the cerebral cortex* (pp. 285–319). Cambridge, MA: MIT Press.

Green, D.M., & Swets, J.A. (1966). *Signal detection theory and psychophysics.* New York: Wiley.

Green, M., Corwin, T., & Zemon, V. (1976). A comparison of Fourier analysis and feature analysis in pattern-specific color aftereffects. *Science, 192,* 147–148.

Grosof, D.H., Skottun, B.C., & De Valois, R.L. (1985). Linearity of cat cortical cells: Responses to 2-D stimuli. *Invest. Ophthalmol. Vis. Sci. (Suppl.), 26,* 265.

Guilford, J.P., & Dallenbach, K.M. (1928). A study of the autokinetic sensation. *Am. J. Psychol., 40,* 83–91.

Gullstrand, A. (1924). In H. von Helmholtz, *Handbook of physiological optics, vol. 1* (pp. 261–482), (3rd ed., J.P.C. Southall, Trans.). Rochester, NY: Optical Society of America, (Original work published 1909).

Guth, S.L., Donley, N.J., & Marrocco, R.T. (1969). On luminance additivity and related topics. *Vision Res., 9,* 537–575.

Hagins, W.A. (1972). The visual process: Excitatory mechanisms in the primary photoreceptor cells. *Annu. Rev. Biophys. Bioeng., 1,* 131–158.

Hagins, W.A., & Yoshikami, S. (1974). A role for Ca^{++} in excitation of retinal rods and cones. *Exp. Eye Res., 18,* 229–305.

Hammond, P., & MacKay, D.M. (1975). Differential responses of cat visual cortical cells to textured stimuli. *Exp. Brain Res., 22,* 427–430.

Hänny, P., von der Heydt, R., & Poggio, G.F. (1980). Binocular neuron responses to tilt in depth in the monkey visual cortex. Evidence for orientation disparity processing. *Exp. Brain Res., 41,* A26.

Hartline, H.K. (1940). The receptive fields of optic nerve fibers. *Am. J. Physiol., 130,* 690–699.

Helmholtz, H. von (1877). *On the sensations of tone.* New York: Dover (reprinted in 1954)

Helmholtz, H. von (1924). *Handbook of physiological optics* (3rd ed., J.P.C. Southall, Trans.). Rochester, NY: Optical Society of America, (Original work published 1909)

Helson, H. (1963). Studies of anomalous contrast and assimilation. *J. Opt. Soc. Am., 53,* 179–184.

Helstrom, C.W. (1966). An expansion of a signal in Gaussian elementary signals. *IEEE Trans. Inf. Theory, IT-13,* 81–82.

Henning, G.B., Hertz, B.G., & Broadbent, D.E. (1975). Some experiments bearing on the hypothesis that the visual system analyses spatial patterns in independent bands of spatial frequency. *Vision Res., 15,* 887–898.

Henning, G.B., Hertz, B.G., & Hinton, J.L. (1981). Effects of different hypothetical detection mechanisms on the shape of spatial-frequency filters inferred from masking experiments: I. Noise masks. *J. Opt. Soc. Am., 71,* 574–581.

Henry, G.H., & Bishop, P.O. (1972). Striate neurons: Receptive field organization. *Invest. Ophthalmol., 11,* 357–368.

Henry, G.H., Bishop, P.O., & Dreher, B. (1974). Orientation, axis and direction as stimulus parameters for striate cells. *Vision Res., 14,* 767–777.

Henry, G.H., Dreher, B., & Bishop, P.O. (1974). Orientation specificity of cells in cat striate cortex. *J. Neurophysiol., 37,* 1394–1409.

Henry, G.H., Harvey, A.R., & Lund, J.S. (1979). The afferent connections and laminar distribution of cells in the cat striate cortex. *J. Comp. Neurol., 187,* 725–744.

Hess, R., & Woo, G. (1978). Vision through cataracts. *Invest. Ophthalmol. Vis. Sci., 17,* 428–435.

Hicks, T.P., Lee, B.B., & Vidyasagar, T.R. (1983). The response of cells in macaque lateral geniculate nucleus to sinusoidal gratings. *J. Physiol. (Lond.), 337,* 183–200.

Hilz, R.L., & Cavonius, C.R. (1970). Wavelength discrimination measured with square wave gratings. *J. Opt. Soc. Am., 60,* 273–277.

Hilz, R.L., & Cavonius, C.R. (1974). Functional organization of the peripheral retina: Sensitivity to periodic stimuli. *Vision Res., 14,* 1333–1337.

Hitchcock, P.F., & Hickey, T.L. (1980). Ocular dominance columns: Evidence for their presence in humans. *Brain Res., 182,* 176–178.

Hochstein, S., & Shapley, R.M. (1976a). Quantitative analysis of retinal ganglion cell classifications. *J. Physiol. (Lond.), 262,* 237–264.

Hochstein, S., & Shapley, R.M. (1976b). Linear and non-linear spatial subunits in Y cat retinal ganglion cells. *J. Physiol. (Lond.), 262,* 265–284.

Hoffman, K.-P., & Stone, J. (1971). Conduction velocity of afferents to cat visual cortex: A correlation with cortical receptive field properties. *Brain Res., 32,* 460–466.

Hogan, M.J., Alvarado, J.A., and Weddell, J.E. (1971). *Histology of the human eye.* Philadelphia: W.B. Saunders.

Holt, J.J., & Ross, J. (1980). Phase perception in the high spatial frequency range. *Vision Res., 20,* 933–935.

Horton, J.C. (1984). Cytochrome oxidase patches: A new cytoarchitectonic feature of monkey cortex. *Phil. Trans. R. Soc. Lond. (B), 304,* 199–253.

Horton, J.C., & Hedley-White, E.T. (1984). Mapping of cytochrome-oxidase patches and ocular dominance columns in human visual cortex. *Phil. Trans. R. Soc. Lond. (B), 304,* 255–272.

Horton, J.C., & Hubel, D.H. (1981). Regular patchy distribution of cytochrome oxidase staining in primary visual cortex of macaque monkey. *Nature, 292,* 762–764.

Hubbell, W.L., & Bownds, M.D. (1979). Visual transduction in vertebrate photoreceptors. *Annu. Rev. Neurosci., 2,* 17–34.

Hubel, D.H., & Wiesel, T.N. (1959). Receptive fields of single neurones in the cat's striate cortex. *J. Physiol. (Lond.), 148,* 574–591.

Hubel, D.H., & Wiesel, T.N. (1962). Receptive fields, binocular interaction and functional architecture in the cat's visual cortex. *J. Physiol. (Lond.), 160,* 106–154.

Hubel, D.H., & Wiesel, T.N. (1965). Receptive fields and functional architecture in two nonstriate visual areas (18 and 19) of the cat. *J. Neurophysiol., 28,* 229–289.

Hubel, D.H., & Wiesel, T.N. (1967). Cortical and callosal connections concerned with the vertical meridian of visual fields in the cat. *J. Neurophysiol., 30,* 1561–1573.

Hubel, D.H., & Wiesel, T.N. (1968). Receptive fields and functional architecture of monkey striate cortex. *J. Physiol. (Lond.), 195,* 215–243.

Hubel, D.H., & Wiesel, T.N. (1970). Cells sensitive to binocular depth in area 18 of the macaque monkey cortex. *Nature, 225,* 41–42.

Hubel, D.H., & Wiesel, T.N. (1972). Laminar and columnar distribution of geniculo–cortical fibers in the macaque monkey. *J. Comp. Neurol., 146,* 421–450.

Hubel, D.H., & Wiesel, T.N. (1974a). Sequence regularity and geometry of orientation columns in the monkey striate cortex. *J. Comp. Neurol., 158,* 267–294.

Hubel, D.H., & Wiesel, T.N. (1974b). Uniformity of monkey striate cortex: A parallel relationship between field size, scatter and magnification factor. *J. Comp. Neurol., 158,* 295–306.

Hubel, D.H., & Wiesel, T.N. (1977). Functional architecture of macaque visual cortex. *Proc. R. Soc. Lond. (B), 198,* 1–59.

Hubel, D.H., Wiesel, T.N., & Stryker, M.P. (1978). Anatomical demonstration of orientation columns in macaque monkey. *J. Comp. Neurol., 177,* 361–380.

Hurvich, L.M. (1981). *Color vision.* Sunderland, MA: Sinauer Associates.

Hyde, J.E. (1959). Some characteristics of voluntary human ocular movements in the horizontal plane. *Am. J. Ophthalmol., 48,* 85–94.

Ives, H.E. (1912). Studies in the photometry of lights of different colors. IV. The addition of luminosities of different colors. *Phil. Mag., 24,* 845–853.

Ives, H.E. (1922). Critical frequency relations in scotopic vision. *J. Opt. Soc. Am., 6,* 254–268.

Jacobs, G.H. (1965). Effects of adaptation on the lateral geniculate response to light increment and decrement. *J. Opt. Soc. Am., 55,* 1535–1540.

Jacobs, G.H. (1977). Visual capacities of the owl monkey (*Aotus trivirgatus*) —II. Spatial contrast sensitivity. *Vision Res., 17,* 821–825.

Jennings, J.A.M., & Charman, W.N. (1981). Off-axis image quality in the human eye. *Vision Res., 21,* 445–455.

Jones, R.M., & Tulunay-Keesey, U. (1975). Local retinal adaptation and spatial frequency channels. *Vision Res., 15,* 1239–1244.

Julesz, B. (1971). *Foundation of cyclopean perception.* Chicago: University of Chicago Press.

Julesz, B. (1975). Experiments in the visual perception of texture. *Sci. Am., 232,* 34–43.

Julesz, B. (1980). Spatial nonlinearities in the instantaneous perception of textures with identical power spectra. *Phil. Trans. R. Soc. Lond., 290,* 83–94.

Julesz, B., & Schumer, R.A. (1981). Early visual perception. *Annu. Rev. Psychol., 32,* 575–627.

Julesz, B., Gilbert, E.N., & Victor, J.D. (1978). Visual discrimination of textures with identical third-order statistics. *Biol. Cybern., 31,* 137–140.

Kabrisky, M. (1966). *A proposed model for visual information processing in the human brain.* Urbana, IL: University of Illinois Press.

Kaplan, E., & Shapley, R. (1982). X and Y cells in the lateral geniculate nucleus of macaque monkeys. *J. Physiol. (Lond.), 330,* 125–143.

Kato, H., Bishop, P.O., and Orban, G.A. (1978). Hypercomplex and simple/complex cell classifications in cat striate cortex. *J. Neurophysiol., 41,* 1071–1095.

Kelly, D.H. (1961). Visual responses to time-dependent stimuli. I. Amplitude sensitivity measurements. *J. Opt. Soc. Am., 51,* 422–429.

Kelly, D.H. (1974). Spatio-temporal frequency characteristics of color-vision mechanisms. *J. Opt. Soc. Am., 64,* 983–990.

Kelly, D.H. (1975). Luminous and chromatic flickering patterns have opposite effects. *Science, 188,* 371–372.

Kelly, D.H. (1976). Pattern detection and the two-dimensional Fourier transform: Flickering checkerboards and chromatic mechanisms. *Vision Res., 16,* 277–287.

Kelly, D.H. (1979a). Manipulation of two-dimensionally periodic stimulus patterns. *Behav. Res. Methods Instrum., 11,* 26–30.

Kelly, D.H. (1979b). Motion and vision. II. Stabilized spatio-temporal threshold surface. *J. Opt. Soc. Am., 69,* 1340–1349.

Kelly, D.H. (1983). Spatiotemporal variation of chromatic and achromatic contrast thresholds. *J. Opt. Soc. Am., 73,* 742–750.

Kelly, D.H. (1984). Retinal inhomogeneity. I. Spatiotemporal contrast sensitivity. *J. Opt. Soc. Am. A., 1,* 107–113.

Kelly, D.H., & Magnuski, H.S. (1975). Pattern detection and the two-dimensional Fourier transform: Circular targets. *Vision Res., 15,* 911–915.

Kelly, J.P., & Van Essen, D.C. (1974). Cell structure and function in the visual cortex of the cat. *J. Physiol. (Lond.), 238,* 515–547.

Kinsbourne, M., & Harrington, E.K. (1964). Observations on color agnosia. *J. Neurol. Neurosurg. Psychiatry, 27,* 296–299.

Klein, S., Stromeyer, C.F., & Ganz, L. (1974). The simultaneous spatial frequency shift: Dissociation between the detection and perception of gratings. *Vision Res., 14,* 1421–1432.

Koffka, K. (1935). *Principles of gestalt psychology.* New York: Harcourt.

Kohler, W., & Wallach, H. (1944). Figural after-effects: An investigation of visual processes. *Proc. Am. Phil. Soc., 88,* 269–357.

Kuffler, S.W. (1953). Discharge patterns and functional organization of mammalian retina. *J. Neurophysiol., 16,* 37–68.

Kulikowski, J.J. (1971). Effect of eye movements on the contrast sensitivity of spatio-temporal patterns. *Vision Res., 11,* 261–273.

Kulikowski, J.J. (1978). Limit of single vision in stereopsis depends on contour sharpness. *Nature, 275,* 126–127.

Kulikowski, J.J., & Bishop, P.O. (1981). Linear analysis of the responses of simple cells in the cat visual cortex. *Exp. Brain Res., 44,* 386–400.

Kulikowski, J.J., & King-Smith, P.E. (1973). Spatial arrangement of line, edge and grating detectors revealed by subthreshold summation. *Vision Res., 13,* 1455–1478.

Kulikowski, J.J., & Vidyasagar, T.R. (1982). Representation of space and spatial frequency in the macaque striate cortex. *J. Physiol. (Lond.), 332,* 10–11P.

Kulikowski, J.J., Abadi, R.V., & King–Smith, P.E. (1973). Orientation selectivity of grating and line detectors in human vision. *Vision Res., 13,* 1479–1486.

Kulikowski, J.J., Marcelja, S., & Bishop, P.O. (1982). Theory of spatial position and spatial frequency relations in the receptive fields of simple cells in the visual cortex. *Biol. Cybern., 43,* 187–198.

Latour, P.L. (1962). Visual threshold during eye movements. *Vision Res., 2,* 261–262.

Lawden, M.C. (1983). An investigation of the ability of the human visual system to encode spatial phase relationships. *Vision Res., 23,* 1451–1463.

Lee, B.B., Cleland, B.G., & Creutzfeldt, O.D. (1977). The retinal input to cells in area 17 of the cat's cortex. *Exp. Brain Res., 30,* 527–538.

Legge, G.E. (1976). Adaptation to a spatial impulse: Implication for Fourier transform models of visual processing. *Vision Res., 16,* 1407–1418.

Legge, G.E., & Foley, J.M. (1980). Contrast masking of human vision. *J. Opt. Soc. Am., 70,* 1458–1471.

Le Grand, Y. (1957). *Light, colour and vision* (R.W.G. Hunt, J.W.T. Walsh, & F.R.W. Hunt, Trans.). New York: Wiley.

Lennie, P., Derrington, A., & Krauskopf, J. (1982). Spatio-chromatic properties of neurones in the macaque's LGN. *Invest. Ophthalmol. Vis. Sci. (Suppl.), 22,* 10.

Le Vay, S., Hubel, D.H., & Wiesel, T.N. (1975). The patterns of ocular dominance columns in macaque visual cortex revealed by a reduced silver stain. *J. Comp. Neurol., 159,* 559–575.

Leventhal, A.G., Rodieck, R.W., & Dreher, B. (1981). Retinal ganglion cell classes in the Old World monkey: Morphology and central projections. *Science, 213,* 1139–1142.

Levinson, E., & Blake, R. (1979). Stereopsis by harmonic analysis. *Vision Res., 19,* 73–78.

Liebman, P.A., & Pugh, E.N. Jr. (1979). The control of phosphodiesterase in rod disk membranes: kinetics, possible mechanisms and significance for vision. *Vision Res., 19,* 375–380.

Lillywhite, P.G. (1978). Coupling between locust photoreceptors revealed by a study on quantum bumps. *J. Comp. Physiol., 125,* 13–27.

Lindsay, P.M., & Norman, D.A. (1972). *Human information processing.* New York: Academic Press.

Livingstone, M.S., & Hubel, D.H. (1984). Anatomy and physiology of a color system in the primate visual cortex. *J. Neurosci., 4,* 309–356.

Lund, J.S. (1973). Organization of neurons in the visual cortex, area 17, of the monkey (*Macaca mulatta*). *J. Comp. Neurol., 147,* 455–496.

Lund, J.S., Lund, R.D., Hendrickson, A.E., Bunt, A.H., & Fuchs, A.F. (1975). The origin of efferent pathways from primary visual cortex, area 17, of the macaque monkey as shown by retrograde transport of horseradish peroxidase. *J. Comp. Neurol., 164,* 287–304.

MacKay, D.M. (1973). Lateral interactions between neural channels sensitive to texture density? *Nature, 245,* 159–161.

MacKay, D.M. (1981). Strife over visual cortical function. *Nature, 289,* 117–118.

Maffei, L., & Fiorentini, A. (1973). The visual cortex as a spatial frequency analyzer. *Vision Res., 13,* 1255–1267.

Maffei, L., & Fiorentini, A. (1976). The unresponsive regions of visual cortical receptive fields. *Vision Res., 16,* 1131–1139.

Maffei, L., Fiorentini, A., & Bisti, S. (1973). Neural correlates of perceptual adaptation to gratings. *Science, 182,* 1036–1038.

Maffei, L., Morrone, C., Pirchio, M., & Sandini, G. (1979). Responses of visual cortical cells to periodic and non–periodic stimuli. *J. Physiol. (Lond.), 296,* 27–47.

Mansfield, R.J.W. (1974). Neural basis of orientation perception in primate vision. *Science, 186,* 133–135.

Marc, R.E., & Sperling, H.G. (1977). Chromatic organization of primate cones. *Science, 196,* 454–456.

Marcelja, S. (1980). Mathematical description of the responses of simple cortical cells. *J. Opt. Soc. Am., 70,* 1297–1300.

Marr, D. (1982). *Vision.* San Francisco: W.H. Freeman & Co.

Marr, D., & Poggio, T. (1976). Cooperative computation of stereo disparity. *Science, 194,* 283–287.

Marr, D., & Poggio, T. (1979). A computational theory of human stereo vision. *Proc. R. Soc. Lond. (B), 204,* 301–328.

Marron, J.A., & Bailey, I.L. (1982). Visual factors and orientation-mobility performance. *Am. J. Optom. Physiol. Opt., 59,* 413–426.

May, J.G., & Matteson, H.H. (1976). Spatial frequency-contingent color aftereffects. *Science, 192,* 145–147.

Mayhew, J.E.W., & Frisby, J.P. (1976). Rivalrous texture stereograms. *Nature, 264,* 53–56.

McCollough, C. (1965). Color adaptation of edge-detectors in the human visual system. *Science, 149,* 1115–1116.

McKee, S.P., & Westheimer, G. (1978). Improvement in vernier acuity with practice. *Percept. Psychophys., 24,* 258–262.

Michael, C.R. (1978a). Color vision mechanisms in monkey striate cortex: Dual opponent cells with concentric receptive fields. *J. Neurophysiol., 41,* 572–588.

Michael, C.R. (1978b). Color vision mechanisms in monkey striate cortex: Simple cells with dual opponent-color receptive fields. *J. Neurophysiol., 41,* 1233–1249.

Michael, C.R. (1978c). Color-sensitive complex cells in monkey striate cortex. *J. Neurophysiol., 41,* 1250–1266.

Missotten, L. (1974). Estimation of the ratio of cones to neurons in the fovea of the human retina. *Invest. Ophthalmol., 13,* 1045–1049.

Missotten, L.E., & van den Dooren, E. (1966). L'ultrastructure de la retine humaine. Les contacts lateraux des pedoncules de cônes de la fovea. *Bull. Soc. Belge Ophthalmol., 144,* 800–805.

Mitchell, D.E. (1969). Qualitative depth localization with diplopic images of dissimilar shape. *Vision Res., 9,* 991–993.

Mitchell, O.R. (1976). Effect of spatial frequency on the visibility of unstructured patterns. *J. Opt. Soc. Am., 66,* 327–332.

Morrone, M.C., Burr, D.C., & Maffei, L. (1982). Functional implications of cross-orientation inhibition of cortical visual cells. I. Neurophysiological evidence. *Proc. R. Soc. Lond. (B), 216,* 335–354.

Movshon, J.A. (1975). Velocity tuning of single units in cat striate cortex. *J. Physiol. (Lond.), 249,* 445–468.

Movshon, J.A., & Blakemore, C. (1973). Orientation specificity and spatial selectivity in human vision. *Perception, 2,* 53–60.

Movshon, J.A., & Lennie, P. (1979a). Pattern–selective adaptation in visual cortical neurones. *Nature, 278,* 850–852.

Movshon, J.A., & Lennie, P. (1979b). Spatially selective adaptation in cat striate cortical neurons. *Invest. Ophthalmol. Vis. Sci. (Suppl.), 18,* 135.

Movshon, J.A., Bonds, A.B., & Lennie, P. (1980). Pattern adaptation in striate cortical neurons. *Invest. Ophthalmol. Vis. Sci. (Suppl.), 19,* 93.

Movshon, J.A., Thompson, I.D., & Tolhurst, D.J. (1978a) Spatial summation in the receptive fields of simple cells in the cat's striate cortex. *J. Physiol. (Lond.), 283,* 53–77.

Movshon, J.A., Thompson, I.D., & Tolhurst, D.J. (1978b). Receptive field organization of complex cells in the cat's striate cortex. *J. Physiol. (Lond.), 283,* 79–99.

Movshon, J.A., Thompson, I.D., & Tolhurst, D.J. (1978c). Spatial and temporal contrast sensitivity of neurones in areas 17 and 18 of the cat's visual cortex. *J. Physiol. (Lond.), 283,* 101–120.

Movshon, J.A., Adelson, E.H., Gizzi, M.S., & Newsome, W.T. (1985). The analysis of moving visual patterns. In C. Chagas, R. Gattass, & C. Gross (Eds.), *Pattern recognition mechanisms, (Pontificiae Academiae Scientiarum Scripta Varia, 54)* (pp. 117–151). Rome: Vatican Press.

Mullen, K.T. (1985). The contrast sensitivity of human colour vision to red-green and blue-yellow chromatic gratings. *J. Physiol. (Lond.), 359,* 382–400.

Mullikin, W.H., Jones, J.P., & Palmer, L.A. (1984). Periodic simple cells in cat area 17. *J. Neurophysiol., 52,* 372–387.

Myers, R.E. (1962). Commissural connections between occipital lobes of the monkey. *J. Comp. Neurol., 118,* 1–16.

Myerson, J., Manis, P.B., Miezin, F.M., & Allman, J.M. (1977). Magnification in striate cortex and retinal ganglion cell layer of owl monkey: A quantitative comparison. *Science, 198,* 855–857.

Nachmias, J., & Weber, A. (1975). Discrimination of simple and complex gratings. *Vision Res., 15,* 217–224.

Nachmias, J., Sansbury, R., Vassilev, A., & Weber, A. (1973). Adaptations to square-wave gratings: In search of the elusive third harmonic. *Visions Res.,* 13, 1335–1342.

Neisser, U. (1967). *Cognitive psychology.* New York: Appleton Press.

Nelson, J.I. (1975). Globality and stereoscopic fusion in binocular vision. *J. Theor. Biol., 49,* 1–88.

Nelson, J.I., & Frost, B.J. (1978). Orientation-selective inhibition from beyond the classic visual receptive field. *Brain Res., 139,* 359–365.

Nelson, R., Famighetti, E.V., Jr., & Kolb, H. (1978). Intracellular staining reveals different levels of stratification for on- and off-center ganglion cells in the cat retina. *J. Neurophysiol., 41,* 472–483.

Nikara, T., Bishop, P.O., & Pettigrew, J.D. (1968). Analysis of retinal correspondence by studying receptive fields of binocular single units in cat striate cortex. *Exp. Brain Res., 6,* 353–372.

Norman, R.A., & Werblin, F.S. (1974). Control of retinal sensitivity. I. Light and dark adaptation of vertebrate rods and cones. *J. Gen. Physiol., 63,* 37–61.

Northmore, D.P.M., & Dvorak, C.A. (1979). Contrast sensitivity and acuity of the goldfish. *Vision Res., 19,* 255–261.

Ochs, A.L. (1979). Is Fourier analysis performed by the visual system or by the visual investigator? *J. Opt. Soc. Am., 69,* 95–98.

Ohm, G.S. (1843). Ueber die Definition des Tones, nebst daran geknupfter Theorie der Sirene und ahnlicher tonbildener Vorrichtungen. *Ann. Phys. Chem., 135,* 497–565.

Ohzawa, I., Sclar, G., & Freeman, R.D. (1982). Contrast gain control in the cat's visual cortex. *Nature, 298,* 5871–5872.

Ohzu, H., & Enoch, J.M. (1972). Optical modulation by the isolated human fovea. *Vision Res., 12,* 245–251.

Ohzu, H., Enoch, J.M., & O'Hair, J. (1972). Optical modulation by the isolated retina and retinal receptors. *Vision Res., 12,* 231–244.

Østerberg, G.A. (1935). Topography of the layer of rods and cones in the human retina. *Acta Ophthalmol. (Suppl.), 6,* 1–102.

Pantle, A. (1974). *Visual information processing of complex imagery.* Report AMRL-TR-74-43. Aerospace Medical Research Laboratory, Wright–Patterson Air Force Base, Ohio.

Pantle, A., & Sekuler, R. (1968). Size detecting mechanisms in human vision. *Science, 162,* 1146–1148.

Patel, A.S. (1966). Spatial resolution by the human visual system. *J. Opt. Soc. Am., 56,* 689–694.

Patmos, P., & van Norren, D. (1975). Cone systems interaction in single neurons of the lateral genic-ulate nucleus of the macaque. *Vision Res., 15,* 617–619.

Peichl, L., & Wässle, H. (1979). Size, scatter and coverage of ganglion cell receptive field centers in the cat retina. *J. Physiol. (Lond.), 291,* 117–141.

Perry, V.H., & Cowey, A. (1985). The ganglion cell and cone distributions in the monkey's retina: Implications for central magnification factors. *Vision Res., 25,* 1795–1810.

Pettigrew, J.D. (1973). Binocular neurones which signal change of disparity in area 18 of cat visual cortex. *Nature, 241,* 123–124.

Pieron, H. (1939). La dissociation de l'adaptation lumineuse et de l'adaptation chromatique. *Ann. Psychol., 40,* 1–14.

Pinto, L.H., & Pak, W.L. (1974). Light-induced changes in photoreceptor membrane resistance and potential in gecko retinas. I. Preparations with active lateral interactions. *J. Gen. Physiol., 64,* 49–69.

Poggio, G.F., & Fischer, B. (1977). Binocular interaction and depth sensitivity of striate and prestriate cortical neurons of behaving rhesus monkeys. *J. Neurophysiol., 40,* 1392–1405.

Poggio, G.F., Baker, F.H., Mansfield, R.J.W., Sillito, A., & Grigg, P. (1975). Spatial and chromatic properties of neurons subserving foveal and parafoveal vision in rhesus monkey. *Brain Res., 100,* 25–59.

Pollen, D.A., & Ronner, S.F. (1981). Phase relationships between adjacent simple cells in the visual cortex. *Science, 212,* 1409–1411.

Pollen, D.A., & Ronner, S.F. (1982). Spatial computation performed by simple and complex cells in the visual cortex of the cat. *Visual Res., 22,* 101–118.

Polyak, S. (1957). *The vertebrate visual system.* Chicago: University of Chicago Press.

Ratliff, F. (1965). *Mach bands: Quantitative studies on neural networks in the retina.* San Francisco: Holden-Day.

Ratliff, F., Knight, B.W., Toyoda, J., & Hartline, H.K. (1967). Enhancement of flicker by lateral inhib-ition. *Science, 158,* 392–393.

Raviola, E., & Gilula, N.B. (1973). Gap junctions between photoreceptor cells in the vertebrate retina. *Proc. Natl. Acad. Sci. USA, 70,* 1677–1681.

Regan, D., & Beverley, K.I. (1978). Looming detectors in the human visual pathway. *Vision Res., 18,* 415–421.

Regan, D., & Cynader, M. (1979). Neurons in area 18 of cat visual cortex selectively sensitive to changing size: Nonlinear interactions between responses to two edges. *Vision Res., 19,* 699–711.

Regan, D., & Neima, D. (1983). Low–contrast letter charts as a test of visual function. *Ophthalmol-ogy, 90,* 1192–1200.

Regan, D., & Tyler, C.W. (1971). Some dynamic features of colour vision. *Vision Res., 11,* 1307–1324.

Regan, D., Bartol, S., Murray, T.J., & Beverley, K.I. (1982). Spatial frequency discrimination in nor-mal vision and in patients with multiple sclerosis. *Brain, 105,* 735–754.

Richards, W., & Kaye, M.G. (1974). Local versus global stereopsis: Two mechanisms? *Vision Res., 14,* 1345–1347.

Riggs, L.A., Ratliff, F., Cornsweet, J.C., & Cornsweet, T.N. (1953). The disappearance of steadily fixated visual test objects. *J. Opt. Soc. Am., 43,* 495–501.

Robson, J.G. (1966). Spatial and temporal contrast sensitivity functions of the visual system. *J. Opt. Soc. Am., 56,* 1141–1142.

Robson, J.G. (1975a). Receptive fields: neural representation of the spatial and intensive attributes of the visual image. In E.C. Carterette & M.P. Friedman (Eds.), *Handbook of perception: Vol.5* (pp. 81–112). New York: Academic Press.

Robson, J.G. (1975b). *Regional variation of contrast sensitivity in the visual field.* Paper presented at ARVO, Sarasota, FL.

Robson, J.G. (1980). Neural images: The physiological basis of spatial vision. In C.S. Harris (Ed.), *Visual coding and adaptability.* (pp. 177–214), Hillsdale, NJ: Lawrence Erlbaum Assoc.

Robson, J.G., & Graham, N. (1981). Probability summation and regional variations in contrast sensitivity curves across the visual field. *Vision Res., 21,* 408–418.

Rodieck, R.W. (1965). Quantitative analysis of cat retinal ganglion cell response to visual stimuli. *Vision Res., 5,* 583–601.

Rodieck, R.W. (1973). *The vertebrate retina.* San Francisco, Freeman.

Rodieck, R.W., & Stone, J. (1965). Analysis of receptive fields of cat retinal ganglion cells. *J. Neurophysiol., 28,* 833–848.

Rogers, B., & Graham, M. (1982). Similarities between motion parallax and stereopsis in human depth perception. *Vision Res., 22,* 261–270.

Rolls, E.T., & Cowey, A. (1970). Topography of the retina and striate cortex and its relationship to visual acuity in rhesus monkeys and squirrel monkeys. *Exp. Brain Res., 10,* 298–310.

Rose, A. (1948). The sensitivity performance of the human eye on an absolute scale. *J. Opt. Soc. Am., 38,* 196–208.

Rose, B., & Lowenstein, W.R. (1971). Junction membrane permeability. *J. Membr. Biol., 5,* 20–50.

Rose, D. (1979). Mechanisms underlying the receptive field properties of neurons in cat visual cortex. *Vision Res., 19,* 533–544.

Rose, D., & Blakemore, C. (1974). Effects of bicuculline on functions of inhibition in visual cortex. *Nature, 249,* 375–377.

Rovamo, J., Virsu, V., & Nasanen, R. (1978). Cortical magnification factor predicts the photopic contrast sensitivity of peripheral vision. *Nature, 271,* 54–56.

Rushton, W.A.H. (1957). Physical measurements of cone pigment in the living human eye. *Nature, 179,* 571–573.

Rushton, W.A.H. (1972). Visual pigments in man. In H.J.A. Dartnall (Ed.), *Handbook of sensory physiology: VII/1* (pp. 364–394). New York: Springer Verlag.

Sachs, M.B., Nachmias, J., & Robson, J.G. (1971). Spatial frequency channels in human vision. *J. Opt. Soc. Am., 61,* 1176–1186.

Said, F.S., & Weale, R.A. (1959). The variation with age of the spectral transmissivity of the living crystalline lens. *Gerontologia, 3,* 213–231.

Sakitt, B., & Barlow, H.B. (1982). A model for the economical encoding of the visual image in cerebral cortex. *Biol. Cybern., 43,* 97–108.

Sarmiento, R.F. (1975). The stereoacuity of macaque monkey. *Vision Res., 15,* 493–498.

Schade, O.H. (1956). Optical and photoelectric analog of the eye. *J. Opt. Soc. Am., 46,* 721–739.

Schein, S.J., Marrocco, R.T., & de Monasterio F.M. (1982). Is there a high concentration of color-selective cells in area V4 of monkey visual cortex? *J. Neurophysiol., 47,* 193–213.

Schiller, P.H., & Malpeli, J.G. (1978). Functional specificity of lateral geniculate nucleus laminae of the rhesus monkey. *J. Neurophysiol., 41,* 788–797.

Schiller, P.H., Finlay, B.L., & Volman, S.F. (1976a). Quantitative studies of single-cell properties in monkey striate cortex. I. Spatiotemporal organization of receptive fields. *J. Neurophysiol., 39,* 1288–1319.

Schiller, P.H., Finlay, B.L., & Volman, S.F. (1976b). Quantitative studies of single-cell properties in monkey striate cortex. II. Orientation specificity and ocular dominance. *J. Neurophysiol., 39,* 1320–1333.

Schiller, P.H., Finlay, B.L., & Volman, S.F. (1976c). Quantitative studies of single-cell properties in monkey striate cortex. III. Spatial frequency. *J. Neurophysiol., 39,* 1334–1351.

Schor, C.M., & Tyler, C.W. (1981). Spatio-temporal properties of Panum's fusional area. *Vision Res., 21,* 683–692.

Schor, C.M., & Wood, I. (1983). Disparity ranges for local stereopsis as a function of luminance spatial frequency. *Vision Res., 23,* 1649–1654.

Schor, C.M., Wood, I., & Ogawa, J. (1984). Binocular sensory fusion is limited by spatial resolution. *Vision Res., 24,* 661–665.

Schumer, R.A., & Ganz, L. (1979). Disparity averaging in random–dot stereopsis. *J. Opt. Soc. Am., 69,* 1479.

Schwarz, E.A. (1975). Rod-rod interaction in the retina of the turtle. *J. Physiol. (Lond.), 246,* 617–638.

Schwartz, E.L. (1980). Computational anatomy and functional architecture of striate cortex: A spatial mapping approach to perceptual coding. *Vision Res., 20,* 645–669.

Sekuler, R., Rubin, E.L., & Cushman, W.H. (1968). Selectivities of human visual mechanisms for direction of movement and contour orientation. *J. Opt. Soc. Am., 58,* 1146–1150.

Shapley, R.M., & Tolhurst, D.J. (1973). Edge-detectors in human vision. *J. Physiol. (Lond.), 229,* 165–183.

Sholl, D.A. (1956). *The organization of the cerebral cortex.* New York: Wiley.

Sidman, R.L. (1957). The structure and concentration of solids in photoreceptor cells studied by refractometry and interference microscopy. *J. Biophys. Biochem. Cytol., 3,* 15–30.

Sillito, A.M. (1975). The contribution of inhibitory mechanisms to the receptive field properties of neurones in the striate cortex of the cat. *J. Physiol. (Lond.), 250,* 305–329.

Sillito, A.M., Kemp, J.A., Milson, J.A., & Berardi, N. (1980). A re-evaluation of the mechanisms underlying simple cell orientation selectivity. *Brain Res., 194,* 517–520.

Silverman, M.S. (1984). *Deoxyglucose and electrophysiological evidence for spatial frequency columns in cat striate cortex.* Doctoral dissertation, University of California, San Francisco.

Sjøstrand, F.S. (1953). The ultrastructure of the outer segments of rods and cones of the eye as revealed by the electron microscope. *J. Cell Comp. Physiol., 42,* 15–44.

Skottun, B.C., Grosof, D., & De Valois, R.L. (1985). Responses of simple and complex cells in the cat visual cortex to visual dot stimuli. *Neurosci. Abstr., 11, Part 1,* 651.

Smith, T.G., Baumann, F., & Fuortes, M.G.F. (1965). Electrical connections between visual cells in the ommatidium of Limulus. *Science, 147,* 1446–1448.

Sokolov, L., Reivich, C., Kennedy, C., Des Rosiers, M.H., Patlack, C.S., Pettigrew, K.D., Sakurada, O., & Shinohara, M. (1977). The [^{14}C] deoxyglucose method for the measurement of local cerebral glucose utilization: Theory, procedure, and normal values in the conscious and anesthetized albino rat. *J. Neurochem., 28,* 897–916.

Stecher, S., Sigel, C., & Lange, R.V. (1973). Composite adaptation and spatial frequency interactions. *Vision Res., 13,* 2527–2531.

Steinman,R.M. (1965). Effect of target size, luminance and color on monocular fixation. *J. Opt. Soc. Am., 55,* 1158–1165.

Stell, W.K. (1967). The structure and relationships of horizontal cells and photoreceptor–bipolar synaptic complexes in goldfish retina. *Am. J. Anat., 121,* 401–423.

Stephan, F.K., & Zucker, I. (1972). Circadian rhythms in drinking behavior and locomotor activity of rats are eliminated by hypothalamic lesions. *Proc. Natl. Acad. Sci. USA, 69,* 1583–1586.

Stiles, W.S., & Crawford, B.H. (1933). The luminous efficiency of rays entering the eye pupil at different points. *Proc. R. Soc. Lond. (B), 112,* 428–450.

Stone, J. (1972). Morphology and physiology of the geniculo-cortical synapse in the cat: The question of parallel input to the striate cortex. *Invest. Ophthalmol., 11,* 338–346.

Stromeyer, C.F., & Julesz, B. (1972). Spatial-frequency masking in vision: Critical bands and spread of masking. *J. Opt. Soc. Am., 62,* 1221–1232.

Stromeyer, C.F., Lange, A.F., & Ganz, L. (1973). Spatial frequency phase effects in human vision. *Vision Res., 13,* 2345–2360.

Sullivan, G.D., Georgeson, M.A., & Oatley, K. (1972). Channels for spatial frequency selection and detection of single bars by the human visual system. *Vision Res., 12,* 383–394.

Swindale, N.V. (1979). How ocular dominance strips may be formed. In R.D. Freeman (Ed.), *Developmental neurobiology of vision* (pp. 267–273). New York: Plenum Press.

Switkes, E., & De Valois, K.K. (1983). Luminance and chromaticity interactions in spatial vision. In J.D. Mollon & L.T. Sharpe (Eds.), *Colour vision, (pp. 465–470). London: Academic Press.*

Switkes, E., Mayer, M.J., & Sloan, J.A. (1978). Spatial frequency analysis of the visual environment: Anisotropy and the carpentered environment hypothesis. *Vision Res., 18,* 1393–1399.

Switkes, E., Tootell, R.B.H., Silverman, M.S., & De Valois, R.L. (1986). Picture processing techniques applied to autoradiographic studies of visual cortex. *J. Neurosci. Methods, 15,* 269–280.

Szentagothai, J. (1973). Neuronal and synaptic architecture of the lateral geniculate nucleus. In R. Jung (Ed.), *Handbook of sensory physiology: VII/3* (pp. 141–176). Berlin: Springer Verlag.

Talbot, S.A., & Marshall, W.H. (1941). Physiological studies on neural mechanisms of visual localization and discrimination. *Am. J. Ophthalmol., 24,* 1255–1264.

Thomas, J.P. (1970). Model of the function of receptive fields in human vision. *Psychol. Rev., 77,* 121–134.

Thomas, J.P., & Shimamura, K.K. (1975). Inhibitory interaction between visual pathways tuned to different orientations. *Vision Res., 15,* 1373–1380.

Thorell, L.G. (1981). *The role of color in form analysis.* Doctoral dissertation, University of California, Berkeley.

Thorell, L.G., De Valois, R.L., & Albrecht, D.G. (1984). Spatial mapping of monkey V1 cells with pure color and luminance stimuli. *Vision Res., 24,* 751–769.

Tolhurst, D.J. (1972a). On the possible existence of edge detectors in the human visual system. *Vision Res., 12,* 797–804.

Tolhurst, D.J. (1972b). Adaptation to square-wave gratings: Inhibition between spatial frequency channels in the human visual system. *J. Physiol. (Lond.), 226,* 231–248.

Tolhurst, D.J., & Barfield, L.P. (1978). Interactions between spatial frequency channels. *Vision Res., 18,* 951–958.

Tolhurst, D.J., & Thompson, P.G. (1975). Orientation illusions and after-effects: Inhibition between channels. *Vision Res., 15,* 967–972.

Tootell, R.B.H. (1985). *Studies of the functional anatomy of the monkey visual cortex,* Doctoral dissertation, University of California, Berkeley.

Tootell, R.B.H., Silverman, M.S., & De Valois, R.L. (1981). Spatial frequency columns in primary visual cortex. *Science, 214,* 813–815.

Tootell, R.B.H., Silverman, M.S., De Valois, R.L., & Jacobs, G.H. (1983). Functional organization of the second visual cortical area in primates. *Science, 220,* 737–739.

Tootell, R.B.H., Silverman, M.S., Switkes, E., & De Valois, R.L. (1982a). Deoxyglucose analysis of retinotopic organization in primate striate cortex. *Science, 218,* 902–904.

Tootell, R.B.H., Silverman, M.S., Switkes, E., & De Valois, R.L. (1982b). The organization of cortical modules in primate striate cortex. *Soc. Neurosci., 8,* 707.

Toyoda, J., Nosaki, H., & Tomita, T. (1969). Light-induced resistance changes in single photoreceptors of *Necturus* and *Gekko. Vision Res., 9,* 453–463.

Tyler, C.W. (1975). Stereoscopic tilt and size aftereffects. *Perception, 4,* 187–192.

Tyler, C.W., & Julesz, B. (1978). Binocular cross-correlation in time and space. *Vision Res., 18,* 101–105.

Tyler, C.W., & Sutter, E.E. (1979). Depth from spatial frequency difference: An old kind of stereopsis? *Vision Res., 19,* 859–865.

van der Horst, G.J.C., & Bouman, M.A. (1969). Spatiotemporal chromaticity discrimination. *J. Opt. Soc. Am., 59,* 1482–1488.

van der Horst, G.J.C., de Weert, C.M.M., & Bouman, M.A. (1967). Transfer of spatial chromaticity-contrast at threshold in the human eye. *J. Opt. Soc. Am., 57,* 1260–1266.

van Doorn, A.J., Koenderink, J.J., & Bouman, M.A. (1972). The influence of the retinal inhomogeneity on the perception of spatial patterns. *Kybernetik, 10,* 223–230.

Van Essen, D.C., & Maunsell, J.H.R. (1980). Two-dimensional maps of the cerebral cortex. *J. Comp. Neurol., 191,* 255–281.

Van Essen, D.C., & Maunsell, J.H.R. (1983). Hierarchical organization and functional streams in the visual cortex. *Trends Neurosci., 6,* 370–375.

Van Essen, D.C., Newsome, W.T., & Maunsell, J.H.R. (1984). The visual field representation in striate cortex of the macaque monkey: Asymmetries, anisotropies, and individual variability. *Vision Res., 24,* 429–448.

van Nes, F.L., Koenderink, J.J., Nas, H., & Bouman, M.A. (1967). Spatiotemporal modulation transfer in the human eye. *J. Opt. Soc. Am., 57,* 1082–1088.

Vautin, R.G., & Berkley, M.A. (1977). Responses of single cells in cat visual cortex to prolonged stimulus movement: Neural correlates of visual aftereffects. *J. Neurophysiol., 40,* 1051–1065.

Volkmann, F.C. (1962). Vision during voluntary saccadic eye movements. *J. Opt. Soc. Am., 52,* 571–578.

von Blanckensee, H.T. (1981). *Spatio-temporal properties of cells in monkey lateral geniculate nucleus.* Doctoral dissertation, University of California, Berkeley.

von der Heydt, R. (1979). *Stereoskopische Wahrnehmung der Orientierungs-disparation,* Doctoral dissertation, Eidgenossische Technische Hochschule, Zurich, Switzerland.

von der Heydt, R., Adorjani, Cs., & Hänny, P. (1977). Neuronal mechanisms of stereopsis: sensitivity to orientation disparity. *Experientia, 33,* 786.

von der Heydt, R., Hänny, P., & Dursteller, M.R. (1981). The role of orientation disparity in stereoscopic perception and the development of binocular correspondence. In E. Grastyan & P. Molnar (Eds.), *Advances in physiological science: vol. 16* (pp. 461–470). Oxford: Pergamon.

von der Heydt, R., Adorjani, Cs., Hänny, P., & Baumgartner, G. (1978). Disparity sensitivity and receptive field incongruity of units in the cat striate cortex. *Exp. Brain Res., 31,* 523–545.

Wald, G. (1949). The photochemistry of vision. *Documenta Ophthalmol. 3,* 94–137.

Wald, G. (1964). The receptors of human color vision. *Science, 145,* 1007–1017.

Wald, G. (1967). Blue–blindness in the normal fovea. *J. Opt. Soc. Am., 57,* 1289–1301.

Wald, G., & Griffin, D.R. (1947). The change in refractive power of the human eye in dim and bright light. *J. Opt. Soc. Am., 37,* 321–336.

Walls, G.L. (1937). Significance of the foveal depression. *Arch. Ophthalmol. NY, 18,* 912–919.

Walraven, P.L., & Bouman, M.A. (1960). Relation between directional selectivity and spectral response curves in human cone vision. *J. Opt. Soc. Am., 50,* 780–784.

Watanabe, A., Sakara, H., & Isono, H. (1976). Chromatic spatial sine-wave response of the human visual system. *NHK Lab. Note., 198,* 1–10.

Waterman, T.H. (1981). Polarization sensitivity. In H. Autrum (Ed.), *Handbook of sensory physiology: VII/6B* (pp. 281–469). New York: Springer Verlag.

Watkins, D.W., & Berkley, M.A. (1974). The orientation selectivity of single neurons in cat striate cortex. *Exp. Brain Res., 19,* 433–446.

Watson, A.B. (1982). Summation of grating patches indicates many types of detectors at one retinal location. *Vision Res., 22,* 17–25.

Watson, A.B., & Nachmias, J. (1980). Summation of asynchronous gratings. *Vision Res., 20,* 91–94.

Weale, R.A. (1959). Photo–sensitive reactions in foveae of normal and cone-monochromatic observers. *Opt. Acta, 6,* 158–174.

Webster, M.A., & De Valois, R.L. (1985). Relationship between spatial-frequency and orientation tuning of striate-cortex cells. *J. Opt. Soc. Am., A, 2,* 1124–1132.

Weisstein, N., & Harris, C.S. (1980). Masking and unmasking of distributed representations in the visual system. In C.S. Harris (Ed.), *Visual coding and adaptability* (pp. 317–364). Hillsdale, NJ: Lawrence Erlbaum Assoc.

Weisstein, N., Harris, C.S., Berbaum, K., Tangney, J., & Williams, A. (1977). Contrast reduction by small localized stimuli. Extensive spatial spread of above-threshold orientation-selective masking. *Vision Res., 17,* 341–350.

Werblin, F.S., & Dowling, J.E. (1969). Organization of the retina of the mudpuppy, *Necturus maculosus. II. Intracellular recording. J. Neurophysiol., 32,* 339–355.

Westheimer, G. (1964). Pupil size and visual resolution. *Vision Res., 4,* 39–45.

Westheimer, G. (1977). Spatial frequency and light–spread descriptions of visual acuity and hyperacuity. *J. Opt. Soc. Am., 67,* 207–212.

Westheimer, G. (1978). Spatial phase sensitivity for sinusoidal grating targets. *Vision Res., 18,* 1073–1074.

Westheimer, G. (1979). The spatial sense of the eye. *Invest. Ophthalmol. Vis. Sci., 18,* 893–912.

Westheimer, G. (1981). Visual hyperacuity. In *Progress in sensory physiology: Vol. 1* (pp. 1–30). Berlin: Springer Verlag.

Westheimer, G., & McKee, S.P. (1975). Visual acuity in the presence of retinal-image motion. *J. Opt. Soc. Am., 65,* 847–850.

Westheimer, G., & McKee, S.P. (1977). Spatial configurations for visual hyperacuity. *Vision Res., 17,* 941–947.

Westheimer, G., & McKee, S.P. (1978). Stereoscopic acuity for moving retinal images. *J. Opt. Soc. Am., 68,* 450–455.

Westheimer, G., & Tanzman, I.J. (1956). Qualitative depth localization with diplopic images. *J. Opt. Soc. Am., 46,* 116–117.

Wheatstone, C. (1838). On some remarkable, and hitherto unresolved, phenomena of binocular vision. *Phil. Trans. R. Soc. Lond., 2,* 371–394.

Wheeler, G.L., & Bitensky, M.W. (1977). A light-activated GTPase in vertebrate photoreceptors: Regulation of light-activated cyclic GMP phosphodiesterase. *Proc. Natl. Acad. Sci. USA, 74,* 4238–4242.

Wiesel, T.N. (1960). Receptive fields of ganglion cells in the cat's retina. *J. Physiol. (Lond.), 153,* 583–594.

Wiesel, T.N., & Hubel, D.H. (1966). Spatial and chromatic interactions in the lateral geniculate body of the rhesus monkey. *J. Neurophysiol., 29,* 1115–1156.

Wiesel, T.N., Hubel, D.H., & Lam, D.M.K. (1974). Autoradiographic demonstration of ocular-dominance columns in the monkey striate cortex by means of transneuronal transport. *Brain Res., 79,* 273–279.

Williams, D.R., MacLeod, D.I.A., & Hayhoe, M.M. (1981). Punctate sensitivity of the blue–sensitive mechanism. *Vision Res., 21,* 1357–1375.

Wilson, H.R. (1976). The significance of frequency gradients in binocular grating perception. *Vision Res., 16,* 983–989.

Wilson, H.R., & Bergen, J.R. (1979). A four mechanism model for threshold spatial vision. *Vision Res., 19,* 19–32.

Wilson, H.R., McFarlane, D.K., & Phillips, G.C. (1983). Spatial frequency tuning of orientation selective units estimated by oblique masking. *Vision Res., 23,* 873–882.

Wilson, J.B., & Sherman, S.M. (1976). Receptive-field characteristics of neurons in cat striate cortex: Changes with visual field eccentricity. *J. Neurophysiol., 39,* 512–533.

Wilson, M.E., & Cragg, B.G. (1967). Projections from the lateral geniculate nucleus in the cat and monkey. *J. Anat., 101,* 677–692.

Woodruff, M.L., & Bownds, M.D. (1979). Amplitude, kinetics, and reversibility of a light-induced decrease in guanosine 3′, 5′-cyclic monophosphate in frog photoreceptor membranes. *J. Gen. Physiol., 73,* 629–653.

Wurtz, R.H., & Goldberg, M.E. (1971). Superior colliculus responses to eye movements in awake monkeys. *Science, 171,* 82–84.

Yarbus, A.L. (1967). *Eye movements and vision.* New York: Plenum Press.

Yellott, J.I., Jr. (1982). Spectral analysis of spatial sampling by photoreceptors: Topological disorder prevents aliasing. *Vision Res., 22,* 1205–1210.

Yoshikami, S., & Hagins, W.A. (1971). Ionic basis of dark current and photocurrent of retinal rods. *Biophys. J., 10,* 60a.

Young, R.A. (1986). The Gaussian derivative model for machine vision: Visual cortex simulation. *General Motors Research #5323,* 1–24.

Young, R.W. (1971). The renewal of rod and cone outer segments in the rhesus monkey. *J. Cell Biol., 49:* 303–318.

Yund, E.W., & Armington, J.C. (1975). Color and brightness contrast effects as a function of spatial variables. *Vision Res., 15,* 917–929.

Yund, E.W., Snodderly, D.M., Hepler, N.K., & De Valois, R.L. (1977). Brightness contrast effects in monkey lateral geniculate nucleus. *Sensory Processes, 1,* 260–271.

Zeki, S.M. (1973). Colour coding in rhesus monkey prestriate cortex. *Brain Res., 53,* 422–427.

Zeki, S.M. (1974). Cells responding to changing image size and disparity in the cortex of the rhesus monkey. *J. Physiol. (Lond.), 242,* 827–841.

Zeki, S.M. (1978). Functional specialization in the visual cortex of the rhesus monkey. *Nature, 274,* 423–428.

Zeki, S.M. (1985). Colour coding in the cerebral cortex: The reaction of cells in monkey visual cortex to wavelengths and colours. *Neuroscience, 9,* 741–765.

Zrenner, E. (1983). Neurophysiological aspects of colour vision mechanisms in the primate retina. In J.D. Mollon & L.T. Sharpe (Eds.), *Colour vision* (pp. 195–210). London: Academic Press.

Author Index

Subject Index